Commercial Leases and Insolvency

Commercial Leases and Insolvency

Third edition

Patrick McLoughlin   BA, LLM, Solicitor

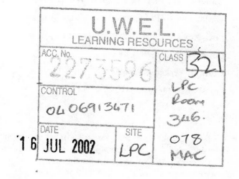

Butterworths
LexisNexis™

Members of the LexisNexis Group worldwide

United Kingdom	LexisNexis Butterworths Tolley, a Division of Reed Elsevier (UK) Ltd, Halsbury House, 35 Chancery Lane, LONDON, WC2A 1EL, and 4 Hill Street, EDINBURGH EH2 3JZ
Argentina	LexisNexis Argentina, BUENOS AIRES
Australia	LexisNexis Butterworths, CHATSWOOD, New South Wales
Austria	LexisNexis Verlag ARD Orac GmbH & Co KG, VIENNA
Canada	LexisNexis Butterworths, MARKHAM, Ontario
Chile	LexisNexis Chile Ltda, SANTIAGO DE CHILE
Czech Republic	Nakladatelství Orac sro, PRAGUE
France	Editions du Juris-Classeur SA, PARIS
Hong Kong	LexisNexis Butterworths, HONG KONG
Hungary	HVG-Orac, BUDAPEST
India	LexisNexis Butterworths, NEW DELHI
Ireland	Butterworths (Ireland) Ltd, DUBLIN
Italy	Giuffrè Editore, MILAN
Malaysia	Malayan Law Journal Sdn Bhd, KUALA LUMPUR
New Zealand	Butterworths of New Zealand, WELLINGTON
Poland	Wydawnictwo Prawnicze LexisNexis, WARSAW
Singapore	LexisNexis Butterworths, SINGAPORE
South Africa	Butterworths SA, DURBAN
Switzerland	Stämpfli Verlag AG, BERNE
USA	LexisNexis, DAYTON, Ohio

© Reed Elsevier (UK) Ltd 2002

A CIP Catalogue record for this book is available from the British Library.

ISBN 0 406 91347 1

Typeset by J&L Composition Ltd, Filey, North Yorkshire
Printed and bound by Bookcraft (Bath), Midsomer Norton

Visit Butterworths LexisNexis *direct* at www.butterworths.com

Foreword to the third edition

I am very pleased to have been asked to provide the foreword to the third edition of McLoughlin's *Commercial Leases and Insolvency*. In my career as an insolvency practitioner with a particular interest in property, I have been at various times landlord, tenant and even developer. Both then and now an authoritative guide to the position of a landlord or tenant is a necessity.

In dealing with property in an insolvency situation, traps and pitfalls abound. A mistaken action can materially alter the position of the landlord or the tenant, and can easily cause substantial loss or expense. Patrick McLoughlin's book is a vital guide to the issues. Whilst not shrinking from explaining the legal background, he also succeeds in illuminating the practical situations that complicate the lives of landlords and tenants following an insolvency.

Given the current changes in insolvency law, and those proposed for the near future, the position of those interested in property is in flux. This book will guide the non-specialist away from ill-judged actions and will be a valuable reference work for those experienced in insolvency.

Roger Oldfield
Partner, KPMG
February 2002

Preface to the third edition

This third edition comes at a time of flux for insolvency law and practice. The Insolvency Act 2000 has been partly implemented so that where a company is in administration a lease cannot now be forfeited by a landlord making a peaceable re-entry upon land without leave. Upon full implementation of the Insolvency Act 2000 a moratorium on peaceable re-entry will also apply to an individual voluntary arrangement.

The same Act will also have the wider impact of allowing a 'small' corporate tenant to propose a company voluntary arrangement ('CVA') incorporating a statutory moratorium, and this new procedure will probably be used instead of administration in many cases. But the introduction of a CVA with a moratorium will not necessarily result in administration being less frequently used if proposals contained in the recent White Paper 'Productivity and Enterprise' are introduced. The White Paper proposes that administration will be the prescribed procedure for dealing with most types of case which traditionally have been the subject of administrative receivership.

Apart from legislative developments the period since the second edition has also seen the courts at work providing guidance on a number of important and difficult issues. In *Hindcastle Ltd v Barbara Attenborough Associates Ltd* the House of Lords has explored further the nature of that 'dormant volcano' – the disclaimed lease; and their Lordships have sought to quantify the damage caused by a disclaimer in *Christopher Moran Holdings Ltd v Bairstow*. All chapters of this work have been affected as areas of uncertainty are tested and new problems encountered, and I have attempted to state the law as at December 2001.

Patrick McLoughlin
Theodore Goddard
February 2002

Preface to the first edition

The law of insolvency was reviewed in 1982 by a committee chaired by Sir Kenneth Cork. The review led to the amendment and consolidation of the law, which is now contained in the Insolvency Act 1986. The amendment and consolidation of the law was the seed which has engendered a spate of new books on insolvency. This book, however, is not the product of the seed of the 1986 reform but is instead a product of the recession of 1991 to 1992. As a practitioner advising on the insolvency of tenants in commercial leases I found myself and others struggling to solve problems thrown up by the recession. There were many books on insolvency law, and many texts on the law of landlord and tenant; but there was nothing to bridge the gap between the two areas of law, and to explain specifically how the relationships between commercial property owners, their tenants, and mortgages of commercial leases are affected by a tenant's insolvency. It is the purpose of this book to bridge that gap.

Spurred on by the recession, and urged by fellow professionals to produce something in the shortest possible time, I have limited the scope of this first edition to the law of England and Wales, and the law relating to registered companies and individuals. Some of the law differs in Scotland, and in the cases of unregistered companies and partnerships.

Although I am a lawyer and primarily equipped to write for the benefit of other lawyers, I am very aware that the law on this subject is as much of interest to various non-lawyers, including accountants who are insolvency practitioners, property managers, surveyors, and banks whose loans are secured on commercial leases. I have, where appropriate, attempted to consider the needs of such persons in so far as a work of such a technical nature will allow.

Thanks are due to those who have assisted me in progressing the book from the inception of the idea to the point of publication. In particular I acknowledge the assistance of Susan Prevezer, barrister, of the chambers of Michael Crystal QC, who read and commented on the draft in full. I also thank my colleagues Christine Lerry, Gary Russell, and Caroline Sielle, who each commented on parts of the draft. I must, of course, accept responsibility for any errors or imperfections which remain. My gratitude is due also to the quasi-corporate entity of Theodore Goddard for allowing me time to complete this book and recognising that the need for knowledge has a value which has its place alongside financial concerns.

Patrick McLoughlin
Theodore Goddard

Contents

Table of statutes

Table of statutory instruments

Table of cases

PAGE

I

J

K

PAGE

CHAPTER 1

Tenant insolvency

When a tenant of a commercial lease suffers serious financial difficulties, one of several possible scenarios might arise. In a less serious case a tenant might be able to extricate itself from its predicament by refinancing and restructuring, without the need for any formal insolvency procedure. In other cases formal insolvency procedures may be invoked and a receiver, administrator, liquidator or trustee in bankruptcy might be appointed. It is not the purpose of this work to examine the full range of the powers and duties of such persons. Instead, this first chapter aims to give an overview of the various procedures available in insolvency and of the different contexts within which a lease may operate, and to help landlords, tenants (including any receiver, administrator, liquidator or trustee for the tenant) and other persons interested in commercial leases to understand how their respective rights and obligations under a lease are affected by insolvency.

The law of insolvency was comprehensively reviewed by a committee chaired by Sir Kenneth Cork, and the ensuing report (*Cork Report 1982* (Cmnd 8558)) led to the amendment and consolidation of the law which is now contained in the Insolvency Act 1986 ('IA 1986') and the Insolvency Rules 1986 ('IR 1986') as amended. The IA 1986 has been supplemented so as to make specific provision for partnerships and in particular to apply to the newly created commercial vehicle and legal personality of the limited liability partnership.

1.1 Refinancing, restructuring and informal moratoria

A tenant may borrow money or otherwise reorganise its business in an attempt to solve its immediate problems. A reorganisation may include the making of redundancies, the selling of assets, and participation funding. Where the tenant is a company there may be an issue of new shares, the alteration of rights of existing shareholders, the conversion of debt into equity, and the use of vehicle companies. Such arrangements might include an informal moratorium; i e, an informal agreement by some or all creditors not to enforce their rights. Since bankruptcy, receivership, administration or liquidation may be on the horizon such a reorganisation is fraught with both practical and technical difficulties. From a practical point of view an informal moratorium can be unstable, since a creditor might break ranks at any time and insist upon enforcing security or taking proceedings to make the tenant bankrupt or, in the case of a company, to petition for winding up. Sometimes the risk of this occurring may be reduced by all the major creditors entering into a multipartite agreement whereby they agree not to break ranks except in certain defined circumstances.

Apart from the instability of 'informal' techniques for dealing with insolvency, there may be legal obstacles and risks involved in such arrangements, particularly if they involve the giving to creditors of fresh security or the making of other dispositions of property. The giving of security, for example, may fall foul of 'negative pledges', that is, clauses in existing debentures, mortgages or other agreements, prohibiting the giving of further security. This might cause existing securities which were not previously enforceable to become enforceable, unless the persons entitled to such securities consent to the further security. The giving of security which extends to current debt also runs the risk that if the tenant becomes bankrupt or, being a company, enters into liquidation or administration, the security may be challenged as a 'preference' (IA 1986, ss 239, 340; see para 7.1.2) in favour of one creditor over the other creditors. The security might also be considered to be a transaction at an undervalue and might later be set aside on an application to the court by a trustee, liquidator or administrator (IA 1986, ss 238, 339; see para 7.1.3). If a fresh floating charge (i e normally a charge over all of the assets from time to time of a tenant company) is given by a tenant company, and the company giving the charge becomes insolvent or is put into administration within the 'relevant time', it will only be valid to secure any fresh consideration given (IA 1986, s 245; see para 7.1.6). If a petition in bankruptcy or liquidation has been presented at any time before the arrangement is put in place, any disposition of property pursuant to the arrangement will be void (IA 1986, ss 127, 284; see para 7.1.1). There are also other provisions of the IA 1986 and other rules of law which might cause difficulty (see para 7.1).

Where the debtor has a lease or leases of commercial property, any refinancing or restructuring is likely to involve the lease or leases. Any new charge over the lease may need the landlord's consent, and the charge may be a disposition which is void or voidable on the grounds mentioned in the paragraph above. A reorganisation may include an assignment or surrender of the lease, which again is likely to require the involvement of the landlord, and such a surrender or assignment might be void or voidable.

Despite the difficulties attendant on an 'out of court' solution to the tenant's problems, such remedies do sometimes suffice to heal the ills of an insolvent or near insolvent tenant, particularly where management strategies are altered so as to eradicate practices which may have caused or contributed to the problems in the first place, and perhaps with the assistance of a 'company doctor'. In many cases, however, the insolvency of the tenant cannot be treated with 'home-made' remedies, and the tenant, or its creditors, may have to resort to the harsh medicine of a formal insolvency procedure. It is with these more formal procedures that this work is principally concerned.

1.2 Voluntary arrangements

A tenant whose insolvency is actual or imminent might, in the first instance, consider the benefits of entering into a voluntary arrangement with its creditors. By doing so it might be able to avoid the more severe procedures of bankruptcy or liquidation described below. Before the IA 1986 there existed procedures for deeds of arrangement under the Deeds of Arrangement Act 1914 and the Companies Act 1985, s 425 and for administration orders under the County Courts Act 1984. The IA 1986 makes provision for binding voluntary arrangements in the cases of both individuals and companies, and these new arrangements have now largely taken over from the previous procedures.

1.2.1 INDIVIDUAL VOLUNTARY ARRANGEMENTS

An individual debtor can make an arrangement with his creditors to deal with his financial problems. Use of the statutory procedure for doing so will give the debtor the benefit of a statutory moratorium, giving him time to make the necessary arrangement. The IA 1986 allows the debtor to 'make a proposal to his creditors for a composition in satisfaction of his debts or a scheme of arrangement of his affairs' (IA 1986, s 253). A composition is an agreement between the debtor and some or all of his creditors whereby the creditors agree to accept lesser payment than they would otherwise be entitled to. A scheme of arrangement usually involves the transfer of the debtor's property to a third party for its realisation, and distribution of the proceeds of sale (3(2) *Halsbury's Laws of England* (4th edn) para 75). The voluntary arrangement procedure is quite often used, accounting in 1999 for about 25% of the incidence of individual insolvency (Insolvency Service General Annual Report, 1999).

Application to court

If a tenant debtor decides to propose such a 'voluntary arrangement' the first step is for the tenant to apply to the court for an interim order nominating some person (the 'nominee') to act as trustee or supervisor of the arrangement (IA 1986, s 253). Whilst an application is being made there is an immediate semi-moratorium in that the court may upon application stay actions taken by creditors against the tenant or the tenant's property (IA 1986, s 254). The tenant is thereby given a provisional instant breathing space which may acquire more permanence if an interim order is made on the application. There are modified procedures where the tenant debtor is already bankrupt and the trustee in bankruptcy or Official Receiver makes an application for a voluntary arrangement. The modified procedures are not discussed below (see the IA 1986, Pt VIII and the IR 1986, Pt 5). There is also to be a modified procedure where the tenant may, if desired, arrange for the making of a proposal without the benefit of a moratorium (IA 1986, s 256A as amended).

Grounds for an interim order

The court may make an order if it thinks that it would be appropriate to do so for the purpose of facilitating the consideration and implementation of the tenant's proposal, but it cannot make an order unless four conditions are satisfied (IA 1986, s 255):

1. the court must be satisfied that the tenant intends to make a voluntary arrangement;
2. on the day of the application the tenant must be able to petition for his own bankruptcy or must be an undischarged bankrupt (see para 1.5);
3. no previous application for an order must have been made by the tenant debtor within the preceding 12 months;
4. the nominee under the tenant's proposal must be a person qualified to act as an insolvency practitioner in relation to the tenant, and must be willing to act in relation to the proposal.

Effect of interim order

Once an order is made no bankruptcy petition may be presented or proceeded with, and no other proceedings, and no execution or other legal process, may be commenced or continued against the tenant or his property except with the leave of the court (IA 1986, s 252). The interim order establishes a moratorium which can only be breached with the leave of the court, and it gives the tenant debtor valuable time to put proposals to creditors. Whilst the moratorium continues a landlord will not be able to take proceedings against the tenant including court proceedings for forfeiture (*Re Mohammed Naeem (a bankrupt) (No 18 of 1988)* [1990] 1 WLR 48). Under the Insolvency Act 2000 the moratorium also now applies to any peaceable re-entry or distress for rent. Prior to that Act the moratorium did not impede forfeiture by peaceable re-entry (*Re a Debtor (No 13A 10 of 1995)* [1996] 1 All ER 691) nor distress for rent arrears (*McMullen & Sons Ltd v Cerrone* (1993) 66 P & CR 351), since these procedures do not require the intervention of the court. The interim order will cease at the end of 14 days unless extended (IA 1986, s 255).

Report to court and meeting of creditors

During the period allowed by the order the nominee must obtain details of the proposal and a statement of affairs from the debtor. He must then prepare a report stating whether a meeting of creditors should be held (and under provision being brought in by the Insolvency Act 2000 whether the proposal has a reasonable prospect of being approved and implemented), and must submit the report to the court two days before the interim order expires (IA 1986, s 256, IR 1986, r 5.10). If the nominee so recommends, then unless the court directs otherwise, a meeting of the creditors will be held to consider proposals for dealing with the tenant's debts, and the effect of the interim order will be extended. The meeting is normally chaired by the nominee.

Entitlement to vote

Creditors who are notified of the meeting in accordance with the rules are entitled to vote at the meeting (IR 1986, r 5.17(1)). Most importantly, in cases prior to full implementation of the Insolvency Act 2000, notification is a prerequisite to causing a person to be bound by an arrangement. For such purpose a creditor has been taken to have been given notice even if a notification has gone astray in the post. In *Beverley Group plc v McClue* [1995] BCC 751, a notice was sent but had apparently not been received by the creditor. The creditor was, however, informed of the meeting by a third party and was aware of the proposals. In these circumstances he was taken to have notice of the meeting, was entitled to vote, and was bound by the arrangement. Similarly, a person not in receipt of formal notice, but who independently finds out about the meeting, has been held to be entitled to vote (in *Re Debtors (Nos 400 and 401 of 1996)* [1997] BPIR 431). Under the Insolvency Act 2000 (when fully implemented), however, notification of the meeting will not be of such importance, since a person will be bound whether or not they have received notification of the meeting – but subject to the right to challenge the outcome of the meeting (see below).

Level of voting rights

Subject to the rules summarised below, creditors generally vote according to the amount of debt owed at the date of the meeting (IR 1986, r 5.17(2)). A landlord will, of course, be entitled to vote in respect of arrears of rent then owing.

With regard to future rents there are a number of issues which arise. First, there is the question as to whether future rent is a simple debt and valued as such, or is rent a debt for an unliquidated amount or whose value is not ascertained and may be subject to the chairman agreeing an estimated minimum value?

An unascertained debt is one 'the amount of which cannot be estimated until the happening of some future event'; and the term 'unliquidated debt' refers to 'cases of damages to be ascertained by a jury, but beyond that, extends to any debt where the creditor fairly admits that he cannot state the amount' (Mellish LJ in *Re Dummelow, ex p Ruffle* (1873) 8 Ch App 997). Although it might be thought that future rent is liquidated or ascertained, since a landlord will be able to state the amount of the future rent contracted for, future rent has nevertheless been treated as if it is an unascertained amount (*Doorbar v Alltime Securities Ltd* [1996] 1 WLR 456, CA). It is not clear why this should be the case. Admittedly it could be argued that the value of the debt is not clear since the likelihood of it being paid is uncertain and the tenant might later default or become bankrupt, or the lease might be forfeited or disclaimed (see *Re Lucania Temperance* [1966] Ch 98). To this argument, however, it might be objected that similar argument could be – but is not – applied to many other debts. For instance, the value of a debt for a fixed sum due at the date of the arrangement could be regarded as uncertain if the possibility of non-payment were to be taken into account; or a contract debt might be treated as unascertained on the basis that a future breach might entitle rescission.

Irrespective of whether or not future rent may technically be classified as unascertained or unliquidated it is submitted that the correct approach is to allow the landlord to vote to the extent that rent is the subject of the arrangement. For example, if the arrangement provides that two years' future rent is to be affected by the arrangement then the landlord's vote should include a weighting for that rent. This would put the landlord on a footing consistent with that of other creditors. It would be unfair to reduce the landlord's vote to, say, one year's rent by speculating that the rent, for one reason or another, might not be paid, whilst not entering into similar speculation with regard to sums due to other creditors.

The position may be more complex, perhaps with the lease containing a tenant's break clause. It is suggested that the possibility or even the probability of the tenant operating the break clause should not be taken into account. The tenant's proposal in respect of rents ought rather to extend only to those due up to the date of the break. If the tenant anticipates the continuation of the lease after the break date and the arrangement deals with rents following such date then those rents should be taken into account in full.

A further problem could be encountered where the rents are subject to periodic review and the tenant's proposal is to include rents extending beyond a review date. In such a case it is likely that debt beyond the review date is for an unliquidated amount or unascertained value and it may be that the chairman will take into account valuation evidence in order to estimate the minimum value of the debt.

If the claim is not a claim against the tenant under the lease but is a claim against a surety for possible future liability for rent, the claim may be treated as a contingent liability for an unascertained amount (*Doorbar v Alltime Securities Ltd*, above); this is consistent with the traditional view that a surety's liability is contingent. Also, claims under a lease in respect of service charges and defective works will usually be treated as unliquidated or unascertained (*Re Cranley Mansions Ltd* [1994] 1 WLR 1610).

Unliquidated sums and unascertained amounts

If a claim is for an unliquidated amount or a debt of unascertained value a creditor has no vote 'except where the chairman agrees to put upon the debt an estimated minimum value for the purpose of entitlement to vote' (IR 1986, r 5.17(3)). It is unclear from this wording whether the agreement of estimated minimum value needs to be a bilateral agreement between creditor and chairman or whether the chairman can unilaterally estimate the minimum value of the claim to enable the landlord or other creditor to vote. If the rule requires a bilateral agreement, a creditor could disqualify himself from voting by refusing to agree a value with the effect that the creditor, not being entitled to vote, would not (prior to the new rules under the Insolvency Act 2000) be bound by the voluntary arrangement (see *Re Cranley Mansions Ltd* [1994] 1 WLR 1610). For this reason it has been held that the chairman can act unilaterally (*Doorbar v Alltime Securities Ltd* [1996] 1 WLR 456, CA), but it is likely that the chairman should make a proper attempt to value the claim and not simply set a nominal value of £1 (see *Doorbar v Alltime Securities* [1995] 1 BCLC 316 and *Re Sweatfield Ltd* [1998] BPIR 276). The creditor will be able to vote to the extent of the value ascertained and will be bound by the arrangement, subject to the right to appeal in respect of the amount of the estimate.

Buying of debt

As the effect of the proposals may be more beneficial to some creditors than others, a creditor or creditors might be tempted to buy up debt in order to increase their voting power. Under the old law prior to 1986 such a ruse would, at least in some circumstances, render the arrangement voidable at the instance of a non-assenting creditor (*Re Burrs & Co, ex p Fore St Warehouse Co Ltd* (1874) 30 LT 624). Nowadays the mere buying up of debt will probably not render an arrangement void – but in appropriate circumstances manipulation of debt and voting rights will likely render the arrangement subject to challenge; e g if an associate of the debtor secretly offers to a creditor an inflated price for his debt on condition that the creditor votes in favour of the proposed arrangement (*Somji v Cadbury Schweppes plc* [2001] 1 BCLC 498, CA).

Procedure and cases of doubt

The chairman has power to admit or reject a creditor's claim for the purpose of his entitlement to vote, subject to the right of the creditor (or the debtor) to appeal to the court, within 28 days of the chairman's report to the court (IR 1986, r 5.17(4)(5) and (8)).

In cases of doubt the chairman should admit the claim to vote. If the claim or the extent of the claim is disputed the proper course is to allow the vote, and to hear the dispute in court afterwards, in which case the court has power to declare the vote invalid (*Re a Debtor (No 222 of 1990)* [1992] BCLC 137, Harman J). If the vote is declared invalid the court will consider whether it is necessary for a fresh meeting of creditors to be held to reconsider the proposals (*Re a Company (No 4539 of 1993)* [1995] 1 BCLC 459; IR 1986, r 5.17(8)).

Requisite majorities and secured creditors

For the proposal to be approved there must be a majority in excess of three-quarters of the value of the creditors voting on the resolution. In relation to any other resolutions a simple majority is adequate (IR 1986, r 5.18). The proposal can be approved with or without modifications, but no modification is effective unless approved by the debtor (IA 1986, s 258).

Although a secured creditor of the tenant may vote, the vote is to be left out of account in calculating the requisite majority (IR 1986, r 5.18). If the creditor is partly secured, his vote should be taken into account to the extent that he is undersecured (*Re a Debtor (Nos 31/32/33 of 1993)* [1994] 2 BCLC 321).

Notwithstanding that a resolution may have been passed with the requisite majority (after discounting or partial discounting of secured creditors' votes) the resolution may be avoided if there is a sufficiently large body of creditors voting against the resolution, and for this purpose the votes which would otherwise be discounted may be taken into account. The IR 1986, r 5.18(4) states that a resolution is invalid if those voting against it include more than half in value of the creditors, but counting in these latter only those to whom notice of the meeting was sent, whose votes are not to be left out of account, and who are not associates of the debtor. That is, the value (a) of all votes (without any discounting) lodged against the resolution must be compared with (b) the value of the debt owed to creditors (excluding the value of discounted votes and votes of associates) who were entitled to vote at the meeting and whether or not such creditors did in fact vote. If the value of (a) exceeds 50% of the value of (b) then the resolution is invalid.

The meeting should not approve a proposal which will affect the rights of a secured creditor to enforce his security, without his consent, and must not prejudice the priority of preferential creditors without their consent (IA 1986, s 258). For these purposes an execution creditor in respect of whom a sheriff has taken possession of goods is secured, and the meeting should not approve an arrangement to sell the debtor's business as a going concern (including such goods) without the consent of the execution creditor (*Peck v Craighead* [1995] 1 BCLC 337). A landlord with a right to forfeit is not regarded as a secured creditor for these purposes (*Razzaq v Pala* [1997] 1 WLR 1336; cf *March Estates v Gunmark* [1996] 2 EGLR 38), and his consent is not required for the proposal.

Outcome of meeting

The chairman of the meeting must report its outcome to the court within four days of the meeting (IR 1986, rr 5.22–5.24). If the proposal is rejected the court may discharge the interim order. If it is accepted the chairman must give notice to the Secretary of State for entry in the register of voluntary arrangements (IR 1986, r 5.19).

The decision may then be challenged within 28 days of the report being made to the court (IA 1986, s 262), by the debtor, the nominee or anyone eligible to vote at the meeting. The challenge may be made on one or both of two grounds: first, that the arrangement unfairly prejudices the interests of a particular creditor; and second, that there has been some material irregularity at or in relation to the meeting. If either ground is proven the court may revoke or suspend the arrangement and may direct that a further meeting be held to consider a revised proposal (IA 1986, s 262), and the interim order may be extended.

A challenge on the ground of unfair prejudice must prove that a particular creditor or group of creditors is, under the scheme, treated differently to other creditors (*Re a Debtor (No 87 of 1993) (No 2)* [1996] 1 BCLC 63) and, in addition, that a prejudicial effect has occurred through such differential treatment (*Re a Debtor (No 101 of 1999)* [2001] 1 BCLC 54). If, for example, it is proved that there was an arrangement to give some secret payment to particular creditors, this will probably provide a good ground for challenging the arrangement, even if the payment is to be made by a third party (*Re Milner* (1885) 15 QBD 605, CA).

Conversely a creditor may be unfairly prejudiced through not being treated differently to others, if a term of the arrangement, in practice, impacts to prejudice only a particular creditor or class of creditors. In *Sea Voyager Maritime Inc v Bielecki* [1999] 1 All ER 628, a particular creditor had a claim in negligence against the debtor which might entitle the creditor to a statutory right to make a claim against the debtor's insurers. The terms of the arrangement included a prohibition upon suing the debtor. The High Court decided that regard was to be had to prejudice which a scheme causes to a particular class of creditor, and the creditor in this case had good cause to challenge the scheme.

'Material irregularity' will justify a challenge if material financial information has not been included in the tenant debtor's statement of affairs (*Re a Debtor*

(No 87 of 1993) (No 2) [1996] 1 BCLC 63); and probably also if the details of the proposed arrangement are not clear (*Re Pilling* [1903] 2 KB 50, CA). It is not an irregularity if a chairman, in putting a value on a landlord's voting rights in respect of future rent, applies a discount to reflect the fact that the lease might terminate early through forfeiture (*Doorbar v Alltime Securities* [1996] 1 WLR 456, CA). Failure to notify a particular creditor is not a material irregularity if that creditor has no voting rights (*Re a Debtor (No 259 of 1990)* [1992] 1 WLR 226).

Effect of approved arrangement

The approved arrangement binds every person who had notice of and who was entitled to vote at the meeting, whether or not that person was actually present at the meeting (IA 1986, s 260). Under the IA 1986 as originally provided, a person who had not received notice was not bound and was free to serve upon the debtor a statutory demand to the full amount owed and, if necessary, proceed to bankrupt the debtor (*Re a Debtor (No 64 of 1992)* [1994] 2 All ER 177); but amendment to the IA 1986, s 260 being introduced by the Insolvency Act 2000 will provide that any person who is within the class of persons eligible to vote is bound by the arrangement whether or not such person is notified of the meeting.

The approved arrangement is not necessarily an accord and satisfaction which extinguishes for all purposes debt to the extent of any reduction agreed. Accordingly, a third party who is liable for a particular debt along with the insolvent tenant does not necessarily benefit from any reduction of liability in respect of which the insolvent tenant and the third party are both responsible. Thus in *Mytre Investments Ltd v Reynolds* [1995] 3 All ER 588, Burton QC held that an original tenant was liable in full to a landlord notwithstanding that the landlord's rights against the insolvent assignee had been reduced by virtue of a voluntary arrangement binding upon the landlord. As, however, the original tenant was not (in the particular circumstances) bound by the terms of the voluntary arrangement, he was entitled to claim indemnity in full from the insolvent assignee. Similarly in *Johnson v Davies* [1998] 3 EGLR 72, CA the terms of an individual voluntary arrangement releasing a debtor from liability did not preclude a creditor from pursuing a co-debtor.

A landlord who is entitled to vote may be concerned that a vote in favour of the voluntary arrangement will act as a waiver of an existing right to forfeit the lease, but this fear is unfounded following the decision in *Re Mohammed Naeem (a bankrupt) (No 18 of 1988)* [1990] 1 WLR 48. In that case an insolvent tenant sought the approval of the court to a voluntary arrangement. The scheme which included the sale of the tenant's lease was approved. The landlord as a creditor for arrears of rent made an application under the IA 1986, s 262 (see above), arguing that the scheme was unfairly prejudicial to his interests since it would prevent a forfeiture of the lease pending the sale of the lease in accordance with the terms of the arrangement. It was determined that the landlord's right to forfeit (subject to the court's discretion to grant the tenant relief from forfeiture) would be preserved (though altered so as to be security for the modified debt) and that the arrangement should stand. Hoffmann J said that the arrangement 'was only intended to bind the creditors in their character as creditors. It did not affect proprietary rights such as those of the landlord to forfeit the lease.'

9

Execution of approved arrangement

Once the scheme is approved the nominee normally becomes the supervisor of the scheme, and will carry it out in accordance with its terms and the IR 1986, rr 5.20–5.30. The supervisor can apply to the court for directions as required. If the debtor or a creditor or any other person is 'dissatisfied by any act, omission or decision of the supervisor' the person dissatisfied can apply to the court, which can confirm, reverse or modify any act or decision of the supervisor, give him directions, or make such other order as it thinks fit (IA 1986, s 263).

The supervisor can continue to carry out the approved arrangement notwithstanding a later bankruptcy order against the debtor. The assets which are the subject of the voluntary arrangement are regarded as being held upon trust according to the terms of the voluntary arrangement so as to be excluded from the debtor's estate and are not available to the debtor's trustee in bankruptcy (*Re Bradley-Hole* [1995] 1 WLR 1097).

Variation of voluntary arrangement

There is no provision in the IA 1986 for variation of a voluntary arrangement once approved. If the arrangement itself includes an express provision enabling variation then such provision is valid (*In Re Debtor (No 638-IO-1994)* (1998) Times, 3 December). Such a provision will not, however, necessarily be implied (*Raja v Rubin* [2000] Ch 274, CA). In the absence of an express provision for variation it may be that an express agreement between the debtor and the majority of creditors will be binding in contract as between them; but such an agreement will not directly bind any creditor or creditors who is not a party to it (*Raja v Rubin*, above). If such agreement indirectly prejudices a non-consenting creditor then such creditor may apply under the IA 1986, s 263(3) asking for the court's intervention (*Raja v Rubin*, above).

Unlimited liability partnerships

Insolvency in the case of a partnership can give rise to a complex situation. Due to the lack of separate legal personality in a traditional partnership an insolvency can result in a series of individual inter-relating voluntary relationships. The procedures have been streamlined somewhat by the Insolvent Partnerships Order 1994 (SI 1994/2421) which provides for the procedures described above to be applied with modification to a partnership.

1.2.2 COMPANIES AND LIMITED LIABILITY PARTNERSHIPS

Just as an individual can make a voluntary arrangement with creditors (para 1.2.1), so can a company or limited liability partnership. But in the case of a company or limited liability partnership there is no automatic statutory moratorium whilst an application is made. In the case of large companies the absence of an automatic moratorium can conveniently be dealt with by first initiating a formal administration and then proposing a voluntary arrangement under the umbrella of the statutory moratorium which arises in administration under the IA 1986, ss 10 and 11. In the case of small companies, however, such a combined procedure may be inappropriately costly. In order to redress the balance the Insolvency Act 2000 is to allow a small company to propose a voluntary arrangement which includes a moratorium.

The following discussion proceeds on the presumption that the proposal is made by the directors of the company. The procedure is modified slightly in the case of an application made by an administrator or liquidator (see IA 1986, Pt I and IR 1986, Pt 1) or by partners of a limited liability partnership (Limited Liability Partnerships Act 2000).

Procedure

The proposal is not made to the court but is made to the company and its creditors. A nominee acts as trustee or supervisor. The directors must prepare a document with the terms of the proposal and a statement of the company's affairs for submission to the nominee. The nominee must, within 28 days of being given notice of the proposal for a voluntary arrangement, submit a report to the court stating whether meetings of the company and its creditors should be summoned to consider the proposal. Unless the court directs otherwise such meetings as are proposed by the nominee will be held (IA 1986, s 23).

The two meetings, of the company and the creditors, must be held on the same day in the same place, and the creditors' meeting has to be fixed for a time in advance of the company meeting (IR 1986, r 1.13).

The creditors' meeting

At the creditors' meeting the creditors are able to vote according to the amount of debt owed at the date of the meeting (IR 1986, r 1.17). No creditor may vote in respect of any unliquidated amount, nor in respect of a debt of unascertained value, but the chairman may decide to estimate the minimum value of a debt for the purpose of allowing a creditor to vote. Any person aggrieved by the decision of the chairman can appeal to the court within 28 days from the day upon which the outcomes of the meetings are reported to the court. The meeting shall not approve a proposal which will affect the rights of a secured creditor to enforce his security without his consent and shall not prejudice the priority of preferential creditors without their consent (IA 1986, s 4).

The necessary majority for approval of an arrangement is three-quarters in value of the creditors voting, whether in person or by proxy, and the requisite majority for any other resolution is one-half. As with an individual voluntary arrangement (see para 1.2.1 above) the landlord can vote in respect of arrears of rent, and if the arrangement affects future rents the landlord's vote can include a weighting in respect of such rents (*Re Cancol Ltd* [1996] 1 All ER 37) .

The meeting of the company

The company's meeting is held according to the articles of association of the company and the members vote according to the voting rights attached to their shares. Members whose shares do not carry voting rights may nevertheless vote (IR 1986, r 1.18) but their vote is to be disregarded in determining whether any necessary majority has been obtained (IR 1986, r 1.20). The necessary majority is a simple majority, but the statutory rules are subject to any express provision in the company's articles (IR 1986, r 1.20).

Decision and appeal

The meetings must consider the proposed arrangement, and may consider modifications, but any modifications approved must be approved in identical form at both meetings. The outcome of each meeting must be reported to the court within four days. Any person entitled to vote, the nominee or, if the company is in liquidation or administration, the liquidator or administrator, then has 28 days to appeal to the court on one or both of two grounds. First, that the arrangement unfairly prejudices the interests of a creditor member or contributory of the company; second, that there was some material irregularity at or in relation to either of the meetings (IA 1986, s 6). If the outcome of the company's meeting differs from that of the creditors' meeting the decision of the creditors will prevail but under new rules a company member will be able to apply to court to challenge such decision (IA 1986, s 4A, as amended by the Insolvency Act 2000).

Effect of approved arrangement

The effect of an approved arrangement is similar to that described above in respect of an individual voluntary arrangement. An approved arrangement takes effect as if made by the company at the creditors' meeting. Under the IA 1986 as originally enacted, it bound every person who had notice of and who was entitled to vote at the meeting (IA 1986, s 5). New rules introduced by the Insolvency Act 2000 bind every person who would be eligible to vote at the meeting – even if such person was not notified of the meeting – but subject to the right to appeal. Any reduction in liability of an insolvent tenant will not inure for the benefit of an original tenant and such original tenant can be pursued in full for the original debt (*RA Securities Ltd v Mercantile Credit Co Ltd* [1995] 3 All ER 581). If the company was being wound up or was in administration whilst the proposal was considered, the court may stay further proceedings in the winding up or may discharge the administration order.

Execution of approved arrangement

Once approved, the arrangement will be carried out by the supervisor of the arrangement. The terms of the voluntary arrangement may include provision for the supervisor to carry on the business of the company, and he may be authorised to realise assets on behalf of the company, in which case he will presumably be acting as an agent of the company. If a creditor is dissatisfied with any act, decision or omission of the supervisor the creditor may apply to court under the IA 1986, s 7. Such an application may be made to challenge a supervisor's refusal to allow a claim under the voluntary arrangement even if the supervisor is also administrator of the company and is refusing consent to proceedings in respect of the same claim under the IA 1986, s 11 (*Holdenhurst Securities plc v Cohen* [2001] 1 BCLC 460).

Funds which are the subject of the arrangement may be regarded as held on trust for the purpose of the arrangement and may be not be available in an ensuing liquidation, depending upon the terms of the scheme (*Re Maple Environmental Services* [2000] BCC 93; *Re Brelec Installation Ltd* [2000] 2 BCLC 576).

Company voluntary agreement with moratorium

In the case of a 'small' company (as defined by the Company Act 1985, s 247(3)) full implementation of the Insolvency Act 2000 will allow an application for a moratorium (IA 1986, Sch A1, as amended). Such application cannot, however, be made if the company is an insurance company, a banking institution or is trading on the investment market. Nor can a moratorium be obtained if the company is subject to other formal insolvency procedure (including an existing voluntary arrangement) or was subject to a voluntary arrangement or moratorium in the previous 12 months.

Where the voluntary arrangement is to include a moratorium the procedures for approval and implementation of the voluntary arrangement are modified as set out in the IA 1986, Sch A1 as amended by the Insolvency Act 2000. For the approval of the voluntary arrangement with moratorium the following key points apply:

- The directors' proposal to the nominee includes the proposed moratorium.
- The nominee submits to the directors a statement in prescribed form including the nominee's opinion as to whether the proposal has a reasonable prospect of approval and implementation and whether the company will have sufficient funds during the moratorium to continue business.
- The directors lodge with the court papers describing the proposal including statements as to the company's affairs; that the company is eligible for a moratorium; that the nominee has consented to act; and a statement from the nominee confirming his opinion that the proposal has a reasonable prospect of approval and implementation and the company has sufficient funds to enable it to continue business during the moratorium.
- The moratorium begins when the necessary documents are lodged with the court at which point the directors must notify the nominee. The nominee, in turn, must advertise the fact of the moratorium and notify the registrar of companies and any creditor who has presented a winding up petition.
- The moratorium continues until the day upon which meetings of the company and its creditors are to be held or, if the nominee fails to summon such meetings, after 28 days (whichever is earlier). The moratorium can be extended by resolution of the meetings called by the nominee but

not for more than two months beginning on the day on which the later of the two meetings is held. When the moratorium ends, the nominee must again advertise that fact and notify the court, the Registrar of Companies, the company and any creditor of whom the nominee is aware.

- The interim moratorium pending approval of the voluntary arrangement establishes a complete protection for the company against the commencement of any other insolvency proceeding or (except with the leave of the court) any enforcement action by any creditor whether by formal proceedings or self-help remedy such as peaceable re-entry or distress.
- The IA 1986, Sch A1, para 13 postpones, for the period of the moratorium, the crystallisation of any floating charge and any restriction upon the disposal of the property of the company.
- The moratorium counteracts the effect of the IA 1986, s 127 so that dispositions of property made by the company during the moratorium are effective, notwithstanding the presentation of a petition for winding up (except where the petition is on the grounds of public interest or under the Financial Services Act 1986 or the Banking Act 1987).
- During the moratorium, there is a restriction upon the company obtaining credit of £250 or more.
- Property charged by way of security may be disposed of subject to the charge. By the leave of the court or with consent of the chargee the property can be disposed of as if it were not subject to the charge, but on terms that do not prejudice the chargee's rights in respect of sale proceeds.
- Any clause of a floating charge is void if it provides that the obtaining of a moratorium (or any step towards obtaining a moratorium) is an event of default causing the floating charge to crystallise or causing restrictions upon the disposal of property (IA 1986, Sch A1, para 43).
- The effect of an approved arrangement with moratorium is similar to that described above in respect of a proposed arrangement without moratorium.

Variation

There is no provision in the IA 1986 for variation of a voluntary arrangement once approved but if the arrangement itself includes an express provision enabling variation then such provision is likely to be valid; and some or all creditors may, subject to the usual rules of contract, agree modifications which can be binding upon such creditors who agree such modification (see *Raja v Rubin* [2000] Ch 274, CA involving an individual voluntary arrangement; para 1.2.1).

1.3 Appointment of receiver

Often the insolvent tenant will have borrowed money on the security of property, being or including a lease. In the case of commercial premises the lease is likely to be a short or medium term lease (normally up to 25 years) at a rack rent, not having a capital value; rather than a long lease at a ground rent, with a capital worth. The lease may be the subject of a fixed charge, that is, a mortgage specifically of the lease itself. Where the tenant is a company the lease may be one of many things affected by a floating charge over the whole or part of the tenant company's assets, which on the happening of an event of default or a formal insolvency procedure, will become a fixed charge, attaching to the assets of the tenant company available at that time, including the lease.

If the lease is specifically mortgaged, a receiver appointed to enforce the mortgage is governed by the terms of the mortgage and rules laid down in the Law of Property Act 1925, and is colloquially termed an 'LPA receiver'. If there is no specific charge over the lease, but the tenant is a company (whether registered or unregistered; *Re International Bulk Commodities Ltd* [1993] Ch 77) and there is a debenture containing a charge over the whole or substantially the whole of a company's assets, a receiver appointed to enforce the charge is known as an 'administrative receiver'. A person is also an administrative receiver if he would be a receiver of the whole or substantially the whole of the company's property but for the appointment of some other person as the receiver of part of the company's property (IA 1986, s 29). The powers and duties of an administrative receiver are regulated by the debenture which created the charge and by the IA 1986.

1.3.1 THE APPOINTMENT

Once there has been a default under the terms of a mortgage or of a floating charge the creditor with the benefit of the mortgage or charge may decide to appoint a receiver. If the charge was a floating charge over the whole or substantially the whole of a company's assets, including the company's undertaking, the receiver appointed will be an administrative receiver for the purposes of the IA 1986 (IA 1986, s 29), and must be a licensed insolvency practitioner. A receiver, whether an administrative receiver or not, of a company's property must be an individual and not a corporation (IA 1986, s 30).

Joint appointments

Although normally one or more persons may be appointed as receiver (Law of Property Act 1925, s 61) a question about the appointment which often arises in practice is whether the receivers are able to act severally as well as jointly. The document making the appointment ought to state whether the appointment is joint or joint and several, and in the case of administrative receivers there is a statutory requirement for the appointment to state this (IA 1986, s 231). A landlord or other person dealing with receivers should therefore check the terms of the appointment. In addition the terms of the mortgage or debenture should be considered since if the mortgage or debenture only authorises a joint appointment, a purported joint and several appointment is not valid as it is outside of the powers of the creditor making the appointment (see Picarda *The Law Relating to Receivers, Managers and Administrators* (3rd edn) p 60).

Formality

The appointment itself must comply with any formalities required by the terms of the mortgage or debenture, or by statute. In the case of a receiver appointed under the terms of the Law of Property Act 1925 the appointment must be in writing (Law of Property Act 1925, s 109). Unless the mortgage or debenture requires an appointment by deed, a deed is not necessary. This is so even if the receiver is empowered, by the mortgage or debenture, to act as attorney for the tenant debtor since the power to act as attorney is given by the mortgage or debenture and not by the document of appointment (*Phoenix Properties Ltd v Wimpole Street Nominees Ltd* [1992] BCLC 737).

A formality required by a mortgage or debenture may be waived by acquiescence of the debtor. For example, failure to make formal demand for the debt as required by a debenture may not invalidate actions of a receiver if following a purported appointment the debtor acquiesces and the receiver thereby acquires ostensible authority to act as agent of the debtor (*Village Cay Marina Ltd v Acland* [1998] 2 BCLC 327).

In addition, for the appointment to be effective, it is necessary that the person nominated as receiver must accept the appointment. In the case of a receiver of property of a company the appointment is of no effect unless it is accepted by the appointee before the end of the next business day following the day upon which he receives the instrument of appointment (IA 1986, s 33). The initial acceptance may be done informally but the appointee must, within seven days, confirm his acceptance in writing. The acceptance must state the time and date of receipt of the instrument of appointment and the time and date of acceptance. The appointment is deemed to be effective at the time at which the instrument of appointment was received by the receiver (IA 1986, s 33). If the appointment is a joint one there must be a separate acceptance by each of the appointees, and the appointment does not take effect unless all of them accept (IA 1986, s 46; IR 1986, r 3.1).

Notification

Following the appointment of a receiver of property of a company the creditor making the appointment must, within seven days, notify the Registrar of Companies (Companies Act 1985, s 405). Any invoices, orders or business letters of the company must bear a statement that a receiver has been appointed (IA 1986, s 39), and an administrative receiver must send notices to the company and its creditors containing prescribed information (IR 1986, r 3.2), and must advertise his appointment in the London Gazette.

Invalid appointments

If an appointment is invalid the purported receiver may be treated as a trespasser in relation to the assets of the company (*Re Simms, ex p Trustee* [1934] Ch 1, CA) and the purported appointment will confer no power to bind the company (*Jaffe Ltd (in liquidation) v Jaffe (No 2)* [1932] NZLR 195). If, however, the receiver acts with the consent or acquiescence of the company for some time then the receiver may acquire ostensible authority to act notwithstanding the invalid appointment (*Village Cay Marina Ltd v Acland* [1998] 2 BCLC 327, PC). Further, in the case of an administrative receiver, the acts of the person appointed are deemed valid notwithstanding a defect in an appointment (IA 1986, s 232), but an analogous authority suggests that this protection might not apply if the charge under which he was appointed is invalid or there is for some reason no power to make the appointment. *Morris v Kanssen* [1946] AC 459, HL was concerned with the purported appointment of a director by persons who themselves were not directors at the time of the appointment. The Companies Act 1929, s 143 stated that 'The acts of a director or manager shall be valid notwithstanding any defect that may afterwards be discovered in his appointment or qualification.' The House of Lords held that the protection of the section applied where there was a substantively good appointment, and some slip or minor error had occurred, but it did not extend to a case where the appointment was wholly invalid.

1.3.2 THE AGENCY OF THE RECEIVER

Although a receiver is appointed by the secured creditor, the receiver is almost invariably the agent, not of the creditor, but of the tenant debtor. The agency is normally created by the express terms of the mortgage or debenture. But in the absence of an express term an agency will be deemed to arise under the Law of Property Act 1925, s 109 in the case of a receiver appointed under a mortgage; or under the IA 1986, ss 44 and 109, in the case of an administrative receiver appointed under a debenture. It may seem strange to the layperson that the receiver is agent of the tenant rather than the mortgagee or debenture holder, but the rationale behind the rule is that the mortgagee or debenture holder should be paid by the tenant and the receiver is acting for the tenant in order to pay its debt. The main advantage of the arrangement to the mortgagee or debenture holder is that he is not responsible for any defaults of the receiver, since the receiver is not his agent.

Where the tenant is a company it should be noted that the agency of the receiver ceases upon the winding up order (*Gosling v Gaskell* [1897] AC 575, HL), or the resolution for voluntary winding up (*Thomas v Todd* [1926] 2 KB 511). If the company is already in liquidation when the receiver is appointed, the appointment is valid but the receiver does not normally become the agent of the company (*Re Northern Garage Ltd* [1946] Ch 188). But the fact that the receiver is not agent of the company does not necessarily make the receiver agent for the mortgagee or debenture holder (*Gosling v Gaskell*, see above). This can have serious consequences for the receiver, who may then become solely responsible for any contracts entered into by him (*Thomas v Todd*, see above), and if he is purporting to be agent of the company he will be liable for breach of warranty that he has authority to act on the company's behalf (*Gosling v Gaskell*, see above). Third parties contracting with the receiver will not be able to look to the company for performance of the contract. In an appropriate case, where the receiver is acting on the constant instructions of the mortgagee or debenture holder, the receiver will become agent of the mortgagee or debenture holder (*American Express International Banking Corpn v Hurley* (1985) 2 BCC 98, 993). In exceptional cases it may be found that the receiver is an agent of the company after liquidation, if the liquidator has authorised the receiver to act as such (*Re Northern Garage Ltd* [1946] Ch 188).

Notwithstanding the cessation of the agency of the receiver upon liquidation, some at least of the receiver's powers remain. The receiver retains the powers of disposition given to him by the mortgage or debenture (*Sowman v David Samuel Trust Ltd (in liquidation)* [1978] 1 WLR 22; see chapter 7, para 7.2.3) and the receiver can continue to take proceedings in the name of the company. In *Gough's Garages Ltd v Pugsley* [1930] 1 KB 615, a company was a tenant of commercial property. The lease was within the protection of the Landlord and Tenant Act 1927 (now Pt II of the Landlord and Tenant Act 1954), with the consequence that the company was entitled to apply to the court for a new lease at the expiry of the old one. The company served the necessary notice that it wished to take a new lease. Subsequently debenture holders appointed a receiver in respect of the whole of the company's property. The landlord did not comply with the request for a new lease, so the receiver commenced an action in the county court, in the name of the company, for a new lease. The company then went into a compulsory liquidation. The landlord objected to the continuation of the proceedings by the receiver, on the ground that the winding up order terminated the receiver's power to continue the proceedings. The Court of Appeal held that the power of the receiver to pursue proceedings in the name of the company was given by way of security by the debenture, and the order for winding up did not take away the power.

1.3.3 LIABILITY OF TENANT AND RECEIVER IN CONTRACT

The tenant as contracting party will remain liable upon all contracts entered into prior to the receivership. The receiver cannot free the tenant from the obligations in the contract, there being no power to disclaim onerous contracts. If the receiver decides not to perform or observe the terms of the contract he will render the tenant liable for breach. The other party to the contract can seek to enforce the contract, and can rely upon any lien arising out of the contract (*George Barker (Transport) Ltd v Eynon* [1974] 1 WLR 462, CA).

All the usual remedies are available against the tenant, including an order for specific performance of a contract for the sale of land (*Freevale Ltd v Metrostore Holdings Ltd* [1984] Ch 199). If a company has contracted to purchase an interest in land and subsequently a receiver is appointed, the contract is specifically enforceable and the mere fact that an order for specific performance will prejudice creditors is not sufficient reason to persuade a court to refuse an order (*AMEC Properties Ltd v Planning Research and Systems plc* [1992] BCLC 1149). Neither will a court refuse an order on the ground that the receiver might become personally liable under the terms of a lease granted pursuant to an order, since the court has a discretion to require the lease to contain an express exclusion of liability on the part of the receiver (*AMEC Properties Ltd v Planning Research and Systems plc*, above).

The receiver, on the other hand, is not personally liable on existing contracts, and if the receiver decides, on behalf of the tenant, not to honour an existing contract, the receiver is not liable for the tort of inducing the tenant to breach its contract, although a receiver may be liable for acting in bad faith or outside of his authority. The rule was stated by Sir Neil Lawson in *Lathia v Dronsfield*

Bros Ltd [1987] BCLC 321, that 'all the authorities establish that a receiver (in the circumstances of this case) is immune in actions for breach of contract and procurement of a breach of contract unless he did not act bona fide or in the course of his authority.'

In the case of fresh contracts the basic rule of agency is that the tenant, as principal, is bound by the acts of its agent, the receiver, acting within the scope of the receivership. The receiver is not, however, personally liable (*Montgomerie v United Kingdom Mutual Steamship Association* [1891] 1 QB 370). So a receiver who carries on the business of the tenant is not liable on contracts entered into by him, nor personally liable upon any claim for money had and received (*Owen & Co v Cronk* [1895] 1 QB 265, CA). However, this basic rule is modified in the case of a receiver of property of a company, in which case the Insolvency Act 1986, ss 37 and 44 provide that a receiver of property of a company will be personally liable on any contract entered into by him except in so far as the contract provides otherwise, subject to the right to be indemnified from the assets of the company. In practice, solicitors for receivers will ensure that any fresh contracts entered into by them contain exclusions of liability.

If for some reason the receiver, acting as agent for a tenant company, is contracting with the bank or other person who appointed him, the same rule as to personal liability as discussed above applies. The receiver will be personally liable upon the contract with the mortgagee or debenture holder unless personal liability is excluded by the terms of the contract or the terms of the mortgage or debenture (*Hill Samuel & Co Ltd v Laing* (1988) 4 BCC 9, Sc). In practice the receiver should, upon appointment, try to bargain so that the mortgagee or debenture holder gives an express indemnity against all liabilities that may be incurred in any dealings with any person whosoever, including the mortgagee or debenture holder.

The mortgagee or debenture holder is not liable on any contract entered into by the receiver, since the receiver is agent of the tenant (*Cully v Parsons* [1923] 2 Ch 512), except that the mortgagee may become liable if its actions show that the receiver is really agent for it rather than for the tenant.

1.3.4 CRIMINAL LIABILITY

A receiver may also commit some crime in the course of the receivership. The receiver may thereby incur personal liability, and in the case of a company may make the company liable, for instance, for a tax offence (*Re John Willment (Ashford) Ltd* [1980] 1 WLR 73). In *Meigh v Wickenden* [1942] 2 KB 160, a receiver and manager of factory premises was held to be the occupier of the premises for the purpose of the Factories Acts and was personally responsible for failure to comply with safety requirements. This was so notwithstanding that the receiver was an accountant with no knowledge of factory management, and even though the directors were still exercising general control of the factory.

1.3.5 RECEIVER'S LIABILITY FOR RATES

A receiver of commercial premises may be faced with a claim by a local authority for payment of business rates. The weight of precedent indicates that it is only in rare cases (if at all) that liability for such rates will be imposed upon the receiver personally. Rates are normally levied upon the occupier of commercial premises, or, if the premises are vacant, upon the person entitled to possession. Although in a sense a receiver of an insolvent tenant may be occupying or entitled to possession of premises, a receiver normally occupies as agent of the insolvent tenant rather than on the receiver's own behalf. Accordingly, the receiver will not usually be held personally liable for rates (*Ratford v Northavon District Council* [1987] QB 357, CA) and an early case (*Banister v Islington London Borough Council* (1972) 71 LGR 239) holding a receiver so liable must now be regarded as quite exceptional.

Neither will a receiver be guilty of 'fraudulent trading' merely because the receiver decides to defer the sale of commercial premises and thereby allow a debtor's (unsecured) liability for rates to continue (*Brown v City of London Corpn* [1996] 1 EGLR 139). Furthermore, the receiver will not usually be required to pay rates by virtue of the Law of Property Act 1925, s 109(8) and the rates will not be payable as a priority expense of the receivership (*Re Sobam BV and Saletscoop BV* [1996] 1 WLR 1070).

The position is arguably different if during receivership a liquidation ensues; in such case the agency of the receiver is usually deemed to end (see para 1.3.2 above), following which it might be thought that the receiver could incur liability for rates as the occupier. Even in such circumstances it has been held that such liability will not be imposed unless the receiver shows an intention to act as principal, and a receiver continuing to manage the business of the debtor will not thereby incur liability for rates (*Re Beck Foods Ltd* [2001] 2 BCLC 663 contd *Boston Borough Council v Rees* [2002] 02 EG 101, CA).

1.3.6 RECEIVER'S LIABILITY IN TORT

A third party may also be concerned as to whether a receiver is liable for damage caused by his negligence, or for nuisance or some other tort. Although the receiver is normally agent of the tenant, this does not absolve him from torts perpetrated by him. The general rule of law is that an agent who commits a tort in the course of the agency is a joint tortfeasor with the principal, so that the person injured by the tort may sue either or both of the agent and the principal (see *Clerk & Lindsell on Torts* (18th edn) paras 8–152 and 8–153). So, for example, if in the course of realising assets of the tenant, a receiver causes damage to the premises leased, both the tenant and the receiver may be liable to the landlord for the tort of waste (*Mancetter Developments Ltd v Garmanson* [1986] QB 1212, CA). It should be noted that the tenant will not be liable if the acts which the receiver was doing at the time of commission of the tort were outside the scope of his agency.

If the receiver interferes with goods or materials belonging to a third party the receiver will be personally liable for the tort of interference with goods. A receiver may encounter difficulty in respect of goods which were supplied to the tenant under a contract which contained a title retention clause, providing that ownership of the goods did not pass to the tenant until payment. Sometimes such a clause will only create a charge which if not registered will be unenforceable against the receiver. In some cases, however, the clause will be effective to reserve ownership to the seller of the goods or materials, and if the receiver uses or sells the goods or materials the receiver will be personally liable in tort (*Clough Mill v Martin* [1985] 1 WLR 111, CA). An administrative receiver's liability for wrongful interference with goods is mitigated by the effect of the IA 1986, s 234 which provides that where an administrative receiver seizes or disposes of property which is not property of the company, but he had reasonable grounds for believing that he was entitled to deal with the property, he is not liable to any person in respect of any loss or damage resulting from the seizure or disposal except in so far as he has acted negligently, and he has a lien on the property or the proceeds of sale for the expenses incurred in connection with the seizure or disposal.

A receiver appointed under a floating charge will also be liable in tort if he sells assets of the company and pays money to ordinary creditors and thereby causes a deficiency for preferential creditors (*Westminster Corpn v Haste* [1950] Ch 442).

1.3.7 DUTY OF CARE TO TENANT, CHARGEE AND OTHER CREDITORS

Where a receiver is managing the insolvent tenant's business and possibly selling assets in the course of the receivership, the receiver's primary duty is to the debenture holder or mortgagee. The main objective is to realise assets of the tenant in order to discharge the sums owing. If the receiver has powers of management the receiver is not under a duty to manage the business of the tenant at the expense of the chargee (*Re B Johnson & Co Builders Ltd* [1955] Ch 634, CA).

Subject to the receiver's overriding duty to the debenture holder or other chargee the receiver owes a secondary duty to the tenant. A duty is also owed to any guarantor of the tenant's obligations under the charge (*American Express International Banking Corpn v Hurley* [1985] 3 All ER 564), since a sale at less than the amount secured will leave the guarantor exposed to a claim or larger claim than would otherwise be the case (*Standard Chartered Bank Ltd v Walker* [1982] 1 WLR 1410, CA). Accordingly, the receiver's claim against a guarantor may be reduced by the amount of the 'undersell'; but the guarantor's liability will not necessarily be wholly extinguished (*Skipton Building Society v Stott* [2000] 2 All ER 779, CA). It seems that a duty is also owed to any other chargees of the property (*Downsview Nominees Ltd v First City Corpn Ltd* [1993] AC 295, PC). But no duty is owed to any unsecured creditor of the tenant. In *Hemlata Lathia v Dronsfield Bros Ltd* [1987] BCLC 321, Sir Neil Lawson said:

> 'On authority, we must look at the context to determine to whom the duties are owed. Primarily [receivers] owe a duty to their debenture holders, and also, as agents, to the company. In my judgment, they do not owe a duty to the general creditors, to contributors, to officers of the company and members. They also owe a duty to guarantors. But that is a secondary liability. It is clear on the authorities, and no authority has been cited to the contrary, that the receivers do not owe a duty to the general creditors of the company or to contributors.'

If the property is held upon trust no direct duty is owed to the beneficiaries. The duty is owed to the trustee and the trustee alone can sue (*Parker-Tweedale v Dunbar Bank plc* [1991] Ch 12, CA).

The duty is a duty for the receiver to take reasonable care in the exercise of his powers. In selling assets the duty is a duty to obtain the true market value of the property (*Cuckmere Brick Co Ltd v Mutual Finance Ltd* [1971] Ch 949, CA). What is reasonable in any particular case will, of course, depend upon the particular facts. In the *Cuckmere Brick* case the breach of duty was a failure to advertise planning permission for the property sold. Another clear example of failure to take care is if the receiver chooses to execute an immediate 'crash sale' with no regard for the interest of anyone other than the mortgagee or debenture holder (*Predeth v Castle Phillips Finance Co Ltd* [1986] 2 EGLR 144, CA). It is also probable that the receiver should not sell to the mortgagee or debenture holder, although a sale to a company in which the mortgagee or debenture holder is interested may be permissible if the circumstances show that the sale was a fair one (*Tse Kwong Lam v Wong Chit Sen* [1983] 1 WLR 1349, PC). But the duty is not set too high and in general the receiver may choose the time of sale and is not under any duty to wait for the market to improve (Salmon LJ in *Cuckmere Brick Co Ltd v Mutual Finance Ltd*, see above), or to sell quickly so as to avoid any decrease in the value of the assets charged (*China and South Sea Bank Ltd v Tan Soon Gin (alias George Tan)* [1990] 1 AC 536, PC).

There is also a duty to take reasonable care in exercising powers of management, so that a receiver has, for example, been found to be in breach of duty for failing to serve rent review notices upon tenants of the property (*Knight v Lawrence* [1993] BCLC 215). The duty to the tenant is a duty to manage the property with due diligence. The receiver is not under a duty to continue the business of the tenant, but if the receiver chooses to continue the business the receiver should take reasonable steps to do so profitably (*Medforth v Blake* [2000] Ch 86, CA).

The duty owed does not extend to a duty to consult before sale with the tenant debtor nor any surety for the debt owed by the tenant (*Mahomed v Morris* [2000] 2 BCLC 536, CA).

1.3.8 STATUTORY LIABILITY OF RECEIVER

Apart from the possibility of common law liability on contracts, in tort or for crimes, a receiver may be liable under the specific terms of the IA 1986. Where a company is in the course of being wound up, the IA 1986, s 212 provides that if an administrative receiver or other person who has taken part in the management of the company has misapplied, or retained, or become accountable for, any money or other property of the company, or been guilty of any misfeasance or breach of fiduciary or other duty, the court may compel him to repay, restore or account for the money or property or any part of it with interest at such rate as it thinks just, or to contribute such sum to the company's assets by way of compensation as it thinks just. An application may be made by the Official Receiver, the liquidator, any creditor, or, with the leave of the court, any contributory.

A receiver may also be liable for fraudulent trading under the IA 1986, s 213 which provides that if in the course of the winding up of a company it appears that any business of the company has been carried on with intent to defraud creditors of the company or any other person, or for any fraudulent purpose, the court may on the application of the liquidator declare that any person who was knowingly party to the carrying on of the business is liable to make such contributions to the company's assets as the court thinks proper.

1.3.9 DUTIES OF ADMINISTRATIVE RECEIVER

An administrative receiver has certain statutory duties which will directly or indirectly affect a landlord or other person, such as a mortgagee, interested in the lease. The receiver must obtain from the company a statement of affairs, prepare a report on the state of the company, and must present the report to a meeting of unsecured creditors. All known creditors must be notified of the meeting. Voting is according to the amount of the debt owed to the creditor at the date of appointment of the receiver, after deducting any sums paid by the company after that date. For the purpose of voting, mortgagees and other secured creditors of the tenant are required to put a value on their security, and they can only vote in respect of the balance, if any. A creditor is not entitled to vote in respect of any unliquidated amount or unascertained debt, but the chairman of the meeting has a discretion to estimate the value of the debt and allow the creditor to vote. Clearly a landlord is a creditor entitled to vote in respect of any arrears of rent but it is not clear whether the landlord is a 'debtor' in respect of future rent (cf rules for voluntary arrangements above). The meeting of creditors may establish a creditors' committee to liaise with the receiver and to assist the receiver in an agreed manner from time to time (IA 1986, ss 46–49).

1.3.10 POWERS OF RECEIVERS

A receiver of specific property will have the powers given by the Law of Property Act 1925, s 109, namely, power to demand and recover all the income of the property, by action, distress, or otherwise, and to give effective receipts, to insure, and to exercise any powers which may have been delegated to him by the mortgagee. In practice the mortgage is likely to give to the receiver substantially greater powers than the basic powers provided by the IA 1986, s 109.

A receiver appointed under a floating charge has the powers set out in the debenture under which he was appointed. An administrative receiver has, in addition, except in so far as they are inconsistent with the debenture, the powers in the IA 1986, Sch 1 (IA 1986, s 42). The powers in Sch 1 include amongst others: power to collect the property of the company and take proceedings; power to dispose of property; power to borrow money and give security; power to appoint solicitors; power to bring proceedings in the company's name; power to refer to arbitrators; power to effect insurance; power to use the company seal; power to appoint agents; power to carry on the business of the company; power to create subsidiaries; and power to grant leases. In addition, there is a power, with the leave of the court, to dispose of charged property as if it was not charged, thus enabling the receiver to dispose of property subject to a charge which ranks ahead of that under which he is appointed (IA 1986, s 43: see para 7.2.3).

Where a receiver is given powers to carry on the business of a tenant company the position of the directors is by and large supplanted by the receiver, and the directors cannot generally interfere with the receiver's exercise of his powers (see Picarda, *The Law Relating to Receivers, Managers and Administrators* (3rd edn) pp 104–108).

A person dealing with an administrative receiver ought not to be concerned that the receiver is acting within his powers, since the IA 1986, s 42(3) provides that a person dealing with the administrative receiver in good faith and for value is not concerned to inquire whether the receiver is acting within his powers. In the case of a receiver of specific property appointed under the Law of Property Act 1925 any person paying money to the receiver is not to be concerned to inquire whether any case has happened to authorise the receiver to act (Law of Property Act 1925, s 109(4)).

1.3.11 DISTRIBUTION OF ASSETS

The main function of a receiver is to use or to dispose of the assets subject to the charge in order to repay the creditor and to discharge the charge. In realising assets a receiver should be careful not to use property which is owned by third parties. Property which is in the possession and apparent ownership of the tenant may in fact belong to a third party due to there being a trust for the third party (see *Barclays Bank Ltd v Quistclose Investments Ltd* [1970] AC 567, HL), or because materials were supplied to the tenant under a contract which reserved title to the seller until payment (*Clough Mill v Martin* [1985] 1 WLR 111, CA).

In the case of a mortgage of the lease, any income received in respect of the property is to be applied as provided under the Law of Property Act 1925. Section 109 states that the income must be applied by the receiver as follows: first, in discharging outgoings on the property; second, in paying annual sums and interest due on all principal sums owed to any prior mortgagees; third, in payment of his commission, and of the premiums on fire, life, or other insurances, and the cost of doing necessary repairs (if so directed in writing by the mortgagee); fourth, in payment of interest due under the mortgage; and fifth, in discharge of the principal money (if so directed in writing by the mortgagee). Any balance is to be paid to the person who, but for the possession of the receiver, would have been entitled to receive the income of which he was appointed receiver, or who is otherwise entitled to the mortgaged property.

If a receiver appointed under a mortgage has an express power to sell, the Law of Property Act 1925, s 109 does not apply for the purpose of determining the application of the proceeds of sale, since the power of a receiver to sell is an independent express power rather than an extension of any statutory power (*Phoenix Properties Ltd v Wimpole Street Nominees Ltd* [1992] BCLC 737). Instead, it is likely that the proceeds should be applied in accordance with the Law of Property Act 1925, s 105 (*Re GL Saunders Ltd* [1986] 1 WLR 215); first, in discharging prior mortgages; second, in payment of the costs of the sale; third, in discharge of the mortgage money, interest, and costs; and last, any balance should be paid to the person entitled to the mortgaged property.

If the charge is a floating charge, and the tenant is a company which is 'not at the time in the course of being wound up', the receiver must pay the preferential debts of the company before discharging principal or interest in respect of the debenture (IA 1986, s 40). The reference to the company not being in the course of being wound up means that the company must not have passed a resolution for winding up nor been subject to an order for compulsory winding up (*Re Christonette Ltd* [1982] 1 WLR 1245). The preferential debts are also to be paid in priority to the holder of any prior charge (*Re H & K (Medway) Ltd* [1997] 2

All ER 321; cf *Griffiths v Yorkshire Bank plc* [1994] 1 WLR 1427). In a case where the creditor has the benefit of fixed and floating charges any surplus from the realisation of the fixed charge is not affected by s 40, so that the creditor can be repaid interest and capital without first settling preferential debts, and any surplus can be paid to the tenant. It is not right to pay the surplus to preferential creditors (*Re GL Saunders Ltd* [1986] 1 WLR 215).

The preferential debts are listed in the IA 1986, Sch 6. There are six categories, these being: debts due to the inland revenue; debts due to customs and excise; social security contributions; contributions to occupational pension schemes; remuneration of employees; and levies on coal and steel production.

Usually a receiver realising assets is entitled, under the terms of the legal charge, debenture or appointment, to discharge his own fees and expenses before accounting to the chargee or debenture holder for the amount secured upon the property. Where there is a prior charge the receiver should note that the debt secured by the charge must be paid before the receiver's costs and expenses, and the court has no power to order them to have priority over prior sums secured (*Choudhri v Palta* [1992] BCC 787, CA). A receiver should also note that if he pays his appointing chargee or debenture holder before subtracting his costs he runs the risk that there will be insufficient proceeds remaining to discharge his fees and expenses, and if the debtor challenges the level of costs claimed the receiver may be unable to realise further assets while any dispute over fees continues (*Rottenberg v Monjack* [1992] BCC 688).

1.4 Appointment by court of administrator

The Cork Report 1982 noted that appointment of a receiver and manager could sometimes lead to the rescue of a company through the management of the receiver, but that this process was only available where there was a floating charge in favour of a debenture holder, and provided that the debenture holder exercised the power to appoint a receiver and manager. The Cork Report 1982 recommended that the process should be available even where there is no floating charge enabling the appointment of a manager. In order to permit this, the office of administrator was created by the Insolvency Act 1985, and is now regulated by the IA 1986. The principal purpose of administration is to provide a statutory means of rescue in an attempt to avoid liquidation.

In some respects, therefore, administration is akin to administrative receivership but with the manager being appointed by the court rather than a debenture holder. The procedure has proved to be quite popular, perhaps partly because under the IA 1986, s 214 the directors of a company may more easily avoid personal liability for wrongful trading if they can show that they have taken every step, including considering an administration order, to minimise the loss to creditors from an insolvent liquidation. These are considered below the general effects which landlords may face in dealing with a company in administration. There are modified procedures in the case of both ordinary partnerships (Insolvent Partnerships Order 1994; *Re Greek Taverna* [1999] BCC 153) and limited liability partnerships (Limited Liability Partnership Regulations 2001).

Since the administration procedure was introduced there have been many orders made, although the procedure is more suited to cases where there is a lot of money involved, since the procedure is costly, usually entailing substantial professional fees.

1.4.1 EFFECT OF PETITION

Appointment of an administrator is achieved by a petition to the court presented by the company, the directors, any creditor or creditors, or the court (IA 1986, s 9). When an application is made for an administration order there is an immediate moratorium which effectively precludes any action by a landlord or other creditor, such as distress, forfeiture or execution of a judgment, without the leave of the court, except that a debenture holder can appoint an administrative receiver, and a creditor can present a petition for the winding up of the company, but the petition cannot be heard unless the application is dismissed (IA 1986, s 10). An administrative receiver is free to carry out his functions in the period between petition and order. The moratorium precludes not only civil action but also criminal proceedings, such as proceedings for breach by the company of a waste management licence (*Environment Agency v Clark* [2000] 1 EGLR 113, CA).

1.4.2 THE HEARING AND ORDER

If the court is satisfied that a company is or is likely to become unable to pay its debts (IA 1986, s 8) the court may make an administration order if it is likely that one or more of the following purposes will be achieved:

1. the survival of the company and its undertaking as a going concern;
2. the approval of a voluntary arrangement;
3. the sanctioning under the Companies Act 1985, s 425 of a compromise or arrangement;
4. a more advantageous realisation of the company's assets than on a winding up.

If there is an administrative receiver an order is not to be made without the consent of the administrative receiver unless the court is satisfied that, if an administration order were made, any security by virtue of which the receiver was appointed would be void or liable to be set aside as a preference, a transaction at an undervalue, or as a floating charge not given for fresh consideration, under the IA 1986, ss 238–245.

An administration order is an order directing that during the period for which the order is in force the affairs, business and property of the company shall be managed by a person appointed for the purpose by the court (the administrator).

The person appointed must be a licensed insolvency practitioner (IA 1986, s 230). If more than one person is appointed to the office the appointment must state whether they are able to act separately as well as jointly (IA 1986, s 231(2)). The formalities of appointment may not be of great import to a landlord or other person dealing with the administrator since the appointment is by the court, and by the IA 1986, s 232 the acts of an administrator are valid in law notwithstanding any defect in his appointment, nomination or qualifications (cf para 1.3.1).

1.4.3 CIRCUMSTANCES IN WHICH AN ORDER WILL BE MADE

One of the purposes for which an administration order may be made is that the order will result in a more advantageous realisation of the company's assets than on a winding up. In a case where a lease is a major asset of the company the preservation of the lease can be a good enough reason to justify an order. In *Re Dallhold Estates (UK) Pty Ltd* [1992] BCLC 621, a major asset of an Australian company was a lease of agricultural property in England, said to be worth £1m. The company was the subject of an application for its winding up in Australia and provisional liquidators had been appointed in both Australia and England, but the lease was liable to be ended by forfeiture if the tenant went into liquidation. Since the lease was an agricultural lease a court would not, following forfeiture, have any jurisdiction to grant relief from forfeiture and reinstate the lease. It would therefore be undesirable for a winding up order to be made. Apart from the threat of forfeiture the value of the lease was in question because of an alleged surrender, an alleged termination by notice and an alleged proprietary interest in favour of a third party. The English provisional liquidator disputed the claims and the English court was requested by the Australian court to make an administration order as a means of preserving the lease and for its better realisation. Chadwick J was of the view that if an administration order was made it was probable that the administrator would be able to preserve the lease (whether subject to the alleged proprietary interest or not) and he made an administration order on the condition that the administrator, before embarking upon litigation concerning the lease, would satisfy himself that he was adequately funded for the litigation.

It may be appropriate to make an administration order notwithstanding that the motivation of a petitioner is to thwart a claimant from obtaining assets of the company. In *Re Dianoor Jewels Ltd* [2001] 1 BCLC 450, it was proper to make an administration order where a company was insolvent even though the petition was presented by the beneficial owner and director whose purpose included to frustrate an order of the family court in favour of his wife, which included various directions for the transfer to the wife of assets belonging to the company.

1.4.4 EFFECT OF ORDER

If an order is made, its effect is to make more permanent the moratorium in that any petition for winding up is dismissed and any administrative receiver must vacate office. The administrator may also require a receiver of part of the company's property to vacate office. Otherwise creditors cannot take steps to enforce security, to distrain, to take legal proceedings or execute judgments without the leave of the court or the consent of the administrator (IA 1986, s 11). Creditors will generally be on notice that an administration order has been made by the requirement that every invoice, order for goods or business letters of the company issued after the order is made must contain the administrator's name and a statement that the affairs of the company are being managed by the administrator (IA 1986, s 12).

1.4.5 POSITION OF ADMINISTRATOR

The role of the administrator, in accordance with the policy mentioned above, is very much modelled upon the role of an administrative receiver, and, like the administrative receiver, the administrator is deemed to be acting as agent of the company (IA 1986, s 14). A landlord or other person dealing with an administrator can therefore deal with him on a similar footing to an administrative receiver (see para 1.3.2 above). It should be noted, however, that an administrator is also an officer of the court and as such a higher standard of conduct is expected of him. He must act responsibly and must make his decisions speedily (*Re Atlantic Computer Systems plc* [1992] Ch 505, CA).

The administrator as agent will not be personally liable upon the company's contracts, so long as the agency is disclosed. There is no statutory provision, unlike in the case of an administrative receiver, for the administrator to be personally liable on contracts entered into by him without an express exclusion of liability.

The administrator may be liable in tort, subject to the protection given by the IA 1986, s 234 to a conversion of property done by the administrator in good faith (cf para 1.3.6). If a company is being wound up an administrator may be held liable under the IA 1986, s 212 for any misapplication of money or property of the company, or for any 'misfeasance or breach of any fiduciary or other duty in relation to the company'. The court may on the application of the Official Receiver or liquidator, or of any creditor or (with the leave of the court) any contributory, examine the conduct of the administrator and compel him to make restitution to the company. Once the administrator has been released from his duties an application cannot be made except with the leave of the court. An administrator might also be liable under the IA 1986, 213 for fraudulent trading (cf para 1.3.8).

Where an administrator is guilty of some default in the management of the company, relief may be obtained under the Companies Act 1985, s 727 which provides that an officer of the company may be relieved from liability for negligence, default, breach of duty or breach of trust, if the officer has acted honestly and reasonably and ought fairly to be excused. It has been held that an administrator is an 'officer' of the company for the purpose of the statute (*Re Home Treat* [1991] BCLC 705).

1.4.6 POWERS OF ADMINISTRATOR

An administrator may do all things necessary for the management of the company's affairs and property including removing directors (IA 1986, s 14). Without prejudice to the generality of the wide power given by s 14 an administrator has the powers in the IA 1986, Sch 1. These include: power to manage and to deal with the company's property; power to borrow money and grant security; power to appoint solicitors, accountants and other professionals and agents; power to pursue legal proceedings in the company's name; power to refer disputes to arbitration; power to insure; power to use the company's seal and to execute deeds and other documents for the company; power to make payments; power to carry on the business of the company and to establish subsidiaries, and to transfer business or property to subsidiaries;

power to enter into compromises; power to call up uncalled capital; power to claim or prove in the insolvency of any debtor of the company; power to present or defend a petition for winding up of the company; power to change the company's registered office; and power to do all other things incidental to the specific powers described.

In addition, by the IA 1986, ss 14 and 15, the administrator may remove or appoint any director of the company; the administrator may call a meeting of members or creditors at any time so as to consult with such persons about ways of proceeding which might be acceptable to them; and the administrator may, without the leave of the court '... dispose of or otherwise exercise his powers in relation to any property of the company which is subject to a [floating charge] ..., as if the property were not subject to the security'. This enables the administrator to rationalise the assets of the company, but the chargee will have 'the same priority in respect of any property of the company directly or indirectly representing the property disposed of as he would have had in respect of the property subject to the security' (see para 7.2.5).

The administrator may also, with the leave of the court, dispose of property free from a fixed charge. In this case the 'net proceeds of sale' and 'where those proceeds are less than such amount as may be determined by the court to be the net amount which would be realised on a sale of the property ... in the open market by a willing vendor, such sums as may be required to make good the deficiency' shall be applied in discharging the sums secured. So in this case the administrator takes a risk since if he does not realise the full open market value, the deficiency must be made good from the company's assets (para 7.2.5).

The administrator in exercising his powers is an agent of the company; there is no magic to his powers. So s 14 does not give the administrator any ability to do on behalf of the company acts which are ultra vires (*Re Home Treat* [1991] BCLC 705). He can exercise his powers, including any power to dispose of a lease, upon his appointment, without waiting for any meeting of creditors (*Re NS Distribution* [1990] BCLC 169).

Protection of purchaser

The IA 1986 provides that a person dealing with the administrator in good faith and for value is not concerned to inquire whether the administrator is acting within his powers (IA 1986, s 14(6)). It seems that a person dealing needs only to satisfy himself that the administrator has been appointed. Since the powers are drafted so widely it is unlikely that this provision will often need to be invoked, although the protection might perhaps be relevant to a purchaser of property free from a fixed charge, in which case it might not be necessary to check that the leave of the court has been obtained, as required by the IA 1986, s 15.

1.4.7 DUTIES OF ADMINISTRATOR

On his appointment the administrator must take into his custody or control all the property of the company, and must manage the affairs and business of the company. At a time before approval of any proposals the administrator must act in accordance with the court's directions (IA 1986, s 17). Once a proposal is approved the administrator can act in accordance with its terms. The administrator must notify various persons of the administration order, including creditors of the company and the registrar of companies, and he must advertise the order in the London Gazette (IA 1986, s 21; IR 1986, r 2.10).

The administrator must obtain from the company a statement of affairs, and must prepare proposals to give effect to the purpose for which the administration order was made. The proposal must be put to a meeting of the company's creditors. The creditors vote at the meeting in accordance with the debt owed to them at the date of the administration order, but secured creditors must first deduct the value of their security. A creditor cannot vote in respect of any unliquidated debt or unascertained amount, except where the chairman agrees to put upon the debt an estimated minimum value. A resolution is passed if there is an ordinary majority of voting power in favour of it. If the administrator's proposals are approved he must inform the court and give notice to the registrar of companies. If the proposals are not approved the court may discharge the administration order or make any other order that it thinks fit (IA 1986, s 24; IR 1986, ss 2.18–2.30).

1.4.8 RELEASE OF ADMINISTRATOR

An administrator may, at any time, apply to the court for the administration order to be discharged (IA 1986, s 18). Such a discharge will not, however, automatically be given. It may not be right, for example, for an administration to be terminated and for a company to go into liquidation where an administrator has not properly dealt with an outstanding application by a landlord for consent to forfeit a lease or to take other action. Even if the administration order is discharged and a winding-up order obtained, a court may refuse to release the administrator while a claim is outstanding against him (*Barclays Mercantile Business Finance Ltd v Sibec Developments Ltd* [1993] 2 All ER 195).

1.5 Bankruptcy

Where the tenant is an insolvent individual (or partnership other than a limited liability partnership) and the voluntary procedures (see above paras 1.1 and 1.2), short of bankruptcy, for dealing with the insolvency are not adequate, then the tenant's affairs may be wound up by the long-established procedure of bankruptcy. Although much old law will remain relevant today it should be borne in mind when considering established principles that the law of bankruptcy was overhauled by the IA 1986. The basic procedure involved is the presentation of a petition, followed by the making of a bankruptcy order for the winding up of the tenant's affairs. There are modified procedures in the case of partnerships and a partnership may alternatively be wound up as an unregistered company (Insolvent Partnerships Order 1994, SI 1994/2421).

1.5.1 PRESENTATION OF A PETITION

A petition for bankruptcy may be presented by a creditor, the supervisor of a voluntary arrangement, or any person (other than the debtor) who is for the time being bound by a voluntary arrangement, or by the debtor himself (IA 1986, s 264).

Creditor's petition

A creditor may present a petition if there is or are a liquidated debt or debts of £750 or more and the debtor is unable to pay or has no reasonable prospects of paying (IA 1986, s 267). A secured creditor can only petition if he is willing to surrender his security or if he puts a value on the security and the petition is expressed to be made in respect of the unsecured balance only (IA 1986, s 269).

The petitioning process incorporates some important limitations and safeguards which must be taken into account by the petitioning creditor. The requirement that the debt be liquidated will, for example, prevent a landlord from petitioning on the ground of breach of a covenant, such as a covenant to repair the premises leased. If there is such a breach the landlord will not be able to petition without first obtaining judgment for damages.

A second important restriction is that the debtor must be unable to pay the liquidated debt. The IA 1986 recognises only two ways in which such inability may be proven. Inability to pay will be shown if the creditor serves on the tenant a demand in statutory form (the 'statutory demand') in respect of a liquidated debt and the demand is not satisfied within three weeks (see paras 2.9.1, 2.9.2). Alternatively, inability to pay will be proved if execution or other legal process issued in respect of a debt on a judgment or order of a court has been returned unsatisfied in whole or in part (IA 1986, s 268(1)).

A petition may be dismissed if the court is satisfied that the debtor is able to pay all his debts or if the debtor has made an offer to the petitioning creditor which has been unreasonably refused (IA 1986, s 271). A proposed voluntary arrangement is not an offer within section 271 and a vote by a creditor against the arrangement is not an unreasonable refusal justifying dismissal of the creditor's petition (*Re a Debtor (No 2389 of 1989)* [1991] Ch 326).

Debtor's petition

A tenant who is in severe financial difficulties might consider presenting a petition for his own bankruptcy. In this way the tenant may provide for the orderly payment of creditors and eventual discharge from bankruptcy, to start again with a clean slate. In the past debtors sometimes abused the procedure by presenting petitions for the sole purpose of staving off creditors, and then, when matters improved, the debtor would withdraw the petition. There are now a number of safeguards which act so as to minimise the risk of the debtor invoking his own bankruptcy as an abuse of process.

First, the tenant can only present a petition for his own bankruptcy on the ground that he 'is unable to pay his debts' (IA 1986, s 272). In *Re A Debtor, ex p Debtor v Allen (No 17 of 1966)* [1967] Ch 590, the debtor had suffered a court order that he make periodic payments to a person who had been physically injured by the debtor. The debtor then petitioned for his own bankruptcy on inability to pay debts. It was held that the only question which was relevant was whether he was able to make the periodic payments as they fell due, and that as he was so able there was no reasonable ground for his petition.

Even if the debtor is unable to pay his debts the court can still exercise its discretion not to make a bankruptcy order, since the IA 1986, s 264 provides only that the court 'may make a bankruptcy order on any such petition'. So, if an order is inappropriate it need not be made. Of course, at the time of hearing the petition the court may not be aware of any impropriety, and in practice the bankruptcy order is often made in the first instance and allegations of impropriety may follow by way of an application for annulment of the bankruptcy order (*Re Hester* (1889) 22 QBD 632, CA). An application may be made under the IA 1986, s 282. At the hearing of an application the court can rule that the bankruptcy order ought not to have been made. It will probably be a good ground for an application that the debtor is using the bankruptcy procedure improperly so as to avoid his debtors, as in *Re Betts, ex p Official Receiver* [1901] 2 KB 39, where a debtor had presented successive petitions for his own bankruptcy in order to avoid the effect of a court execution. Now a debtor is precluded from withdrawing a petition without the leave of the court (IA 1986, s 266), making it difficult for a debtor to abuse the process in this way.

Effect of petition

The presentation of a petition does not actually establish a moratorium but during the period between petition and order the court can stay any action, execution or other legal process against the property or person of the tenant debtor (IA 1986, s 285(1)). Any disposition of property made by the tenant in this period is void (see para 7.1.1).

1.5.2 ROLE OF OFFICIAL RECEIVER

The Official Receiver has the general role of supervising the bankruptcy procedure. The duties of the Official Receiver begin once a petition is presented. Following the presentation of a petition, if necessary, the Official Receiver may be appointed as an interim receiver to manage the debtor's property pending the making of a bankruptcy order and the vesting of the debtor's property in the trustee in bankruptcy (IA 1986, s 286). During the period up to the making of an order the Official Receiver, as interim receiver, has the powers which he would otherwise not get until a bankruptcy order is made.

If a bankruptcy order is made, the Official Receiver automatically becomes the receiver and manager of the bankrupt's estate until a trustee in bankruptcy is appointed. During the period that he is either interim receiver, or receiver and manager, his role is a caretaking one. He is entitled to sell perishable goods and any other goods comprised in the estate the value of which is likely to diminish, but otherwise he should preserve the bankrupt's property rather than dispose of it (IA 1986, s 287).

1.5.3 COMMITTEE OF CREDITORS

The Official Receiver may call a meeting of the bankrupt's creditors, and the meeting can establish a committee of between three and five creditors (the 'committee of creditors') to supervise the trustee, but may not do so if the Official Receiver is trustee. Whilst the Official Receiver is trustee the functions of the committee are vested in the Secretary of State. The IR 1986 contain detailed provisions in relation to the constitution and operation of such a committee (IR 1986, rr 6.150–6.166).

1.5.4 EFFECT OF BANKRUPTCY ORDER

Once a petition is heard and a bankruptcy order made the tenant carries the title of undischarged bankrupt. From that moment on the tenant is subject to a number of substantial disabilities. Until the appointment of a trustee in bankruptcy the tenant is under a duty to deliver possession of his estate to the Official Receiver. The Official Receiver acts as receiver or manager of the tenant's estate, with the same powers as if he were acting as a receiver or manager appointed by the court (IA 1986, s 287). The Official Receiver has all the powers relating to the lease during the period leading up to appointment of a trustee. The Official Receiver's role is to preserve the estate, not to wind it up. He will not normally therefore sell the lease unless there are special circumstances making it likely that its value will diminish if it is not sold (IA 1986, s 287(2)). Meanwhile, any disposition made by the bankrupt without the consent of the court or without being ratified by the court is void (IA 1986, s 284).

The Official Receiver's stop-gap role includes the investigating of the affairs of the tenant and the tenant is under a duty to deliver a statement of affairs to the Official Receiver within 21 days of the order. The Official Receiver may, and must if required by the court, convene a meeting of creditors to consider the affairs of the bankrupt tenant. The Official Receiver may also, at any time before the bankruptcy ends by discharge, apply to the court for the public examination of the tenant.

Once an order is made, the landlord and any creditor is not to have any remedy against the property or person of the bankrupt in respect of a debt provable in the bankruptcy, and must not commence any action or other legal proceedings against the bankrupt except with the leave of the court and on such terms as the court may impose (IA 1986, s 285(3)). The provisions do not affect the right of a secured creditor to enforce his security (IA 1986, s 285(4)), and do not prevent a landlord from exercising his right to forfeit a lease or distrain for rent (see paras 3.6.3, 4.4.4).

1.5.5 SUMMARY ADMINISTRATION

In some cases of bankruptcy the cost of the bankruptcy may be reduced by the new summary administration procedure. The procedure is intended to apply to 'small' bankruptcies, that is, those bankruptcies where the aggregate amount of unsecured debts is less than the prescribed amount (currently £20,000: SI 1986/1996). In such cases the bankruptcy may be administered without a full enquiry into the affairs of the bankrupt (IA 1986, s 289(5)); discharge will follow at the end of two years rather than the usual three; and there is an exemption from criminal liability for failure to keep proper accounts. The procedure is only available where the bankruptcy results from a debtor's petition rather than a creditor's, and provided that within the period of five years ending with the presentation of the petition the debtor has not been adjudged bankrupt, and has not made a composition with his creditors, nor a scheme of arrangement of his affairs (IA 1986, s 275).

1.5.6 APPOINTMENT OF TRUSTEE IN BANKRUPTCY

Following the bankruptcy order it is the duty of the Official Receiver to decide whether to convene a meeting of creditors within 12 weeks, in order to appoint a trustee in bankruptcy (IA 1986, s 293). The Official Receiver does not normally have to call such a meeting, although he must do so if requested to by at least one-quarter in value of the tenant's creditors (IA 1986, s 294). Usually the only reason why the Official Receiver might fail to call a meeting for the appointment of a trustee is if the tenant is so insolvent that the fees of an insolvency practitioner appointed as trustee would contribute to a deficiency for the preferential creditors. In such a case the Official Receiver may decide to act as trustee himself at public expense.

1.5.7 VESTING OF PROPERTY

Immediately upon a trustee being appointed, the bankrupt's property, including any lease, option for lease or right of pre-emption (*Dear v Rees* [2001] 1 BCLC 643) vests in the trustee. If the Official Receiver is to act as trustee the bankrupt's property will vest in the Official Receiver upon his becoming trustee. The vesting takes effect automatically without the need for any conveyance, assignment or transfer (IA 1986, s 306). If the bankrupt only has an option to take a lease, the option vests in the trustee (*Buckland v Papillon* (1866) 2 Ch App 67).

Excluded property

The bankrupt's estate excludes tools, books, vehicles and such other items of equipment as are necessary to the bankrupt for use personally by him in his employment, business or vocation, and such clothing, bedding, furniture, household equipment and provisions as are necessary for satisfying the basic domestic needs of the bankrupt and his family. If any of these excluded items could on sale realise more than the cost of a reasonable replacement the trustee can opt to claim the item as part of the estate by serving notice, and by providing funds for a reasonable replacement (IA 1986, ss 308–9).

Trust property

The estate does not include property held by the bankrupt on trust for some other person or persons (IA 1986, s 283). This is so even if the bankrupt is entitled to part of the beneficial interest in the property. The law is summarised well by a statement made by Roxburgh J in *Re a Solicitor* [1952] Ch 328:

> 'The words "on trust for any other person" in my judgment, are of very wide import ... If it can be said of any asset that though the title is in the bankrupt, a beneficial interest therein resides in some person other than the bankrupt, even though the bankrupt himself may also have a beneficial interest therein, the asset does not vest in the trustee [in bankruptcy], though the beneficial interest, if any, which the bankrupt himself has would vest in the trustee [in bankruptcy].'

After acquired property

After acquired property is not part of the estate, since it is not property belonging to the bankrupt at the commencement of the bankruptcy, but the trustee can serve notice upon the bankrupt claiming the property for the estate (IA 1986, s 307). If the bankrupt, after acquiring the property, sells it to a purchaser in good faith without notice of the bankruptcy the purchaser is protected and the trustee has no remedy against him (IA 1986, s 307(4)). If a contract for sale of an after acquired lease has been entered into, the contract is valid and may be enforced by the bankrupt against the purchaser (*Re Clayton and Barclays Contract* [1895] 2 Ch 212).

It is the duty of the bankrupt within 21 days of acquiring the property to give notice to the trustee, giving the trustee 42 days to decide whether he wishes to take a vesting of the property (IA 1986, s 333). During the 42-day period the bankrupt must not dispose of the property. If the bankrupt sells to a purchaser without notifying the trustee of the acquisition, or without allowing the requisite 42 days the trustee may trace the property into the hands of the purchaser and recover it, by serving notice within 21 days of his becoming aware of the purchaser's identity (IR 1986, rr 6.200–6.201). It is doubtful that this rule overrides the protection given to a purchaser in good faith by s 307.

Tenancies protected by statute

Certain residential tenancies which are protected by statute do not vest in the trustee in bankruptcy, although he can serve notice requiring their vesting (see chapter 6, para 6.1.2).

1.5.8 POSITION OF THE BANKRUPT

Subject to limitations the bankrupt may enter into fresh contracts. If the bankrupt contracts to take a lease, or an assignment of one, specific performance may lie against a landlord or vendor (*Dyster v Randall & Sons* [1926] Ch 932).

The bankrupt will, however, be guilty of a criminal offence if he obtains credit above the prescribed amount (currently £250) without giving the person from whom he obtains the credit the relevant information about his status. The bankrupt will also be guilty of an offence if he engages in any business under a name other than that in which he was adjudged bankrupt without disclosing to all persons with whom he enters into any business transaction the name in which he was adjudged bankrupt. The bankrupt is further restricted by the requirement not to dispose of after acquired property without first giving the trustee the chance to claim it as part of the estate (see para 1.5.7 above).

1.5.9 ROLE AND POWERS OF THE TRUSTEE

The trustee's primary role is to 'get in, realise and distribute the bankrupt's estate'. He is also, if he is not the Official Receiver, to furnish the Official Receiver with information, papers, records and assistance (IA 1986, s 305). In order to facilitate the carrying out of these duties wide powers are bestowed upon the trustee enabling him to take possession of the bankrupt's property, books and records (IA 1986, s 312).

Powers subject to permission

Some of the trustee's powers are exercisable only with the permission of the court or of the creditors' committee, if there is one (IA 1986, s 314). The powers are listed in s 314 and Pt I of the IA 1986, Sch 5 and include, amongst others: the power to carry on the bankrupt's business; power to engage in litigation in relation to the bankrupt's property; power to sell assets upon credit terms; power to borrow money on security of the bankrupt's property; and power to compromise claims. If the trustee acts without the necessary permission the court or the creditors' committee may, for the purpose of enabling him to meet his expenses out of the bankrupt's estate, ratify what he has done, but the committee (as opposed to the court) can only do so if it is satisfied that the trustee acted out of urgency and sought its ratification without undue delay (IA 1986, s 314).

A purchaser in good faith from the trustee is not to be concerned with the question as to whether the requisite permission has been given (IA 1986, s 314(3)).

Powers not subject to permission

The trustee's general powers, exercisable without permission are catalogued in the IA 1986, Sch 5, Pt II. They are: power to sell any assets; give valid receipts for money; prove, rank claim and draw a dividend in respect of debts due to the bankrupt; exercise any powers given to him by the IA 1986, Pts VIII–XI of the Act; where goods of the bankrupt are held by any person by way of security, to serve notice upon that person requiring a right to inspect the goods and preventing the person from realising the security without the leave of the court or to exercise the bankrupt's right of redemption in respect of the goods; to summon a general meeting of the bankrupt's creditors; to determine when and where the creditors' committee shall meet; to employ a solicitor; and to apply to the court for a direction that the bankrupt do specific things for the purposes of the bankruptcy.

Ancillary powers

The trustee has certain ancillary powers described in the IA 1986, Sch 5, Pt III that he may by his official name hold property, make contracts, sue and be sued, enter into engagements binding on himself and his successors in office, employ agents and execute any power of attorney, deed or other instrument. He may also do any other act which is necessary or expedient for the purpose of or in connection with the exercise of his powers.

Other restrictions on powers

There are several powers the exercise of which must be notified to the creditors' committee if there is one. Notice must be given if the trustee, not being the Official Receiver, disposes of any property to an associate of the bankrupt (IA 1986, s 314(6)). The term 'associate' is defined in the IA 1986, s 435, and includes, amongst others, relatives of the bankrupt. Notice must also be given if the trustee, not being the Official Receiver, employs a solicitor. If the trustee disposes of property to an associate of his the transaction may be set aside (IR 1986, r 6.147).

Any person dissatisfied with the trustee's exercise of his powers can apply to the court to have the trustee's decision modified or reversed (IA 1986, s 303), but the court is unlikely to interfere in the absence of fraud (*Re a Debtor, ex p Debtor v Dodwell (Trustee)* [1949] Ch 236).

1.5.10 LIABILITY OF TRUSTEE

The trustee in bankruptcy, as officer of the court, is expected to act with a high degree of conduct and care. A trustee must not act in a wasteful or vexatious manner (*Re Smith, ex p Brown* (1886) 17 QBD 488, CA). If the trustee receives money paid under a mistake of law he should refund it, even though money paid under a mistake of law is normally not recoverable by the payer (*Re Condon, ex p James* (1874) 9 Ch App 609).

Contracts entered into by the bankrupt prior to bankruptcy pass to the trustee who can enforce such contracts, and who becomes liable to perform them, unless he disclaims them or they are otherwise discharged. The trustee does not, however, become personally liable for debt on an existing contract, and the other contracting party has a right of proof only. If, however, the contract is a continuing one such as a lease, the trustee will become personally liable for future obligations if he elects to take the continuing benefit of the lease or other contract for the purpose of the bankruptcy (para 2.4, cf para 2.3.2). The other contracting party may, if he wishes, apply under the IA 1986, s 345 which gives the court a discretion to order the discharge of obligations under a contract on such terms as to payment by the applicant or the bankrupt of damages for non-performance as the court thinks fit, but damages payable by the bankrupt are only provable as a bankruptcy debt.

The trustee may be liable personally for any torts committed by him, but in so far as the trustee may inadvertently have converted property belonging to a third party, the trustee may be relieved, except to the extent that he may have been negligent, if he believed, and had reasonable grounds for believing, that he was entitled to seize or dispose of the property (IA 1986, s 304).

The trustee in occupation is the occupier for the purposes of non-domestic rates, is personally liable, and is not relieved by disclaimer (*Re Lister, ex p Bradford Overseers and Bradford Corpn* [1926] Ch 149, CA).

If the trustee has misapplied or retained, or become accountable for money or other property comprised in the bankrupt's estate, or if the bankrupt's estate has suffered any loss in consequence of any 'misfeasance' or 'breach of fiduciary or other duty' the court may order the trustee to repay, restore or account for money or other property, together with interest at such rate as the court thinks just, or, to pay such sum by way of compensation in respect of the misfeasance or breach of duty as the court thinks just (IA 1986, s 304).

1.5.11 PRIORITY OF DEBTS

One of the most important considerations in the mind of a creditor of an insolvent tenant, such as a landlord or mortgagee of the lease, is in what order of priority will the assets of the insolvent tenant be distributed in the event of bankruptcy. Apart from the position governing the rights of secured creditors, the basic order of priority of distribution of the bankrupt's assets is as follows:

1. Expenses of the bankruptcy (IR 1986, r 6.224).
2. Pre-preferential debts (see below).
3. Preferential debts (IA 1986, s 328).
4. Ordinary debts (IA 1986, s 328).
5. Interest (IA 1986, s 328).
6. Postponed debts (see below).
7. Surplus to bankrupt.

Mortgagees

A creditor with a specific mortgage over the lease is in the strongest position, since unless he surrenders the security the security remains, and the lease cannot be disposed of free from the charge. If the value of the lease exceeds the amount of the outstanding debt the mortgagee is quite secure and can rely upon his powers as mortgagee so as to ensure payment of the debt. No leave is required for the enforcement of the mortgage (IA 1986, s 285(4)), unless for some reason court proceedings are necessary in relation to the debt. A mortgagee has the following choices:

1. Do nothing, leaving the charge over the asset for the time being.
2. Surrender the security for the general benefit of creditors and prove in the bankruptcy as an ordinary unsecured creditor (IR 1986, r 6.109).
3. Value the security (IA 1986, ss 269, 383), and prove for the balance (if any) as an ordinary unsecured creditor.
4. Realise the security and prove for any balance as an ordinary creditor (IR 1986, rr 6.109, 6.119).
5. Apply to the court for an order that the land be sold (IR 1986, r 6.197). In this case the proceeds of sale will be applied firstly in payment of the expenses of the trustee, and occasioned by the application to the court, of the sale; secondly, in payment of the amount found due to any mortgagee, for principal, interest and costs, and the balance (if any) must be retained by or paid to the trustee.
6. Put the trustee to an election whether he will or will not exercise his power to redeem at the value put upon it. The trustee then has six months within which to redeem (IR 1986, r 6.117).

The trustee, on the other hand has the following options:

1. Redeem the charge at the value specified by the creditor, giving the creditor the opportunity, normally 21 days, to revalue (IR 1986, r 6.117). The trustee is likely to choose this option if he thinks that the creditor has undervalued the security.
2. Test the security's value by offering it for sale (IR 1986, r 6.118). This is likely to occur if the trustee suspects that the creditor has overvalued the property. This option is not open to the trustee if the security has been revalued previously and the revaluation has been approved by the court.

A secured creditor can with the agreement of the trustee or the leave of the court alter the value which he has in his proof of debt put upon his security. If, however, the creditor is the petitioner and has put a value on the security in the petition, or the creditor has voted in respect of the unsecured balance of the debt, he can only revalue with the leave of the court (IR 1986, r 6.115). Leave will probably be given if the property has increased in value (*Re Becher* [1944] Ch 78), but probably not once the creditor has put the trustee to an election to redeem and the trustee has so elected (*Re Sadler, ex p Norris* (1886) 17 QBD 728, CA).

A secured creditor can normally allocate the security to whatever part of the debt he wishes so that if there is a preferential debt and a non-preferential one the mortgagee can use the security to discharge the non-preferential debt and claim the preferential debt in the normal way (*Re William Hall (Contractors) Ltd (in liquidation)* [1967] 2 All ER 1150). But the mortgagee cannot increase his proof by applying the proceeds of realisation of his security to payment of interest accruing after the date of the bankruptcy order (*Quartermaine's Case* [1892] 1 Ch 639).

Although discharge from bankruptcy releases all bankruptcy debts it does not affect the secured creditor's power to realise the security for the debt and all interest to the date of realisation (IA 1986, s 281).

Bankruptcy expenses

The expenses of the bankruptcy must be paid before any other claims. The expenses are listed in IR 1986, r 6.224, and include: expenses incurred in preserving, realising or getting in any of the assets of the company; expenses incurred in carrying on the business of the debtor; the fees of the Official Receiver or an interim receiver, or special manager; the costs of the petitioner; the costs of preparing a statement of affairs; any necessary disbursements by the trustee; fees of other persons involved in providing services for the trustee; and the remuneration of the trustee.

Pre-preferential debts

After the trustee has dealt with the costs of administering the bankruptcy he is next to use any available funds for several special types of debt which are prescribed by statute. Examples include any fees paid to the bankrupt by any apprentice or articled clerk (IA 1986, s 348), and, in the case of a deceased bankrupt, reasonable funeral, testamentary and administrative expenses.

Preferential debts

The debts which are next in line are preferential debts, being mainly debts relating to tax liability and employer's liability. They are described in IA 1986, Sch 6 and are:

1. debts due to the Inland Revenue;
2. debts due to Customs and Excise;
3. social security contributions;
4. contributions to occupational pensions schemes;
5. remuneration owed to employees; and
6. levies on coal and steel production.

Ordinary debts

Ordinary unsecured creditors will be paid after preferential creditors, if there is enough in the kitty, in accordance with their proofs of debts (IA 1986, s 328). If there is a partial deficiency each creditor's claim will abate proportionately, so that the creditors will be entitled to a dividend expressed in terms of a number of pence in every pound.

Interest

If ordinary creditors are paid in full and there is a surplus, interest may be paid on all debts, whether preferential or not, in respect of the periods during which they have been outstanding since the commencement of the bankruptcy. Interest on preferential debts ranks equally with interest on other debts.

Postponed debts

Some debts are specifically postponed by statute, for e g under the Partnership
Act 1890, s 3 the claim of a lender to a partnership who receives a rate of interest varying with the profits of the business, or the claim of a seller of goodwill
of a business, who takes as part of the consideration for the goodwill a profit
share in the business.

Surplus

In the unlikely event of there being any surplus after payment of creditors, it will
pass to the bankrupt.

1.6 Liquidation

Where the tenant is a company it may become necessary or desirable at some
stage for the company to be wound up; i e for its assets to be liquidated
and distributed amongst creditors and contributories. Very often such winding up will be the result of insolvency, but a solvent company may also be
wound up, usually for the purpose of reconstruction or amalgamation. So
different companies may be wound up for different reasons, and for the purpose of achieving the differing objectives there are three procedures available,
namely: a compulsory winding up by the court; a creditors' voluntary winding up; and a members' voluntary winding up. The procedures apply with
modification to a limited liability partnership (Limited Liability Partnership
Act 2000).

1.6.1 VOLUNTARY LIQUIDATION

A voluntary liquidation arises where the company passes a resolution for its own
winding up, or where its articles provide that it should be wound up after the
expiry of a specified period of time (IA 1986, s 84). A voluntary winding up is
in the control of the company and, in the case of an insolvent voluntary winding up, its creditors, and does not require the involvement of the court or the
Official Receiver.

Members' voluntary liquidation

If the directors make a statutory declaration of solvency under the IA 1986, s 89
to the effect that the company will be able to pay its debts within a specified
period not exceeding 12 months, the winding up is a members' voluntary winding up (IA 1986, s 90). A liquidator will be appointed in general meeting to put
the winding up into effect. If, despite the directors' statutory declaration of
solvency, it appears to the liquidator that the company is insolvent then the

liquidator must summon a meeting of creditors and the winding up may be converted to a creditors' voluntary winding up (IA 1986, ss 95–96).

Creditors' voluntary liquidation

If the directors have not made a statutory declaration of solvency the winding up is a creditors' winding up (IA 1986, s 90). Meetings of both creditors and the company will be held which will both vote on the appointment of a liquidator. If the meeting of the company votes for a person different from that chosen by the creditors, the liquidator will be as chosen by the creditors' meeting unless the court orders otherwise (IA 1986, s 100). At the creditors' meeting a liquidation committee may be appointed to fix the liquidator's remuneration, to determine what powers the directors should continue to have, if any, and generally to supervise the liquidation (IA 1986, ss 97–106).

Effect of voluntary liquidation

Where a resolution for voluntary winding up is passed, and until a liquidator has been appointed or nominated the powers of the directors continue (IA 1986, ss 91, 103) but must not be exercised except with the sanction of the court or, in the case of a creditors' voluntary winding up, so far as is necessary for the purpose of the creditors' meeting and statement of affairs. But the directors may dispose of perishable goods and wasting goods, and do all such other things as are necessary for the protection of the company's assets (IA 1986, s 114). Upon the appointment of a liquidator the powers of the directors cease; except that in a members' winding up the general meeting or the liquidator may sanction the continuance of powers, and in a creditors' winding up the creditors' committee or the creditors may sanction the continuance of powers (IA 1986, ss 91, 103).

Although the company should cease to carry on its business once the resolution has effect, the powers of the company continue so as to enable the company to wind up its affairs, and notwithstanding anything in the articles of association of the company.

There is no automatic moratorium in a voluntary winding up, but under the IA 1986, s 112 the liquidator or any contributory or creditor may make an application to the court which can exercise any powers which a court might exercise if there were a compulsory winding up. This includes the court's power under the IA 1986, s 126 to stay or restrain any action or proceedings.

Powers of liquidator in voluntary liquidation

A liquidator in a voluntary winding up has the powers specified in the IA 1986, s 165. In a creditors' winding up the powers conferred cannot be exercised, except with the sanction of the court, in the period between the liquidator's appointment and the time of the holding of a creditors' meeting under the IA 1986, s 98, except that he can take the company's property into his custody or control, dispose of goods which might perish or which might diminish in value, and do whatever is necessary for the protection of the company's assets (IA 1986, s 166).

The general powers available and freely exercisable are those described in the IA 1986, s 165, including those listed in Pts II and III of Sch 4. The powers include power to manage the company's business in so far as is necessary for the winding up, and power to dispose of the company's assets. The liquidator must pay the company's debts, in accordance with the correct priority of claims. Powers listed in the IA 1986, Sch 4 Pt I are also available, including power to pay any class of creditors in full or make compromises or arrangements with creditors, but these powers are only available with the sanction of an extraordinary resolution (in a members' winding up) or the liquidation committee, or in the absence of one, the creditors (in a creditors' winding up). If the liquidator disposes of property of the company to a person who is connected with the company he must, if there is a liquidation committee, give notice to the committee of that exercise of his powers.

1.6.2 COMPULSORY WINDING UP BY COURT

A compulsory winding up of a company by court order and under the court's supervision probably occurs most commonly following the hostile act of a petitioning creditor. This, however, is not necessarily the case, as a petition may be presented by the company, the directors, or, in limited circumstances, shareholders (IA 1986, s 124).

The circumstances in which a company may be compulsorily wound up by the court are described in the IA 1986, s 122, and are as follows:

1. The company has by special resolution resolved that the company be wound up by the court.
2. Being a public company which was registered as such on its original incorporation, the company has not been issued with a certificate under the Companies Act 1985, s 117 (public company share capital requirements) and more than a year has expired since it was so registered.
3. It is an old public company, within the meaning of the Companies Consolidation (Consequential Provisions) Act 1985.
4. The company does not commence its business within a year from its incorporation or suspends its business for a whole year.
5. Except in the case of a private company limited by shares or guarantee the number of members is reduced to below two.
6. The company is unable to pay its debts.
7. The court is of the opinion that it is just and equitable that the company should be wound up.

The ground which is likely to be of most interest to a landlord or mortgagee of commercial property is point 6 above, that the company is unable to pay its debts. By the IA 1986, s 123 a company is deemed unable to pay its debts in four circumstances:

1. if a creditor to whom the company is indebted in a sum exceeding £750 then due serves on the company a written demand (in the prescribed form) and the company neglects to pay the sum within three weeks;
2. if execution or other process issued on a judgment is returned unsatisfied in whole or in part;
3. the company is unable to pay its debts as they fall due; or

4. the value of the company's assets is less than the amount of its liabilities, taking into account its contingent and prospective liabilities.

It may be observed from the above that a company may be considered unable to pay its debts on a 'cash flow' basis, or on a 'balance sheet' basis. It might seem harsh that a company might be wound up on the basis that it has liabilities exceeding assets, particularly if the liability for future rents is to be taken into account, but the harshness may be tempered by the fact that the court has a discretion whether or not to make an order for the company's winding up.

A petition may be presented and an order made notwithstanding that the tenant company is already the subject of a voluntary liquidation. The circumstances in which this occurs may be rare but the landlord might, for instance, have grounds to suspect that the voluntary liquidation is being operated in a manner which will cause him unfair prejudice and favour other creditors (*Re Gordon & Breach Science Publishers Ltd* [1995] BCC 261).

1.6.3 PROCEDURES FOLLOWING PETITION AND ORDER

Once a petition has been presented, a provisional liquidator (often the Official Receiver) may be appointed by the court to preserve the assets and status quo and to prevent any events which might result in an alteration of the priority of debts which will have effect in the winding up (IA 1986, s 135). The powers of the provisional liquidator may be limited by the court order, which must state the functions to be carried out by him (IR 1986, r 4.26). On a winding up order the Official Receiver becomes liquidator until another person is appointed. A permanent liquidator may be appointed after meetings of the creditors and contributories. The creditor's meeting may also appoint a liquidation committee to exercise supervision in the winding up (see the IA 1986, ss 135–141).

1.6.4 EFFECT OF COMPULSORY WINDING UP

If it is determined that a company be wound up by the court, the winding up is deemed to commence from the the date of presentation of the petition, or if the petition was presented after a voluntary winding up had begun it is deemed to commence from the date of the resolution for winding up (IA 1986, s 129). Any disposition of the company's property made after the commencement is void, unless the court orders otherwise (IA 1986, s 127; see para 7.1.1). From the date that a winding up order is made, or from the date of appointment of a provisional liquidator, if earlier, no action or proceeding shall be proceeded with or commenced against the company or its property except with the leave of the court (IA 1986, s 130). This will generally prevent a landlord from taking action without leave (see chapters 2, 3 and 4), but a mortgagee of the tenant's lease will not be prevented from enforcing his security (*Lloyd (David) & Co., Re Lloyd v David Lloyd & Co* (1877) 6 Ch D 339, CA).

The custody of the company's property is given to the provisional liquidator, if any, from the date of his appointment, and from the date of the order it will normally be in the control of the Official Receiver until a permanent liquidator takes over. The company's property does not actually vest in the liquidator, although the court may order the vesting of company property in the liquidator if this is seen to be desirable (IA 1986, s 145). The winding up order terminates the powers of the directors (*Fowler v Broad's Patent Night Light Co* [1893] 1 Ch 724), although they may be allowed to retain specific powers (*Re Mawcon Ltd* [1969] 1 All ER 188) and may instruct solicitors and counsel to appeal against the winding up order.

Certain preliquidation transactions at an undervalue, or which prefer one or more creditors over others, including dealings with leases of the company, are liable to be set aside once liquidation commences (see chapter 7).

1.6.5 POSITION OF LIQUIDATOR

The liquidator must 'secure that the assets of the company are got in, realised and distributed to the company's creditors and, if there is a surplus, to the persons entitled to it'. Where the liquidator is not the Official Receiver the liquidator must furnish the Official Receiver with information (IA 1986, s 143).

A liquidator is an agent of the company. In a compulsory winding up he is an officer of the court, and, as such, a high standard of conduct is expected of him (*Re Wyvern Developments Ltd* [1974] 2 All ER 535) and he must exercise a reasonable degree of care and skill (*Re Silver Valley Mines* (1882) 21 Ch D 381, CA). He may even be bound by a promise which he has made even though no value was given to him in return for it (*Re Wyvern Developments Ltd* above). A liquidator in a voluntary winding up is an agent of the company, but is not an officer of the court (*Re Bateson (John) & Co* [1985] BCLC 259).

The liquidator must not be in a position where his self-interest might conflict with his duties. He is not therefore allowed to make any profit above his remuneration (*Silkstone and Haigh Moor Coal Co v Edey* [1900] 1 Ch 167) and if he is too close to the directors of the company he may be removed if the relationship might inhibit the proper exercise of his powers and duties (*Re Charterland Goldfields Ltd* (1909) 26 TLR 132; *Re Sir John Moore Gold Mining Co* (1879) 12 Ch D 325, CA; IA 1986, ss 108, 171, 172).

The liquidator is a person who is subject to the IA 1986, s 212, so that if he has misapplied or retained, or become accountable for, any money or other property of the company, or been guilty of any misfeasance or breach of any fiduciary or other duty in relation to the company, the court may examine his conduct and order him to make restitution to the company (cf paras 1.3.8, 1.4.5). If, for example, the liquidator makes payments to creditors without making proper allowance for a landlord's claim and proof then the liquidator may have to make good the shortfall to the landlord (in *Re AMF International Ltd* [1996] 1 WLR 77). Once the liquidator has been released from his duties an application cannot be made except with the leave of the court.

1.6.6 POWERS OF LIQUIDATOR

The liquidator in a compulsory winding up has the powers conferred by the IA 1986, ss 167 and 168, which incorporate the powers in Sch 4 of the Act.

The powers in Pt III of Sch 4 can be exercised freely by the liquidator without any authorisation, and include the power to sell any of the company's property. The powers in Pts I and II of the Sch are exercisable only with the sanction of the court, and include power to carry on the business of the company, power to conduct legal proceedings in the company's name, and powers to make compromises or arrangements with creditors.

In the absence of fraud the court will not interfere with a proposed transaction by a liquidator unless he is acting in a way that no reasonable liquidator could act (*Leon v York-O-Matic Ltd* [1966] 3 All ER 277). There is a specific statutory provision in the IA 1986, s 168(5) allowing any person aggrieved by an act or decision of the liquidator to challenge such act or decision; the section is, however, construed restrictively so as not to permit persons other than direct creditors and contributories to invoke it (*Mahomed v Morris* [2000] 2 BCLC 536) and cannot be used so as to impose personal liability upon liquidators (*Mahomed v Morris*).

If the liquidator disposes of property to a connected person (see IA 1986, s 249) or if he employs a solicitor he must, if there is a liquidation committee, give notice to the committee.

If the liquidator enters into any transaction with a person who is an 'associate' of his (IA 1986, s 435), the court has a discretion to set it aside on an application by any person interested, and can order the liquidator to compensate the company (IR 1986, s 4.149). The court has no such discretion if the transaction was entered into with the prior consent of the court, or if the transaction was for value, and the liquidator entered into it without knowing or having reason to know that the person involved was an associate.

1.6.7 ORDER OF PRIORITY OF DEBTS

The landlord and any mortgagee of the lease are likely to want to know the order of distribution of assets in the winding up. It may be that the tenant's obligations to the landlord are adequately 'secured' by the landlord's rights to distrain and forfeit, but whether this is so will depend upon the value and terms of the lease. If there is insufficient distress upon the property, and assuming the lease is a lease at a full market rent, having no capital value, the rights to distrain and forfeit will not compensate the landlord in the event that the company is wound up without the lease being assigned to a solvent tenant. In such a case the landlord may wish to prove for the loss which he suffers as a result of the winding up, and he will be concerned with the order of priority of debts.

Subject to the rights of secured creditors the basic order of priority of debts is as follows:

1. Expenses of the liquidation (IR 1986, r 4.218). These may include instalments of rates where the company continues to occupy and trade from the premises (*Re Nolton Business Centres Ltd* (1995) unreported).
2. Preferential debts (IA 1986, s 175).
3. Ordinary debts (IR 1986, r 4.181).
4. Interest (IA 1986, s 189).
5. Postponed debts.
6. Surplus to shareholders (IA 1986, ss 154, 165).

Mortgagees

The position of a mortgagee in liquidation is similar to that in bankruptcy (see para 1.5.11). No leave is required to enforce the mortgage out of court. If court proceedings are necessary for some reason, leave to pursue an action is required in a compulsory winding up, but leave will normally be given to a mortgagee (*Lloyd (David) & Co., Re, Lloyd v David Lloyd & Co* (1877) 6 Ch D 339). The mortgagee has the following options:

1. Do nothing, leaving the charge over the asset for the time being.
2. Surrender the security for the general benefit of creditors and prove as an ordinary creditor (IR 1986, r 4.88).
3. Value the security (IR 1986, r 4.75), proving for the amount of the valuation as a secured creditor and proving for any balance as an ordinary creditor.
4. Realise the security and prove for any balance as an ordinary creditor (IR 1986, rr 4.88, 4.99).
5. Put the liquidator to an election whether he will or will not exercise his power to redeem at the value put upon it. The liquidator then has six months within which to redeem (IR 1986, r 4.97).

The liquidator has the following choices:

1. Redeem the charge at the value specified by the creditor, giving the creditor the opportunity to revalue (IR 1986, r 4.97). The liquidator is likely to make this choice if he thinks that the creditor has undervalued the security.
2. Test the security's value by offering it for sale (IR 1986, r 4.98). The liquidator is likely to take this course of action if he suspects that the creditor has overvalued the property.

In a compulsory winding up a secured creditor can, with the agreement of the liquidator or the leave of the court, alter the value which he has in his proof of debt put upon his security (IR 1986, r 4.95). If a secured creditor as petitioner has put a value on his security or has voted in respect of the unsecured balance of the debt he can only revalue with the leave of the court (cf generally para 1.5.11).

Liquidation expenses

The expenses of the liquidation must be paid before any other claims. The order of priority in a compulsory winding up or a creditors' voluntary winding up is set out in the IR 1986, r 4.218. The main items in order of priority are: expenses incurred in preserving, realising or getting in any of the assets of the company; expenses incurred in carrying on the business of the company; the fees of the Official Receiver or an interim receiver, or special manager; the costs of the petitioner; costs of preparing a statement of affairs; any necessary disbursements incurred by the liquidator; fees of other persons involved in providing services for the liquidator; and the remuneration of the liquidator.

A liquidator should take utmost care before embarking upon liquidation to get in assets since legal fees for an unsuccessful attempt to get in assets may not be an expense of the liquidation (*RS&M Engineering Co Ltd Re, Mond v Hammond Suddards (No 2)* [1999] 2 BCLC 485).

Preferential debts

The debts which are next in line are preferential debts, being mainly debts relating to tax liability and employer's liability. They are described in the IA 1986, Sch 6 and are:

1. debts due to the Inland Revenue;
2. debts due to Customs and Excise;
3. social Security Contributions;
4. contributions to occupational pensions schemes;
5. remuneration owed to employees; and
6. levies on coal and steel production.

Floating charges

A creditor who is secured by a floating charge has his priority postponed to preferential claims and liquidation expenses, and assets which were subject to the charge may be disposed of in order to satisfy the two categories of debt which have priority. Previously, holders of floating charges often procured the same priority as a mortgagee with a fixed charge by providing that on certain events the floating charge 'crystallised' into fixed charges over the assets of the company, thus giving the creditor the absolute priority of a fixed chargee. The new legislation applies to 'a charge which, as created, was a floating charge' so that enhanced priority can no longer be obtained in this way.

Ordinary debts

Ordinary unsecured creditors will be paid after preferential creditors, assuming that a balance remains. If there is a partial deficiency each creditor's claim will abate proportionately, so that the creditors will be entitled to a dividend expressed in terms of a number of pence in every pound.

Interest

If ordinary creditors are paid in full and there is a surplus, interest may be paid on all debts, whether preferential or not, in respect of the periods during which they have been outstanding since the commencement of the liquidation. Interest on preferential debts ranks equally with interest on other debts.

Postponed debts

Certain debts are postponed so as to be paid last, but before any distribution to shareholders. These include sums owed to a lender to a company where the return varies with the profitability of the company, and the claim of a seller of business goodwill, who takes as part of the consideration for the goodwill a profit share in the business (the Partnership Act 1890, ss 2, 3).

Surplus

In the event of there being any surplus after payment of creditors, it will pass to the members of the company according to their rights and interests in the company (IR 1986, rr 4.179–4.186, 4.221, 4.222).

Finality of dissolution

Where a company is wound up by a liquidator and finally dissolved, all existing actions by or against the company cease to exist. Nevertheless, in certain circumstances, and for certain limited purposes the company can be restored to the register (see para 5.1.2 below). If there has been no formal insolvency procedure and the company has simply been struck off the register as a dormant company having failed to file accounts, then by virtue of the Companies Act 1985, s 653 any restoration of the company to the register restores the company to the position prior to dissolution in respect of any actions by or against the company (*Top Creative Ltd v St Albans District Council* [2000] 2 BCLC 379, CA). If the restoration of a tenant company might directly affect a landlord then the landlord may be permitted to make representations in respect of the proposed restoration, e g if the restoration might cause reinstatement of a lease which has been determined (*Re Blenheim Leisure (Restaurants) Ltd* [2000] BCC 554, CA). Such representations might include a request that upon restoration the company should be subject to formal insolvency procedures if it proves to be insolvent following restoration (*Re Blenheim Leisure (Restaurants) Ltd (No 2)* [2000] BCC 821).

1.7 Law reform

Notwithstanding the comprehensive review of the law and practice undertaken for the purpose of the Cork Report and the consequent introduction of the IA 1986, the laws on insolvency are the subject of continuing review. Recent changes continue to emphasise a 'recovery' culture aiming to achieve the possible continuation of a business or at least the best possible realisation of assets for creditors. The government's White Paper 'Productivity and Enterprise' (Cm 5234, July 2001) continues this trend. The White Paper proposes that personal insolvency be changed to allow a reduction in the discharge period for bankrupts from three years to 12 months and other possible reforms to reduce the stigma of bankruptcy. For corporate insolvency the White Paper suggests a reduction in the role played by administrative receivership and an increase in the role played by administration so that the focus is more on a balanced solution to corporate financial difficulty and not so much on a single secured major creditor.

CHAPTER 2

Liability for rent and other obligations under a lease

Often a tenant's failure to pay rent is the first signal to a landlord of the tenant's impending insolvency. This failure may be followed closely by the appointment of a receiver, administrator, liquidator or trustee in bankruptcy. In these circumstances the landlord's ability to recover the rent or enforce other obligations in the lease will depend upon the degree of insolvency, and upon whether the tenant is subject to some formal insolvency procedure.

2.1 Liability in receivership

Where a receiver has been appointed in respect of the whole or part of the tenant's property there is little effect upon the tenant's liability for rent or other obligations in the lease. This is so even if the receiver is an administrative receiver. The tenant remains liable under the terms of the lease and there is no statutory moratorium to prevent the landlord from taking action to recover the rent. The landlord can sue for rent and damages for breach of the terms of the lease (see para 2.6.1). The landlord may also have rights to forfeit the lease (see chapter 4), or to distrain for rent (see chapter 3). Anomalously the landlord's right to execute a judgment is restricted (see para 2.7.1).

The position of the receiver personally depends to some extent upon whether the receiver is appointed in respect of property of an individual tenant, a partnership or of a company. Usually the receiver is deemed to be merely the agent of the tenant (Law of Property Act 1925, s 109, Insolvency Act 1986 ('IA 1986'), s 44) and, as such, does not take on any personal liability for rent or other obligations in an existing lease. If the receiver takes a fresh lease for the purpose of the receivership the position is not substantially different. A receiver of an individual tenant's property, acting as agent of the tenant, is governed by the normal rules of agency and will not be liable upon any fresh lease, so long as the agency is disclosed. A receiver of property of a company (or limited liability partnership), on the other hand, is prima facie liable on any fresh lease entered into for the purpose of the receivership unless there is an express exclusion of personal liability (IA 1986, ss 37, 44). In practice, however, it is unlikely that any fresh lease would be entered into, and if there were it is likely that there would be an express exclusion of personal liability on the part of the receiver.

Thus, although a receiver might be using the premises for the purposes of the receivership and continuing the tenant's business, the receiver is not personally liable for rent (*Re Atlantic Computer Systems plc* [1992] Ch 505, CA) and a court will not order that in honour the receiver should pay (*Hand v Blow* [1901] 2 Ch 721). The landlord's position is simply that there is a tenant who is not paying rent and the landlord must consider the remedies normally available for non-payment (see paras 2.6–2.10 and chapters 3–5).

2.2 Liability in administration

Where the tenant is a company or limited liability partnership in respect of which an administrator has been appointed the position is not much different. Liability for the rent, past, present and future, continues but there is no guarantee that the rent will be paid. Even if the premises are being used for the purpose of the administration there is no strict doctrine of 'administration expenses' requiring the administrator to pay the current rent from the company's assets as an expense of the administration in priority to other debts (*Re Atlantic Computer Systems plc* [1992] Ch 505, CA). Notwithstanding the absence of any such strict doctrine a landlord will in many cases be able to procure that the current rent is paid. The administrator as officer of the court must act responsibly in deciding whether or not to pay rents as they fall due and many of the considerations which caused the courts to adopt the 'liquidation expenses' principle (see para 2.3.2) in the case of liquidations may apply in administrations. If the administration order was made for the survival of the company or limited liability partnership as a going concern the business should generally be sufficiently viable to hold down current outgoings and the administrator ought normally to pay the current rent. Even if the administration order was made as a prelude to winding up, but for the better realisation of assets the administrator ought to pay over to the landlord any subrents received by the administrators since their appointment from the use of the premises, at least to the extent that the subrents do not exceed the headrents (*Re Atlantic Computer Systems plc*, see above). In addition to the above the administrator must take into account all circumstances when deciding whether to pay rents, and must make a decision speedily, and ought to state reasons for any refusal to make payment.

A landlord who is aggrieved by a decision of an administrator not to pay rent can rely upon the right to forfeit, or to sue or distrain for rent, but leave of the court is necessary and the landlord's ability to enforce the terms of the lease is severely restricted (see paras 2.6 and 2.7 and chapters 3–5). If the landlord makes an application to court for leave to enforce the terms of the lease the court has a discretion to order the administrator to pay rents as they become due as a condition of refusing leave. If the administrator has acted unreasonably in refusing to pay rent an order for costs may be made in favour of the landlord so that the landlord is not prejudiced by the administrator's behaviour (*Re Atlantic Computer Systems plc*, see above).

The personal position of the administrator is that the administrator is deemed to act as agent (IA 1986, s 14(5)) but, like a receiver of a company's property, the administrator will not become liable under pre-existing contracts and will no doubt enter into any new contracts without personal liability. The administrator therefore does not become liable personally for the rent, or otherwise upon the terms of the lease.

2.3 Liability in liquidation

A company or limited liability partnership in liquidation (whether compulsory or voluntary) remains liable to comply with the terms of the lease unless and until the lease is disclaimed (see chapter 6) or the company or partnership is dissolved. In practice the landlord's ability to recover rent will differ for the periods before and after commencement of the winding up. For this purpose the rent, if payable in arrears, may, by the Apportionment Act 1870, be apportioned on a daily basis for the periods before and after commencement of the winding up (*Re South Kensington Co-operative Stores* (1881) 17 Ch D 161).

2.3.1 RENT PRIOR TO COMMENCEMENT OF THE WINDING UP

Rent due prior to the winding up is an unsecured debt of the tenant and the landlord has his usual remedies but subject to any statutory restrictions that there may be (see paras 2.6–2.10 and chapters 3–4). The landlord will also have the right to submit a proof of debt in the liquidation (see para 2.10) and receive a dividend – if there is anything left for unsecured creditors after payment of secured creditors and preferential debts (see para 1.6.7).

2.3.2 RENT AFTER COMMENCEMENT OF THE WINDING UP

Rent accruing due after commencement of the winding up will in many, but not necessarily all, cases be recoverable as an expense of the liquidation having priority over the claims of other creditors and the remuneration of the liquidator, at least unless and until the liquidator disclaims. The court has a general discretion as to the priority which one expense should have over another (IA 1986, ss 115, 156) but the general rule as to the order of priority is set out in Insolvency Rules 1986 ('IR 1986') r 4.218 for a compulsory winding up or a creditors' voluntary winding up.

Rent as an 'expense' of the liquidation

The test which was used in the past to consider whether an expense was an expense of the liquidation was whether the liquidator had retained possession 'for the convenience of the winding up' (Plowman J in *Re ABC Coupler and Engineering Co Ltd (No 3)* [1970] 1 All ER 650). Now IR 1986, r 4.218 provides that the first item in order of priority is normally the 'expense(s) properly chargeable or incurred by the Official Receiver or liquidator in preserving, realising or getting in any assets of the company'. This equates roughly, but not necessarily exactly, with the old test of whether property was retained for the convenience of the winding up. If the liquidator does not disclaim the lease but retains it, taking active steps to sell it or surrender it, the rent will be an expense which has priority over all others. In addition, if the liquidator pays rent in order to avoid forfeiture of the lease the payment may properly be regarded as an expense properly incurred in preserving the lease (see Warner J in *Re Linda Marie Ltd* [1989] BCLC 46). But mere inactivity, allowing goods to remain upon the property, while not seeking to surrender was not enough under the old law. Also, if the lease was retained by arrangement with and for the benefit of the landlord, the retention of possession was not solely for the benefit of the company and the landlord was not able to claim that the rent should be paid 'for the convenience of the winding up' (*Re Bridgewater Engineering Co* (1879) 12 Ch D 181; see further para 3.6.5).

Rent as a 'necessary disbursement'

Even if the claim to rents does not have priority as a claim for expenses incurred in 'preserving' or 'realising' the lease, the rents may be regarded as 'necessary disbursements' in the liquidation which are listed in IR 1986, r 4.218 as twelfth in priority, ahead of the liquidator's remuneration which ranks fourteenth. It is possible that liability for rent might fall within this head even though the lease is not retained for the convenience of the liquidation. In *Re Linda Marie Ltd* (see above), the company was subject to a creditor's voluntary liquidation and the liquidator went into occupation intending to continue trading with a view to assigning or surrendering the lease on beneficial terms. The liquidator did not take many active steps in relation to the lease, did not assign and eventually surrendered, but without paying the rent and service charges. The contested question was whether the landlord's claim to rent ranked ahead of the liquidator's claim to his fees. The parties accepted that rent was not an expense incurred in preserving or realising the lease. Liability for rent was simply 'an inevitable consequence' of allowing the lease to run on. Warner J decided that the landlord's claim had priority as rent was a 'necessary disbursement' within IR 1986, r 4.218. Unfortunately the facts are not reported as precisely as they might have been and it is not clear whether rents will be considered to be necessary disbursements in all cases where a liquidator has failed to disclaim. If in the future the rents will so be considered the cases concerned with whether the lease was retained for the convenience of the liquidation will have a substantially reduced importance. There is, however, at least one instance where it is likely that the rent will be neither an expense incurred in preserving or realising the lease, nor a necessary disbursement; i e where a company (or limited liability partnership) is in liquidation but a receiver is using the property (*Re House and Land Investment Trust, ex p Smith* (1894) 42 WR 572).

Claim for rent where liquidator disclaims

If the liquidator disclaims, the question may arise as to whether the rent due for the period from commencement of the winding up to the date of disclaimer is an expense of the liquidation. It was previously held that rent would be an expense of the liquidation for such part of the period between petition and disclaimer as the lease was in fact retained for the convenience of the liquidation (*Re HH Realisations Ltd* (1975) 31 P & CR 249). This might exclude a period while the liquidator decides whether or not to disclaim, or a period of delay following the giving of a notice of disclaimer by the liquidator. It might now be argued, following *Re Linda Marie Ltd* (see above) that, although the rent does not have the first priority awarded to an expense incurred in preserving or realising the lease, the rent may be considered a necessary disbursement while the lease is vested in the company, with the slightly lesser priority available to such disbursements. Such rent, being a liability for periodic payments arising after the commencement of the winding up, cannot be the subject of a proof in the liquidation (see para 2.10.2).

Discretion of the court

As mentioned above the order of priority listed in IR 1986, r 4.218 is a general guide only and the question of priority of expenses is a matter for the discretion of the court (IA 1986, ss 115, 156), which may in appropriate cases order that the liquidator's expenses shall have priority over the landlord's claim for rent. But if the court is to be persuaded to alter the general rules as to priority so as to favour the liquidator, the onus is upon the liquidator to put before the court by affidavit evidence of all the facts which he relies upon in support of his contention that his expenses should have priority. In *Re Linda Marie Ltd* (see above) Warner J refused to exercise his discretion so as to afford priority to the liquidator's remuneration, where the liquidator had not prepared a detailed case and argument to justify priority.

2.3.3 OTHER OBLIGATIONS UNDER THE LEASE

Other sums due under the lease may also be liquidation expenses in respect of which the landlord may have priority over other creditors. Service charges, for example (*Re Linda Marie Ltd* [1989] BCLC 46) may be sums in respect of which a priority claim may lie. Other liability under the lease, for example, for disrepair continues but the landlord's claim for damages for breach of the terms of the lease is not a liquidation expense and is provable only as an unsecured claim (*Re ABC Coupler Engineering Co Ltd (No 3)* [1970] 1 All ER 650, and see para 2.10.3).

2.3.4 PERSONAL LIABILITY OF THE LIQUIDATOR

The liquidator, like a receiver or administrator, is agent only, and will not be personally liable upon the terms of an existing lease. Even if, under the IA 1986, s 145, an order is made vesting the lease in the liquidator, it is possible that the liquidator will not be personally liable. It should be borne in mind, however, that the decision to this effect (*Graham v Edge* (1888) 20 QBD 683, CA) was based upon a differently worded statute. In addition, the Court of Appeal in its reasoning was influenced by the fact that, at the time, the liquidator had no power to disclaim a lease, and that it would be unjust to make the liquidator personally liable in such circumstances.

2.4 Liability in bankruptcy

In the case of bankruptcy the lease vests in the trustee in bankruptcy who accordingly becomes the tenant upon his appointment. The trustee is in the position of an assignee of the lease (see para 5.2) and will be personally liable for the rent and for all other tenant's obligations, including inter alia liability for dilapidations, unless he disclaims (*Re Solomon, ex p Dressler* (1878) 9 Ch D 252, CA). Liability includes liability for future payments of rent as they become due, which rent is not a debt provable in the bankruptcy. Even after discharge of the bankrupt the landlord may sue the trustee for rent accruing due, assuming that the trustee has not disclaimed the lease, because the trustee remains the tenant until disclaimer (*Metropolis Estates Co Ltd v Wilde* [1940] 2 KB 536, CA; see para 6.8). The trustee is, of course, entitled to be indemnified out of the assets of the bankrupt, unless there is some special reason for not giving an indemnity (*Lowrey v Barker* (1880) 5 Ex D 170, CA). If the trustee does disclaim he does not incur any personal liability for rent or on the terms of the lease and the court cannot order the trustee to pay any sum for the use and occupation of the premises for the time that the lease was vested in the trustee (see para 6.5.2).

The position of the bankrupt is that he will remain liable upon the terms of the lease. Even if the lease is a 'new tenancy' the vesting of it in the trustee is not an event which will release the bankrupt from liability as former tenant (see para 5.1.6). Liability may continue despite the discharge of the bankrupt (*Metropolis Estates Co v Wilde*, see above; see further para 6.8). If the lease is disclaimed the liability of the bankrupt ceases on the date of disclaimer. The landlord can lodge a proof for the rent due up to the date of the bankruptcy order, and if it is payable in arrears liability can be apportioned on a daily basis up to the date of the order (see para 2.10.2), but what of the liability for the period between the date of the bankruptcy order to the date of disclaimer? It is arguable that rent for this period might be recoverable as an expense of the bankruptcy under principles similar to those which apply in liquidation (see paras 2.3.2, 6.5.2 and the IR 1986, r 6.224).

2.5 Liability of mortgagee

The position of a mortgagee of a lease (where a receiver has been appointed, see para 2.1 above) depends upon whether the lease was granted before the commencement of the Landlord and Tenant (Covenants) Act 1995, or after; and upon whether the mortgagee is or is not in possession. The basic rule is that a mortgagee does not, by taking a charge, become liable upon the terms of the lease. If, however, the lease is a 'new tenancy' (see chapter 5, para 5.1.6) and the mortgagee enters into possession, then the Landlord and Tenant (Covenants) Act 1995, s 15 provides that the tenant's covenants will be enforceable against the mortgagee. As there is no equivalent provision to make covenants enforceable against a receiver appointed by a mortgagee it must be assumed that the instances in which a mortgagee of a lease will take possession rather than appoint a receiver will become increasingly rare.

2.6 Suing for arrears of rent or breach of other lease terms

The landlord may of course consider suing the tenant for the rent arrears or in respect of a breach of the terms of the lease. In the majority of cases, however, this is not a viable course of action for a number of possible reasons: if the tenant is insolvent leave of the court or consent of some other person, such as an administrator, may be required to commence or continue proceedings; the proceedings are likely to take some time; costs will be incurred which might not be easily recoverable; the tenant in many cases will be unable to satisfy any judgment which is obtained; forfeiture or distress may be more effective remedies; and leave of the court may be required if the landlord wishes, by execution, to enforce any court order obtained (see para 2.7).

In cases where leave is required there may be little point in applying for leave to commence or continue proceedings simply for arrears of rent since a court is likely to consider the landlord's action as an attempt to obtain priority over other creditors, although if the premises are needed for the purposes of the insolvency and the landlord might otherwise forfeit or distrain, payment of rent to prevent a forfeiture or distress may be seen as desirable. In general a court will not give leave to take any proceedings for debt unless the debt is a new debt incurred for the purposes of a bankruptcy, liquidation or administration (*Re Atlantic Computer Systems plc* [1992] Ch 505, CA).

2.6.1 RECEIVERSHIP

Contrary to popularly held belief no leave is required to commence an action against a tenant in respect of which a receiver, even an administrative receiver, has been appointed (unless the tenant is also in liquidation or bankrupt). The receiver is simply the agent of the tenant and the appointment of such an agent does not prevent a landlord from suing the tenant. It should be noted, however, that if in any proceedings issued against the tenant the court has a discretion, the court is likely to take into account the needs of the receivership, when deciding how to exercise the discretion. In addition it should be appreciated that it will be difficult to execute any court order obtained (see para 2.7).

2.6.2 VOLUNTARY LIQUIDATION

If there is a voluntary liquidation no leave is required to commence proceedings, but an application may be made, by the liquidator or any contributory or creditor, to the court to determine any question in the winding up and the court can exercise any power which it would have in a compulsory winding up (IA 1986, s 112), including the powers to stay or restrain proceedings under the IA 1986, s 126 (see para 2.6.3).

2.6.3 COMPULSORY LIQUIDATION

After a petition has been presented but before a winding-up order is made leave is not required to sue for rent or other breach but the company, a creditor or contributory may apply to court for a stay of proceedings (IA 1986, s 126). Once a winding-up order has been made or a provisional liquidator appointed leave is required to proceed with or commence proceedings (IA 1986, s 130). The court has power to give leave subject to such terms as it thinks fit. A court would not normally give leave to a landlord seeking to recover arrears of rent in priority to other creditors, although the landlord might be able to claim current rent as an expense of the liquidation (see para 2.3.2). Proceedings begun without leave are a nullity and the court has no power retrospectively to authorise their commencement (*Re National Employers' Mutual General Insurance Association* [1995] 1 BCLC 232).

2.6.4 ADMINISTRATION

Since the purpose of administration is to give a company or limited liability partnership breathing space in order to find a solution for its problems, the general effect of the IA 1986 is to prohibit any action or proceedings. Leave of the court is required to commence or continue an action for rent, or breach of other obligation, during the period between petition and making of the order (IA 1986, s 10) but if there is an administrative receiver leave is not required unless the person appointing the receiver consents to the making of the administration order (IA 1986, s 10(3)). Once an administration order has been made the leave of the court or the consent of the administrator is required to commence or continue proceedings (IA 1986, s 11). If the administrator is approached for his consent he must act responsibly and promptly in considering the request. In appropriate cases he ought to pay the rent as an expense of the administration (see para 2.2).

2.6.5 BANKRUPTCY

After presentation of a petition for bankruptcy the court can stay any action commenced for rent or breach of obligation (IA 1986, s 285(1)). After a bankruptcy order has been made leave of the court is required to commence any action (IA 1986, s 285(3)), and the landlord will not be able to take steps to recover rent arrears (but see paras 3.6.3, 4.4.4), since no person is to have any remedy 'in respect of a debt provable in the bankruptcy'.

2.7 Execution of judgments

A landlord who has obtained judgment for arrears of rent or other breach of obligation by the tenant, or another judgment creditor of the tenant may wish to enforce that judgment (eg by seizure and sale of goods of the tenant), particularly once it becomes apparent that the tenant is insolvent. If the landlord or other creditor manages to enforce the court order by execution before any liquidation, administration or bankruptcy the basic rule is that the benefit of the execution may be retained in priority to all other parties. If, however, execution is not complete the execution creditor may be restrained from completing the execution or may have to disgorge the benefits of the execution to a liquidator or trustee.

A landlord will only rarely utilise the court procedures for enforcement of any judgment for rent or damages for other breach, since under the terms of the lease the rights to forfeit the lease or to distrain upon the tenant's goods may be relied upon. Use of the right to forfeit or distrain will usually be more effective than execution of judgment, although it should be noted that once the landlord has obtained judgment in respect of arrears of rent he can only enforce the judgment through the means of execution available through the court and cannot utilise the right to distrain (see para 3.10).

2.7.1 RECEIVERSHIP

It might have been thought that execution could be freely pursued notwithstanding the appointment of a receiver in respect of the goods of the tenant, but in a series of decided cases the courts have held that once a charge has crystallised over goods the rights of the chargee have preference over any subsequent sale of chattels by a sheriff on behalf of an execution creditor, even if the sheriff has already bound and seized the goods (*Re Standard Manufacturing Co* [1891] 1 Ch 627, CA; *Re Opera Ltd* [1891] 3 Ch 260, CA; *Re London Pressed Hinge Co Ltd* [1905] 1 Ch 576). The preference which this gives debenture holders over execution creditors has been criticised (*Hare and Milman* [1981] LMCLQ 57; *Calnan* (1982) 10 NZULR 111) and is in marked contrast to a landlord's right to levy distress notwithstanding the appointment of a receiver (see para 3.6.7). The position is not clear where the sheriff has sold the goods and still has the proceeds of sale, although it is likely that in such a case the execution creditor will have priority (see *Robson v Smith* [1895] 2 Ch 118; *Taunton v Sheriff of Warwickshire* [1895] 2 Ch 319, CA).

2.7.2 COMPULSORY LIQUIDATION

Where the tenant is in a compulsory liquidation the success of an execution will depend upon when it is begun, when it is completed, and upon the amount for which it is made.

Execution begun after commencement of winding up

If an execution is 'put in force' after the commencement of a winding up it is void (IA 1986, s 128). Presumably the phrase 'put in force' refers to the initiation of the execution, so that an execution begun after presentation of the petition will be void.

Execution begun, but not completed, before commencement of winding up

If a judgment creditor has begun execution and subsequently there is a winding up the creditor is not entitled to retain the benefit of the execution against the liquidator unless it was completed before the petition for winding up (IA 1986, s 183). To be complete the sheriff or bailiff must have seized and sold the goods (*Re Dickinson* (1888) 22 QBD 187). If the sheriff has not completed the sale the execution is not complete and the execution creditor will lose the benefit of the execution even though the delay was the fault of a third party, and not the fault of the execution creditor (*George v Tompson's Trustee* [1949] Ch 322).

Upon receiving written notice (sent by hand or recorded delivery) of a winding-up order or appointment of a provisional liquidator, and upon being required to do so, the sheriff must deliver to the liquidator the goods seized and any money received in part satisfaction of the execution, but the costs of the execution are a first charge on the goods or money and the liquidator may sell any goods seized in order to satisfy that charge (IA 1986, s 184).

Execution begun and completed before commencement of winding up

Even if a sale of goods is complete before commencement of the winding up the judgment creditor may still lose the benefit of the execution if it is for a sum exceeding the prescribed amount, currently £500 (IA 1986, s 346(3) and Insolvency Proceedings (Monetary Limits) Order 1986, SI 1986/1996) and if within 14 days a notice is served on the sheriff that a petition for winding up has been presented, in which case the sheriff must pay the balance to the liquidator.

Discretion of court

The court does have a discretion to allow the execution creditor to retain the proceeds of execution but weighty reasons are needed to justify the court in exercising its discretion so as to interfere with the normal rule that all unsecured creditors rank pari passu in a winding up (*Re Caribbean Products (Yam Importers) Ltd* [1966] Ch 331, CA). It may be a weighty enough reason if the execution could have been completed before the winding up but was not so completed because the execution creditor was induced to delay by trickery or pressure on the part of the insolvent tenant (*Re Grosvenor Metal Co Ltd* [1950] Ch 63). But if the insolvent tenant is stalling creditors generally it might be considered unjust to give preference to one stalled execution creditor over the other creditors who may have been induced not to commence action or execution (*Re Redman (Builders) Ltd* [1964] 1 All ER 851).

Protection for purchaser from sheriff

Although the judgment creditor may not be able to retain the benefit of an exe-cution which is not completed in time, any sale done in execution is valid so that a purchaser in good faith obtains a good title against the liquidator (IA 1986, s 183).

2.7.3 VOLUNTARY LIQUIDATION

In a voluntary liquidation there is no provision stating that an execution begun during the winding up is void, and it has been held that the predecessor to the IA 1986, s 128 (see above) does not apply in a voluntary liquidation (*Westbury v Twigg & Co* [1892] 1 QB 77); but the question can be referred to the court under s 112 of the IA 1986 and it is probable that if the court considered that the execution would confer an unfair preference it would restrain it (*Westbury v Twigg*, see above). If an execution is put in force but not completed before the resolution for winding up the IA 1986, s 183 (see para 2.7.2) applies so that the execution creditor is not entitled to retain the benefit of the execution against the liquidator. If the creditor has notice of a meeting having been called at which a resolution for voluntary winding up is to be proposed, the date upon which he had notice is the relevant date upon which the execution should be complete, in order that the creditor can retain the benefit of it.

As is the case in a compulsory winding up (see para 2.7.2) the sheriff must, upon receiving notice that a resolution for voluntary winding up has been passed, disgorge the benefit of the execution to the liquidator, subject to his right to deduct the costs of the execution. Again, the court has a discretion to allow the execution creditor to retain the benefit of the execution, and again there is protection for a purchaser from the sheriff in good faith. If an execution for a sum exceeding the prescribed amount is complete, but within 14 days the sheriff is notified of a resolution for winding up, the sheriff must pay the balance, after deducting costs, to the liquidator.

2.7.4 ADMINISTRATION

Where the tenant is a company or limited liability partnership in administration a landlord needs leave of the court to execute during the period between a peti-tion and the making of an administration order (IA 1986, s 10), but if there is an administrative receiver leave is not required unless the person appointing the receiver consents to the making of the administration order (IA 1986, s 10(3)). Once an administration order has been made the leave of the court or the con-sent of the administrator is required (IA 1986, s 11) before enforcing a judgment by execution.

2.7.5 BANKRUPTCY

As in the case of a liquidation the efficacy of an execution against an insolvent individual depends very much upon the timing of the execution. Once a petition for bankruptcy has been presented the court can stay any execution (IA 1986, s 285(1)); and after a bankruptcy order has been made leave of the court is required to execute (IA 1986, s 285(3)).

As in liquidation, if a creditor has issued execution and bankruptcy intervenes the creditor is not entitled as against the trustee in bankruptcy to retain the benefit of the execution unless it was completed before the commencement of bankruptcy (IA 1986, s 346). Even if the execution is complete before commencement of bankruptcy (i e the date of the order) if a sheriff has actually seized and sold goods for a sum exceeding the prescribed amount currently £500, IA 1986, s 346(3): Insolvency Proceedings (Monetary Limits) Order 1986, SI 1986/1996) a sheriff may be made to pay over the proceeds of sale (less expenses) if before the expiry of 14 days following sale or payment the sheriff is given notice that a petition has been presented and subsequently an order is made (IA 1986, s 346(3)).

The court does have a discretion to permit the execution creditor to retain the benefit of the execution (IA 1986, s 346(6)) but special circumstances need to be shown to persuade the court to give the execution creditor such a preference (see para 2.7.2).

2.7.6 VOLUNTARY ARRANGEMENT

Where a sheriff has taken possession of goods on behalf of an execution creditor, the creditor is regarded as a secured creditor, and a meeting of creditors in a voluntary arrangement of the debtor cannot interfere with the execution without the consent of the execution creditor (*Peck v Craighead* [1995] 1 BCLC 337). The execution creditor can proceed with the execution notwithstanding the voluntary arrangement.

2.7.7 LANDLORD'S PRIORITY OVER EXECUTION CREDITORS

Perhaps of more importance to a landlord than the right to execute a judgment is the landlord's right to require payment of arrears of rent from an execution creditor. If a person other than the landlord seeks to execute against the goods of the tenant the landlord has rights under s 1 of the Landlord and Tenant Act 1709 or s 102 of the County Courts Act 1984 to serve a notice on the sheriff or county court bailiff, claiming an amount not exceeding one year's rent. The landlord only has rights against creditors acting in 'execution' of a court order, and not where a person is using some other method of enforcing payment, such as a statutory distress for rates under a justices' warrant (*Potts v Hickman* [1941] AC 212, HL).

Execution of High Court judgments

Where the execution creditor is proceeding under the jurisdiction of the High Court the landlord's rights arise under, the Landlord and Tenant Act 1709, s 1 (8 Annex c14) which simply places the sheriff under a duty to pay off any rent arrears (not exceeding one year's rent) before removing goods from the premises. If the premises are let on a weekly tenancy the landlord is not allowed more than four weeks' arrears; and if the letting is for some other period less than a year the landlord is not entitled to rent in excess of that due for four 'terms or times for payment' (Execution Act 1844, s 67). The 'arrears' of rent which may be claimed by a landlord include rent due to be paid for a period in advance, so long as the sum is due at the time of execution (*Harrison v Barry* (1819) 7 Price 690).

Although a strict interpretation of the Landlord and Tenant Act 1709 would make wrongful any removal of goods before payment of the rent it has become the practice for the sheriff to remove the goods, sell them and then pay the land-lord from the proceeds (*Re Mackenzie, ex p Sheriff of Hertfordshire* [1899] 2 QB 566, CA). This may, however, cause problems. The sheriff may incur personal liability by wrongly deciding that the landlord should (*White v Binstead* (1853) 13 CB 304), or should not (*Forster v Cookson* (1841) 1 QB 419) be paid, and it may be better for the sheriff to notify the execution creditor so that the creditor may pay off the landlord prior to the sheriff continuing with the execution (see *Cocker v Musgrove and Moon* (1846) 9 QB 223).

The statute does not expressly require the landlord to serve any notice upon the sheriff, but it has been decided that it is not the sheriff's duty to inquire as to whether there are any arrears and he is under no liability to the landlord unless he is informed that rent is due (*Waring v Dewberry* (1718) 1 Stra 97; *Palgrave v Windham* (1719) 1 Stra 212). In practice therefore the onus is upon the landlord to inform the sheriff of any arrears. The sheriff's duty to satisfy the arrears of rent arises so long as he has notice of the arrears before parting with the pro-ceeds of sale (*Arnitt v Garnett* (1820) 3 B & Ald 440). It is not necessary that the notification to the sheriff is by means of notice served by the landlord, but so long as the sheriff has knowledge, from whatever source, that there may be a claim by the landlord, the sheriff is under a duty to deal with the claim before parting with the proceeds of sale (*Andrews v Dixon* (1820) 3 B & Ald 645). Upon being told by a landlord that there are arrears of rent the sheriff might ask the landlord to provide evidence that such arrears exist. It is, of course, often diffi-cult to prove a negative, and the landlord may not have written proof of non-payment. In such a case the sheriff may act upon the landlord's word unless the tenant produces to the sheriff some proof of payment (*Harrison v Barry* (1819) 7 Price 690).

Execution of county court judgments

In a county court the landlord's rights are more limited (County Courts Act 1984, s 102). The bailiff can seize the goods without the landlord's consent. The landlord's right to claim the rent must then be exercised at any time within the five days following the seizure, or before removal of the goods. The landlord must make the claim by delivering to the bailiff a claim in writing, signed by himself or his agent, stating the amount of rent in arrear and the period in respect of which it is due. Where such a claim is made the bailiff must distrain upon sufficient goods to satisfy the rent and costs and must not, within five days after seizure, sell any of the goods unless the goods are perishable or the person whose goods have been seized so requests in writing. On sale the bailiff must apply the proceeds in the following order:

(a) first, the costs of and incidental to the sale;
(b) next, the claim of the landlord not exceeding:
    (i) in a case where the tenement is let by the week, four weeks' rent;
    (ii) in a case where the tenement is let for any other term less than a year, the rent of two terms of payment;
    (iii) in any other case, one year's rent; and
(c) lastly, the amount for which the warrant of execution was issued.

It should be noted that although the statute refers to the bailiff levying a distress, the bailiff does not have the right to take goods of a third party. Although a landlord would normally be able to take third-party goods whilst levying a distress, the right is exceptional and should not be extended to other instances where a distress is permitted by statute (*Beard v Knight* (1858) 8 E & B 865; *Foulger v Taylor* (1860) 5 H & N 202). The landlord's right to require payment of rent applies even where the debtor is not the tenant, but the debtor's goods are found upon the premises. Since a landlord would be able to distrain upon the debtor's goods the bailiff should pay the rent before accounting to the creditor for the proceeds of sale (*Hughes v Smallwood* (1890) 25 QBD 306).

Effect of insolvency

The landlord's rights are reduced in bankruptcy by the IA 1986, s 347(6) which provides that if the tenant against whom the execution is levied is adjudged bankrupt before the notice of claim is served on the sheriff or county court bailiff, the right of the landlord is restricted to a claim for an amount not exceeding six months' rent and does not extend to any rent payable in respect of a period after the notice of claim is served. Otherwise the landlord's claim is unaffected by the bankruptcy or liquidation of the tenant and the sheriff or bailiff may pay the rent to the landlord before releasing the benefit of the execution to the trustee or liquidator under the IA 1986, ss 184 or 346 (*Re Neil Mackenzie, ex p Sheriff of Hertfordshire* [1899] 2 QB 566, CA, see above). The landlord does not need leave of the court to rely upon these rights, so that if an execution creditor has been given leave to proceed, the sheriff must pay the arrears of rent to the landlord before accounting to the execution creditor, and in priority to other creditors (*Re British Salicylates Ltd* [1919] 2 Ch 155).

Execution against the lease

The landlord may also find that an execution creditor has rights against the lease itself by the terms of a charging order, or possibly a writ of *fieri facias*, which in a subsequent bankruptcy or liquidation would give the execution creditor priority to the proceeds of sale of the lease over other unsecured creditors, including the landlord. This would not normally cause a landlord too much of a problem because the landlord will retain the right to forfeit for any arrears of rent, although while the lease is subject to a charging order the execution creditor will have a right to apply for relief from forfeiture.

In the case of a charging order under the Charging Orders Act 1979 the position depends upon whether at the commencement of the liquidation a charging order is absolute or not. If the charge is absolute the execution creditor will have become a secured creditor and will have a corresponding priority when assets are distributed. If the court has only made a charging order nisi and there is an intervening insolvency the court is very unlikely to look favourably upon an application by the creditor to have the order made absolute as this would in many cases be an unfair preference. The House of Lords in *Roberts Petroleum Ltd v Bernard Kenny Ltd* [1983] 2 AC 192, accepted that the charging order nisi itself constituted a charge but held that the charge was a defeasible one which was dependent upon the court's exercising its discretion to make the order absolute. Insolvency of the debtor would normally be sufficient cause for the court to refuse its discretion and to discharge the charge created by the order nisi. If, however, there are special circumstances, the order may be made absolute notwithstanding the insolvency of the debtor. Such circumstances may include the case where there are no bankruptcy proceedings and where a debtor's proposed voluntary arrangement cannot properly be approved without the consent of the execution creditor (*Re a Debtor (Nos 31/32/33 of 1993)* [1994] 2 BCLC 321).

Prior to the Charging Orders Act 1979 the only means of execution against the lease would have been a writ of *fieri facias* whereby a sheriff may 'seize' the lease and sell it, using the proceeds of sale to pay off the execution creditor. This right would be subject to the normal restrictions against execution in bankruptcy, liquidation and administration (see above).

2.8 Recovery of subrents from subtenant

One very useful practical remedy for a landlord when a tenant defaults in payment of rent is provided by the Law of Distress Amendment Act 1908. Under s 6 of that Act where rent is in arrears under a headlease the head landlord may receive subrents from subtenants by service of a notice requiring the subtenants to pay the subrents directly to him. The right will have priority over the rights of an administrative receiver and even over the right of a receiver of a fixed charge to receive rents. In *Rhodes v Allied Dunbar Pension Services Ltd* [1989] 1 All ER 1161, CA, a tenant company had given a debenture and a mortgage of a lease to a bank. The bank appointed receivers under the debenture, which receivers did not pay rent to the landlord. The landlord accordingly served notices under the Law of Distress Amendment Act 1908, s 6, upon the subtenants. Entitlement to the subrents was litigated and the Court of Appeal held that the subrents were payable to the landlord since the receiver as agent of the company had no better right to the rents than the tenant company which had appointed him. Whether the result would be the same in the case of liquidation, bankruptcy or administration is unclear.

In compulsory liquidation leave of the court is required for any 'action or proceeding against the company or its property' (IA 1986, s 130(2)). Arguably service of a notice is not an action or proceeding and service on a subtenant is not done against the company or its property. But the contrary argument would also appear to be viable, particularly since distress for rent has been held to fall within the definition of an 'action or proceeding' (*Re Memco Engineering Ltd* [1986] Ch 86).

In administration, leave of the court is required 'to enforce any security over the company's property' (IA 1986, s 10), and in administration and bankruptcy leave is required for any 'legal process' (IA 1986, ss 10, 285).

It is arguable that the right to serve s 6 notice in lieu of distress is a right of security for non-payment of rent and restricted by the IA 1986.

The term 'legal process' has been held to apply to a distress for rates by a local authority (*Re Smith (a bankrupt) v Braintree District Council* [1990] 2 AC 215, HL). On the other hand in *Re Fanshaw and Yorston, ex p Birmingham and Staffordshire Gas Light Co* (1871) LR 11 Eq 615, Sir James Bacon CJ held that a distress by a landlord for rent was not a legal process which could be restrained in bankruptcy because 'no legal process whatever is necessary; and the landlord may, if he thinks proper, distrain with his own hands'. This line of reasoning was adopted in *McMullen & Sons Ltd v Cerrone* (1993) 66 P & CR 351, where a restraint upon 'other legal process' in the IA 1986 s 252(2)(b) was held insufficient to outlaw a distress against a tenant in a voluntary arrangement, and in *Re Olympia and York Canary Wharf Ltd* [1993] BCLC 453, Millet J decided that the words did not catch the service of a contractual notice making time of the essence in respect of a contract. On the basis of these authorities it is likely that the service of a notice under the Law of Distress Amendment Act 1908 is not restricted in bankruptcy.

In other circumstances it has been held that leave of the court is not needed before relying upon the Law of Distress Amendment Act 1908. *Wallrock v Equity and Law Life Assurance Society* [1942] 2 KB 82, CA, was concerned with the Courts (Emergency Powers) Act 1939, s 1 which prohibited the exercise of any remedy by way of levying of distress or the taking of possession of any property without the leave of the court. It was decided by the Court of Appeal that the service of a notice under the 1908 Act, s 6, did not require the leave of the court.

2.8.1 PROCEDURE

The landlord's notice need not be in prescribed form but must state the amount of the arrears and require all future payments of the subrents, whether they have accrued due or not, to be made directly to the head landlord until the arrears have been satisfied. The notice may be served by registered post or personally (*Jarvis v Hemmings* [1912] 1 Ch 462), and upon the premises.

2.8.2 EFFECT OF NOTICE

The effect of the notice is to transfer to the head landlord the right to recover, receive and give a discharge for such rent (Law of Distress Amendment Act 1908, s 6), thereby establishing an immediate relationship of landlord and tenant between head landlord and subtenant (s 3). The head landlord can therefore recover the sums from the subtenant by an action for rent or by distress. The head landlord can concurrently pursue his claim against the immediate tenant for the headrent and may prove in bankruptcy or liquidation for any balance due (*Re A Debtor (No 549 of 1928)* [1929] 1 Ch 170, CA). The subtenant may, of course, deduct any sums paid from the amount due to his immediate landlord (s 3), and the immediate landlord has no remedies against the subtenant (*Rhodes v Allied Dunbar Pension Services Ltd* [1989] 1 All ER 1161, CA).

2.9 Petitioning for bankruptcy or winding up

A landlord faced with a defaulting tenant may consider the possibility of taking steps to bankrupt or wind up the tenant. A threat to bankrupt or wind up the tenant by service of a statutory demand for the rent will often induce payment in cases where the financial difficulties of the tenant are not severe and the tenant does not wish to have its business disrupted. In the case of a seriously insolvent tenant who cannot pay the rent it is questionable whether the threat should be followed through with a petition since if the landlord precipitates a bankruptcy or winding up he will create a situation whereby secured creditors and preferential creditors will have the first bite of the cherry, perhaps leaving nothing for the landlord; and in the bankruptcy or winding up the landlord's remedies of forfeiture and distress will be restricted.

2.9.1 STATUTORY DEMAND

If the threat to bankrupt or wind up is to be made the landlord will normally (although there are other grounds for bankrupting or winding up) serve a statutory demand in prescribed form on the tenant in respect of a debt exceeding the prescribed amount (currently £750). If the tenant fails to satisfy the demand within three weeks of service a petition may be presented (IA 1986, ss 123, 267).

The debt

In case of a winding up the debt may be one which is immediately payable. This does not include a contingent debt if the contingency giving rise to liability to pay has not yet occurred (*JSF Finance & Currency Exchange Co Ltd v Akma Solutions Inc* [2001] 2 BCLC 307). In the case of bankruptcy, the debt may be one already due or which is payable at some certain future time. If the debt is one which is already payable the tenant is required to pay it or to secure or compound for it to the satisfaction of the landlord or other creditor. If, in bankruptcy, the debt is not immediately payable the tenant is required to establish to the satisfaction of the landlord or other creditor that there is a reasonable prospect of the tenant being able to pay it when it falls due.

Set-off

If the debtor has a counterclaim, set-off or cross-demand which equals or exceeds the amount of the debt specified in the statutory demand then the statutory demand may be set aside (IR 1986, r 6.5(4)(a)). There must be a good arguable case of set-off if the statutory demand is to be set aside (*McDonald's Restaurants Ltd v Urbandivide Co Ltd* [1994] 1 BCLC 306) and not a remote possibility of creating a genuine triable issue (*Hurst v Bennett* [2001] 2 BCLC 290, CA).

Form and content

The demand must be in writing and must be dated and signed by the creditor or its authorised agent. It must state the amount of the debt and the consideration for it. If there is interest payable which was not previously notified to the debtor (e g default interest for late payment) such interest must be separately identified. The demand must also state its purpose, the time limit for compliance and modes of compliance, and the fact that if it is not complied with bankruptcy or winding-up proceedings may be commenced. The demand must also specify one or more named individuals with whom the tenant may enter into communication with a view to securing or compounding for the debt to the satisfaction of the creditor, or, if the demand was served in respect of a future debt in bankruptcy, establishing to the creditor's satisfaction that there is a reasonable prospect of the debt being paid. There must be given the address and telephone number, if any, of any person named (IR 1986, rr 4.4–4.6 and 6.1–6.5).

In the case of bankruptcy the demand must in addition, if the creditor is secured, specify the security and the value which the creditor puts upon it, and the demand must be for the amount of the debt less the amount of the security. It must also inform the tenant of his right to apply for the statutory demand to be set aside.

Service of demand

In the case of a winding up the demand must be served upon the debtor's registered office, either personally or by post, provided that it is proved that it was actually delivered (*Re A Company (No 008790 of 1990)* [1991] BCLC 561; IA 1986, s 123).

In the case of bankruptcy of an individual the creditor must 'do all that is reasonable for the purpose of bringing the statutory demand to the debtor's attention and, if practicable in the particular circumstances, to cause personal service of the demand to be effected.' Where personal service is not possible service may be effected by first class post or insertion through a letter box (*Practice Direction* [1987] 1 All ER 604). If the statutory demand is in respect of a judgment debt and the landlord or other creditor knows or believes with reasonable cause that the debtor tenant has absconded or is keeping out of the way with a view to avoid service and there is no reasonable prospect of the sum being recovered by execution, the demand may be advertised in one or more newspapers; and the time for compliance with the demand runs from the date of the advertisement (IR 1986, r 6.3). If the statutory demand is to be followed up by a bankruptcy petition service of the demand must be evidenced by an affidavit of service (IR 1986, r 6.11).

Defective demands

Prior to the IA 1986 the law governing statutory demands in individual bankruptcy were very technical. The new law governing statutory demands on both individuals and companies is modelled upon the rules previously applicable to companies, and is designed to avoid the technicalities which previously complicated the law of individual bankruptcy. The general approach of the courts is to treat the demand as valid unless the tenant would be prejudiced by the defect.

Defective demands upon companies/limited liability partnerships

If a statutory demand which has been served upon a tenant company or limited liability partnership is substantially defective a petition cannot be served in reliance upon it. A minor defect will, however, be disregarded and the demand may found an effective petition. This may be so even if the demand has by error incorrectly stated an amount greater than the debt, since the tenant is required by the IA 1986, s 123, to pay the sum actually due, and not the sum demanded, if different (*Cardiff Preserved Coal and Coke Co v Norton* (1867) 2 Ch App 405). But the demand for a greater sum can only be relied upon if the tenant knows the correct amount due. If the debt is a matter which is the subject of a substantial dispute between landlord and tenant, perhaps a disputed service charge, the demand for the greater amount will not justify the presentation of a petition (*Re A Company (No 003729 of 1982)* [1984] 3 All ER 78) and may be an abuse of process (*Re A Company (No 0012209 of 1991)* [1992] 1 WLR 351).

Defective demands upon individuals

In the case of bankruptcy a debtor who has been served with a demand has 18 days, from the date of its service upon him (or the date of its advertisement, if advertised), to apply to the court to have the demand set aside (IR 1986, r 6.4). Although the law of bankruptcy has been drawn closer to that applicable in liquidation it should be noted that differences may arise.

Difference may arise, for example, from the fact that an individual served with a demand is required to 'comply' with the demand, rather than to pay the sum actually due (IA 1986, ss 123, 267). In *Re A Debtor (No 10 of 1988)* [1989] 2 All ER 39, Hoffmann J noted the distinction. He said that an individual, in order to comply with a demand, would either have to pay the whole sum demanded, or have the demand set aside under the insolvency rules (IR 1986, r 6.5).

Difference may also arise because the function of a demand in the case of bankruptcy is to establish inability to pay the debt in question whereas in liquidation the demand is simply one means of establishing the company's general inability to pay debts. This might lead a court to give such weight to a counterclaim on a bankruptcy statutory demand so as to set aside the demand (*Re a Debtor (No 544/SD/98)* [2000] 1 BCLC 103.

The Court of Appeal has, however, held that a defect in a statutory demand will not cause the demand to be set aside so long as there is no prejudice to the debtor. In *Re A Debtor (No 1 of 1987)* [1989] 2 All ER 46, CA, the statutory demand was made in respect of a judgment debt. It was made on the wrong form and the amount was incorrectly calculated, but there was no evidence that the debtor had been misled. Accordingly, the court refused to exercise its discretion to set the demand aside. The decision should not, however, be taken to give carte blanche for the service of defective notices. Nicholls LJ emphasised that:

'The new statutory code affords the court a desirable degree of flexibility when confronted with an application to set aside a statutory demand containing one or more

69

defects. But this is not to be taken by banks or others as a charter for the slipshod preparation of statutory demands. The making of a bankruptcy order remains a serious step so far as a debtor is concerned, and the prescribed preliminaries are intended to afford protection to him. If a statutory demand is served in an excessive amount or is otherwise defective, the court will be alert to see whether those mistakes have caused or will cause any prejudice to the debtor.'

Where a statutory demand overstates the debt the demand will not generally be set aside. The proper course of action on the part of the debtor is to pay the amount which the debtor believes to be due and then to apply to have the demand set aside on the basis that the balance is disputed (*Re a Debtor (No 490/SD/91), ex p Debtor v Printline* [1992] 2 All ER 664). But if the undisputed amount is below the statutory minimum required to support a petition the demand may be set aside in any event (*Re a Debtor (Nos 49 and 50 of 1992)* [1995] Ch 66, CA).

Where there is a serious dispute relating to a statutory demand in the case of an individual tenant the demand may be set aside. If the court is of the view that a defence raised by the tenant is sketchy or weak it may order that the demand be set aside upon terms, for example, that the tenant pays a sum into an account in the joint names of the landlord's and tenant's solicitors to meet the landlord's claim if successful (*Re a Debtor (No 517 of 1991)* (1991) Times, 25 November). Where the tenant is a solvent company (or limited liability partnership) and there is a bona fide dispute as to the demand, the landlord should not present a petition upon the basis of it. To do so would be an abuse of process and the landlord may be ordered to pay the tenant's costs on an indemnity basis (*Re a Company (No 0012209 of 1991)* [1992] 2 All ER 797).

2.9.2 PRESENTATION OF PETITION

If a statutory demand is not complied with the landlord may consider the next step of issuing a petition in bankruptcy or liquidation. In many cases it is likely that a landlord would be better off relying upon one of his remedies for non-payment of rent rather than formally petitioning for bankruptcy or winding up, for the reasons stated above (para 2.9.1).

It should be remembered that a creditor of a company or limited liability partnership cannot petition for winding up while there is an administration (IA 1986, s 11). If there is a voluntary liquidation, a petition for winding up may be presented but the court will not make a winding up order unless it is satisfied that the voluntary winding up cannot be continued with due regard to the interests of creditors or contributories (IA 1986, s 124(5)).

Winding up

There are a number of grounds for winding up a company or limited liability partnership (see para 1.6.2). The main ground for winding up which will concern a landlord is that the tenant is unable to pay its debts. It was noted in chapter 1 (para 1.6.2) that a company or limited liability partnership is deemed unable to pay its debts in the following circumstances: if it fails to satisfy a statutory demand (para 2.9.1); if execution or other process issued on a judgment is returned unsatisfied in whole or in part; or it is proved to the satisfaction of the court that it is unable to pay its debts as they fall due. A company is also deemed unable to pay its debts if it is proved to the satisfaction of the court that the value of assets is less than the amount of liabilities (IA 1986, s 123).

In these cases a landlord may present a petition by filing it in court with copies for service on the company (or partnership), for attaching to an affidavit verifying service, and for other interested parties. The petition must be properly served on the registered office of the company or limited liability partnership and must be advertised, normally in the London Gazette. The contents of the petition must also be verified by an affidavit. The petitioner has to lodge a deposit (currently £500, Insolvency Fees Order 1986, SI 1986/2030, as amended) to cover the fee of the Official Receiver. The deposit is returnable if the petition is withdrawn or dismissed (see generally IR 1986, rr 4.7–4.21).

Bankruptcy

In bankruptcy a landlord's petition must be in respect of a debt exceeding the 'bankruptcy level', currently £750. The debt must be for a liquidated sum and must be unsecured and the tenant must appear unable to pay or to have no reasonable prospect of paying. The tenant will be deemed unable to pay if he has not satisfied the statutory demand (see para 2.9.1) or if an execution has been returned unsatisfied in whole or part (IA 1986, s 267).

The petition must clearly identify the tenant, the amount owed and the consideration for it and must identify any interest element. The petition is normally presented in the county court for the area in which the tenant resides or carries on business, but if the tenant has resided or carried on business in the London insolvency district during the major part of the immediately preceding six months the petition should be presented in the High Court. The petition must be filed in court with copies for the debtor and for an affidavit verifying service, and other interested parties may be entitled to a copy. The contents of the petition must also be verified by affidavit. The petition must be served personally on the tenant unless an order for substituted service is obtained. The petitioner has to lodge a deposit (currently £300, Insolvency Fees Order 1986, SI 1986/2030, as amended), which is returnable if the petition is withdrawn or dismissed (see generally IR 1986, rr 6.6–6.36).

2.10 Proving in bankruptcy or liquidation

In liquidation (whether compulsory or voluntary) or bankruptcy a landlord may prove for rent due or for damages for breach of the terms of the lease. In other words the landlord may inform the liquidator or trustee in bankruptcy of the amount owing and claim a dividend in the bankruptcy as an ordinary creditor. The remedy will be of no value if there is no surplus after payment of claims of secured and preferential creditors, but in some cases the landlord will by proof be able to recover the rent or part of it. If, for example, a landlord is owed £1,000 rent by a tenant company and the liquidator is paying a dividend to ordinary creditors of 50 pence in every pound, the landlord will recover £500.

2.10.1 PROCEDURE

The rules for proving vary according to whether there is compulsory liquidation, voluntary liquidation or bankruptcy. In a compulsory liquidation forms of proof must be sent out by the liquidator to every creditor who is known to him. The forms must accompany the notice to creditors of the Official Receiver's decision to call meetings under the IA 1986, s 136, or the first notice calling a meeting of creditors, or the notice of the appointment of the liquidator by the court, whichever is the first to occur. Where with the leave of the court the liquidator advertises his appointment he must send proofs to creditors within four months after the winding-up order. A landlord who wishes to prove for arrears of rent must submit a claim in the prescribed form, or a substantially similar form, which must be signed by the landlord or its agent. The liquidator may require the proof to be in the form of an affidavit, or he may require a supporting affidavit. The cost of the proof is borne by the landlord. The liquidator must decide whether to accept or reject the proof. A creditor who is dissatisfied can appeal to the court against the liquidator's decision (IR 1986, rr 4.73–4.85). A proof can be withdrawn or varied at any time by agreement between the creditor and the liquidator. The court may fix a time limit within which creditors are to prove or to be excluded from any distribution made before the debt is proved. If the time limit is missed the debt may still be proved up until the dissolution and paid out of a subsequent dividend, if any (IA 1986, s 153, IR 1986, rr 4.182, 11.2).

In a voluntary winding up the liquidator may, at his discretion, require creditors to lodge proofs of debt. If the liquidator does so there is no prescribed form, but the proof must be in writing. The liquidator may require the proof to be in the form of an affidavit, or may require a supporting affidavit. The liquidator may require such information and evidence as the liquidator thinks fit. The liquidator must decide whether to accept or reject a proof, subject to the creditor's right to appeal. The proof may be withdrawn or varied at any time by agreement between the creditor and the liquidator. The cost of the proof will be borne by the landlord or other creditor.

The procedure for lodging a proof in bankruptcy is similar to that in a compulsory liquidation. Forms must be sent to creditors with whichever is the first of: a notice to creditors of the Official Receiver's decision not to call a meeting of creditors under the IA 1986, s 293; the first notice calling a meeting of creditors; where there is a summary administration, the notice of the bankruptcy order; and, where a trustee is appointed by the court, the notice of his appointment. A landlord wishing to prove must do so on the prescribed form, or in a substantially similar form. The trustee must decide whether to accept or reject a proof. There is a right for the creditor to appeal to the court against the decision (IR 1986, rr 6.96–6.107).

2.10.2 RENT PROVABLE

In the case of liquidation the landlord proves for the rent due and unpaid 'up to the date when the company went into liquidation' (IR 1986, r 4.92), i e the date of presentation of the petition or the date of the passing of a resolution for voluntary winding up (IA 1986, s 129); whereas in bankruptcy the rent is claimed for the period up to the date of the bankruptcy order and not the earlier date of presentation of the petition (IR 1986, r 6.112).

If rent is payable quarterly in advance and bankruptcy or liquidation occurs during a quarter the landlord can prove for the quarter's rent then due. When the next quarter's rent becomes due the landlord may be able to look to the trustee or liquidator for payment (see paras 2.3.2, 2.4). If rent is payable in arrears a payment which is not yet due, but which is accruing due, at the beginning of the liquidation or at the date of the bankruptcy order may be apportioned so that the landlord can prove for so much as would have fallen due at that date if the rent was accruing on a daily basis (IR 1986, rr 4.92 and 6.112; *Re South Kensington Co-operative Stores* (1881) 17 Ch D 161).

Rent accruing due afterwards should be claimable as an expense of the bankruptcy or liquidation (see para 2.3.2), or claimable against the trustee in bankruptcy personally (see para 2.4) unless and until the liquidator or trustee disclaims the lease. It is possible, however, that payments due in advance cannot be recovered and that the trustee or liquidator might pay on a daily basis only (see para 3.6.5).

If the trustee or liquidator disclaims the lease, such disclaimer ends the liability for rent from the date of disclaimer (IA 1986, ss 178, 315), and in the case of bankruptcy absolves the trustee from all personal liability, but presumably without prejudicing the landlord's claim to treat the rent as an expense of the bankruptcy up to the date of the disclaimer (IR 1986, r 6.224).

Although in a liquidation rent is only provable up to the date of presentation of the petition, the landlord will be concerned to see that liability for future rents is met so far as is possible. If the lease is disclaimed the landlord will be able to prove for loss of future rents as a loss caused by the disclaimer (for the measure of damages see para 6.9). If the lease is assigned the landlord can look to the assignee for the rent, and prove for the loss of the right to sue the insolvent tenant (see para 7.3.5).

If the lease is neither disclaimed nor assigned, and if the landlord does not accept a surrender, the problem is more complex. The inability to prove for future rent in such cases has caused the courts some problems, particularly in the case of a solvent voluntary liquidation. It might be feared that a tenant could, by putting itself into voluntary liquidation, avoid the future obligations under the lease, and distribute the company's assets amongst creditors and shareholders. In order to avoid this result the courts have sometimes shown a willingness to order that, after payment of creditors, any balance of assets cannot be paid to shareholders until a sufficient fund has been set aside to meet the landlord's future claims (*Oppenheimer v British and Foreign Exchange and Investment Bank* (1877) 6 Ch D 744). In other cases the courts have not thought it appropriate to set aside a fund to cover possible future default. In *Re London and Colonial Co, Horsey's Claim* (1868) LR 5 Eq 561, Sir GM Giffard V-C refused to adopt this approach for the reason that the landlord could rely upon remedies of forfeiture and distress in the event of future default. More recently Roxburgh J in *Re House Property and Investment Co Ltd* [1954] Ch 576, doubted that it was correct to set a fund aside, although in that case the lease had been assigned and his Lordship was only considering a company's contingent liability as assignor of the lease (see also *Re Lucania Temperance Billiard Halls (London) Ltd* [1966] Ch 98).

It should be noted that the earlier cases were decided at a time when a liquidator had no power to disclaim. Following the introduction of the power of disclaimer it is suggested that the best analysis is as follows. If the liquidator is aware of the lease, the liquidator should (pursuant to the liquidator's role in winding up assets) dispose of the lease or disclaim it. If there is a disclaimer the landlord can prove for the loss arising from the disclaimer (see chapter 6). There should be no question of the liquidator allowing the lease obligations to continue and setting aside a fund to satisfy them. If the lease is overlooked it will, on the dissolution of the company, vest in the Crown as *bona vacantia* (see para 6.8). The Crown then has to decide whether to disclaim the lease. If it does not disclaim it becomes liable upon the covenants in the lease and the only loss suffered by the landlord is the loss of the dissolved tenant's covenant. If the Crown does disclaim the effect is that the lease is deemed not to have vested in the Crown, and there is a deemed disclaimer by the liquidator immediately prior to the dissolution. In this case the landlord ought theoretically to be entitled to prove for the loss of future rent on the basis discussed in chapter 6 (para 6.9). As disclaimer by the Crown will, however, have occurred after the conclusion of the winding up there will in all probability be no money remaining to satisfy the landlord. The landlord will be left to repossess or relet the property.

Set-off

In bankruptcy and liquidation a landlord may be able to take advantage of the provisions allowing for mutual set-off (IA 1986, s 323, IR 1986, r 4.90). If, for example, a landlord owes money to a tenant – say, as a capital contribution to works – the landlord may wish to set off the sum against rent due, and to prove for the net arrears only (after deduction of the amount due to the tenant). As the effect of set-off, however, may be to prefer the landord over other creditors the right of set-off is applied restrictively (*Bank of Credit and Commerce International SA v Al-Saud* [1997] 1 BCLC 457). If the sum owing by the landlord is a statutory sum due to the tenant, e g compensation for disturbance under the Landlord and Tenant Act 1954, it may be that the landlord cannot rely upon the statutory right of set-off and may have to pay the statutory compensation in full whilst proving for the full amount of arrears of rent (see *Alloway v Steere* (1882) 10 QBD 22 and *Re Wilson, ex p Lord Hastings* (1893) 62 LJQB 628).

2.10.3 PROOF FOR DAMAGES FOR DISREPAIR OR OTHER BREACH

Even though a claim for damages for disrepair is an unliquidated claim it may nevertheless be the subject of a proof of debt. The IR 1986, r 12.3 provides that all claims of creditors are provable as debts whether they are 'present or future, certain or contingent, ascertained or sounding only in damages'. A trustee in bankruptcy (IA 1986, s 322) or liquidator (IR 1986, r 4.86) can estimate the value of the claim for the purpose of allowing the proof. The liquidator or trustee is likely in many cases to require the claim to be supported by affidavit evidence (IR 1986, rr 4.77 and 6.98). In cases where the creditor is aggrieved by the amount of the estimate an application can be made to the court which has power to alter the estimate (IA 1986, ss 168, 303).

One method of reducing room for dispute as to the quantum of damages would be for the landlord to enter into the property and carry out the repairs at his own cost and then to prove for that amount. The landlord will only be able to do so if he has expressly reserved the right to enter for this purpose by the terms of the lease.

2.10.4 PROOF FOR INTEREST

Leases often contain provisions for payment of interest on late payment of rent, service charges or other sums. Where such interest is expressly reserved it may be proved for as part of the debt. Even if not expressly reserved the landlord's claim may include interest in the circumstances provided by the rules.

In the case of a lease in writing interest may be claimed at the rate specified in the Judgments Act 1838, s 17, from the due date to the commencement of the liquidation or in bankruptcy to the date of the order. In the case of an oral lease (see the Law of Property Act 1925, s 54(2)), provided that the landlord serves a written demand for the rent or other sum due, he will be able to claim interest from the date of the demand until the commencement of liquidation or the bankruptcy order (see the IR 1986, rr 4.93 and 6.113). The statutory rate of interest is varied from time to time by statutory instrument (currently 8% – Judgment Debts (Rate of Interest) Order 1993, SI 1993/564).

2.10.5 PROOF AS WAIVER OF DISTRESS

It has been suggested that if a landlord decides to prove for rent he may be held to have waived his right to distrain for such rent. The question is considered in depth at para 3.10.

CHAPTER 3

Distress for rent

Distress is a remedy of the common law, reinforced by statute, arising independently of the terms of the lease, whereby a landlord who is owed rent is able to take possession of goods which are on the demised premises and either hold them as security for the rent, or sell them and use the proceeds of sale to satisfy the arrears of rent.

In appropriate cases the remedy can be remarkably effective, but it can sometimes give rise to complications and costs which make it ineffectual. In a case where distress is effective a landlord, who might otherwise be an ordinary creditor without priority, will achieve priority to the tenant's goods over unsecured creditors. There are, however, statutory restrictions which may check the exercise of distress in cases of bankruptcy and liquidation.

The law of distress is a maze of complexity which it is not intended to investigate fully within this present work; its purpose is to emphasise and examine the special restrictions which are applicable in cases where a tenant is insolvent. Public authorities also have rights to distrain. The most well-known of these are the rights to distrain for rates or for taxes. Such rights are governed by their own statutes and the rules discussed below do not necessarily apply to them in the same way.

3.1 Is a distraint worthwhile?

Whether it is worthwhile distraining is in most cases a commercial decision which depends upon the particular factual matrix and financial circumstances. If the ultimate objective of the distraint is to sell the goods in order to satisfy rent arrears then the realisation value of the goods will be an important consideration; this will often be less than their book value because of the fact that there will be a forced sale. Whether there are sufficient goods to make distress fruitful will depend upon the nature of the premises. There is likely to be more of value to distrain upon in the case of industrial or retail premises, for example, than in the case of office premises where there will be little by way of stock and much of the equipment will be rented from third parties. The proportion of the goods on the premises which belong to third parties will be another factor affecting the efficacy of the distress, since there is a statutory procedure whereby third parties can avoid having their goods sold in distress (see para 3.5.3).

In cases where sale of the goods is not a viable option a distress may nevertheless be beneficial in another way. Preventing the receiver, trustee, administrator or liquidator from using the goods in the course of business may trigger a payment of rent, or, if the landlord is attempting to negotiate a surrender, distraint may speed up the process of negotiation and give the landlord bargaining strength.

3.2 The right to distrain

3.2.1 WHO CAN DISTRAIN?

The right to distrain on a tenant's goods is only available to the person who is legally entitled to the landlord's interest, both at the time when the rent falls due and at the time of the distress. So if a landlord transfers his interest without having distrained for arrears due at the date of the transfer, neither the transferring landlord nor the new landlord will be able to distrain for those arrears. If the landlord is himself a tenant under a superior lease and the superior lease is ended by forfeiture, the landlord's right to distrain ends with his lease, and any mortgagee of the headlease or receiver appointed by such mortgagee, will lose the right to distrain upon the subtenant's goods when the headlease ends (*Serjeant v Nash, Field & Co* [1903] 2 KB 304, CA).

Where a landlord has mortgaged his interest he is entitled to distrain for the rent so long as the mortgagee has not enforced the mortgage (*Turner v Walsh* [1909] 2 KB 484, CA). Once the mortgagee exercises his right to possession he is regarded as the person entitled to the landlord's interest, and the mortgagee has the right to distrain in respect of any lease of the property granted before the mortgage or not prohibited by it. Where the mortgagor is a tenant who has mortgaged a lease the mortgagee, if in possession, is the landlord in respect of any sublease (*Re Ind Coope & Co Ltd* [1911] 2 Ch 223, Landlord and Tenant (Covenants) Act 1995, s 15), and may distrain on the goods of the subtenant.

If a lease is granted by a mortgagor after the mortgage and in breach of the mortgage terms, the tenancy is binding by estoppel between the mortgagor and the tenant. But no relationship is created between the mortgagee and the tenant, and the mortgagee cannot distrain unless by payment and acceptance of rent, or other acts, a tenancy arises between the mortgagee and the tenant (*Rogers v Humphreys* (1835) 4 Ad & El 299).

If a mortgagee of the landlord's interest appoints a receiver as agent of the landlord, the receiver may collect the rents and distrain either in the name of the mortgagee or the landlord mortgagor (Law of Property Act 1925, s 109), and while a receiver is appointed the landlord may not distrain without the consent of the receiver (*Woolston v Ross* [1900] 1 Ch 788). The receiver can distrain for arrears of rent even though the due date for payment was prior to the date of his appointment (*Moss v Gallimore* (1779) 1 Doug KB 279).

In some cases a receiver of property is appointed by a court. Such a receiver has an automatic power to distrain for rents and does not need to make an application to the court prior to distraining unless there is some doubt as to who is entitled to the rents (*Bennett v Robins* (1832) 5 C & P 379).

3.2.2 AND AGAINST WHOM?

Distress is a remedy which is only available in respect of rent. For there to be 'rent' in the legal sense there must be a lease of the land and not a mere licence. An owner of land will therefore be able to distrain if there is a tenant, even if only a tenant at will (*Doe d Davies v Thomas* (1851) 6 Exch 854), but not if the occupier is a licensee (*Rendell v Roman* (1893) 9 TLR 192). Where the insolvent occupier holds under the terms of an enforceable contract for a lease there is likewise a right to distrain (*Walsh v Lonsdale* (1882) 21 Ch D 9). Where a business tenancy is continuing by virtue of the Landlord and Tenant Act 1954, s 24 there is a statutory extension of the contractual tenancy and it is likely that the right to distrain continues to be available.

Distress cannot be levied against the Crown, or upon property which is in the possession of the Crown (*Secretary of State for War v Wynne* [1905] 2 KB 845).

Although distress may usually be levied upon any goods upon the premises regardless of their ownership, a landlord may find that he cannot distrain upon the goods of a lawful assignee in respect of arrears due from a former tenant (*Wharfland Ltd v South London Co-operative Building Co Ltd* [1995] 2 EGLR 21, see para 3.7.1).

3.3 Rent distrainable

3.3.1 WHAT SUMS MAY BE DISTRAINED FOR?

Strictly speaking, distress is a right to enable a landlord to recover rent, i e 'a payment made to him in consideration of the enjoyment by a tenant of land belonging to the landlord,' (per Templeman LJ in *T & E Homes Ltd v Robinson* [1979] 2 All ER 522, CA). A landlord may, in addition to distraining for rent, wish to distrain for other sums, such as service charges, interest and landlord's costs. The basic rule is that the common law right of distress only applies to rent and the costs of the distress itself (Distress for Rent Act 1689, s 1), but it is possible that an appropriately drafted lease can reserve to the landlord a right to distrain for other sums which is similar to the common law right.

Service charges

Many leases state that service charges are reserved as rent and may be distrained for. It is doubtful whether calling such payments rent makes them rent, since the payments are plainly not rent in the strict sense. Where the lease goes further to state that service charges (whether or not reserved as rent), 'are to be recoverable in the same manner as rent' or 'are to be recoverable by distress', the provision should be prima facie binding in contract (*Escalus Properties Ltd v Dennis* [1995] 3 WLR 524, CA), but it may be subject to certain statutory requirements governing bills of sale by individuals and charges given by companies.

The right to distrain for service charges was considered to be valid by Vinelott J in *Concorde Graphics Ltd v Andromeda Investments SA* (1982) 265 Estates Gazette 386, although the right would only be exercisable once the amount of the service charge had been conclusively fixed in accordance with the terms of the lease. On the facts of *Concorde* itself his Lordship declared that distress could not be levied because the amount of the service charge due was in dispute, and the provisions in the lease for 'arbitration' had not been exhausted. There was not therefore a certain sum in respect of which to distrain. This line of reasoning is consistent with a basic rule relating to distress for rent – that the sum can only be distrained for if it is certain at the time that it falls due.

Even if the amount of service charge owing in *Concorde* had been indisputable it is not clear to what extent the right to distrain would have been valid, as such a right may fall foul of statutory provisions imposing special requirements in respect of creditors' rights to take goods for debts due. In the case of an individual tenant the Bills of Sale Acts 1878 and 1882 impose strict conditions upon any agreement whereby rights over personal chattels are given to secure debts. In *Stevens v Marston* (1890) 60 LJQB 192, CA, a landlord let a hotel under an agreement which provided that the tenant was to take supplies of liquor from the landlord and that the landlord should have power to distrain upon the demised premises for money due for liquor delivered by him to the tenant during the term. The Court of Appeal held that the power to distrain amounted to a licence to take possession of personal chattels as security for a debt within the Bills of Sale Act 1878, s 4 and the power was void for non-registration. It is possible that the effect of *Stevens v Marston* was reversed by the Law of Property Act 1925, s 189 which states that 'A power of distress given by way of indemnity ... against the breach of any covenant or condition in relation to land, is not ... a bill of sale', but as there is no authority confirming this it is arguable that the rule in *Stevens v Marston* applies to a right to distrain for service charges where the tenant is an individual.

If the tenant is a company any right to distrain for service charges may need to comply with the Companies Act 1985, s 396, which provides that an agreement entered into by the company, which if executed by an individual would require registration as a bill of sale, should be registered as a charge over the company's property. If a registrable charge is not registered within 21 days of its creation it is void against a liquidator, administrator or creditor of the company.

If, however, a rent is payable both in respect of the property and for other items such as furniture, and there is no separate payment for the use of the furniture, the rent is deemed to be a rent for the land only so that the right of distress is available (*Newman v Anderton* (1806) 2 Bos & PNR 224). So also, if under a lease a landlord provides services, but the rent is an inclusive one, the right to distrain is probably available without the need for its registration as a bill of sale or charge over company assets.

Mortgage payments

Similarly problems arise in relation to a right in a mortgage whereby the mortgagor becomes tenant of the mortgagee at a rent equivalent to interest, and the mortgagee as landlord has a right to distrain for arrears. Such a clause is known as an 'attornment', and the right reserved, being by way of security for money owed is regarded as a security bill of sale within the Bills of Sale Acts 1878 and 1882 (*Re Willis, ex p Kennedy* (1888) 21 QBD 384, CA). Such a right is not strictly a bill of sale which by the 1882 Act, s 9, has to be in the cumbersome scheduled form; but under the 1878 Act, s 6 the right is 'deemed to be a bill of sale' and as such is subject to the requirement of registration under the 1882 Act, s 8 (*Green v Marsh* [1892] 2 QB 330, CA). Non-registration will make the right to distrain void, but will not otherwise affect the attornment clause or the mortgage (*Mumford v Collier* (1890) 25 QBD 279).

Where the borrower is a company the Bills of Sale Acts have no direct application and a simple right to distrain for sums due will be valid, with or without an attornment clause (*Re Higginshaw Mills and Spinning Co* [1896] 2 Ch 544, CA). It seems, however, that the right is registrable under the Companies Act 1985, s 396 since if it was executed by an individual it would require registration as a bill of sale. In practice many lenders giving credit to a company on security of land will combine a fixed charge of the land with either or both of a fixed and floating charge over other and possibly all of the company's assets. Any such charge or charges will also be registrable under s 396, but will generally be seen as preferable to a right to distrain, since the chargee will have remedies which are usually more freely exercisable than distress.

Even assuming that a right to distrain for sums other than rent is valid in a particular case, the provision authorising distress cannot be effective to invoke the full common law right of distress. Such a contractual provision could not, for instance, entitle a landlord to distrain against the goods of a third party (see para 3.5) since the contract would be binding between the landlord and tenant only.

Reviewed rent

In law, rent properly so-called is a sum which must be ascertained upon the date that it is effective. Where a lease contains provision for rent review there is usually a specified rent review date from which the revised rent is to be effective. It is common, however, for the review to take place later than the specified date and for the backlog of increased rent from the review date to be paid in the future once the new rent is fixed. In such a case it is likely that the backlog is not rent properly so-called since it is not ascertained at the date from which it is effective and it is unlikely that the sum is distrainable (*United Scientific Holdings v Burnley Borough Council* [1978] AC 904, HL).

Interim rent

Where at the end of its contractual term a commercial lease has continued by virtue of the Landlord and Tenant Act 1954, Pt II a temporary rent may be determined by an application to court by the landlord to set an 'interim rent'. It is possible that the difference between the contractual rent and the interim rent (if any) is not strictly rent so as to form the basis of a distress for rent. It has at least been decided that a landlord cannot distrain for such rent pending an appeal by the tenant against its determination by a court at first instance. Nourse LJ in *Eren v Tranmac Ltd* [1997] 2 EGLR 211, held that in such circumstances the interim rent was not sufficiently certain to found a distress. It may be doubted, however, that it is right to say that a debt determined by a court is to be regarded as uncertain simply because an appeal is pending.

Set-off

The early authorities indicated that a tenant could not set off against the rent sums owed to him by the landlord so as to negate or reduce the landlord's right of distress (*Townrow v Benson* (1818) 3 Madd 203). The Court of Appeal has now decided, however, that an equitable set-off is available against a claim to levy a distress (*Eller v Grovecrest Investments Ltd* [1995] QB 272, CA). This decision could have a serious impact upon exercise of the right of distress, particularly where the tenant is seeking to exercise a counterclaim for an unliquidated amount and the landlord will be unable to determine what sum may be regarded as undisputed. In the *Eller* case, for instance, the tenant was alleging a cross-claim in respect of nuisance and breach of covenant on the part of the landlord. Perhaps worse for landlords is the recent decision in *Fuller v Happy Shoppper Markets Ltd* [2001] 1 WLR 1681, where Lightman J held not only that an equitable right of set-off was available to a tenant, but that it was the landlord's reponsibility to ascertain whether there might be any such right prior to levying distress. Further, it was decided that a landlord might be interfering with the tenant's rights to respect for privacy and home under the European Convention of Human Rights, art 8 by distraining without first taking into account any possible set-off

3.3.2 WHEN MAY DISTRESS BE LEVIED?

The right to distrain for unpaid rent arises on the first moment following the day upon which the payment became due. Most modern commercial leases provide that rent is payable quarterly in advance, and it is settled that such rent is distrainable on the day following that appointed for payment.

A landlord of commercial premises is only entitled to recover arrears of rent accrued due during the six years preceding an action for the rent, so only arrears accrued due in the six years ending with the day of levy can be distrained for (Limitation Act 1980, s 19). The rule is different in the case of agricultural property.

3.3.3 AMOUNT DISTRAINABLE IN BANKRUPTCY

Even though a tenant, being an individual, is bankrupt the landlord is still entitled to distrain for rent (see para 3.6.3). The right is, however, cut down by the Insolvency Act 1986, s 347(1) which provides that the landlord's right to distrain upon the goods and effects of an undischarged bankrupt for rent due to him is limited to a right to distrain for a maximum of six months' rent accrued due before the commencement of the bankruptcy. If a landlord has distrained after presentation of a petition but before a bankruptcy order, and an order is subsequently made, any sum recovered in excess of six months' rent is to be held for the bankrupt or his estate (IA, 1986, s 347(2)). If any amount recovered is in respect of rent for a period following the levying of the distress it is also to be held for the bankrupt.

Otherwise the landlord is free to distrain for all rent due and where a bankruptcy occurs during a quarter the landlord can distrain at the end of the quarter for the whole quarter's rent (*Re Howell, ex p Mandleberg & Co* [1895] 1 QB 844). If the trustee in bankruptcy disclaims the lease it is likely that liability for rent payable in arrears can be apportioned up to the date of disclaimer, but it is not clear whether the landlord can distrain for the arrears after the lease has been determined in this way (see para 3.7.1).

Distress for rent due after commencement

The restriction limiting the right to six months' rent only applies to rent due before the onset of bankruptcy. If the trustee in bankruptcy remains in possession after the lease vests in him and does not disclaim, all rent accruing after commencement of bankruptcy may be distrained for even if payable in advance (*Re Binns, ex p Hale* (1875) 1 Ch D 285). The IA 1986, s 347(9) expressly preserves the landlord's right to distrain against property comprised in a bankrupt's estate notwithstanding that the property has vested in the trustee.

Goods owned by or charged to third parties

The restriction only protects the goods of the bankrupt and not those of a third party (*Brocklehurst v Lawe* (1857) 7 E & B 176), since the third party goods would not be available to the general creditors in the bankruptcy, and distress upon them by the landlord does not amount to a preference over other creditors (*Railton v Wood* (1890) 15 App Cas 363, PC). It has been held, for instance, that property which the bankrupt tenant has mortgaged is liable to distress in full, on the basis that property in the goods passes to the mortgagee and is not property comprised in the bankrupt's estate. This will of course be a very harsh blow to a secured creditor of the bankrupt who finds that his security has been distrained upon by a landlord and left the creditor to prove unsecured in the bankruptcy. If the creditor has advance warning of the landlord's intention to distrain he might be able to remove the goods from the premises in order to avoid the distress (*Tomlinson v Consolidated Credit and Mortgage Corpn* (1889) 24 QBD 135, CA). But once the landlord has begun to distrain it is doubtful that there is anything that the secured creditor can do.

3.4 Charge in favour of preferential creditors

Where a landlord distrains and soon after the tenant (being an individual) becomes bankrupt or (being a company or limited liability partnership) is forced into compulsory liquidation the landlord may find that the priority given by the distress is less than absolute, since in some circumstances a landlord who has distrained shortly before the bankruptcy or liquidation will have to hold the goods distrained or the proceeds of sale to satisfy preferential claims, such as for rates, taxes, salaries and wages. This is in accordance with the general policy of the insolvency legislation that preferential creditors should have priority over others.

If a distress has occurred within the three months prior to a bankruptcy order and at the time of the bankruptcy order it transpires that the bankrupt's estate is insufficient to satisfy the claims of preferential creditors then the goods distrained or their proceeds of sale are to be charged, for the benefit of the bankrupt's estate, with the preferential debts (IA 1986, s 347(3)). The position is similar in a compulsory winding up of a company, by virtue of the IA 1986, s 176. The section provides:

> 'Where any person . . . has distrained upon the goods or effects of the company within the period of three months ending with the date of the winding-up order, those goods or effects, or the proceeds of their sale, shall be charged for the benefit of the company with the preferential debts of the company to the extent that the company's property is for the time being insufficient for meeting them.'

If the distress was initiated more than three months before the adjudication or winding-up order but not completed by sale before the date of the adjudication or order it is not clear whether there will be a charge upon the goods or proceeds of sale. The charge attaches where the landlord 'has distrained' in the period of three months. It is clear that if the whole process took place within the period the distress is caught, the more difficult question is whether completing within the period a distress which started outside of the period amounts to distraining within the period. On the slightly different wording of the Companies Act 1948, s 319 it has been held (*Re Memco Engineering Ltd* [1986] Ch 86) that distress is not completed until sale occurs so that a person has not 'distrained' until sale. Thus if sale of the goods has not taken place prior to the three months immediately preceding the order, the sale within the period falls within the section and the goods and proceeds will be subject to a charge.

Although the charge is a charge for the benefit of preferential creditors the proper person to enforce the charge is the trustee in bankruptcy or liquidator (*Re Caidan, ex p Official Receiver v Regis Property Co Ltd* [1942] Ch 90).

Problems of tracing

The provisions for the making of a charge over any goods or money still in the hands of the person distraining should give rise to few problems, but there may be difficulties where the goods have been sold and the proceeds dissipated or mixed with other moneys prior to the adjudication or winding-up order. If the proceeds of sale have been given by the bailiff to the landlord the charge will be enforceable against the landlord, who is regarded as the person who has distrained, albeit through his bailiff (*Re Caidan*, see above).

If, however, the proceeds of sale have been given to the landlord, who has dissipated them, consumed them, or mixed them with other money prior to the bankruptcy order or winding-up order the problem is more complex. It is likely that the charge does not arise until the date of the bankruptcy order or winding-up order (*Re Caidan*, see above). Thus, if the proceeds are not easily identifiable at the date of the order it is arguable that there is nothing for the charge to attach to, and that the preferential creditors lose out. Presumably the law of restitution and tracing will have to be relied upon to determine whether there are money or assets to which the charge can attach.

Preferential rights of landlords

Although a landlord may have to release distrained goods or their proceeds of sale to a trustee in bankruptcy or liquidator the landlord may through the distraint gain some priority over other creditors. The IA 1986, s 347(4) and 176(3) provide that the landlord will rank as a preferential creditor in respect of the amount of the proceeds of sale of any goods surrendered or any payment of money by the landlord to the trustee or liquidator, except that the landlord is not to have preference in respect of the amount available to the preferential creditors by virtue of the surrender of goods or payment of money by the landlord. So the landlord gains a priority in the bankruptcy or liquidation ranking as a preferential creditor – but just below the other preferential creditors, and only so long as there are still proceeds of the distraint available.

3.5 What goods may be taken?

Distress is a right to take goods, i e physical matter, in order to enforce payment of rent. Choses in action, such as patent rights or bills of exchange, cannot be the subject of distress. The basic rule is that a landlord can distrain on all goods found upon the property let and whether the goods are those of the tenant, a subtenant, or a stranger to the property, including a mortgagee of the tenant's goods. The reason why a third party's goods may be taken is that the landlord has a lien on goods in respect of the place where they are found and not in respect of the person to whom they belong. A third party may, however, avoid the distress by removing his goods from the premises before the distress begins (*Tomlinson v Consolidated Credit and Mortgage Corpn* (1889) 24 QBD 135, CA); and in some cases by serving a notice upon the landlord after commencement of the distress (see para 3.5.3 below).

There are exceptions, and if a landlord distrains upon goods which should not have been distrained upon the landlord may be liable for wrongful or excessive distress.

3.5.1 GOODS WHICH CANNOT BE DISTRAINED UPON

Some goods are 'absolutely privileged' and if a landlord distrains against them he will be liable for illegal distress. The goods which have absolute privilege are:

(a) property of the Crown (*Secretary of State for War v Wynne* [1905] 2 KB 845);
(b) property of persons enjoying diplomatic privilege;
(c) tenant's fixtures – these cannot be distrained upon even if they are goods being acquired on hire purchase (*Crossley Bros Ltd v Lee* [1908] 1 KB

86). The exception includes keys and title deeds (*Hellawell v Eastwood* (1851) 6 Exch 295 at 311);

(d)   things in actual use at the time of distraint (*Simpson v Hartopp* (1744) Willes 512);

(e)   perishable articles;

(f)   loose money;

(g)   wild animals – since by law these are incapable of ownership;

(h)   fresh food (*Morley v Pincombe* (1848) 2 Exch 101);

(i)   wearing apparel and bedding – to the value of £100 (Law of Distress Amendment Act 1888, s 4, SI 1980/26);

(j)   goods already in the custody of the law;

(k)   items of public trade – where items are on the premises for some temporary purpose of trade, such as for sale or repair, they are not distrainable, as it is in the interest of public trade that a person should be able to deposit his goods with another for the purpose of trade, without the fear of their being taken by distress. Thus a motor car sent to a garage for repair is not distrainable, or jewellery sent to a jeweller for appraisal. Items left at a pawnbroker shop as a pledge are not distrainable. Goods warehoused are not distrainable (*Thompson v Mashiter* (1823) 1 Bing 283). The goods of guests at an hotel (Bac Abr 'Inns and Innkeepers' (B)) or goods sent to an auctioneer (*Adams v Grane* (1833) 1 Cr & M 380) are not distrainable.

The exception does not apply where goods have been deposited on the premises for the mere convenience of a third party and not with the intent that the tenant should perform any service in relation to the goods. So brewers' casks left with a publican until he emptied them have been held not to be exempt (*Joule v Jackson* (1841) 7 M & W 450). The goods must have been goods delivered to the tenant. Goods being manufactured by the tenant to the order of a third party are not exempt (e g a ship, *Clarke v Millwall Dock Co* (1886) 17 QBD 494, CA, or a painting, *Von Knoop v Moss and Jameson* (1891) 7 TLR 500);

(l)   property of statutory undertakers;

(m)   books of record – e g day books, ledgers and other business papers (*Gauntlett v King* (1857) 3 CBNS 59);

(n)   frames, looms, machines and materials – belonging to third parties in use in the textile trade (Hosiery Act 1843, s 18);

(o)   railway rolling stock – belonging to third parties (Railway Rolling Stock Protection Act 1872, s 3);

(p)   water, gas and electrical appliances – and fittings of a public utility body which are clearly marked as such (Water Industry Act 1991, s 179(4)(b), Gas Act 1986, Sch 5, Electricity Act 1989, Sch 7).

3.5.2 GOODS WHICH CAN ONLY BE DISTRAINED UPON IF THERE IS NO OTHER SUFFICIENT DISTRESS

Some goods have the partial protection afforded by 'qualified privilege'. The effect of qualified privilege is that a landlord distraining should if possible seize goods which are not the subject of qualified privilege before distraining upon those which have the privilege so that if the arrears of rent can be satisfied from non-privileged goods the privileged goods should not be subject to the distraint. Most of the goods to which qualified privilege attaches are primarily of relevance to agricultural tenancies only, but in relation to 'commercial' leases there is the important category of tools and implements of a person's trade to the value of £150 (Law of Distress Amendment Act 1888, s 4, SI 1980/26). This may include the professional books of a professional person (on Distress and Replevin 33). If a landlord or his bailiff fails to observe the privilege he risks a claim for excessive distress (see para 3.9.3).

3.5.3 GOODS OF SUBTENANTS, MORTGAGEES AND OTHER THIRD PARTIES

Special considerations apply to the goods of subtenants, 'lodgers' and other strangers to the landlord and tenant relationship whose goods do not have privilege, whether absolute or conditional (see paras 3.3.1 and 3.3.2 above). The normal rule is that their goods may be distrained upon to satisfy the arrears of rent, even though they were not blameworthy.

At common law a person who suffered in this manner did have some remedies available. Such a person could tender the rent to the landlord in order to avoid the distress, and the person would have a right of indemnity against the tenant (*Exall v Partridge* (1799) 8 Term Rep 308). Alternatively, once the goods of the third party had been sold he could claim an indemnity from the tenant in the sum of the value of the property (*Edmunds v Wallingford* (1885) 14 QBD 811, CA). There might also be available to the third party the right to stand in the shoes of the landlord (i e to be subrogated to the landlord's rights), so as to have the landlord's remedies, including the right to distrain upon any goods of the tenant. If the third party makes the payment at the request of the creditors, or perhaps the trustee or liquidator, it is further arguable that the person paying should then have a priority right to reimbursement, presumably on the basis that the payment is an expense of the bankruptcy or liquidation (*Re Humphreys, ex p Kennard* (1870) 21 LT 684).

If some of the tenant's goods are subject to a charge the landlord should distrain first upon the goods which are not charged, according to the doctrine of marshalling. The doctrine has been stated (Halsbury's Laws, Vol 16, para 876) as follows:

> 'Where one claimant, A, has two funds, X and Y, to which he can resort for satisfaction of his claim, . . . and another claimant, B, can resort to only one of these funds, Y, equity interposes so as to secure that A shall not by resorting to Y to disappoint B. Consequently, if the matter is under the court's control, A will be required in the first place to satisfy himself out of X, and only to resort to Y in case of deficiency; and if A has already been paid out of Y it will allow B to stand in his place as against X.'

The principle has been held to apply to the right to distrain, so that if a landlord has distrained upon goods which the tenant has charged to a third party, the third party can claim a lien over other goods of the tenant in priority to the other creditors of the tenant, notwithstanding the fact that the tenant is bankrupt (*Re Stephenson, ex p Stephenson* (1847) 10 LTOS 310).

Now third parties, in some circumstances, have the stronger statutory rights given them by the Law of Distress Amendment Act 1908 ('LDAA 1908'), which provides that a third party can protect his goods from distress by serving a notice upon the landlord making it clear that the goods do not belong to the tenant. If the person serving the notice is a subtenant or lodger, relief is conditional upon him paying his subrent or licence fee direct to the landlord. The subtenant or lodger will in the meantime be relieved of any obligation to the tenant, and is thus relieved of the necessity of seeking indemnity from the tenant.

Which third parties can protect their goods?

It is clear that lawful subtenants whose goods are upon the premises can rely upon the LDAA 1908. To be protected a subtenant must be liable to pay rent equal to the full rental value (*Parsons v Hambridge* (1917) 33 TLR 346, CA) in instalments not less often than quarterly. An unlawful subtenant cannot rely upon the Act for the protection of goods from distress (LDDA 1908, s 5).

Otherwise the LDAA 1908 is not as clear as one would wish it to be in respect of defining the persons who are protected by it. Lodgers are protected so long as they pay their rent to the superior landlord, but the meaning of the term 'lodger' is unclear. In the context of residential property the House of Lords decision in *Street v Mountford* [1985] AC 809, HL, probably provides sufficient clarification. In that case Lord Templeman said that if a residential occupier has exclusive occupation at a rent for a term, he is a tenant; if not, he is a lodger. What, however, of commercial premises? Is a contractual licensee or tenant at will a lodger? It is likely that such a person would be regarded as a lodger. Otherwise, it would appear that a commercial licensee who has entered premises to negotiate a lease, or who is holding over at the end of a lease to negotiate a new one, and is a tenant at will or licensee (*Javad v Aqil* [1991] 1 All ER 243, CA) will not have the benefit of the LDAA 1908 in order to avoid the distress.

It is also unclear what other third parties are included. To have protection a third party must be a person 'not being a tenant of the premises or of any part thereof, and not having any beneficial interest in any tenancy of the premises or any part thereof'. It has been held that a chargee of the lease does have a beneficial interest in the lease for these purposes so as to be excluded from protection (*Cunliffe Engineering Ltd v English Industrial Estates Corpn* [1994] BCC 972).

A further difficulty is that the person relying upon the LDAA 1908 must serve a notice stating that the tenant has no right of property or beneficial interest in the goods distrained. A chargee might argue that where goods have been mortgaged they do not form part of the insolvent tenant's property, at least where the value of the goods is not greater than the amount of the debt (*Re New City Constitutional Club & Co, ex p Purssell* (1887) 34 Ch D 646, CA) and where any floating charge has crystallised and become fixed (*Ramsbottom and Benzie v Luton Borough Council; Re ELS Ltd* [1994] 1 BCLC 743). It has been decided, however, that the tenant is the owner of charged goods for the purpose of the LDAA 1908 and a chargee is not entitled to serve a notice stating that the tenant has no right of property in them (*Cunliffe Engineering Ltd v English Industrial Estates Corpn,* see above). The reasoning in *Cunliffe* to this effect does not rest easily with the principle in *Re ELS Ltd* (see above); but even if this reasoning is wrong, and the goods are actually owned by the chargee, they may nevertheless be excluded from the protection of the Act as goods in the 'reputed ownership' of the tenant (see *Cunliffe* above and see below).

Accordingly, it appears that the only way in which the chargee will be able to gain priority to the goods is by removing them from the demised premises before the landlord distrains (*Tomlinson v Consolidated Credit and Mortgage Corpn* (1889) 24 QBD 135, CA).

What third party goods cannot be protected from distress?

The protection from distress which the LDAA 1908 bestows is limited by the 11 exceptions stated. The most important of these exceptions for present purposes are as follows:

(1) Goods belonging to the spouse of the tenant – so that the tenant cannot avoid distress by transferring ownership of goods to the spouse.

(2) Goods comprised in any hire purchase agreement – as this effectively excludes hire purchase companies from the protection of the LDAA 1908 it has become common for such companies to insert in hire purchase agreements clauses that the agreements will terminate upon distress, so that they can then rely upon the LDAA 1908. Such clauses have sometimes been held ineffective on the ground that even though they might terminate a licence to possess the goods, nevertheless the goods are still comprised in the agreement until the owner recovers them (*Jay's Furnishing Co v Brand & Co* [1915] 1 KB 458, CA). In others the courts have managed to find that the agreement is terminated and that the company's right to possession does not depend upon the continuance of the agreement (*Smart Bros Ltd v Holt* [1929] 2 KB 303). But even if the goods are no longer comprised in a hire purchase agreement they may nevertheless be goods excluded from the protection of the LDAA 1908 as goods in the reputed ownership of the tenant (see below).

(3) Goods in possession of the tenant with the consent of the true owner under such circumstances that the tenant is the reputed owner of them – goods belonging to a third party may appear to belong to the tenant. If so, the third party goods are not protected by the LDAA 1908. One example of this is that goods which were subject to a hire purchase arrangement may continue in the reputed ownership of the tenant, even after termination of the agreement. In *Times Furnishing Co Ltd v Hutchings* [1938] 1 KB 775, a clause in a hire purchase agreement provided that the agreement and the company's consent to the hirer's possession of the goods should automatically determine 'if any landlord of the hirer threatens or takes any step to levy a distress for rent ...' It was held by Humphreys J that the clause was effective to determine the agreement upon the landlord signing a distress warrant, but the goods remained in the reputed ownership of the tenant after such determination. It is not clear what steps a company would need to take to take the goods outside of the reputed ownership of the tenant. In *Times Furnishing v Hutchings* (see above) Humphreys J thought that the company would need to take

steps for the recovery of the goods, but in *Perdana Properties Bhd v United Orient Leasing Co* [1982] 1 All ER 193, the Privy Council thought that a letter from the company to the tenant was enough to take the goods out of the tenant's reputed ownership. The advantage to a landlord of this line of authority may have been weakened by the recent court of Appeal decision of *Salford Van Hire (Contracts) Ltd v Bocholt Developments* [1995] 2 EGLR 50. In that case the tenant of premises was in possession of a van on hire. When the landlord of the premises levied a distress, the owners of the van notified the landlord of their interest, but the landlord proceeded to sell. The Court decided that the van was not in the reputed ownership of the tenant. Hirst LJ stated that to be in the reputed ownership of the tenant goods must be in the tenant's possession in circumstances which suggest that the goods *must* be the tenant's. In applying this test the Court could take judicial notice of the 'huge expansion of hiring ... since the Second World War', and that the landlord could make simple enquiries as to the ownership of the van, e g by making a telephone call to the DVLC. Even if there was an initial presumption of reputed ownership, this could be rebutted by actual evidence or evidence of trade custom.

(4) Goods comprised in any bill of sale – goods comprised in a bill of sale may be distrained upon, except that goods comprised in a hire purchase agreement, consumer hire agreement, or agreed to be sold under a conditional sale agreement within the meaning of the Consumer Credit Act 1974 may not be distrained upon during the period between service of a default notice and the date upon which the default notice expires.

(5) Goods of a partner of the immediate tenant.

(6) Goods on premises where any trade or business is carried on in which both the immediate tenant and the subtenant have an interest – so, for example, where the tenant and subtenant both have an interest in a business carried on at the premises, the subtenant cannot rely upon the LDAA 1908 for the protection of its goods.

(7) Goods belonging to and in the offices of any company on premises the immediate tenant of which is a director or officer, or in the employment of such company.

(8) Goods on premises used as offices or warehouses where the owner of the goods neglects for one calendar month after notice to remove the goods and vacate the premises – the protection given to third party goods can seriously weaken the effect of distress as a weapon in the landlord's hands, since if the goods belong to third parties the tenant, perhaps through its receiver, can continue to occupy and use the premises without the worry of distress. In the case of offices and warehouses the landlord has the option to serve notice upon third parties requiring them to remove their goods, and if the goods are not removed within one month the protection of the LDAA 1908 is lost and the third parties' goods may be distrained upon.

The owner's notice

The notice may be served upon either the landlord or his bailiff and must be a written declaration stating that the immediate tenant has no property or beneficial interest in the goods, and are not goods to which the LDAA 1908 does not apply (*Druce & Co Ltd v Beaumont Property Trust Ltd* [1935] 2 KB 257). A subtenant or lodger must also set out in writing the amount of his own rent and the amount and dates of future instalments, and must undertake to make future payments to the landlord until the relevant arrears are cleared. The notice must attach an inventory specifying the goods which are to be protected from the distress. The notice can be signed by the owner or by his solicitor (*Lawrence Chemical Co Ltd v Rubenstein* [1982] 1 All ER 653, CA).

Timing

The LDAA 1908 does not specify any time limit within which the notice may be served, so, presumably, a notice may be served at any time after the distress has commenced (*Thwaites v Wilding* (1883) 12 QBD 4, CA), but before the distress is complete. Accordingly if a landlord is distraining, the quicker he can complete the distraint, the less likely he is to be notified by a third party, who, once the distraint is complete, will lose the right to serve notice under the LDAA 1908.

Each time that a landlord levies a new distress any interested third party must serve a fresh notice to assert rights under the LDAA 1908. A notice served by a third party at the time of a previous distraint will not remain operative to protect the third party in the event of a subsequent distraint (*Thwaites v Wilding*, see above).

Effect of notice

The service of a valid notice precludes the landlord from proceeding with a distress and the goods may be recovered on application by the tenant or third party to a stipendiary magistrate or two justices of the peace (LDAA 1908, s 2). Where the person serving notice is a subtenant or lodger the service creates a direct relationship of landlord and tenant between head landlord and subtenant until the arrears of head rent are paid off. There is a statutory assignment of the tenant's right to the subrents (i e the 'chose in action', *Wallrock v Equity and Law Life Assurance Society* [1942] 2 KB 82, CA). It follows that the head landlord can sue or distrain against the subtenant for failure to pay the subrent. The statutory assignment of the right to the subrents does not, however, deprive the landlord of his remedies against the tenant. He can for example, serve a statutory demand for the bankruptcy or winding up of the tenant (*Re a Debtor (No 549 of 1928)* [1929] 1 Ch 170, CA).

3.6 When is leave of the court required?

In some cases of insolvency the leave of the court is required before a distress can be levied. It should be noted in passing that the restrictions upon issuing 'execution', mentioned in chapter 2 do not affect distress which is not an 'execution'. Lord Russell pointed out in *Herbert Berry Associates Ltd v IRC* [1978] 1 All ER 161, that the legislation draws a clear distinction between distress and execution for these purposes. The word 'execution' is properly limited to the execution of a court order and does not include distress (see chapter 2).

3.6.1 RESIDENTIAL PREMISES

In the case of most residential lettings leave of the court is required before the landlord can distrain. Statutory provisions so restrict the right to distrain in the case of Rent Act-protected or statutory tenancies (Rent Act 1977, s 147), assured tenancies under the Housing Act 1988 (s 19) and protected or statutory occupancies within the meaning of the Rent (Agriculture) Act 1976. There is no restriction upon distress where the tenancy is a secure tenancy and public landlords have often used the remedy of distress.

3.6.2 INDIVIDUAL VOLUNTARY ARRANGEMENT

Where the tenant is an individual seeking approval of a voluntary arrangement, by the IA 1986, s 252 the interim order establishes a statutory moratorium so that no proceedings, execution or other legal process may be commenced or continued without the leave of the court. Although it has been held that a landlord's right to distrain is not affected by s 252 (*McMullen & Sons Ltd v Cerrone* (1993) 66 P & CR 351) this loophole is now addressed by amendment contained in the Insolvency Act 2000 which, when fully implemented, will subject distress to the statutory moratorium.

3.6.3 BANKRUPTCY

In contrast to the position where a tenant company is in liquidation (see para 3.6.5 below) a landlord is free to distrain against the goods of a bankrupt tenant. Distress is not an 'execution or other legal process' which needs the leave of the court under the IA 1986, s 285 (*Re Fanshaw and Yorston, ex p Birmingham and Staffordshire Gaslight Co* (1871) LR 11 Eq 615, *cf Smith v Braintree District Council* [1990] 2 AC 215, HL); nor is a distress levied after commencement of the bankruptcy void. On the contrary, the IA 1986, s 347(9) expressly preserves the right to distrain against property comprised in the bankrupt's estate notwithstanding that the property has vested in the trustee. As has been noted above (para 3.3.3) however, the right to distrain for rent accruing due prior to the adjudication is limited to six months' rent. If the trustee in bankruptcy does not disclaim, and he is liable for all rent accruing due after bankruptcy (see para 2.4), it may be distrained for without the leave of the court (*Re Binns, ex p Hale* (1875) 1 Ch D 285); if the law had been otherwise 'the consequence would be that a trustee in bankruptcy might make use of a man's property without paying any rent for it, and might snap his fingers at him' (per Bacon CJ, *Re Binns, ex p Hale*).

3.6.4 VOLUNTARY LIQUIDATION

If a corporate tenant is in voluntary liquidation there is no immediate restriction upon the landlord's right to levy distress. It has been held that the predecessor to the IA 1986, s 128 (see below), which makes void any distress levied after the commencement of a compulsory winding-up, does not apply in a voluntary liquidation (*Westbury v Twigg & Co* [1892] 1 QB 77). So if a landlord acts quickly in a voluntary liquidation he will be able to distrain with impunity.

The landlord's right may, however, be pre-empted or suspended by an application to court. Section 112 of the IA 1986 provides that the liquidator or any contributory or creditor may apply to the court to determine any question arising in the liquidation and the court may exercise any of the powers which it might exercise if there was a compulsory winding-up. The powers available undoubtedly include the power to stay any distress (*Herbert Berry Associates Ltd v IRC* [1978] 1 All ER 161, HL). Whether the court will allow the distress to proceed depends upon similar factors to those discussed below in relation to distress commenced, but not completed, prior to commencement of a compulsory liquidation. The position is summarised as follows:

(a) if distress was begun prior to the liquidation leave to complete it will probably be given;
(b) if distress was begun after liquidation in respect of rent due before the liquidation leave will probably not be given (*Re Margot Bywaters Ltd* [1942] Ch 121);
(c) if distress was begun after liquidation in respect of amounts falling due while the liquidator has the property leave will probably be given.

3.6.5 COMPULSORY LIQUIDATION

Once a corporate tenant is subject to a compulsory liquidation the leave of the court is generally required before the landlord can distrain. The precise position depends upon when the distress was begun, and if begun before the presentation of a petition, when it is completed. The law was summarised by the Court of Appeal in *Re Atlantic Computer Systems plc* [1992] Ch 505.

Distress commenced prior to petition

If a landlord has started to distrain and then a petition is presented the company or any creditor or contributory may apply to the court under the IA 1986, s 126 to stay the distress. Once a winding-up order is made the landlord needs to apply to the court to continue the distress, since the effect of the order is to prevent the sale of distrained goods without the leave of the court under the IA 1986, s 130. Both of these rules are based upon the idea that a distress is an 'action or proceeding' within the meaning of ss 126 and 130. A distress was so held to be an 'action or proceeding' by Mervyn Davies J in *Re Memco Engineering Ltd* [1986] Ch 86, despite the fact that s 126 in particular refers to an 'action or proceeding against the company ... pending in the High Court or Court of Appeal in England and Wales ...', and a distress is not, of course, a court action. Although there must be some doubt as to the correctness in principle of his Lordship's decision, the decision is based upon a proper consideration of previous precedent (*Herbert Berry Associates Ltd v IRC* [1978] 1 All ER 161, HL).

Assuming that the court's leave is required to proceed with a distress begun prior to commencement of the winding up, the court's usual policy is to permit the landlord to complete the distress unless there are special reasons which make it inequitable to distrain (*Re Roundwood Colliery Co, Lee v Roundwood Colliery Co* [1897] 1 Ch 373, CA). It will be most exceptional for a court to restrain the landlord's distress. According to Lord Cozens Hardy MR in *Venner's Electrical Cooking and Heating Appliances Ltd v Thorpe* [1915] 2 Ch 404, CA, 'no equitable ground has ever been made out for restraining the landlord from levying the distress, unless there have been some circumstances outside the levying, such as fraud, or unfair dealing, which would entitle the tenant to an injunction.' In that case the landlord began a distraint for rent due yearly in advance, the tenant company then entered into voluntary liquidation and the liquidator sought an injunction to prevent the landlord from completing the distress. The liquidator argued that it was unjust for the landlord to sweep off the assets of the company to the prejudice of the other creditors. The Court of Appeal refused to exercise its discretion to restrain the landlord as there was no hint of fraud and the landlord was simply exercising his legal rights. The mere fact that a sale under a distress might produce less for the creditors than a sale in a liquidation or by the company carrying on its business is not a special circumstance which will make it inequitable to allow the landlord to continue (*Re Bellaglade Ltd* [1977] 1 All ER 319).

Distress commenced after petition

If a landlord begins a distress after the commencement of a compulsory winding-up, the distress is void (IA 1986, s 128). The right to distrain does not survive so as, in effect, to make the landlord a secured creditor, and a landlord distraining without leave of the court will be liable to an action for illegal distress (*Re Traders' North Staffordshire Carrying Co, ex p North Staffordshire Rly Co* (1874) LR 19 Eq 60).

The court does, however, have power to give leave for any 'action or proceeding' against the company or its property (IA 1986, s 130(2)), and the two sections are to be read together so that a distress put in force after the commencement of the winding up is void under s 128 unless leave of the court is obtained under s 130 (*Re Exhall Coal Mining Co* (1864) 33 LJ Ch 569n; *Re Coal Consumers' Association* (1876) 4 Ch D 625).

If the rent fell due prior to the winding up the court will generally not give a landlord leave to distrain since to do so would put the landlord in a better position than other ordinary creditors. The landlord must prove, like any unsecured creditor, for the arrears of rent (*Re Traders' North Staffordshire Carrying Co* (1874) LR 19 Eq 60).

If, however, rent falls due during the period of the liquidation a landlord will normally be given leave, since the liquidator should pay a rent if he has the use of the premises. So, if the liquidator decides to occupy the property for the purpose of continuing the tenant's business (*Re Silkstone and Dodworth Coal and Iron Co* (1881) 17 Ch D 158), or if the liquidator keeps the lease with a view to selling it, or in order to store goods upon the property (*Re Lundy Granite Co, ex p Heavan* (1871) 6 Ch App 462, CA), the rent must be paid and the landlord will be able to distrain for it, for the landlord should have the same right as any other person providing goods or services for the purpose of the liquidation: 'if the company choose to keep the estates for their own purposes, they ought to pay the full value to the landlord, as they ought to pay any other person for anything else' (per James LJ in *Re Lundy Granite Co*).

In the older cases the landlord was not automatically given leave just because there was a liquidation. If the property is being occupied by a receiver, and the liquidator is unable to use it, the property is not available to the liquidation and the landlord will not be given leave to distrain (*Re House and Land Investment Trust, ex p Smith* (1894) 42 WR 572). Before the court would give leave to distrain the liquidator had to be using the property for the purposes of the liquidation. It was not sufficient that the liquidator had taken no steps to surrender the lease (*Re Oak Pits Colliery Co* (1882) 21 Ch D 322, CA) nor that the liquidator had incidentally benefited from the lease (*Re House and Land Investment Trust, ex p Smith*, see above).

But this was before a liquidator had the power to disclaim the lease, which was not available to the liquidator of a company until 1929. Now that the power to disclaim is available it might be argued that if the liquidator does not disclaim, the rent should be paid in full and the landlord should be able to distrain for it (*Re Linda Marie Ltd* [1989] BCLC 46, para 2.3.2).

In some cases leave has been refused where the use of the property by the liquidator has been for the benefit of both the landlord and the liquidator. In *Re Bridgewater Engineering Co* (1879) 12 Ch D 181, the liquidator, with the co-operation of the landlord was arranging for the sale of plant and machinery on the property and on terms that the purchaser of the plant and machinery would be offered a new lease of the property by the landlord. It was held that the landlord was not entitled to rent for the interim period, since the use of the property was for the mixed accommodation of both the company and the landlord.

If the circumstances are such that leave should be given the right to distrain is only available in respect of an apportionment of the rent from the date of presentation of the petition. If rent is payable quarterly in arrears and liquidation intervenes during a quarter the landlord cannot distrain at the end of the quarter for a full quarter's rent (*Re South Kensington Co-operative Stores* (1881) 17 Ch D 161, but see *Re Howell, ex p Mandleberg & Co* [1895] 1 QB 844). Rent payable in advance is not normally apportioned, so a payment due prior to petition can only be proved for. If a payment falls due after petition it might be thought that the liquidator would have to pay it in full, and that if he did not the landlord would be able to distrain for it as an expense of the liquidation. In *Shackell & Co v Chorlton & Sons* [1895] 1 Ch 378, however, the court refused to allow a landlord to distrain for the rent due in advance. In effect the liquidator will pay in arrears until the property is no longer used by the company.

Goods owned by or charged to third parties

If the goods which a landlord wishes to distrain upon are not the goods of the tenant but are the goods of a third party, the restrictions on distress do not apply since the landlord is not proceeding against goods of the tenant company which is in liquidation. The rule apparently extends to goods which have been charged to a third party, at least if the value of the goods is less than the debt which the charge over the goods secures, since in these circumstances the goods cease to be the property of the company (*Re New City Constitutional Club* (1887) 34 Ch D 646). This is so even if a receiver has not been appointed in respect of the goods (*Re Harpur's Cycle Fittings Co* [1900] 2 Ch 731). But where the assets are not even sufficient to pay preferential creditors a court might not let the landlord distrain so as to rank ahead of such creditors (*Re South Rhondda Colliery Co* [1928] WN 126).

If the third party is in liquidation the restrictions on distraint against the goods of the third party in liquidation do not prevent a landlord from distraining since he is not a creditor of the third party company and will have no right of proof in the winding up, and for this reason his right to distrain is not curbed (*Re Lundy Granite Co, ex p Heaven* (1871) 6 Ch App 462, CA). One would have thought that if the landlord does have a right of proof in the liquidation of the third party, there would be no right to distrain, but in *Re Carriage Co-operative Supply Association, ex p Clemence* (1883) 23 Ch D 154, the company in liquidation was a subtenant of the landlord's property which gave the landlord a promissory note for payment of the head rent. It was held that the fact that the landlord might prove in the liquidation on the promissory note did not preclude the landlord from distraining. Although the decision has been doubted it is suggested that it is correct; otherwise an insolvent company might often evade the landlord's right of distress by the liquidator allowing the landlord to prove in the liquidation for an amount equal to the rent owed by the tenant (*Re Regent United Service Stores* (1878) 8 Ch D 616, CA).

Distress for mortgage interest

Where a mortgage gives a lender a right to distrain on the borrower's goods for mortgage interest it appears that similar principles apply and the lender can distrain after a winding up for interest accrued while the liquidator is in possession, but not for arrears accrued due prior to the winding up (*Re Brown, Bayley & Dixon, ex p Roberts and Wright* (1881) 18 Ch D 649). If, however, the liquidator's possession will benefit the lender, by preserving the property and business as a going concern, the court may refuse leave to the lender to distrain (*Re Higginshaw Mills and Spinning Co* [1896] 2 Ch 544, CA).

3.6.6 ADMINISTRATION

In line with the general moratorium effected by administration both IA 1986, ss 10 (for the period between petition and administration order) and 11 (for the period following the administration order) expressly provide that no distress may be levied except with the leave of the court, or, following an administration order, with the leave of the court or the consent of the administrator. Administration is, of course, a newly-born creature of statute and it is not clear how the court's discretion will be exercised. In *Re Atlantic Computer Systems plc* [1992] Ch 505, however, the Court of Appeal made it clear that the landlord does not have an absolute entitlement to be paid the rent or to distrain for it. If the circumstances are such that the statutory moratorium should be strictly enforced to enable the company to reorganise, the court might refuse leave. But if the administration is a prelude to an insolvent winding up it is more likely that the court will either give leave to the landlord to distrain, or to refuse leave, but upon terms that the current rent is paid.

3.6.7 RECEIVERSHIP

Where the tenant is a company it is likely that goods which the landlord wishes to distrain on will be subject to a charge or charges in favour of third parties. Often the tenant's goods will be subject to a floating charge which the tenant company has given over the whole or substantially the whole of its assets. Where a receiver has been appointed under the terms of a charge the receiver acts as agent of the tenant to use assets to discharge the obligations owed to the secured creditor. The rights of other creditors of the company are not restricted any more than is a necessary result of this process and accordingly a landlord may distrain against goods on the demised premises notwithstanding that the goods are subject to the floating charge under which the receiver was appointed. It has been held that a landlord may distrain whether distress has commenced before or after a receiver of a floating charge is appointed (*Re Roundwood Colliery Co* [1897] 1 Ch 373, CA; *New City Constitutional Club, ex p Purssell* (1887) 34 Ch D 646, CA; *Re Mayhew, ex p Till* (1873) LR 16 Eq 97).

3.7 How to distrain

3.7.1 WHEN TO DISTRAIN

If a landlord is to levy distress he must normally do so whilst the lease exists. But there is an exception – i e that a landlord may within the six months following the end of the lease, distrain for arrears accrued due before its determination; but only so long as his title continues and whilst the tenant remains in occupation (Landlord and Tenant Act 1709, ss 6 and 7). Where a tenant dies shortly before the end of the term, occupation after his death by his personal representatives will suffice to preserve the right to distrain within the six months (*Braithwaite v Cooksey* (1790) 1 Hy Bl 465), but not if the lease ends upon the death of the tenant (*Turner v Barnes* (1862) 2 B & S 435). The Act requires that the tenant be in occupation, so if the tenant has ceased to occupy the landlord cannot distrain upon goods which the tenant has wrongfully left upon the property (*Taylerson v Peters* (1837) 7 Ad & El 110).

The exception only applies if the tenant is 'holding over' either with or without the permission of the landlord (*Nuttall v Staunton* (1825) 4 B & C 51). The lease may have been a fixed term lease which has expired by time, or it may be a tenancy at will or periodic tenancy terminated by notice. But the right to distrain ceases to be available if the landlord has elected to terminate the lease by forfeiture (*Grimwood v Moss* (1872) LR 7 CP 360), or if the tenant remains and by agreement pays a rent, so that a new lease of the premises arises (*Wilkinson v Peel* [1895] 1 QB 516).

If the tenancy is a business tenancy whose original term has expired, but the tenancy is continuing under the terms of the Landlord and Tenant Act 1954, it must be assumed that the right to distrain continues to be available. Once the continuation tenancy is terminated in accordance with the Act it is likely that the landlord may rely upon the right under the 1709 Act, to distrain for arrears of rent during the six months following such termination.

If the defaulting tenant proposes to assign the lease the landlord should deal with the issue of the arrears and distraint prior to giving any consent to assign. If the landlord consents to an assignment the landlord is not entitled to distrain on the goods of the assignee for the arrears of the assigning tenant (*Wharfland Ltd v South London Co-operative Building Co Ltd* [1995] 2 EGLR 21).

The action must be taken during daylight hours (*Tutton v Darke* (1860) 5 H & N 647) on any day except Sunday (*Werth v London and Westminster Loan and Discount Co* (1889) 5 TLR 521). The rent must be in arrears at the time of distress, which means that the due date for payment must have passed. Thus the landlord may distrain on the following day unless the lease allows to the tenant days of grace for payment. Even if the rent is due on a Sunday, and not paid, the landlord may distrain on the Monday following (*Child v Edwards* [1909] 2 KB 753).

3.7.2 IN PERSON OR BY BAILIFF

A landlord can exercise the right in person or by a certificated bailiff (Law of Distress Amendment Act 1888, s 7). Where the landlord is a company it can only act through its agents and it can therefore only distrain through the agency of a bailiff (*Hogarth v Jennings* [1892] 1 QB 907, CA). Otherwise the landlord has the option to distrain in person or by use of a bailiff. The bailiff must be certificated by a county court judge. Any person acting without a valid certificate is acting unlawfully as a trespasser, and in addition is guilty of a criminal offence (Law of Distress Amendment Act 1895, s 2). The bailiff acts as the landlord's agent and the landlord may be liable in respect of the wrongful actions of the bailiff under the normal rules of agency. The bailiff will of course be liable to compensate the landlord for such wrongdoing.

3.7.3 ENTRY

Distress necessarily involves an entry onto the property. It is not possible to distrain by post (*Evans v South Ribble Borough Council* [1992] QB 757). The right to enter for the purpose of distress is an incident of the lease and no express right of entry needs to be reserved. The landlord must not make his initial entry by force, and if he does so there will be a trespass. To use or threaten force is also a criminal offence if there is someone present on the premises opposed to the landlord's entry, and the landlord or bailiff is aware of this (Criminal Law Act 1977, s 6). The landlord or his bailiff may enter through an open door or window (*Tutton v Darke*, above) or even by removing a partition between the premises let and other premises, as in *Gould v Bradstock* (1812) 4 Taunt 562, where the landlord entered a lower floor from an upper floor by taking up wooden boards which divided the two sets of premises. Once inside force may be used to gain access to other parts of the property through internal doors and partitions (*Browning v Dann* (1735) Lee temp Hard 167). If a landlord has made an initial lawful entry and taken walking possession of goods, he can later re-enter by force, at least where the tenant is absent from the premises. (*Khazanchi v Faircharm Investments*

Ltd; *McLeod v Butterwick* (1999) 77 P & CR 29, CA). It is not clear, however, whether the landlord can do so where the tenant opposes the re-entry, or whether the re-entry would fall foul of the Criminal Law Act 1977, s 6. The landlord's entry must not be done with the effect of excluding the tenant, since this will amount to a trespass (*Etherton v Popplewell* (1800) 1 East 139), and, in some circumstances, a criminal eviction (Protection from Eviction Act 1977, s 1).

3.7.4 SEIZURE

Once entry has been achieved the seizure of the goods may take place. The person distraining must take some action which shows which goods are being distrained upon. Such person may, for instance, attach labels to the goods, or might simply say to the tenant that certain goods are being seized. It is not necessary for the landlord or his agent to see the goods. So, if it would cause embarrassment to third parties, such as subtenants of parts of the property, for the landlord to inspect the goods, it may be agreed that the tenant should simply provide a list of goods, which will be deemed seized for the purpose of the distraint (*Tennant v Field* (1857) 8 E & B 336).

3.7.5 IMPOUNDING AND WALKING POSSESSION AGREEMENTS

After seizure the goods may be impounded either on or off the premises (Distress for Rent Act 1737, s 10). They may be impounded on the premises by the landlord or bailiff clearly separating them from other goods. In order to avoid doubt as to which goods are impounded, particularly in respect of third party goods, the goods may be labelled or some other action may be taken to show that they are impounded (*Abingdon RDC v O'Gorman* [1968] 2 QB 811, CA). But if it is undesirable that the landlord or his agent should identify the goods it may be agreed that a list provided by the tenant will show what goods are impounded (*Tennant v Field*, see above). If animals are to be impounded they must be given sufficient quantities of wholesome food and water. If they are not properly cared for, the landlord is liable for any injury caused to them and may be liable to a fine (Protection of Animals Act 1911, s 7).

If the goods are impounded on the premises the landlord or bailiff does not in practice remain to keep possession of the goods. Once impounded they are in the custody of the law, and the landlord or bailiff may leave them unattended on the premises, in which case the landlord is said to be in 'walking possession' of the goods. In order to avoid any dispute over which goods have been impounded it is usual for a 'walking possession' agreement to be signed by the tenant whereby the tenant agrees: to pay the bailiff's fee; that re-entry may be made at any time while the distress is in force; that the goods will not be removed from the premises; that any other person attempting to distrain or levy execution will be informed of the distress; and that if any other person attempts to distrain or execute, the tenant will inform the landlord. A form is provided by the Distress for Rent Rules 1988. The agreement will list the goods. In an appropriate case the agreement may permit the tenant to sell stock in the ordinary course of business provided that it is replaced by similar stock (*Re Dalton (a bankrupt), ex p Herrington and Carmichael (a firm) v Trustee* [1963] Ch 336).

3.7.6 NOTICE OF DISTRESS

If the landlord wishes to be in a position to sell the goods distrained, after seizure a notice must be served upon the tenant containing the following information:

(a) the amount of the rent arrears;
(b) an inventory of the goods taken;
(c) the place where the landlord is impounding the goods (if not on the premises); and
(d) the time when the goods will be sold.

In the case of distress through a bailiff the notice must be in the prescribed form.

3.7.7 SALE

Originally a landlord who had distrained upon goods could only hold them as security for the rent, but the right now includes the power to sell the goods and use the proceeds to discharge the arrears (Distress for Rent Act 1689, s 1). The landlord does not have to sell, but if he chooses to sell he must comply with the appropriate legal requirements as to the time of sale, the place of sale, the price to be obtained, and as to the distribution of the proceeds of sale.

Time of sale

If the landlord wishes to sell he must wait five clear days excluding the day of seizure and the day of sale (Distress for Rent Act 1689, s 1). So if the landlord distrains on a Saturday the goods cannot lawfully be sold until the following Friday. During this time the tenant has the right to the return of the goods upon payment of the arrears together with costs. The tenant or owner of the goods can procure an extension of the period to a period of not more than 15 days by the tenant or the owner making a request in writing to the landlord and giving security for any additional cost which might be incurred by the landlord as a result of the delay (Law of Distress Amendment Act 1888, s 6). The security for such additional cost is settled by the county court registrar under the County Courts Act 1984, s 144. The parties may agree a further extension.

At the expiry of the period the landlord may sell, but need not do so and may instead simply retain the goods until the tenant makes payment. If the goods are impounded upon the premises let the landlord should probably remove them within a reasonable time after the five days has elapsed (*Winterbourne v Morgan* (1809) 11 East 395), unless the tenant agrees to the goods remaining upon the premises.

Place of sale

The goods may be sold where they have been impounded, even if this is on the demised premises themselves (Distress for Rent Act 1737, s 10). This might in some cases cause embarrassment to the tenant, who can avoid such embarrassment by requiring the goods to be removed to a public auction room or other place, provided that he bears any additional cost that this might cause (Law of Distress Amendment Act 1888, s 5).

Duty to obtain best price

By the Distress for Rent Act 1689, s 1 there is a statutory duty to obtain the best price on a sale. The duty is probably similar to that of a selling mortgagee, i e to take reasonable care to obtain the true market value of the goods (*Cuckmere Brick Co Ltd v Mutual Finance Ltd* [1971] Ch 949, CA). In many cases, of course, the forced circumstances of the sale will tend to depress the market value, but this should not in itself expose the landlord to any liability. The landlord can sell by private treaty or by auction. The landlord cannot sell to, or take the goods for, himself (*King v England* (1864) 4 B & S 782); although it is possible that he might sell to a company in which he is interested so long as the deal is a fair one (*Tse Kwong Lam v Wong Chit Sen* [1983] 3 All ER 54, PC).

The tenant may if he wishes arrange at his expense to have the goods valued before sale (Law of Distress Amendment Act 1888, s 5) so as to be in a position to assess whether the landlord has in fact obtained the best price. A written request must be served, presumably upon the landlord, or, if the bailiff is distraining, upon the bailiff.

Proceeds of sale

The landlord may take from the proceeds of sale, the arrears of rent and costs. The balance (the 'overplus') should be left in the hands of the bailiff 'for the owner's use' (Distress for Rent Act 1689, s 1). The landlord does not need to enquire as to who the owner of the goods is. If there is a possibility that the goods or some of them belonged not to the tenant but to a third party the landlord should simply leave the overplus in the hands of the sheriff or bailiff, to whom the third party should look for the overplus. If the landlord does not do so the landlord will be liable for the tort for breach of statutory duty, but will not be liable in conversion or restitution for money had and received (*Yates v Eastwood* (1851) 6 Exch 805).

Protection of purchaser

The sale by the landlord passes good title to the purchaser even if the distress is irregular or excessive (Distress for Rent Act 1737, s 19) but not if it is illegal.

3.7.8 EXPENSES OF DISTRESS

The landlord is entitled to recover the expenses of the distress, but the level of such expenses is limited to a minimal level by the Distress for Rent Rules 1988. When a bailiff levies distress he must specify in his notice to the tenant the fees and expenses authorised by the rules. A bailiff will often charge landlords more than the statutory amount, which additional cost will not be recoverable from the tenant.

3.7.9 SECOND DISTRESS

A landlord can normally not distrain twice for the same rent unless:

(a)   there were insufficient goods on the premises when he first distrained (*Wallis v Savill* (1701) 2 Lut 1532); or

(b)   the value of the goods taken was unreasonably underestimated (*Hutchins v Chambers* (1758) 1 Burr 579); or

(c)   the tenant prevents the landlord from selling the goods (*Rawlence and Squarey v Spicer* [1935] 1 KB 412, CA).

If there was no restriction upon a second or subsequent distress much inconvenience could be caused to the tenant by successive distresses, so the landlord must exercise his rights efficiently and sensibly so as to cause the tenant the minimum inconvenience.

3.8 Action to avoid distress

The tenant, through its receiver, liquidator or trustee in bankruptcy, might consider action to avoid distress. Careful thought must be applied and expert advice sought before taking any such action as ill-conceived steps may expose the person avoiding distress to either or both of civil and criminal liability. In the case of a compulsory winding up there should be little difficulty, since a distress without leave of the court is void. In a voluntary liquidation probably the best course of action is for the liquidator to make an application to court under the IA 1986, s 126 to suppress the distress. In other cases the only option (assuming the distress to be lawful) may be to tender the arrears of rent.

3.8.1 TENDER OF RENT BY OR ON BEHALF OF THE TENANT

A tenant may avoid distress by making a valid tender of rent. To be effective the tender to the landlord must be in full, together with any interest due under the lease. Once the distress has begun any tender must also include any expenses of the distress itself. The distress is considered only to have begun once an entry is made, and not upon the earlier signing of a distress warrant (*Bennett v Bayes, Pennington and Harrison* (1860) 5 H & N 391). The tender should be made to the landlord or to the bailiff, or any agent of the landlord authorised to accept the rent. Early legal decisions had held that tender was only good if it was made before the goods were impounded, but it was subsequently decided (*Johnson v Upham* (1859) 2 E & E 250) that a tender is effective if made at any time before the expiry of the five clear days, or 15 days if extended, allowed under the Distress for Rent Act 1689, and Law of Distress Amendment Act 1888 before the landlord is permitted to sell.

3.8.2 FRAUDULENT REMOVAL TO AVOID DISTRAINT

A tenant who fears that his landlord might levy distress may be tempted to remove goods from the demised premises in order to avoid a distress. If a tenant fraudulently or clandestinely does so, and is found out, his landlord can seize the goods wherever they are, within the 30 days following removal (Distress for Rent Act 1737, s 1), unless a bona fide purchaser has obtained good title. The landlord is, in addition, entitled by way of penalty to recover double the value of the goods removed (Distress for Rent Act 1737, s 3). The landlord can, if necessary, use force to enter upon other premises where the goods have been secured, but should only do so in daytime and with the aid of a constable (Distress for Rent Act 1737, s 7). The difficulty for a landlord is, of course, proving what goods have been removed, and proving that the removal was fraudulent or clandestine. Because of these difficulties, a landlord who is contemplating distress may decide not to warn the tenant in case the tenant removes goods and the landlord is unable to prove such removal or that the removal was fraudulent.

The rights of the landlord to follow goods and to recover double value is only applicable to goods of the tenant. A third party may remove his goods from the premises without penalty. A mortgagee of the tenant's goods, as legal owner, may, under the terms of the charge or by the permission of the tenant, also remove the goods with impunity (*Tomlinson v Consolidated Credit and Mortgage Corpn* (1889) 24 QBD 135, CA).

3.8.3 WRONGFUL RECOVERY OF GOODS BEING DISTRAINED

When a landlord seizes goods the tenant might contemplate trying to recover them. If a bailiff is upon the premises and has just seized the goods the tenant might in the heat of the moment seize them back. Alternatively the tenant might recover the goods after they have been impounded upon the premises. If the distress is illegal the tenant can lawfully recover the goods at any time before impounding but not afterwards (*Cotsworth v Betison* (1696) 1 Salk 247). But if the distress is legal (even though irregular or excessive) the tenant is not entitled to recover the goods once they have been seized.

If the tenant unlawfully recovers the goods he will be guilty of an indictable offence (*R v Butterfield* (1893) 17 Cox CC 598). In the case of wrongful recovery after seizure but before impounding the offence is termed rescue or 'rescous'; in the case of recovery after impounding the tenant is guilty of 'poundbreach'. In the case of third parties recovering their goods, whether they are guilty or not depends upon whether they are aware that the goods have been seized and impounded (*Abingdon RDC v O'Gorman* [1968] 2 QB 811, CA).

As well as probably being criminal offences both rescous and poundbreach give the landlord the right to recover the goods and a right against the tenant for monetary compensation. The level of compensation is penal in that the landlord is entitled to treble damages (Distress for Rent Act 1689, s 3) – calculated as treble the value of the goods siezed (*Cyril Morgan (Holdings) v Dyer* (1995) unreported).

3.9 Tenant's remedies for wrongful distress

A landlord must take care when distraining that the rules of distress are fully complied with; that there are arrears in respect of which to distrain, that the procedures are observed, and that he does not take an excessive amount of goods.

3.9.1 ILLEGAL DISTRESS

Distress is illegal if there are no arrears of rent, or if the initial entry was forcible and so unlawful, or if fully privileged goods have been taken. A distress is also illegal if the landlord sells goods after the receipt of a notice under the Law of Distress Amendment Act 1908 (see the 1908 Act, s 2). The landlord will be regarded as a trespasser on the premises and will be liable for the tort of unlawful interference with goods.

The basic remedy of the tenant is an action to recover the goods and to obtain damages for any loss suffered. In a case where there were no arrears of rent and the landlord has wrongfully sold the goods the tenant has a special statutory remedy for double value, i e to recover by way of penalty double the value of the goods (Distress for Rent Act 1689, s 4). Since the landlord has no title to the goods, any sale to a third party is ineffective and the landlord may be liable in conversion.

The tenant or third party may of course bring a court action to recover the goods. A special swift procedure is available called 'replevin', whereby the owner of the goods first obtains an interim order in the county court for their return, and then later proves the illegality of the distraint (County Courts Act 1984, s 144, Sch 1). To get the interim order the tenant or third party will have to provide such security as the court orders, which may be the payment of money, or the giving of a solicitor's undertaking. The High Court also has jurisdiction to award replevin.

3.9.2 IRREGULAR DISTRESS

Distress is irregular if the initial seizure was lawful but the landlord or the bailiff is guilty of some irregularity later: e g if the landlord sells before the expiry of the prescribed five-day period; or if the landlord continues with the distress after a proper tender (*Evans v Elliott* (1836) 5 Ad & El 142); or for less than market price. In this case the distress cannot be impeached but the tenant, or any third party whose goods are affected (*Sharpe v Fowle* (1884) 12 QBD 385) may sue the landlord for any special damage caused, together with costs (Distress for Rent Act 1737, s 19). The landlord may avoid an action by making a 'tender of amends' to compensate the tenant for any special damage, before the tenant begins any action.

3.9.3 EXCESSIVE DISTRESS

Distress is excessive if the landlord seizes goods which have a value which is obviously disproportionate to the rent owed (Statute of Marlborough 1267, c 1 Distress Act 1267), or if goods which have qualified privilege are taken unnecessarily. The landlord should only take such goods as are reasonably required to meet the arrears. Value is estimated according to the expected realisation value of the goods rather than their value to the tenant (*Wells v Moody* (1835) 7 C & P 59). A single item whose value far exceeds the arrears may be properly taken, so long as there are not other goods on the premises of lower value which might have been taken instead. It might be thought that, since any surplus after sale will pass to the tenant, it should not matter that excessive goods are taken. But the deprivation of the tenant's goods might cause him inconvenience for which he should be compensated. The goods might be essential, for instance, to the carrying on of the tenant's business: so, a landlord who levies excessive distress may not only be liable to account for the proceeds of sale but might find himself paying substantial damages for inconvenience and for the tenant's loss of business (see *Baylis v Usher* (1830) 4 Moo & P 790 and *Smith v Enright* (1893) 69 LT 724). A tenant may, of course, apply for an injunction to prevent a sale following a seizure which is an excessive distress (*Steel Linings Ltd v Bibby & Co* [1993] RA 27, CA).

3.10 Distress and other remedies

Normally where a creditor has several remedies in respect of a debt the creditor's rights are cumulative so that he can rely upon any one or more of the remedies as he wishes. A landlord, however, may find that an election to pursue one particular remedy may have the effect of precluding him from also using another. In particular an exercise of the right to distrain may preclude the landlord from relying upon another remedy, or reliance upon another remedy may bar the landlord from distraining.

3.10.1 DISTRESS AND JUDGMENT FOR RENT

Where, for example, a landlord decides to sue for rent the landlord's right to distrain may be lost. If a judgment for rent is obtained the debt for the rent apparently 'merges' into the judgment debt. The effect of this is that the landlord can rely upon the court procedures for enforcement of judgment debts, but the private right to distrain ceases (*Chancellor v Webster* (1893) 9 TLR 568).

3.10.2 DISTRESS AND PROOF

Another example of the interrelationship between distress and other remedies is that usually a landlord can both distrain and prove, and in bankruptcy the IA 1986, s 347(10) makes it clear that the exercise of the right to distrain does not take away the landlord's right to prove in the bankruptcy in respect of rent, so that the landlord may lodge a proof for the balance after distraining (*Re Bumpus, ex p White* [1908] 2 KB 330).

What is not quite so clear is whether, once a landlord lodges a proof for rent, the landlord can afterwards distrain for the same rent. In *Ex p Grove* (1747) 1 Atk 104, Lord Hardwicke LC refused to allow a landlord, who had proved in the bankruptcy of the tenant, to distrain three years later on goods which had been sold in the bankruptcy to a third party, who continued in occupation of the premises. In *Ex p Devine* (1776), which is reported in *Cooke's Bankruptcy Laws* (8th edn, pp 199, 201), Lord Bathurst LC said that the reason for not allowing the proof in *Ex p Grove* was that the goods had passed to a third party, and that it was irrelevant that there had been an earlier proof. His Lordship thought that the basic principle was that the landlord could distrain at any time after bankruptcy, notwithstanding the proof. A later authority, however, indicates that once a dividend is declared the landlord must choose between the two remedies (*Holmes v Watt* [1935] 2 KB 300, CA), so that distress is barred after declaration of a dividend.

The justification for limiting the landlord's right to distrain after proof is that the landlord's position is analogous to that of a secured creditor. In *Ex p Grove* Lord Hardwicke pointed out that a secured creditor is not allowed to prove for the full amount and have the benefit of the security. He can surrender the security and prove for the full amount, or he can put a value on the security and prove for the balance. Although the landlord is not a secured creditor in the normal sense (*Thomas v Patent Lionite Co* (1881) 17 Ch D 250, CA) the right of distress is a legal lien which places him in a position analogous to that of a secured creditor. It is arguable therefore that he should not be allowed to both prove and distrain for the same debt. This should not mean, however, that he cannot prove in respect of arrears due before the commencement of a bankruptcy or liquidation, and later distrain for amounts due afterwards.

3.10.3 DISTRESS AND FORFEITURE

Before distraining, a landlord should also appreciate that the levying of distress may prevent him from forfeiting the lease for the arrears of rent or other breach of the terms of the lease of which the landlord is aware (see para 4.3.3). Conversely, if the landlord elects to forfeit the lease, and issues a writ for possession or re-enters, the landlord will lose the right to distrain.

3.11 Landlord's right against execution creditors

A landlord will be unable to distrain upon goods which have been seized by a bailiff or sheriff in execution of some court order in favour of some other creditor, since upon such seizure the goods are in the custody of the law and not of the tenant. Although the landlord's right to distrain is stymied, the sheriff or bailiff may be made to account to the landlord for rent before having the benefit of the execution. The landlord is normally entitled to require the execution creditor, through the High Court sheriff or county court bailiff, to pay up to one year's arrears of rent. In bankruptcy the right is reduced to six months. The landlord's rights are considered in depth in chapter 2 (para 2.7.7).

Where a tenant has had a judgment made against him which he is unable to satisfy, in certain circumstances an administration order may be made (County Courts Act 1984, s 112) which will have the effect that named creditors, which may include the landlord, will be unable to petition for bankruptcy nor to exercise any remedy against the tenant (County Courts Act 1984, s 114). There is expressly reserved, however, the landlord's right to distrain for rent for six months' rent accrued due prior to the date of the administration order (s 116).

3.12 Law reform

The law of distress has been subject to the criticisms that it is archaic and unduly complex (see LCWP No 97, 1986), and no doubt these criticisms are justified. But it is the very effectiveness of the remedy which has caused the Law Commission to recommend its abolition. In its report (Law Com 194, 1991) it criticises first the priority given to landlords over other creditors, and then its harshness, and prejudice to debtors and third parties whose goods are distrained upon. From what has been explained in this chapter, however, it can be seen that there are a number of checks upon the exercise of the right of distress which limit the degree of priority give to a landlord. In particular, in the case of liquidation of a company the court has a discretion whether to allow distress and after commencement will generally only exercise the discretion if the liquidator is using the premises for the purposes of the liquidation, which might be considered to be fair enough. The right which might be open to most criticism is a landlord's right in bankruptcy to distrain for six months' rent accrued due prior to the bankruptcy as this puts the landlord in the position of a secured creditor. The question arises, however, as to whether, if distress were to be abolished, a landlord would seek some alternative form of security which would achieve a similar priority.

CHAPTER 4

Forfeiture of the lease

When a tenant becomes insolvent the landlord is sometimes attracted by the possibility of terminating the lease by forfeiture. If the lease has a capital worth the value of the landlord's reversion can be increased by obtaining vacant possession. The landlord can then sell the reversion, relet on a long lease for a premium, or relet without a premium but at an increased rent. Insolvency will almost always be an event which will trigger a landlord's right to forfeit, since failure to pay rent or appointment of a receiver, liquidator or trustee in bankruptcy will usually be events for which the lease permits forfeiture.

As will be seen below, however, a landlord may not find it so easy to forfeit. Where the tenant is insolvent the law must take account of the possibility that forfeiture of the lease might deprive other creditors of a valuable asset, since the lease may have a capital value on a sale or surrender. If the lease does have such value the forfeiture of it will transfer value to the landlord, augmenting the value of the reversion, quite possibly to an extent greater than the value of the obligations owed by the tenant. In these circumstances forfeiture not only puts the landlord in a position similar to that of a secured creditor (such as a mortgagee), but it also operates as a penal provision depriving both the insolvent tenant and creditors of value which in justice they ought to have the benefit of. The House of Lords in *Billson v Residential Apartments Ltd* [1992] 1 AC 494 considered that this would amount to unjust enrichment of the landlord at the expense of the tenant. For these reasons both statute law and judicial precedent lean against forfeiture, and special restrictions apply in the event of insolvency.

4.1 Does the lease give the right to forfeit?

Not every lease carries with it the same right to forfeit. The right will be available if it is expressly reserved by proviso allowing the landlord to re-enter upon breach of covenant by the tenant, or if it is impliedly reserved through the lease being conditional upon some event, so that the landlord has the right to end the lease upon breach of the condition. The landlord will also be justified in re-entering if the tenant denies the landlord's title to the property. Most modern commercial leases incorporate express provisos for re-entry upon breach of any of the terms of the lease by the tenant, and such leases are almost invariably conditional upon the tenant not suffering bankruptcy, liquidation or other events associated with insolvency. The Law Commission (Law Com 221, 1994) has recommended that every lease should carry with it a right to forfeit for breach of obligation, without the necessity for an express term permitting the landlord to re-enter.

4.1.1 EXPRESS RIGHT TO FORFEIT

A commercial lease will normally have an express proviso for re-entry upon breach of tenant's obligation. The basic proviso will often be in a form similar to the following:

> 'Provided that if any part of the rent shall be in arrears for 21 days, whether formally demanded or not, or there shall be any breach of the covenants herein and on the part of the tenant to be performed the lessor may re-enter upon the premises, and immediately thereupon the term shall absolutely determine.'

Sometimes the proviso will not take this standard form, but any clause which in substance reserves to the landlord the right to determine the lease upon the default of the tenant is regarded as a proviso for re-entry, even though it may take an unusual form, such as a form akin to that of an option to determine. In *Richard Clarke & Co Ltd v Widnall* [1976] 3 All ER 301, the lease contained a clause which stipulated that if the tenant was in breach of covenant the landlord could serve upon the tenant a three-month notice to quit the premises. The Court of Appeal held that the clause was a proviso for re-entry and was subject to the same rules relating to forfeiture as any other such right, including the rule which permits the court to grant to the tenant relief from forfeiture. The clause must, however, to constitute a forfeiture clause, be one which permits the landlord to end the lease earlier than its natural determination date. In *Clays Lane Housing Co-operative Ltd v Patrick* (1984) 49 P & CR 72, the Court of Appeal decided that a clause in a weekly tenancy which restricted the landlord's right to end the lease unless the tenant was in default, and then only by the giving of four weeks' notice, was not a forfeiture clause, since it did not allow the landlord to end the lease earlier than would normally have been the case.

The effect of a proviso for re-entry is to make the lease voidable at the option of the landlord. The lease is not automatically void even though the proviso may state that the lease shall end immediately upon a breach of covenant or condition. The reason for construing the clause as making the lease voidable rather than void is to prevent a tenant from avoiding the obligations under a lease by claiming that the lease is void as a result of his own wrongful act (*Davenport v R* (1877) 3 App Cas 115, PC). The rule is now reinforced by the Law of Property Act 1925, s 146(7) which provides that a lease limited to continue as long only as the lessee abstains from committing a breach of covenant shall be and take effect as a lease to continue for any longer term for which it could subsist, but determinable by a proviso for re-entry on such breach.

So the landlord has an option to end the lease, which the landlord may exercise by the doing of some act unequivocally demonstrating an intention to forfeit – usually by making a peaceable entry upon the land or serving a claim for possession, and after complying with any statutory prerequisites.

4.1.2 IMPLIED RIGHT TO FORFEIT

Even if there is no express term allowing re-entry, the law implies a right to re-enter if the continuance of the lease is conditional upon some matter or matters, or if the tenant denies the landlord's title.

Breach of condition

Whether or not the lease in question contains a proviso for re-entry upon a breach of covenant, the lease may as a matter of construction, be subject to some condition or conditions, upon the occurrence of which the landlord will have the option to end the lease. A condition 'is a clause which shows a clear intention upon the part of the landlord, not merely that the tenant shall be personally liable if he fails in his contractual duties, but that the lease shall determine in the event of such a failure' (Cheshire & Burn's *Modern Law of Real Property* (15th edn) p 457). Usually a condition will be preceded by such words as 'upon condition' or 'provided that', although no particular formula is necessary to create a condition. If such a condition subsequent to the lease occurs, the lease does not automatically determine but the landlord may, at his option, re-enter. The condition will pass with the lease to bind any assignee upon the same basis as any tenant covenant which is not purely personal (per Lord Russell CJ in *Horsey Estate Ltd v Steiger and Petrifite Co* [1899] 2 QB 79, CA, see para 5.2.2). Often acts associated with the insolvency of the tenant, such as appointment of a receiver, liquidator or trustee in bankruptcy are drafted so as to be conditions of the lease.

Denial of title

All leases are determinable upon a denial by a tenant of his landlord's title. This rule is a throwback to feudal times when tenants were unfree men who owed duties to their 'lords', and it would have been disloyal for a tenant to deny his relationship with his lord. In recent times the courts have been reluctant to apply the principle (see *WG Clark (Properties) Ltd v Dupre Properties Ltd* [1992] Ch 297). In *Warner v Sampson* [1959] 1 QB 297, CA, Lord Denning MR said that the medieval rule was 'quite inappropriate at the present day', and the Law Commission (Law Com 221, 1994) has recommended its abolition.

4.2 Has the right to forfeit arisen?

Assuming that the lease in question contains an express proviso for re-entry upon breach of tenant's covenant, and there has been such a breach; or if there has been a breach of condition, the landlord will have the option to forfeit. Likely breaches of covenant in the case of an insolvent tenant include failure to pay rent, failure to repair, and wrongful assignment or subletting – perhaps by a receiver or liquidator who is in a hurry to realise any capital value in the lease. The most likely breach of condition is the insolvency of the tenant.

4.2.1 INSOLVENCY AS A FORFEITING EVENT

In the absence of an express stipulation the insolvency of the tenant will not entitle the landlord to forfeit while there is no other breach. Such a stipulation will not be implied into an open contract for a lease, i e a contract for a lease where the parties, the property, the rent and the length of the lease are known, but no other terms have been agreed. Where there is such an open contract the law will normally imply 'usual covenants', but it has been decided that it is not usual for a lease to be determinable upon insolvency of the tenant. The decision to this effect (*Hyde v Warden* (1877) 3 Ex D 72) is, however, an old one decided by the Court of Appeal on its particular facts, Brett LJ saying:

> 'the power of re-entry not only if the lessee (which word is expressly declared to include assigns) should become bankrupt, or make any composition with his creditors, but also if any execution should issue against him, such provision appears to us unusual and unreasonable, especially in the present case, where the defendant would be liable to be evicted for breach of the condition not only by himself, but by the original lessee ...'

The reasoning of Brett LJ may not be so appropriate to the present day, and it is just possible that the condition could be implied in the case of a modern commercial lease (see *Chester v Buckingham Travel Ltd* [1981] 1 All ER 386).

It has also been held that in the absence of an express term of the lease providing for forfeiture on insolvency, the vesting of the lease in a trustee in bankruptcy will not give the landlord an option to forfeit for breach of a restriction upon assignment of the lease, as the vesting of the lease in the trustee is an assignment taking effect by operation of law, rather than by act of the tenant (*Re Riggs, ex p Lovell* [1901] 2 KB 16). This is so even if the tenant has petitioned for his own bankruptcy.

In any case, many leases, and certainly most modern commercial leases, give landlords rights to forfeit upon the insolvency of the tenant, or upon events which might signal that there is an impending insolvency. A usual proviso might take the following form:

> 'Provided that if any part of the said rent shall be in arrears for 21 days, whether formally demanded or not, or there shall be any breach of the covenants herein and on the part of the tenant to be performed or observed, or if a receiver shall be appointed over the property of the tenant or the tenant shall enter into a composition or voluntary arrangement with creditors or the tenant shall become bankrupt, or being a company have an administrator or liquidator appointed, the lessor or his assigns may re-enter upon the premises, and immediately thereupon the term shall absolutely determine.'

Validity of insolvency condition

The general principle of law is that a condition rendering an interest liable to be defeated upon bankruptcy is void since its effect is to alter the operation of the law of bankruptcy which normally requires the vesting of all property of a bankrupt in the debtor's trustee, for the benefit of the general creditors. So, for instance, if a debtor had a freehold interest in land which was stated to be conditional upon the debtor not becoming bankrupt, upon bankruptcy of the debtor the freehold would vest in his trustee in bankruptcy and the condition would not be effective to divest the trustee of the freehold (*Re Machu* (1882) 21 Ch D 838). But, although a clause in a lease providing for its determination upon bankruptcy is construed as a condition, it has been long settled that the condition is valid.

The leading authority establishing the validity of such a condition is *Roe d Hunter v Galliers* (1787) 2 Term Rep 133. In the court the argument that the condition was repugnant to the law of bankruptcy and unfair to creditors was rejected. Buller J (Ashhurst J and Grose J agreeing) first said that other creditors would not have relied upon the lease when giving credit, since if they saw the lease they would know that it was determinable upon bankruptcy; if they did not see it they could only assume that the tenant had bare possession, and no interest. Buller J then continued, saying:

'It is next urged that this is equivalent to a proviso that the lease shall not be seized under a commission of bankrupt; the defendant's counsel having first supposed the lease to be granted absolutely for a certain term, and then that a subsequent proviso is added to that effect. Such a proviso as that indeed would be bad, because it would be repugnant to the grant itself: but here there is an express limitation that the lease shall be void upon the fact of the lessee's becoming bankrupt.'

He and Ashhurst J further equated the clause as equivalent to a covenant against assignment, Ashhurst J reasoning:

'If it be reasonable for [the landlord] to restrain the tenant from assigning, it is equally reasonable for him to guard against such an event as the present, because the consequence of the bankruptcy is an assignment of the property into other hands. Perhaps it may be more necessary for the landlord to guard against this latter event, as there is greater danger to be apprehended by him in this than in the former case. Persons who are put into possession under a commission are still less likely to take proper care of the land than a private assignee of the first tenant.'

So it is settled that a proviso for determination of a lease upon bankruptcy or some other insolvency event is valid, notwithstanding the normal rule that a condition upon bankruptcy is void.

When does the right to forfeit for insolvency arise?

In the absence of a contra-indication the right to forfeit arises on the commencement of the bankruptcy or liquidation, and not at some later time such as the completion of the winding up (*General Share and Trust Co v Wetley Brick and Pottery Co* (1882) 20 Ch D 260, CA). If the right is a right to forfeit for the 'insolvency' of the tenant, this will probably mean a general inability to pay debts, and forfeiture will not be justified by the mere fact of a solvent bankruptcy or liquidation (*Doe d Gatehouse v Rees* (1838) 4 Bing NC 384). If the lease is determinable upon the tenant's 'inability to pay debts' reference may be had to the Insolvency Act 1986 ('IA 1986'), s 123 which defines the circumstances in which a company is deemed unable to pay its debts.

Forfeiture for insolvency of third parties

A lease may also be liable to forfeiture upon the bankruptcy of a third party if the lease so provides. In *Doe d Bridgman v David* (1834) 1 Cr M & R 405, the lease was terminable upon the bankruptcy of the lessee, his executors, administrators or assigns. The court held the provision to be enforceable and that the lease was terminable upon bankruptcy of the tenant's personal representatives, Lord Lydhurst CB commenting:

> 'The object of the lessor was to guard against having an insolvent tenant imposed upon him. He was aware that the obligation to perform the various covenants in the lease would, on the death of the lessee, devolve upon his executor, and he was desirous that the executor, when he became his tenant, should not be insolvent or bankrupt and so deprive him of the benefit of the covenants.'

A landlord may also wish to forfeit upon the insolvency of a guarantor particularly where the guarantee was taken because the covenant of the tenant was a weak one. An express right to forfeit upon the insolvency of the guarantor will be effective (*Halliard Property Co Ltd v Jack Segal Ltd* [1978] 1 All ER 1219). Similarly, where a lease has been assigned, a landlord may wish to be in a position to forfeit if a former tenant becomes bankrupt – at least where the former tenant remains liable for the lease obligations as a guarantor or quasi surety for the assignee (see chapter 5). The landlord will not be able to do so unless the lease expressly reserves the right since in normal circumstances a forfeiture provision will be read to apply only to the insolvency of the assignee who presently has the leasehold estate and will not be operable upon the insolvency of an earlier tenant. In *Smith v Gronow* [1891] 2 QB 394, a lease had been assigned and after the assignment the original tenant was declared bankrupt. The court refused to allow the landlord to forfeit for the original tenant's bankruptcy because the consequences would not be fair to the assignee. In some cases a landlord may well be relying upon the strength of covenant of a former tenant and may well wish to be in a position to forfeit where that tenant is insolvent, notwithstanding that the lease has been assigned. If a landlord wishes to reserve such a right the lease must so state in clear terms to counteract the effect of *Smith v Gronow* (see above).

4.2.2 CONSTRUCTION OF RIGHT TO FORFEIT UPON INSOLVENCY

As the effect of forfeiture is in many cases to penalise the tenant, rather than simply to compensate the landlord, the right to forfeit will be strictly construed so as to give the landlord no greater right than he has clearly reserved. For instance, if the clause simply states that the landlord can re-enter upon 'the tenant's failure to perform' the terms of the lease the clause may be construed so as to give the landlord a right to re-enter only where the tenant has failed to perform a positive obligation such as to keep the premises in repair, but the landlord will have no right upon a breach by the tenant of a negative stipulation, for instance, not to use the premises for a particular purpose. For this reason most clauses which give landlords rights to forfeit are expressed to operate upon breach, non-performance and non-observance. So before a landlord attempts to forfeit it should examine carefully the wording of the lease to determine whether the right has in fact arisen (see further Woodfall, *Landlord and Tenant* para 17.071).

As far as forfeiture for insolvency is concerned the courts have not construed leases too strongly against landlords and have decided, for instance, that if a lease provides that the landlord may forfeit upon the tenant, being a company, entering into liquidation, whether compulsory or voluntary, and there is no qualification that the liquidation must be an insolvent one, then the landlord may forfeit for voluntary liquidation even though the company is solvent and the liquidation is merely for the purpose of reconstruction or amalgamation (*Fryer v Ewart* [1902] AC 187, HL). The same principle has been applied where a tenant has voluntarily taken steps for his own bankruptcy while solvent (*Re Walker, ex p Gould* (1884) 13 QBD 454).

On the other hand the court found against a landlord in a case where a lease was determinable upon the tenant being 'duly found and declared a bankrupt'. The tenant was made bankrupt upon a petition which relied upon a debt stated in the petition to be owed by the tenant to A and B as partners, whereas, in fact, the debt was owed to A, B and C as partners. Even though the proceedings could be validated by amendment to reflect the true facts, the majority of the court held that the tenant had not 'duly' been found bankrupt and the landlord had no right to forfeit (*Doe d Lloyd v Ingleby* (1846) 15 M & W 465).

4.2.3 FORFEITURE FOR NON-PAYMENT OF RENT

It might be thought that the right to forfeit for non-payment of rent arises as soon as rent is due and unpaid. This would be true if the lease in question specified that the right to forfeit arose immediately upon default. In practice, however, most leases give the tenant a period of grace and provide that the right to forfeit arises after a specified number of days, often 21 days following the due date for payment. The right to forfeit will not arise until after the expiry of the specified period.

A landlord can forfeit for non-payment of rent even if the landlord has assigned to a third party the right to recover rent. In *Kataria v Safeland plc* [1998] 1 EGLR 39, the landlord's interest in a let property had been sold on terms that the buyer would assign back to the seller the right to recover rent arrears. After such assignment of arrears the buyer sought to forfeit the lease for non-payment of the arrears but the tenant objected, arguing that a landlord could only forfeit in respect of arrears owed to such landlord. The Court of Appeal decided that as a matter of construction the buyer had a right to forfeit for arrears and nothing in the lease required such arrears to be owed to the buyer. Accordingly the tenant had no defence to the landlord buyer's claim.

4.3 Has the landlord waived the right to forfeit?

It has been seen above that the occurrence of a forfeiting event does not automatically determine the lease. A forfeiting event, such as failure to pay rent for 21 days (if that is the period specified) operates rather to give the landlord an option to end the lease. Once the landlord's right to forfeit has arisen the landlord can elect either that the lease should end, or that it should continue. The landlord cannot have it both ways and take the benefit of the lease while attempting to reserve the right to forfeit. So if the landlord, after becoming aware of the facts which constitute a breach of the terms of the lease, does an act which unequivocally indicates that the lease is to continue, the recognition of the lease is an election that it is to continue and the landlord waives its right to end the lease for the breach; but the election that the lease should continue does not necessarily operate as a waiver by the landlord of the right to pursue other remedies for the breach, such as the right to seek monetary compensation (see para 4.3.5).

4.3.1 KNOWLEDGE OF THE BREACH

In order to make an election that the lease should continue notwithstanding the breach the landlord must, of course, know of the breach. In this context knowledge is knowledge of the facts which constitute the breach rather than knowledge of the law as to whether the facts amount to a breach or not. In *David Blackstone Ltd v Burnetts (West End) Ltd* [1973] 3 All ER 782, the lease in question contained a restriction upon the tenant subletting without the landlord's consent. The landlord consented to a subletting to two individuals in partnership, but the tenant sublet to a company of which the individuals were director and secretary. The landlord became aware of these facts and while the landlord and its solicitors were considering whether the facts amounted to a breach, a routine rent demand was issued. The landlord then decided to serve a notice requiring forfeiture. Meanwhile, the tenant sent a cheque for the rent, which the landlord returned to the tenant uncashed. Swanwick J decided that the landlord had waived the right to forfeit by the making of the routine rent demand after knowledge of the breach. That the landlord was uncertain whether the facts amounted to a breach was irrelevant because '... the knowledge required to put a landlord to his election is knowledge of the basic facts which in law constitute a breach ... his knowledge or ignorance of the law is, in my judgment, irrelevant'.

The effect of this decision may have been reduced somewhat by the later decision of the Court of Appeal in *Chrisdell Ltd v Johnson* (1987) 54 P & CR 257, where the tenant had gone to the United States of America and had asked for consent to assign the tenancy, which the landlord had refused. The tenant then entered into an agreement with a lady which agreement purported to employ her as a housekeeper but also provided for payment by her for the use of furniture. The landlord was suspicious of the arrangement but was uncertain about it. The landlord was told by the tenant that there had been no change of tenant, and the landlord took no action for eight years during which time he accepted rent. After eight years the landlord's interest had been transferred to new landlords who took the view that the agreement was a sham and was in breach of the covenant against subletting, and they sought to forfeit. The court held that there had been no waiver of the landlord's right to forfeit. Glidewell LJ said 'If a landlord receives a representation from his tenant which, if true means that there has been no breach and if the landlord, not being sufficiently confident of the untruth of what the tenant says, proceeds on the basis that what the tenant says is true, then, in my judgment, it cannot later be said that he knew all the necessary facts to establish a breach'. It is not clear to what extent this ratio is accurate. Presumably what should be relevant is not the state of confidence of the landlord, but whether he has or has not been told the truth. If he has been told the truth he must be taken to know the facts; if he has not been told the truth, he does not know the facts. It is submitted that once the truth has been revealed to the landlord he should not be able to say that he has not waived the right to forfeit on the basis that he lacked confidence as to whether the facts were true or false.

Actual and imputed knowledge

The knowledge required may be actual knowledge by the landlord or knowledge imputed to the landlord through a relevant agent of the landlord having notice. In *Metropolitan Properties Co Ltd v Cordery* (1979) 39 P & CR 10, the premises were a flat in a block and the relevant breach was an unlawful subletting. The landlord's porter at the block learned of the facts which constituted the breach, after which the landlord in ignorance of the facts accepted rent. The Court of Appeal found that the knowledge of the porter was imputed to the landlord and that the landlord had by acceptance of rent waived the right to forfeit. Templeman LJ made the additional point that knowledge of the agent is not imputed to the landlord immediately but 'After the lapse of a reasonable time for the porters to appreciate the facts and communicate them to the management, the landlords are deemed to have known that which the porters knew ...'.

Constructive knowledge

Although imputed knowledge is sufficient it seems that constructive notice of the breach will not be. In *Official Custodian for Charities v Parway Estates Developments Ltd* [1985] Ch 151, the lease could be determined upon the tenant company entering into liquidation. The landlord was aware for some time that receivers had been appointed. Later an order was made for the winding up of the company and the order was notified in the usual manner in the London Gazette, and a liquidator appointed. After these latter two events, and in ignorance of them, the landlord accepted rent. The issue was whether the landlord had constructive knowledge of the order and had waived the right to forfeit. The Court of Appeal decided that he had no knowledge and had not waived his right to forfeit for the liquidation, even though he knew that the tenant company was in financial difficulties and that receivers had been appointed.

4.3.2 ACCEPTANCE OF RENT

As is demonstrated by the cases immediately above the classic example of an act of a landlord which, in normal circumstances, unequivocally shows that the lease is to continue is acceptance of rent after the right to forfeit has arisen. The position may be complicated, however, by reason that rent accepted may have fallen due prior to or after the breach, and rent might be payable in advance or arrears (see below).

A demand for rent will cause a waiver in law irrespective of the subjective intention of the landlord, and waiver occurs even though the demand was inadvertent and the landlord had no actual intention to waive. In *Central Estates (Belgravia) Ltd v Woolgar (No 2)* [1972] 1 WLR 1048, the tenant had, in breach of covenant, used the premises as a brothel. On discovering the breach the landlord's managing agents were instructed not to accept rent. One clerk, unaware of these instructions, sent out a routine rent demand. The Court of Appeal decided that the demand for rent should be regarded objectively, and the subjective intention of the landlord, not to waive the breach, was irrelevant. Such a demand indicated the continuance of the lease and was a waiver by the landlord.

The strictness of the above rule has been mitigated by the courts when considering whether the right to forfeit a statutory tenancy under the Rent Acts has been waived. In such a case it has been held that waiver is more a question of fact than law and will depend not only upon whether the landlord has demanded or accepted rent with knowledge of the breach, but also upon the tenant's subjective view as to whether there has or has not been a waiver (*Oak Property Co Ltd v Chapman* [1947] KB 886, CA).

The Law Commission (Law Com 221, 1994) considers that the present strict rule, applicable to contractual tenancies, operates unjustly against landlords in some cases and it has recommended the replacement of the rule with the principle that an act of the landlord will only amount to waiver of the right to forfeit if 'his conduct is such that a reasonable tenant would believe, and the actual tenant does believe, that [the landlord] will not seek a termination order'.

Acceptance or demand for rent due after breach

If, knowing of the facts that establish a breach, a landlord demands rent (*David Blackstone v Burnett's (West End) Ltd* [1973] 3 All ER 782), accepts rent, or commences proceedings for rent (*Dendy v Nicholl* (1858) 4 CBNS 376) due for a period subsequent to the breach, the landlord waives the right to forfeit for the breach, because it shows that the landlord intends the lease to continue for a period following the breach.

> **Example** – Rent is payable quarterly in advance on the usual quarter days (25 March, 24 June, 29 September and 25 December). There is the usual right to forfeit for breach of covenant. In February the tenant carries out a wrongful alteration. On 20 March the landlord's agent sends out a rent demand for the March quarter's rent. The demand for rent for a period following the wrongful alteration will be a waiver of the right to forfeit for the breach.

Acceptance of rent due prior to breach

If the rent was due prior to the breach then acceptance of it will not indicate a waiver on the part of the landlord, since such acceptance does not show that the lease is to continue after the date of the breach (*Marsh v Curteys* (1597) Cro Eliz 528). Even if the rent due prior to the breach is payable in advance, so as to cover a period following the breach, it does not necessarily follow that there is a waiver of all future breaches for the period for which rent is paid. The waiver operates in respect of existing breaches only, and in the case of a continuing breach for the period during which the landlord knows that such breach will continue (*Segal Securities v Thoseby* [1963] 1 QB 887).

> **Example** – Rent is payable quarterly in advance on the usual quarter days (25 March, 24 June, 29 September and 25 December). The tenant defaults in payment of the March quarter's rent, and on 31 March the tenant carries out a wrongful alteration on the property. On 1 April the landlord (knowing of the alteration) demands the rent due on 25 March. The demand for rent is not a waiver of the right to forfeit for the wrongful alteration, since the rent accrued due prior to the breach.

Demand for rent non-payment of which constitutes the breach

If the relevant breach is non-payment of rent the landlord can safely demand the rent without waiving the right to forfeit for the failure to pay on time. This result would clearly be expected where the right to forfeit does not arise immediately upon default, but after a specified period of grace, since a demand during the period of grace could not be taken to be a waiver of a right to forfeit which would arise at the end of such period. Although not quite so obvious it has been held that a demand for the rent will not cause a waiver even though it is made after the days of grace have expired and after the right to forfeit for such non-payment has arisen (in *Re Debtors (Nos 13A10 and 14A10 of 1994)* [1996] BCC 57). If, however, there have been other relevant breaches a demand for rent will waive the right to forfeit which has arisen in respect of such breaches – including any previous failure to pay rent (in *Re Debtors*, above).

> **Example** – Rent is payable quarterly in advance on the usual quarter days (25 March, 24 June, 29 September and 25 December). There is a right to forfeit if the rent is due and unpaid for 21 days and the usual right to forfeit for any other breach of covenant. On 25 March the tenant fails to pay the March quarter's rent. In May the tenant carries out a wrongful alteration. On 24 June the tenant fails to pay the June quarter's rent. On 17 July (after expiry of the days of grace) the landlord demands the rent for the March and June quarters. The demand will not operate to waive the right to forfeit for non-payment of the June quarter's rent. The demand for the June quarter's rent will, however, cause a waiver of the rights which had previously arisen to forfeit for the March quarter's rent and for the unlawful alteration.

The rule that a demand for rent does not cause a waiver of a right to forfeit for such rent applies even if rent is payable in advance. The landlord is entitled to all such rent notwithstanding that he seeks to forfeit within the relevant period (in *Re Debtors*, above).

Acceptance of payment after service of court proceedings

Once the landlord has issued and served a claim for possession he has unequivocally demonstrated an intention to end the lease. If the landlord has done so the taking of other action to recover rent is not likely to amount to a waiver. In *Grimwood v Moss* (1872) LR 7 CP 360, the landlord, after service of a writ for possession, distrained for rent due up to the date upon which the right to forfeit arose. Even though distress can only be levied while a lease continues it was held that this did not amount to a waiver, although the distress by the landlord might be unlawful and a trespass. Similarly a demand for 'rent' after commencement of forfeiture proceedings will not necessarily cause a waiver (*Civil Service Co-operative Society v McGrigor's Trustee* [1923] 2 Ch 347). Strictly, however, rent is only payable up to the date of service of a claim and mesne profits are payable thereafter as compensation for trespass. The claim will normally include a claim for mesne profits, and the landlord is entitled to any rent due in advance prior to service. If rent is payable in arrears the rent may be claimed at a daily rate for the period up to the date of service.

Acceptance of 'rent' is therefore to be regarded as risky since in an exceptional case it might be argued that, although the landlord has commenced proceedings, a subsequent acceptance of rent is evidence of an intention on the part of the landlord to discontinue the proceedings and recognise the lease as continuing. Another risk is that such acceptance might show that a new lease has been granted, if there is evidence that this was intended (*Legal and General Assurance Society Ltd v General Metal Agencies Ltd* (1969) 20 P & CR 953). It is suggested therefore that the safer course for a landlord is not to accept any payments unless the tenant accepts that the lease is at an end and clearly agrees that they are to be considered as mesne profits for the tenant's trespass.

In order to avoid problems of waiver by acceptance of rent after commencement of proceedings a landlord may rely upon the Civil Procedure Rules (CPR 25.6, 25.7(1)(c), (d), (5), 25.8) which permit the courts to order that interim payments be made to the landlord whilst the landlord proceeds with an action for possession.

Payment by bank transfer

In many modern commercial leases rent is paid automatically by bank transfer and the question may arise as to whether the crediting of the landlord's bank account by direct debit of the tenant's will amount to a waiver. It is quite possible that this will amount to a waiver. In *Pierson v Harvey* (1885) 1 TLR 430, the method of payment of rent was direct credit of the landlord's account. Following a breach by the tenant of a term of the lease the landlord instructed his bank not to accept rent. Subsequently the tenant paid rent to the landlord's bankers. The landlord was unaware of the payment for some months, and even when he had become aware of it he had not taken immediate action. At no time did the landlord inform the tenant that the rent would not be accepted. Lord Coleridge concluded that the acceptance of rent by the landlord's bankers was a waiver. It is possible, if the landlord had told the tenant that rent was not going to be accepted, that the court might have decided that there was no waiver, but even then it may be argued that if the landlord's bankers credit his account there is an acceptance of rent which ought to cause a waiver. Of course, if there is a waiver due to the fault of the bank then the landlord may have a right to sue the bank for negligence.

Acceptance of rent 'without prejudice'

It is often wishfully thought that a landlord can accept rent 'without prejudice' to his right to forfeit. But this is not the case, since the rent is only due if the lease continues. Accordingly a 'without prejudice' demand for rent operates as a waiver of the right to forfeit (*Segal Securities Ltd v Thoseby* [1963] 1 QB 887).

Acceptance of rent from subtenant

Whether acceptance of payment from a subtenant or other third party will cause a waiver depends upon whether the payments may properly be looked on as rent. If the tenant has consented to the payment, and the landlord accepts the payment as rent, the payment will be equivalent to a payment of rent and the right to forfeit for the breach will be waived (*Pellatt v Boosey* (1862) 31 LJCP 281). Sometimes a landlord may want to get sums from a subtenant by serving a notice under the Law of Distress Amendment Act 1908, s 6, which enables the landlord to collect rent from a subtenant in order to pay off arrears of head rent. It is not clear whether the exercise of this statutory right will operate as a waiver of the right to forfeit for existing arrears of head rent. Since the obligation to pay future subrent is dependent upon the continuance of the lease and sublease a demand to pay, such future rents ought to cause a waiver. If, however, the landlord is simply seeking to collect subrent which fell due prior to the date upon which the right to forfeit arose it is arguable that the service of a notice under the Law of Distress Amendment 1908 does not cause a waiver.

Use of rent deposit or payment by surety

A question which is likely to arise in the case of an insolvent tenant is whether use of a rent deposit or acceptance of payment from a surety will waive the right to forfeit. It is submitted that resort to such sources of payment should be regarded as similar to payment of rent. The decided cases, however, are not entirely clear on the point.

The effect of the decision of the Court of Appeal in *London and County (A & D) Ltd v Wilfred Sportsman Ltd* [1971] Ch 764, appears to be that acceptance of payment from a guarantor may amount to a waiver of a past breach, but a payment, though made in respect of rent, is not equivalent to payment of rent. If therefore, a guarantor, on a quarter day, pays a sum equal to a quarter's rent in advance, the payment is not rent, and if on the following day there is a default in payment by the tenant, there is a breach by the tenant which the landlord can rely upon as a ground for forfeiture. It is suggested that the judgment of Russell LJ (with whom Lord Donovan and Megaw LJ agreed) is not correct. A payment by a guarantor in respect of rent should be regarded as rent for two reasons. First, a guarantee is usually drafted so that the guarantor agrees that the rent will be paid by the tenant or the guarantor. The terms of such a guarantee envisage therefore that the guarantor will be making a rental payment. Second, a guarantor's implied right of indemnity from the tenant (see para 5.4 below) is based upon the assumption that the guarantor has met the tenant's obligation to pay the rent.

The distinction made by the Court of Appeal between rent and a guarantee payment was not applied in the later Court of Appeal decision of *Milverton Group Ltd v Warner World Ltd* [1995] 2 EGLR 28, where guarantee payments were held to be equivalent to rentals (see para 5.1.8).

By a similar token it is arguable, though less strongly, that a demand made upon a surety or former tenant will amount to a waiver of the right to forfeit in respect of a breach which has taken place prior to the date upon which the rent became due. This point is likely to have added importance following the introduction by the Landlord and Tenant (Covenants) Act 1995 of the statutory requirement for a landlord to serve formal notice upon a former tenant or his surety within six months of relevant sums becoming due (see para 5.1.7).

It is also submitted that where a landlord relies upon a rent deposit similar principles apply and a withdrawal from the deposit will not only operate to waive a pre-existing breach, but, where the withdrawal is in respect of rent for a period not yet expired, will also be equivalent to acceptance of the rent for that period, so that a right to forfeit will not arise until there is a subsequent default by the tenant.

4.3.3 OTHER ACTS OF THE LANDLORD

Although acceptance of rent is the most common cause of waiver of the right to forfeit, it should not be forgotten that the general principle is that any act of the landlord which unequivocally demonstrates that the lease is continuing will amount to a waiver, and once any breach has occurred the utmost caution must be exercised in conducting any dealings with the tenant. In respect of an act other than acceptance of rent the courts have emphasised that all of the circumstances should be considered in order to assess whether the act of the landlord is so unequivocal as to prevent the landlord from forfeiting (see *Expert Clothing Service and Sales Ltd v Hillgate House Ltd* [1986] Ch 340).

Dealing with draft documentation relating to lease

If the landlord, with knowledge of the breach, deals with documentation which is drafted on the basis that the lease continues, such a dealing may amount to an unequivocal election to treat the lease as continuing, and as a waiver of the breach. If, for instance, a deed varying the lease is actually completed, this can only be on the basis that the lease continues. If such a deed is not actually completed, but the landlord deals with a draft the position is not so clear and whether or not there is a waiver will depend upon all the circumstances of the case. In *Expert Clothing Service and Sales Ltd v Hillgate House Ltd* [1986] Ch 340, CA, there was a breach by the tenant of an obligation to carry out work on the demised premises. The landlords served a Law of Property Act 1925, s 146 notice (see para 4.4.2). The tenant made an application for relief from forfeiture. Eight days later the landlord's solicitors forwarded to the tenant's solicitors a draft deed of variation of the lease, in accordance with a court order relating to previous litigation between the landlord and the tenant. A few days later the landlord issued possession proceedings. The Court of Appeal held that the landlord had not, by dealing with the draft documentation, waived its right to forfeit. Slade LJ made a distinction between acceptance of rent which 'is justifiable only on the basis that the tenancy is still subsisting', and other acts where 'the court is ... free to look at all the circumstances of the case' to consider whether the act is 'so unequivocal that, when considered objectively, it [can] only be regarded as ... done consistently with the continued existence of a tenancy...'.

Without prejudice negotiations

Although an acceptance of rent on a 'without prejudice' basis amounts to waiver (see para 4.3.2) the courts have sensibly ruled that the entering into of negotiations by the landlord 'without prejudice' to the right to forfeit is not a waiver (*Re National Jazz Centre Ltd* [1988] 2 EGLR 57). The 'without prejudice' umbrella provides an important protection, reserving to the landlord the right to forfeit while encouraging the landlord and tenant to reach an amicable settlement of the dispute.

Offer to purchase tenant's interest

In appropriate circumstances an offer by a landlord to purchase a tenant's interest in the demised premises may amount to a waiver. The obiter dictum statement by Roskill J in *Bader Properties Ltd v Linley Property Investments Ltd* (1967) 19 P & CR 620, to this effect must be understood in the light of the approach of the Court of Appeal in *Expert Clothing Service and Sales Ltd* (see above), so that all the circumstances must be examined to ascertain whether it is fitting to find that a waiver has occurred.

Assignment of reversion subject to the lease

If the landlord transfers the reversionary interest to a third party, and the transfer is made subject to the lease, it might be said that this is an act of the landlord showing that the lease continues. Although such an act may be regarded as consistent with a continuing lease, it does not amount to an unequivocal election by the landlord that the right to forfeit will not be exercised, partly because it is not a communication or act operating between the landlord and the tenant, but concerns the landlord and third party only. The third party may rely upon the right to forfeit for the breach even though it occurred before the transfer, since an assignee of the landlord's interest takes the benefit of all of the tenant's covenants which affect the land, by virtue of the Law of Property Act 1925, s 141 (*London & County Ltd v Wilfred Sportsman Ltd*, see above).

Agreement to voluntary arrangement

Where a tenant is insolvent a landlord may be asked to agree to a voluntary arrangement (see para 1.2) which involves the continuance of the lease. A landlord does not waive his right to forfeit by agreeing a voluntary arrangement, and is entitled to proceed to forfeit, with the tenant or any assignee having the usual right to apply for relief. In *Re Mohammed Naeem (a bankrupt) (No 18 of 1988)* [1990] 1 WLR 48, a bankrupt sought the approval of the court to a voluntary arrangement under the IA 1986, s 260. The scheme included the sale of the tenant's lease. The landlord as a creditor for arrears of rent argued that his agreement to the scheme would be a waiver of his right to forfeit. Hoffmann J thought that the arrangement '... was only intended to bind the creditors in their character as creditors. It did not affect proprietary rights such as those of the landlord to forfeit the lease'. Consequently he decided that the landlord's right to forfeit (subject to the court's discretion to relieve) would be preserved and the arrangement should stand. The landlord will, however, be bound by the voluntary arrangement in so far as it limits the amount of the rent recoverable.

Inactivity

Mere failure to take action does not in itself amount to a waiver by a landlord of the right to forfeit. So, in *Doe d Sheppard v Allen* (1810) 3 Taunt 78, where a landlord failed to take action for six years while the tenant used the premises in breach of the terms of the lease, in the absence of evidence of acceptance of rent it was held that the landlord had not waived his right to forfeit. But the facts may show that the landlord intended to take no action upon the breach and that he effectively licensed the breach (*Downie v Turner* [1951] 2 KB 112, CA).

Distraining for rent whenever due

If after a right to forfeit has arisen the landlord chooses to distrain for rent this normally shows that the lease is continuing, since distress can only be levied while there is a lease, and by the distress the landlord waives the right to forfeit (*Doe d David v Williams* (1835) 7 C & P 322). This is so even if the distress was in respect of rent due for a period which has expired, since this does not alter the fact that the distress is a recognition of the current existence of the lease.

A distress does not, however, always result in waiver, and all of the circumstances must be examined to see whether there has been an election to affirm the lease. Where, for instance, a landlord is relying upon the Common Law Procedure Act 1852, s 210 to forfeit for non-payment of rent for at least six months' arrears and without making a formal demand for rent (see para 4.4.1), it appears that distress does not amount to waiver since in this case the landlord is only allowed to forfeit if there is insufficient distress upon the premises, and in order to prove this the landlord must actually distrain (*Thomas v Lulham* [1895] 2 QB 400, CA). The same principle applies if the terms of the lease only give the landlord a right to forfeit if there is insufficient distress on the premises (*Shepherd v Berger* [1891] 1 QB 597). Another instance where a distress or purported distress will usually not amount to waiver is where the landlord's action occurs after the commencement of proceedings for possession (*Grimwood v Moss*, see above).

Exercising right to enter to repair

If a landlord relies upon a right given by the lease for him to enter to carry out repairs, he will waive the right to forfeit since by relying upon a right given by the lease he accepts its continuance (*Doe d De Rutzen v Lewis* (1836) 5 Ad & El 277). The waiver occurs as soon as the landlord serves notice upon the tenant requiring him to do the repairs within the period specified in the lease (*Doe d Morecraft v Meux* (1825) 4 B & C 606).

Service of notice to quit

If the tenancy is a periodic one and the landlord serves notice to quit; or, in the case of a fixed term lease, the landlord serves notice to operate a break clause, the action of the landlord will probably bring about a waiver (*Marche v Christodoulakis* (1948) 64 TLR 466), since the landlord is relying upon the terms of the lease. It is not clear, however, that such actions, where expressed to be done 'without prejudice' to the right to forfeit will unequivocally establish that the lease continues, since the landlord's intention is clearly that the lease should end, and the service of the notice may be served in case a forfeiture is not successful before the date specified in the notice. The same principles may apply to the service of statutory notices under the Landlord and Tenant Act 1954.

Service of section 146 notice

It was argued in *Church Comrs for England v Nodjoumi* (1985) 51 P & CR 155, that service of a notice under the Law of Property Act 1925, s 146 (see para 4.4.2), requiring a breach to be remedied was only consistent with the continuance of the lease. The argument was, of course, rejected, since the very function of such a notice is that it is a preliminary step to forfeiture.

Enforcement proceedings

Where there is a breach of a provision in a lease the landlord can elect either to enforce the terms of the lease, or to end the lease. If the landlord chooses to bring proceedings for enforcement there is a clear election to treat the lease as a subsisting one and the right to forfeit is waived (*Cardigan Properties Ltd v Consolidated Property Investments Ltd* [1991] 1 EGLR 64). Even the issuing of proceedings asking for possession or an injunction in the alternative has been ruled to result in a waiver, as not being a sufficiently unequivocal indication that the lease should end (*Calabar Properties Ltd v Seagull Autos Ltd* [1969] 1 Ch 451; cf *GS Fashions Ltd v B & Q plc* [1995] 4 All ER 899).

4.3.4 WAIVER AND CONTINUING BREACHES

The possibility of waiver is not so much of a problem for a landlord in the case of a continuing breach as in the case of once and for all breaches. A continuing breach is one where a new breach occurs each day, so that a new right to forfeit will arise one day even though the right to forfeit for the breach of the previous day has been waived. Waiver only operates in respect of past breaches and not future breaches, except perhaps if the landlord is certain that a particular breach will continue for a particular period. The principle is well exemplified by the case of *Segal Securities Ltd v Thoseby* [1963] 1 QB 887, where there was breach of a tenant's covenant to use the premises as a single household. The landlord accepted rent for a period in advance. The breach continued after the acceptance of rent but it had ceased by the end of the period covered by the advance payment of rent. The tenant argued that the landlord had waived his right to forfeit, not only in respect of past breaches, but also in respect of the whole period for which the landlord had accepted rent in advance. Sachs J rejected the tenant's argument saying:

> 'As regards continuing breaches it seems to me that, in the absence of express agreement, the acceptance of rent in advance can at highest only waive those breaches that are at the time of demand known to be continuing, and to waive them for such period as it is definitely known they will continue.'

Although acceptance of rent in advance will not necessarily constitute a waiver of the breach for the whole period of the rent, other acts amounting to waiver may be such as to show that the waiver is to operate for a period of time in the future notwithstanding a continuing breach. An example is where a landlord serves notice upon a tenant in accordance with the lease terms to remedy disrepair within a specified period, say three months. In such a case the service of the notice by the landlord will prevent the landlord from forfeiting within the three-month period even though the breach continues during that time (*Doe d Morecraft v Meux* (1825) 4 B & C 606). A fresh right to forfeit will not arise unless at the end of the period the tenant has failed to carry out the repairs.

The following division shows acts and omissions which may be regarded as once and for all or continuing breaches (assuming that they are in breach of the terms of the lease):

Once and for all breaches	*Continuing breaches*
Non-payment of rent, rates, service charge etc. (A new right to forfeit will arise each time a payment is due but not paid.)	Disrepair.
Unlawful assignment or subletting.	Unauthorised occupation by a third party (where there is no assignment or subletting).
Appointment of a receiver/trustee/liquidator.	Insolvency (in the sense of inability to pay debts (*Doe d Gatehouse v Rees* (1838) 4 Bing NC 384).

Unlawful alterations (*Iperion Investments Corpn v Broadwalk House Residents Ltd* [1992] 2 EGLR 235).

Wrongful user (*Segal Securities Ltd v Thoseby* [1963] 1 QB 887).

Use of insurance money for reinstatement (*Farimani v Gates* (1984) 128 Sol Jo 615, CA).

Failure to insure.

It may be noted that a landlord may cease to waive the right to forfeit for a continuing breach at any time provided that by his actions he is not estopped from relying upon the breach. In *Cooper v Henderson* (1982) 5 HLR 1, the tenant was in breach of a restriction upon using the premises as a residence. The landlord accepted rent for about a year without objecting, but on deciding to sell his reversion he sought to forfeit. The Court of Appeal decided that his waiver was temporary only and that he could rely upon the forfeiture clause. Cumming Bruce LJ said:

'... in the absence of such conduct as would give rise to a claim for equitable relief on the grounds of acquiescence which involves detriment or to an enforceable variation of the agreement, it was open to the landlord at any time, if he had been polite enough to allow the tenant to begin staying in the business premises with his family, to withdraw that consent at any time.'

So unless the landlord agrees a binding variation of the lease, or there is clear acquiescence in a change of circumstance, the landlord can forfeit for a continuing breach at any time. The sort of circumstance which might show acquiescence is, for example, that the landlord consented to an assignment of the lease in the knowledge that the assignee intended a use not authorised by the lease (*Downie v Turner* [1951] 2 KB 112, CA).

4.3.5 WAIVER AND OTHER REMEDIES

Although an act of a landlord which shows that the lease is to continue operates as a waiver of the landlord's right to forfeit, it does not deprive the landlord of other rights or remedies. For instance an action for an injunction or a claim for damages for the breach is not inconsistent with the continuance of the lease (*Stephens v Junior Army and Navy Stores Ltd* [1914] 2 Ch 516, CA; *Norman v Simpson* [1946] KB 158). It should be remembered, however, that some remedies, such as injunction and specific enforcement, are within the discretion of the court, which might be reluctant to exercise its discretion in some cases where the landlord has waived the right to forfeit.

4.3.6 NON-WAIVER CLAUSES

Many commercial leases contain clauses which state that rent may be accepted and other acts done without waiving the right to forfeit. Since waiver is a question of fact and law such clauses are not effective (*R v Paulson* [1921] 1 AC 271, PC) just as attempts to accept rent 'without prejudice' to the right to forfeit are unsuccessful (see above).

4.4 Preliminaries to forfeiture

In order to give the tenant the opportunity to avoid a forfeiture the law requires that the landlord should take certain steps before exercising any right to forfeit. Before forfeiting a landlord may have to demand payments due, give notice of breaches, and may have to seek leave of the court.

4.4.1 DEMAND FOR RENT

In the case of non-payment of rent the common law requires that prior to forfeiture the landlord must normally make a formal demand for rent in the following manner:

(a) the landlord or his agent must demand the exact sum,
(b) at the place specified in the lease for payment,
(c) on the date that payment is due,
(d) before and until sunset.

In most cases, however, the landlord need not comply with this antiquated rigmarole, since the need for a formal demand may be dispensed with by the terms of the lease, and most modern leases expressly provide that the landlord may forfeit for non-payment of rent whether or not a formal demand has been made. Even if there is nothing in the lease a formal demand need not be made where at least half a year's rent is in arrear and there are insufficient goods on the premises for the landlord to satisfy the arrears through distress (Common Law Procedure Act 1852, s 210), but before forfeiting it may be necessary for the landlord to levy distress so as to prove that there are insufficient goods upon the premises (*Thomas v Lulham* [1895] 2 QB 400, CA).

4.4.2 NOTICE OF OTHER BREACHES

Where the landlord is forfeiting for breach of some other obligation, such as failure to repair, the landlord must serve upon the tenant a notice under the Law of Property Act 1925, s 146 before forfeiting by action or peaceable re-entry. The notice must comply with the following:

(a) it must specify the particular breach complained of; and
(b) if the breach is capable of remedy, it must require the tenant to remedy the breach; and
(c) in any case, it must require the tenant to make compensation in money for the breach.

Upon receipt of a notice the tenant has 'a reasonable time' to remedy the breach, if it is capable of remedy, and to make reasonable compensation in money to the landlord. When serving a notice a landlord may wish to specify what time is given to the tenant to remedy the breach. It is better not to do so in the notice, since if the landlord specifies a time which in law is too short the notice will be invalid. The problem can probably be avoided by specifying in the notice that remedy must be within a 'reasonable time', and by stating in an accompanying letter what period of time the landlord considers to be reasonable in the circumstances.

Irremediable breaches

Some breaches are incapable of remedy, in which case the notice need not require the tenant to remedy the breach (e g breach of a covenant against transferring the lease). In some cases, however, it may not be clear whether or not a breach is remediable. So, for safety's sake it is better for a landlord to state in the notice that the breach should be remedied 'if remediable'. Neither, where a breach is irremediable, should it be relevant to give time to remedy the breach, although a short time, perhaps seven or 14 days, should be allowed for the tenant to consider the position and the need to apply for relief (*Horsey Estate Ltd v Steiger and Petrifite Co* [1899] 2 QB 79, CA).

The columns below show breaches which are often considered to be remediable or irremediable, although not all of the breaches listed have been the subject of a conclusive decision of the court in this respect.

Remediable breaches	*Irremediable breaches*
Insolvency (in the sense of inability to pay debts).	Bankruptcy (*Civil Service Co-operative Society Ltd v McGrigor's Trustee* [1923] 2 Ch 347).
Failure to repair.	Liquidation (*Fryer v Ewart* [1902] AC 187).
Unlawful occupation by third party (where no assignment or subletting).	Unlawful assignment or subletting (*Scala House Ltd v Forbes* [1974] QB 575, CA).
User for other than permitted use.	Immoral user (*Rugby School (Governors) v Tannahill* [1935] 1 KB 87).
Wrongful alteration (but see *Billson v Residential Apartments Ltd* (1990) 60 P & CR 392; revsd [1992] 1 AC 494, HL).	

In the case of insolvency, if the event triggering forfeiture is appointment of a receiver, or the making of an order for bankruptcy, administration or liquidation, the breach is irremediable and the tenant need not be given time to remedy the breach before the landlord proceeds to forfeit, but the landlord should, before forfeiting, consider whether leave of the court is needed to proceed (see below).

It is not always easy to decide whether or not a breach is remediable or not. It might be thought for example that where the lease provides that the tenant should request the landlord's consent prior to doing alterations or prior to some other event, any breach is irremediable since once the works are done the prior consent of the landlord cannot be requested (see at first instance *Billson v Residential Apartments Ltd* (1990) 60 P & CR 392; revsd [1992] 1 AC 494, HL). It has been determined, however, that such breach is capable of remedy so long as the mischief (e g unauthorised alterations) can be removed or rectified (*Savva v Houssein* [1996] 2 EGLR 65, CA).

Continuing breaches

A section 146 notice must be served both in the case of a once and for all breach, and in the case of a continuing breach. It has been argued in the case of continuing breaches that if a notice has been served, and the right to forfeit for the breach is subsequently waived, then the notice becomes inoperative and if the breach continues after the waiver the landlord must serve a further notice under section 146. The courts (*Penton v Barnett* [1898] 1 QB 276, CA; *Greenwich London Borough Council v Discreet Selling Estates Ltd* (1990) 61 P & CR 405, CA) have rejected this argument, and it is clear that a notice may continue to be relied upon by the landlord notwithstanding a temporary waiver of a continuing breach.

Forfeiture for insolvency

Where the landlord is relying upon the tenant's bankruptcy or liquidation as the ground for forfeiting, the position in respect of service of a section 146 notice is governed by the Law of Property Act 1925, sub-ss 146(9) and (10), and is somewhat complicated. In the following cases no section 146 notice is required prior to forfeiture for the bankruptcy or liquidation of the tenant; i e where the lease is of:

(a)   agricultural or pastoral land;
(b)   mines or minerals;
(c)   a house used or intended to be used as a public house;
(d)   a house let as a dwelling, with the use of furniture or any chattels;
(e)   property with respect to which the personal qualifications of the tenant are of importance for the preservation of the value or character of the property, or on the ground of neighbourhood to the lessor, or any person holding under him.

In the cases of a lease other than that mentioned above the Law of Property Act 1925, s 146(10) provides:

'Where a condition of forfeiture on the bankruptcy [or liquidation] of the lessee or on taking in execution of the lessee's interest is contained in any lease ... then –

(a) if the lessee's interest is sold within one year from the bankruptcy or taking in execution, this section applies to the forfeiture condition aforesaid;

(b) if the lessee's interest is not sold before the expiration of that year, this section only applies to the forfeiture condition aforesaid during the first year from the date of the bankruptcy or taking in execution.'

The effect of the section appears to be as follows:

(i)   In a case where the landlord is proceeding to forfeit against the insolvent tenant during the first year of the bankruptcy or liquidation the landlord must serve a section 146 notice upon the tenant. If the landlord is proceeding against the insolvent tenant after the first year, the landlord does not need to serve notice (*Civil Service Co-operative Society v McGrigor's Trustee* [1923] 2 Ch 347, 355).

(ii)   In a case where the trustee in bankruptcy or liquidator has sold the lease, and the landlord wishes to forfeit the lease in the hands of the purchaser, whether or not a section 146 notice is necessary depends upon when the landlord is proceeding and when the lease was sold:

a)   If the landlord is proceeding to forfeit within the first year of the bankruptcy or liquidation a section 146 notice must be served upon the assignee.

b)   If the landlord is proceeding to forfeit after the first year and the lease was sold during the first year a section 146 notice must be served upon the assignee.

c)   If the landlord is proceeding to forfeit after the first year and the lease was not sold until after the first year a section 146 notice need not be served upon the assignee.

The reference in section 146 to the lease being 'sold' includes a contract for sale within the year, but probably not a conditional contract, at least where the contract is a device for obstructing the landlord in enforcement of the right to forfeit (*Re Henry Castle & Sons Ltd* (1906) 94 LT 396). It is possible that the courts might recognise a conditional contract for the purpose of the section if it is entered into bona fide and if the condition is, for example, the obtaining of the landlord's consent to the assignment, since, it is submitted, the landlord should not be able to obstruct the sale so as to take the sale outside of the one-year period by delaying or withholding consent.

It should be noted that if the sale has been done with the landlord's consent there will almost certainly have been a waiver by the landlord of the right to forfeit for the insolvency. If landlord's consent is needed by the terms of the lease but has not been obtained, there will be an additional breach of the lease terms which will give the landlord an extra ground upon which to forfeit.

It should further be noted that section 146 refers to the 'bankruptcy' of the tenant, but by the Law of Property Act 1925, s 205, 'bankruptcy' is defined to include the winding up of a company. The term will embrace both compulsory and voluntary winding up (*Horsey Estate Ltd v Steiger and Petrifite Co* [1899] 2 QB 79, CA). So, in all these cases the operation of section 146 is modified as explained above.

It has been contended that no notice need be served if the insolvency being relied upon is the insolvency of a surety for the tenant, the supposed justification for the contention being that such insolvency is involuntary and outside of the tenant's control, and that as a matter of construction section 146 only applies to voluntary breach of covenant or condition. The suggestion was thrown out by Goulding J in *Halliard Property Co Ltd v Jack Segal Ltd* [1978] 1 All ER 1219, where he decided that a landlord who had omitted to serve a section 146 notice in respect of the surety's insolvency should not be able to rely upon it as a ground for forfeiting.

4.4.3 NOTICE TO SUBTENANTS AND MORTGAGEES

The basic rule is that it is not necessary for a landlord to notify any subtenant or mortgagee of a decision to forfeit, and this rule still applies in the unlikely event that the landlord proceeds by way of a peaceable re-entry. But where the landlord is proceeding by action any subtenant or mortgagee is entitled to be served with a copy of the particulars of claim (CPR Sch 2 CCR Ord 6, r 3).

4.4.4 LEAVE OF THE COURT

In some cases the landlord must also obtain the leave of the court before proceeding to terminate the lease by forfeiture. Ideally leave should be obtained prior to the forfeiture, although leave may be granted retrospectively in appropriate circumstances (*Razzaq v Pala* [1997] 1 WLR 1336). Special protection is given in cases of forfeiture for disrepair, and forfeiture where the tenant is insolvent, as appears below.

Receivership

The landlord's right to forfeit is not affected by the appointment of a receiver (whether an 'LPA receiver' or an administrative receiver), and indeed such an appointment may trigger the right to forfeit. The tenant may, of course, apply for relief from forfeiture, but subject to satisfying such terms as the court may impose (*Transag Haulage Ltd v Leyland DAF Finance plc* [1994] 2 BCLC 88; see para 4.6).

Voluntary liquidation

If the tenant is in voluntary liquidation there is similarly no direct fetter upon the landlord's right to forfeit but an application may be made to the court, by the liquidator or any contributory or creditor, to determine any question in the winding up. The court can then exercise any power which it would have in a compulsory winding up, including, under the IA 1986, s 126, the powers to stay or restrain proceedings (see para 2.5.2).

Forfeiture where tenant in administration

Where the tenant is the subject of an administration order a forfeiture of the lease by the landlord would be contrary to the spirit of the statutory moratorium. Accordingly, a landlord cannot without the leave of the court (once a petition is presented), or without the leave of the court or the consent of the administrator (once an order is made), bring court proceedings for forfeiture (IA 1986, ss 10,11).

These restrictions apply also to any attempted forfeiture by peaceable re-entry where the petition for an administration order is presented on or after 2 April 2001 (IA 1986, ss 10(1)(aa) and 11(3)(ba) – introduced by the Insolvency Act 2000, s 9). Where, however, the petition was presented before 2 April 2001 a landlord may forfeit by peaceable re-entry without the court's leave or the administrator's consent (*Re Lomax Leisure Ltd* [2000] Ch 502).

If the landlord applies for leave to forfeit there is no presumption that leave will or will not be given. The court will examine all of the circumstances in deciding whether to grant leave. The following observations on the exercise of the court's discretion were made by the Court of Appeal in *Re Atlantic Computer Systems plc* [1992] Ch 505:

(1) the landlord must make out the case for leave to be given;
(2) if granting leave is unlikely to impede the purpose for which the administration order was made, leave should be given;
(3) in other cases when a landlord seeks possession the court has to balance the legitimate interests of the landlord and the legitimate interests of the other creditors;
(4) in carrying out the balancing exercise great weight is given to the proprietary interest of the landlord. An administration for the benefit of the unsecured creditors should not be conducted at the expense of those who have proprietary rights which they are seeking to exercise, save to the extent that this may be unavoidable and even then this will usually be acceptable only to a strictly limited extent;
(5) it will normally be sufficient ground for the grant of leave if significant loss would be caused to the landlord by a refusal. For this purpose loss comprises any kind of financial loss, direct or indirect, including loss by reason of delay, and may extend to non-financial loss. But if substantially greater loss would be caused to others by the grant of leave, or loss which is out of all proportion to the benefit which leave would confer on the landlord, that may outweigh the loss to the landlord caused by a refusal;
(6) in assessing these respective losses the court will have regard to matters such as: the financial position of the company, its ability to pay the rental arrears and the continuing rentals, the administrator's proposals, the period for which the administration order has already been in force and is expected to remain in force, the effect of the administration if leave were given, the effect on the applicant if leave were refused, the end result sought to be achieved by the administration, the prospects of that result being achieved, and the history of the administration;
(7) consideration should be given to the probability of the possible consequences;
(8) the conduct of the parties and any other circumstance may be taken into account;
(9) the same considerations may be relevant in deciding whether to impose conditions if leave is granted;
(10) the same considerations may be relevant in deciding whether to impose conditions if leave is refused. Conditions may be imposed; for instance, the administrator may be ordered to pay the current rent.

These guidelines proposed by the Court of Appeal have yet to be fully applied, but they are at least for the time being of substantial assistance to landlords, administrators, and their advisers.

If a landlord, contrary to the moratorium, takes steps equivalent to forfeiture of the lease (e g be granting a lease in possession to a third party) the attempted forfeiture ought to be ineffective. If, however, the administrator is content to allow the forfeiture, the lease will be treated as at an end, and in the event of a later change of heart by the landlord the landlord cannot rely upon the moratorium to establish the continuation of the lease (*Re AGB Research plc* [1995] BCC 1091).

Forfeiture where tenant in compulsory liquidation

If the tenant is a company suffering compulsory liquidation it is not easy for the landlord to forfeit. Before forfeiting the landlord ought to consider whether it would be better to wait, since while the liquidator uses the premises the landlord should be assured of the current rent as an expense of the liquidation (para 2.3.2).

If the landlord intends to proceed to forfeit by action strictly no leave is required between presentation of a petition and the making of the order for winding up but the company, a creditor or a contributory may apply to court for a stay of proceedings. Once a winding-up order has been made or a provisional liquidator appointed, leave is required to proceed with or commence proceedings under the terms of the IA 1986, s 130(2). The court has power to give leave subject to such terms as it thinks fit. It seems that if the liquidator has no defence the court will not normally refuse a possession order (*General Share and Trust Co v Wetley Brick and Pottery Co* (1882) 20 Ch D 260, CA), since 'the company ought not, because it has become insolvent or has been minded to wind up its affairs, to be placed in a better position than any other lessee with regard to his lessor' (James LJ in *Re David Lloyd & Co* (1877) 6 Ch D 339, CA).

Assuming that the court is willing to give leave it is not necessary for the landlord to complicate matters by commencement of separate proceedings since the court has power to make a possession order on summons in the liquidation (*Re Blue Jeans Sales Ltd* [1979] 1 All ER 641). Any possession order made in the liquidation may be made notwithstanding that a third party, such as a licensee is in possession and will be affected by the order. Of course, before the order can be enforced any such person will be given an opportunity to apply to the court to establish any interest which he might claim to have in the premises. In *Re Brompton Securities Ltd (in liquidation)* (1988) 4 BCC 189, the tenant company was being wound up compulsorily by the court. The liquidator agreed to sell the lease to a guarantor of the tenant's liabilities. The guarantor paid a purchase price and went into possession, but the lease was not assigned because the landlord's consent had not been obtained. The landlord issued a summons in the winding-up proceedings and asked for a possession order, which the registrar granted. The liquidator sought to have the order set aside, partly on the basis that separate forfeiture proceedings were appropriate to enable the guarantor to seek relief. Mervyn Davies J held that the landlord was entitled to the possession order. Separate possession proceedings were not necessary and any application for relief by the guarantor could be made before the landlord enforced the possession order.

An order, if made, will be subject to subsequent applications for relief from forfeiture, by the liquidator or another party, such as a receiver of the company's property (see *Re National Jazz Centre Ltd* [1988] 2 EGLR 57).

It is not clear whether peaceable re-entry is restricted by the IA 1986, ss 126 and 130. The sections appear to contemplate actions or proceedings in court rather than out of court procedures such as forfeiture, but in *Re Memco Engineering Ltd* [1986] Ch 86, Mervyn Davies J held that distress was an action or proceeding within the meaning of the Companies Act 1948, s 231, notwithstanding that no court proceedings are necessary, and it is arguable that the same reasoning would apply in the case of forfeiture by peaceable re-entry.

Forfeiture where tenant is bankrupt

Perhaps somewhat surprisingly there is no restriction upon the landlord forfeiting where the tenant is an individual who has been adjudicated bankrupt. Although the IA 1986, s 285 provides that no person shall have any remedy in respect of a debt provable in bankruptcy the Court of Appeal has held that the remedy of forfeiture is available to a landlord (subject to the tenant's right to relief, see para 4.6) since the purpose of the legislation is to inhibit proceedings designed to enforce payment of any debt provable in bankruptcy. It has been decided that forfeiture is not a remedy designed to enforce such payment since its effect is simply to determine the lease (*Ezekiel v Orakpo* [1977] QB 260, CA).

The decision might be criticised in that prima facie it makes it possible for the landlord to take the property in preference to other creditors. It should be borne in mind, however, that the practical effect of the decision will be tempered by the fact that the trustee in bankruptcy (or, if the bankruptcy order is annulled, the tenant) will have the right to apply for relief from forfeiture (see para 4.6). Relief can be given on terms which remedy any breaches which led to the forfeiture (*Razzaq v Pala* [1997] 1 WLR 1336).

Forfeiture where tenant in voluntary arrangement

Where an individual tenant has obtained an interim order under the IA 1986, s 253 a landlord cannot commence court proceedings for forfeiture without the leave of the court (IA 1986, s 252). The same restriction will apply to forfeiture by peacable entry after implementation of the Insolvency Act 2000 (IA 1986, s 252 as amended by the Insolvency Act 2000, Sch 3). Until then, however, a forfeiture by peaceable entry is lawful without the need for a court order (*Re a Debtor (No 13A10 of 1994)* [1995] NPC 50). Similarly, if there is a company voluntary arrangement incorporating a moratorium (see chapter 1) a landlord will be unable to forfeit (whether by court proceedings or peaceable re-entry) without the leave of the court (IA 1986, Sch A1 – introduced by Insolvency Act 2000).

Forfeiture for disrepair

Where the landlord is relying upon disrepair as the ground for forfeiting there is an additional restriction (imposed by the Leasehold Property (Repairs) Act 1938) where the lease was for a term of seven years or more and at least three years remain. In this case, upon receipt of a section 146 notice the tenant (or a mortgagee in possession – *Target Home Loans Ltd v Iza Ltd* [2000] 1 EGLR 23) can within 28 days serve a counter-notice the effect of which will be that leave of the court will be required before the landlord can forfeit.

In order to obtain leave of the court the landlord must prove one of the following:

(a) that the immediate remedying of the breach in question is requisite for preventing substantial diminution in value of his reversion, or that the value thereof has been substantially diminished by the breach;

(b) that the immediate remedying of the breach is required for giving effect in relation to the premises to the purposes of any enactment, or of any byelaw or other provision having effect under an enactment, or for giving effect to any order of a court or requirement of any authority under any enactment or any such byelaw or other provision as aforesaid;

(c) in a case in which the lessee is not in occupation of the whole of the premises as respects which the covenant or agreement is proposed to be enforced, that the immediate remedying of the breach is required in the interests of the occupier of those premises or of part thereof;

(d) that the breach can be immediately remedied at an expense that is relatively small in comparison with the much greater expense that would probably be occasioned by postponement of the necessary work; or

(e) special circumstances exist which in the opinion of the court, render it just and equitable that leave should be given.

The purpose of the statute is to prevent landlords from serving exaggerated lists of dilapidations and then making the tenant forfeit the lease for non-compliance. In order to achieve this the landlord must prove more than an arguable or prima facie case for the exercise of the court's discretion; the landlord must prove a clear breach of covenant and that immediate remedy is necessary (*Associated British Ports v CH Bailey plc* [1990] 2 AC 703, HL).

4.5 Method of forfeiture

Where a breach gives rise to a right to forfeit the landlord has the option to end the lease. The option is exercised by the landlord doing some act which unequivocally and irretractably shows his intention that the lease be ended.

4.5.1 PEACEABLE RE-ENTRY

Peaceable re-entry is one such act, and in the case of commercial leases has in the past often been used. Its usefulness has, however, been reduced by modern developments. One such development is the decision of the House of Lords in *Billson v Residential Apartments Ltd* [1992] 1 AC 494, which determined that a tenant may apply for relief from forfeiture in all cases where the landlord has peaceably re-entered without a court order (see para 4.6.2). Another development hampering peaceable re-entry is the Insolvency Act 2000 which made peaceable re-entry subject to statutory moratorium in cases of administration and voluntary arrangement. Peaceable re-entry cannot be effected where the premises are residential (Protection from Eviction Act 1977, s 2), and in many cases concerning residential tenants a court order on specified statutory grounds must be obtained before the court can order possession.

Letting some third party into physical occupation is equivalent to a physical re-entry, and a landlord can effect a re-entry by an arrangement with an existing subtenant under which the subtenant is to remain in occupation as the tenant of the landlord upon the terms of a new tenancy (*Baylis v Le Gros* (1858) 4 CBNS 537). But simply changing the locks and allowing an existing subtenant to remain in occupation under the terms of the existing subtenancy is not sufficient (*Ashton v Sobelman* [1987] 1 All ER 755). Nor will the landlord be deemed to have re-entered if, unbeknown to the landlord, the tenant has been dissolved and the landlord collects rent from a new entity controlled by the same person who controlled the dissolved tenant (*Cromwell Developments Ltd v Godfrey* [1998] 2 EGLR 62, CA).

Sometimes a landlord will not want to forfeit the lease and lose the right to the rents, but the tenant may have ceased to trade from or use the premises and the landlord may wish to enter in order to secure the premises. This may safely be done provided that the landlords, or preferably its solicitors, make clear to the tenant or its receiver, administrator, liquidator or trustee that entry is for the purpose of security only (*Relvok Properties Ltd v Dixon* (1972) 25 P & CR 1, CA).

4.5.2 COURT PROCEEDINGS

Alternatively a landlord may decide to forfeit by taking court proceedings. In this case it is the service, and not the issue, of the claim which causes the forfeiture (*Canas Property Co Ltd v KL Television Services Ltd* [1970] 2 QB 433, CA). The claim must be an unequivocal request for possession. If it requests alternative remedies it is not an unequivocal election and does not forfeit the lease (*Calabar Properties Ltd v Seagull Auto* [1969] 1 Ch 451).

Where the cause of forfeiture is a wrongful assignment of the lease the landlord must, of course, serve the claim upon the assignee, since the assignment, although wrongfully, vests the lease in the assignee (*Old Grovebury Manor Farm Ltd v W Seymour Plant Sales and Hire Ltd* [1979] 1 All ER 573).

Where the premises are let at not less than three-quarters of the yearly value of the premises, and the tenant has failed to pay a year's rent and has vacated the premises, leaving insufficient distress on the property, there is a special procedure whereby the tenant can apply to a magistrates' court for a possession order (Distress for Rent Act 1737, s 16).

4.6 Relief from forfeiture

As has been mentioned above, the law leans against a forfeiture and tends to give the tenant every opportunity to remedy the breach which has given rise to the landlord's right to forfeit. The law's reluctance to permit a forfeiture manifests itself most clearly in the court's powers to relieve the tenant from a forfeiture of the lease by giving the tenant one last chance to make good the breach. So a tenant may be relieved from forfeiture for non-payment of rent upon finally paying the rent, and the tenant may be relieved from forfeiture for other breaches upon making them good in so far as is possible. Even if the breach is irremediable (see para 4.4.2) the court may still exercise its jurisdiction upon the tenant doing whatever is possible to reduce the effects of the breach.

4.6.1 PERSONS ENTITLED TO RELIEF

The current tenant can apply for relief, and this includes a person who has contracted to take an assignment of the lease even though the assignment is not complete and the person is therefore only an equitable assignee pending completion. Such a person is a 'lessee' for the purpose of the Law of Property Act 1925, s 146 (*High Street Investments Ltd v Bellshore Property Investments Ltd* [1996] 2 EGLR 40). Subtenants and mortgagees too have rights to apply for relief from forfeiture (see para 4.6.5).

4.6.2 RELIEF IN CASES OF NON-PAYMENT OF RENT

In the case of non-payment of rent the historical approach of the courts of equity has been to regard the right to forfeit simply as security for non-payment of rent, and the courts would be willing to grant relief if the tenant paid the arrears and all expenses of the landlord. The equitable jurisdiction has now been reduced by statute in some circumstances. The tenant is normally required to pay all arrears of rent but if the landlord is bound by a voluntary arrangement to accept a lesser amount it seems that relief may be given to the tenant upon paying the amount required by the voluntary arrangement (*Re Naeem (a bankrupt) (No 18 of 1988)* [1990] 1 WLR 48).

The tenant must demonstrate an ability to pay the arrears; it is not sufficient that the tenant shows that it might be able to pay on the basis of money which the tenant might receive – e g if it succeeds in a separate claim against the landlord (*Inntrepreneur Pub Co (CPC) v Langton* [2000] 1 EGLR 34).

Proceedings in the High Court

Where the landlord is proceeding in the High Court the position depends upon how much rent is in arrears. If six months' rent is in arrear the combined effect of the Supreme Court Act 1981, s 38 and the Common Law Procedure Act 1852, s 210 is that the tenant will be entitled to relief upon payment of all arrears and costs before trial, or upon payment into court. If the tenant does not pay in arrears before judgment there is nevertheless an additional right to apply for relief within six months after execution of the judgment, and the court may grant relief on such terms as to rent costs and otherwise as it thinks fit. Generally relief will be granted if the tenant pays all arrears and costs, but if there are exceptional circumstances the court might refuse relief.

If less than six months' rent is in arrears the jurisdiction under the Common Law Procedure Act 1852, s 210 is not available (*Standard Pattern Co Ltd v Ivey* [1962] Ch 432), and the tenant must rely upon the court's inherent discretion as to whether or not it will grant relief. It will normally do so upon the payment of arrears and costs. This has been criticised ((1962) 78 LQR 168), for the obvious reason that it does not make sense to give a right of relief to a tenant who owes six months' rent, but that a tenant who owes less has a mere hope that the court will exercise its general jurisdiction. The rule is, however, well established.

Proceedings in county courts

Where the landlord is proceeding in a county court the County Courts Act 1984, ss 138 and 139 provide that if the tenant pays into court not less than five clear days before the return day all rent and the costs of the action, then the action will cease. In order to have the benefit of the statute, and to have relief upon paying the arrears and the fixed costs of the action only, the tenant must make payment within the specified period, the return day being the date specified in the summons for hearing (*Swordheath Properties Ltd v Bolt* [1992] 2 EGLR 68, CA). The rent payable in order to obtain relief is all rent due and not just that in arrear at the date of service of proceedings (*Maryland Estates Ltd v Joseph* [1998] 2 EGLR 47, CA). For the period from date of service of proceedings to judgment the landlord may claim mesne profits.

Otherwise, assuming that the landlord proves his right to forfeit, the court is to order that possession be given to the landlord at the end of such period not less than four weeks from the date of the order, unless within that period (or any extension given by the court) the tenant pays into court all arrears and costs. If the tenant fails to do so the landlord is entitled to execute the order for possession. The tenant has a further right to apply for relief within six months of the date upon which the landlord takes possession and the court may grant relief upon such terms as it thinks fit.

Peaceable re-entry

Where the landlord proceeds to forfeit by peaceable re-entry upon the premises, the statutory provisions do not apply and the old rules of equity must be relied upon in both the High Court and the County Court (*Lovelock v Margo* [1963] 2 QB 786, CA). Although theoretically there is no time limit upon equity's jurisdiction to grant relief, in practice the courts will adopt as a guide the period of six months by analogy with the statute.

Refusal of relief

In exceptional circumstances a court may refuse relief even if the tenant is willing to pay all arrears of rent and costs. The court might do so where the tenant's behaviour and record has been particularly poor, or where the grant of relief would be an injustice to the landlord or a third party. If, for example, the landlord has spent considerable sums in repairing or improving the property, has let a third party into possession with a view to letting, and in reliance the third party has spent money on plant and machinery, relief may be refused (*Stanhope v Haworth* (1886) 3 TLR 34, CA).

But a landlord should not think that it will be justified in reletting to a third party as a device to avoid the court's jurisdiction. Relief will only be refused if the landlord acted reasonably in reletting. In *Silverman v AFCO (UK) Ltd* (1988) 56 P & CR 185, CA, the tenant had persistently delayed payment of rent. When the landlord began forfeiture proceedings the tenant initially indicated that it would not defend the proceedings, and the landlord proceeded with negotiations to re-let to a third party. The tenant then changed its mind and took out a summons for relief. By the time of the application for relief the tenant had not paid the arrears and only offered a post-dated cheque, without any guarantee of payment. The master hearing the application rejected the claim for relief, and the tenant did not express any intention to appeal. The landlord then granted the lease to the third party, whereupon the tenant appealed against the refusal of relief. The Court of Appeal took the view that the landlord had acted reasonably in granting the lease to the third party and that relief should not be given to the tenant, which had had ample opportunity to protect its position by payment of the arrears and costs.

If the landlord did not act reasonably in re-letting to a third party relief may be given to the tenant, but if the third party acted in good faith without notice of the tenant's right to relief the third party will be entitled to remain upon the property and relief will operate to make the tenant the immediate landlord of the third party (see para 4.6.5).

Payment by third party

In order for relief to be given the payment of rent and costs must be made by or on behalf of the tenant, and not by some stranger, such as a mere licensee. In *Matthews v Dobbins* [1963] 1 All ER 417, the Court of Appeal refused to dismiss a possession action where money had been paid into court on behalf of persons who had, apparently, no lease or sublease of the premises and whose connection with the tenant and the premises was unclear. A subtenant will have a separate right to apply for relief (see para 4.6.4), and it may be that a surety who has covenanted with the landlord that the rent will be paid either by the tenant or by the surety would be sufficiently connected with the tenant to make the payment and obtain relief. A person who has entered into an agreement to take an assignment of the lease, and who occupies the premises, is entitled to apply for relief (*Re Brompton Securities (No 2)* [1988] 3 All ER 677).

4.6.3 RELIEF IN CASES OF OTHER BREACHES

In the case of forfeiture for some ground other than non-payment of rent the tenant's right to apply for relief rests upon the Law of Property Act 1925, s 146(2) which provides as follows:

> 'Where a lessor is proceeding, by action or otherwise, to enforce such a right of re-entry or forfeiture, the lessee may, in the lessor's action, if any, or in any action brought by himself, apply to the court for relief; and the court may grant or refuse relief, as the court, having regard to the proceedings and conduct of the parties under the foregoing provisions of this section, and to all the other circumstances, thinks fit; and in case of relief may grant it on such terms, if any, as to costs, expenses, damages, compensation, penalty, or otherwise, including the granting of an injunction to restrain any like breach in the future, as the court, in the circumstances of each case, thinks fit.'

Timing of application for relief

The statutory jurisdiction to grant relief applies 'where a lessor is proceeding'. So, the right to apply for relief is exercisable where a landlord is 'proceeding, by action or otherwise'. It has been decided that this enables the tenant to apply at any time after service of a section 146 notice (*Pakwood Transport Ltd v 15 Beauchamp Place Ltd* (1977) 36 P & CR 112, CA).

The jurisdiction of the court to grant relief is available even though the landlord has exercised its right to re-enter the property peaceably (*Billson v Residential Apartments Ltd* [1992] 1 AC 494, HL). Once, however, the landlord has re-entered in execution of a court order, the tenant's right to relief is barred and there is no further right for the tenant to apply for relief.

Terms of relief

The tenant will normally be relieved upon terms that the breach is rectified in so far as that is possible. The tenant must put the breach right as soon as is possible, although in exceptional cases time will be given to the tenant. *Duke of Westminster v Swinton* [1948] 1 KB 524, was one such exceptional case in which the tenant (T) had sublet to S1, who, in turn, had sublet to S2. S2 wrongfully converted the house into flats. When the landlord brought proceedings to forfeit, T and S1 were granted relief upon condition that the house was restored to its original state within two years. Denning J took into account the fact that the permission of the local authority was necessary for the reinstatement and that it would take time to find new accommodation for the six families living in the house.

Premises for relief

Under the Law of Property Act 1925, s 146 the court has power to grant relief in respect of part only of the demised premises. It has been considered appropriate to do so where part of the premises were occupied by a subtenant for immoral purposes, but the tenant used a separate part for the purposes of its clothing business (*GMS Syndicate Ltd v Gary Elliott Ltd* [1982] Ch 1). The court gave relief in respect of the part occupied by the tenant.

Conversely, it has been deemed inappropriate to give relief in respect of part only where the party applying for relief wishes to 'cherry pick' – taking part of the premises having best value but not also other premises subject to an onerous service charge obligation (*Barclays Bank plc v Prudential Assurance Co Ltd* [1998] 1 EGLR 44).

Relief for non-payment of sums due

Where the tenant's failure is default in payment of service charge or other sums due other than rent, the court may treat the case as analagous to a case of rent default and grant relief if the tenant pays the sums due (*Khar v Delbounty NLD* [1996] NPC 163, CA).

Relief for unauthorised user

Where the breach is a wrongful user the court will order the cesser of the user, and may even order the tenant to pay an increased rent for the period of the wrongful user (*Southern Depot Co Ltd v British Railways Board* [1990] 2 EGLR 39). If the breach is a continuing one relief will only be granted upon terms that there should be no future breach. The court has no power to sanction the continuing breach (*Wrotham Park Settled Estate v Naylor* (1990) 62 P & CR 233).

Relief for breach of repair obligation

If the landlord is attempting to forfeit for decorative disrepair the Law of Property Act 1925, s 147 gives the court discretion to relieve the tenant from forfeiture if, having regard to the circumstances, and in particular the amount of the term remaining, the court is satisfied that the landlord's notice is unreasonable. But the court has no discretion where the liability arises under an express covenant or agreement to put the property in a decorative state of repair and the tenant has never done so. There is also no discretion to give relief where work is necessary for putting or keeping the premises in a sanitary condition, for the maintenance or preservation of the structure, for making a house fit for human habitation in accordance with statute or where the forfeiture relates to an agreement to yield up the house or other premises in repair at the end of the lease.

Relief for wrongful assignment/subletting

Relief may be given in the case of an unlawful assignment or subletting, even though such is an irremediable breach, but whether or not relief will be available depends upon all of the facts. If, for instance, the tenant wrongfully assigns to an insubstantial assignee the court would be hesitant to require the landlord to be satisfied with the assignee as tenant. If, however, there is a wrongful subletting, and by the time of the court hearing the tenant has managed to unscramble the situation by procuring a surrender by the subtenant, the court might well award relief (*Scala House and District Property Co v Forbes* [1974] QB 575, CA).

Immoral user

In cases of immoral user the court will not normally be willing to give relief and will exercise its discretion most sparingly, and only in exceptional circumstances (per Buckley LJ in *Central Estates (Belgravia) Ltd v Woolgar (No 2)* [1972] 3 All ER 610, CA). An instance where relief might be given is where the immoral use is by a subtenant and the tenant takes prompt steps to stop the user and forfeit the sublease (*Glass v Kencakes* [1966] 1 QB 611). In such a case consideration will be given to the value of the lease, the damage caused to the landlord, the probability that the stigma will be short-lived, whether evicting the head tenant will help remove the stigma, whether the head tenant is a satisfactory tenant, and the health of the head tenant (*Ropemaker Properties Ltd v Noonhaven Ltd* [1989] 2 EGLR 50).

Relief for deliberate breach

In exercising its discretion a court may take into account the culpability of the tenant in participating in the relevant breach and if the breach is calculated and deliberate relief may well be refused (*Crown Estate Comrs v Signet Group plc* [1996] 2 EGLR 200).

Capital value leases

It was noted in the opening paragraph of this chapter that the courts will lean against forfeiture, particularly in the case of a lease which has value, and that the House of Lords in the *Billson* case thought that the forfeiture of such a lease could amount to unjust enrichment. In assessing the justice of the case regard should be had both to the value of the lease and to whether the value of the landlord's reversion has been affected (*Iperion Investments Corpn v Broadwalk House Residents Ltd* [1992] 2 EGLR 235).

Nevertheless the onus is on the tenant to protect the asset by remedying the breach, and if the tenant does not show a willingness to put things right relief will be refused. In *Darlington Borough Council v Denmark Chemists Ltd* [1993] 1 EGLR 62, the tenant had covenanted to erect a pharmacy and surgery. The tenant erected the former but not the latter. The tenant was losing money and had no intention of complying with the covenant. The Court of Appeal refused relief notwithstanding that the landlord would receive the property back with the pharmacy building. Although there might have been some enrichment of the landlord such enrichment was not unjust in view of the tenant's lack of intent to remedy the breach.

If, however, the tenant is unable to remedy the breach the court may consider the enrichment of the landlord to be unjust and may decide to grant relief notwithstanding. In *Van Haarlam v Kasner Charitable Trust* (1992) 64 P & CR 214, the tenant was guilty of illegal use by reason of an offence under the Official Secrets Act 1989. Although the Court of Appeal decided that the breach had been waived by acceptance of rent, the Court stated, obiter dicta, that it would have been proper to relieve taking into account that the tenant had paid a premium for the lease, his use had not been offensive, and the penalty suffered by the tenant would outweigh the loss suffered by the landlord.

It is too early, however, to say whether an English court will adopt a principle of unjust enrichment to prevent a landlord from forfeiting a lease which has capital value. The Scottish courts refused to do so in *Dollar Land (Cumbernauld) Ltd v CIN Properties Ltd* [1998] 3 EGLR 79. In that case the House of Lords recognised that forfeiture of a capital value lease enriched the landlord but decided that, as such enrichment was the result of a clear contract between the parties, the enrichment was not unjust.

Personality of the tenant

If the tenant is judged not to be a proper person to continue to own the lease then the court may, in its discretion, refuse relief. In *Earl of Bathurst v Fine* [1974] 2 All ER 1160, the tenant was a foreign national who, for some unreported reason, had been banned by the Home Office from re-entering the country. The Court of Appeal considered that reason enough to refuse him relief.

4.6.4 RELIEF IN CASES OF INSOLVENCY

If forfeiture is for bankruptcy or liquidation the trustee or liquidator can only apply for relief within the first year of the bankruptcy or liquidation. So long as the application is made during the year, the court's jurisdiction to grant relief does not cease with the expiration of the year (*Gee v Harwood* [1933] Ch 712, CA; affd sub nom *Pearson v Gee and Braceborough Spa Ltd* [1934] AC 272, HL). The jurisdiction is contained within the Law of Property Act, 1925, s 146(10), which ousts any equitable jurisdiction, and if the trustee or liquidator fails to sell the lease within the year the court has no jurisdiction thereafter to relieve from forfeiture (*Official Custodian for Charities v Parway Estates Developments Ltd* [1985] Ch 151, CA).

It will generally be difficult for a company in liquidation to obtain relief, unless perhaps it is a solvent liquidation and there is no prejudice to the landlord (although even this cannot be stated as a principle); but if the liquidator has found an appropriate assignee and will, on the date of the assignment, pay the arrears, it is likely that relief will be granted (*Pakwood Transport Ltd v 15 Beauchamp Place Ltd* (1977) 36 P & CR 112, CA). If, however, the proposal is to assign the lease to an insubstantial solvent subsidiary of the insolvent tenant the court may refuse relief on the ground that the replacement of the tenant by an insubstantial assignee is not to be foisted upon the landlord (*Geland Manufacturing Co v Levy Estates Co* (1962) 181 Estates Gazette 209, see chapter 7). This is so even though there is a substantial guarantor for the assignee (*Geland Manufacturing Co v Levy Estates Co* [1962] CLY 1700).

A liquidator seeking relief does not have to issue proceedings separate to those already on foot; so the application may be made by a summons in the liquidation (*Re Brompton Securities Ltd (No 2)* [1988] 3 All ER 677).

If the tenant has entered into a voluntary arrangement binding the landlord to accept reduced arrears of rent it seems that relief may be given to the tenant upon the tenant paying the lesser amount required by the arrangement (*Re Naeem (a bankrupt)* [1990] 1 WLR 48).

Where relief not available

Under the Law of Property Act 1925, s 146(9) there is no relief from forfeiture on the ground of insolvency where the lease is a lease of any of the following:

(a) agricultural or pastoral land;
(b) mines or minerals;
(c) a house used or intended to be used as a public house;
(d) a house let as a dwelling, with the use of furniture or any chattels;
(e) property with respect to which the personal qualifications of the tenant are of importance for the preservation of the value or character of the property, or on the ground of neighbourhood to the lessor, or any person holding under him.

4.6.5 RELIEF OF SUBTENANTS AND MORTGAGEES

Insolvency of the tenant and forfeiture by the landlord will, of course, affect any mortgagee of the lease and any subtenant, since the effect of forfeiture of the lease will be to deprive the mortgagee of his security and to terminate any sublease. In order to mitigate these harsh effects mortgagees and subtenants have independent rights to apply for relief from forfeiture, so that they may retain the benefit of the property.

It should be noted, however, that the relief is only available where the landlord 'is proceeding' (Law of Property Act 1925, s 146). Thus, a mortgagee or subtenant is not entitled to apply for relief after the landlord re-enters pursuant to a court order for possession except in cases of non-payment of rent where relief may be given up to six months after execution of judgment (*United Dominions Trust Ltd v Shellpoint Trustees Ltd* [1993] 4 All ER 310, CA). A mortgagee or subtenant normally has ample opportunity to apply for relief since if the landlord proceeds to issue court proceedings the subtenant or mortgagee is entitled to be served with a copy of the claim (CPR Sch 2 CCR Ord 6, r 3), and will thereby be notified that the landlord is taking action.

If the landlord peaceably re-enters without a court order it seems likely that a mortgagee applying for relief within a reasonable time would be able to invoke the court's jurisdiction to grant relief, following the decision of the House of Lords in *Billson v Residential Apartments Ltd* [1992] 1 AC 494. It is likely that the earlier cases to the contrary cannot stand (*Egerton v Jones* [1939] 2 KB 702, CA; *Bristol and West Building Society v Turner* [1991] 2 EGLR 52) in the light of *Billson*. If a landlord does peaceably re-enter without taking proceedings it can cause a problem for a mortgagee because the landlord is not under any duty to notify the mortgagee when he peacably re-enters, and a mortgagee may therefore be unaware that the landlord is proceeding.

Sometimes a landlord might retake possession following a disclaimer of a tenant's liability by a liquidator or trustee in bankruptcy. In this circumstance a subtenant or mortgagee may opt either to apply for relief from forfeiture, or to apply under the IA 1986 for a vesting order (see chapter 6, para 6.7 and *Barclays Bank plc v Prudential Assurance Company Ltd* [1998] BCC 928).

Relief of subtenants

Relief may be available to a subtenant in one of two ways: either through reinstatement of the headlease and with it the sublease, or, independent of the head lease, by an application under the Law of Property Act 1925, s 146(4) for a vesting order, giving a fresh lease.

If relief is given by way of a vesting order the new lease created is one basically upon the same terms as the forfeited headlease but the court has a discretion as to the term, the rent and the premises.

In respect of the term the subtenant cannot require a term longer than the term of the original sublease, but the court does have a discretion to give a term of any period up to the length of the original headlease or of any period shorter than the original sublease. It is difficult to anticipate in what circumstances a court might order a shorter term than the original sublease, unless the subtenant requests a shorter term and the landlord agrees (see Tromans [1986] Conv 187). If the sublease is a business tenancy protected by the Landlord and Tenant Act 1954 the court will take into account any statutory continuation and may make a vesting order notwithstanding that the original contractual term has expired (*Cadogan v Dimovic* [1984] 2 All ER 168, CA). In these circumstances the protected subtenant will be given a monthly tenancy (*Hill v Griffin* [1987] 1 EGLR 81, CA).

If the subtenant has part only of the premises demised by the headlease the vesting order may be in respect of that part of the sublet premises only. In *London Bridge Building Co v Thomson* (1903) 89 LT 50, Joyce J would not require the subtenant of part to take a lease of the whole except by agreement. The approach was followed in *Chatham Empire Theatre (1955) Ltd v Ultrans Ltd* [1961] 2 All ER 381, but Salmon J did recognise that there might be cases where 'great hardship could be caused to the head lessor if granting relief to one or two of many subtenants would make it impossible for him to deal with the premises as a whole', so that every case must be considered on its own facts.

If there are arrears of rent, a subtenant of the whole premises who is seeking relief will probably have to pay all arrears under the headlease; but the position is not clear where the subtenant is a subtenant of part only. In spite of earlier authority (*London Bridge Building Co v Thomson*, see above) that all arrears of the head tenant had to be paid, Salmon J in *Chatham Empire Theatre (1955) Ltd v Ultrans Ltd* (see above) gave relief to a subtenant of part upon paying that part of the arrears which could be attributed to the part of the premises held by the subtenant. The point must remain a moot one until determined by a higher authority.

As far as the rent under the new lease is concerned, the court has a discretion to fix 'a fair rent (to be ascertained) of the premises comprised in the sublease, that rent being ascertained upon the basis that the rent and terms of the original lease are fair and proper and right for the whole term'. (Joyce J in *London Bridge Building Co v Thomson*, see above). Normally, a subtenant of the whole of the premises will have to pay the rent reserved by the headlease. But this is not always the case, and the court reserves to itself a wide power to assess such rent as it thinks fit. The powers assumed by the courts are best exemplified by the facts of *Ewart v Fryer* [1901] 1 Ch 499, CA. In that case a landlord let a tavern to a brewery at a rent of £300. The brewery sublet to a publican for £800, or £300 so long as the publican purchased all supplies of liquor from the brewery. The brewery's lease was forfeited for insolvency and the subtenant sought relief. The court was not willing to allow the subtenant to occupy upon payment of the head rent of £300, since it was released from the tie and would therefore benefit from the forfeiture. The Court of Appeal confirmed this view and that there should be an inquiry as to the proper rent.

The other terms of the new lease will normally be on the same terms as the forfeited headlease, at least in so far as they are relevant. If the subtenant refuses to accept a lease on the same terms the court may refuse relief. In *Hill v Griffin* [1987] (see above), the head tenant was insolvent and the premises were in substantial disrepair. The landlord forfeited the head lease and a subtenant applied for relief from forfeiture. The sublease had expired and the subtenant was protected by the Landlord and Tenant Act 1954, and was therefore only entitled to relief by way of a monthly tenancy. The landlord insisted that the subtenant should take the monthly tenancy on the terms of the forfeit headlease, including the onerous repairing obligations. The subtenant was understandably unwilling to take this responsibility, since it is not usually appropriate for a monthly tenancy to place heavy repairing obligations upon the tenant. The Court of Appeal, however, refused to give relief on other terms. The Court cited with approval the statement of Harman J in *Creery v Summersell* [1949] Ch 751:

> 'I think this remains a jurisdiction to be exercised sparingly because it thrusts upon the landlord a person whom he has never accepted as tenant and creates in invitum a privity of contract between them. It appears to me that I ought only to vest the head term in the underlessees upon the footing that they enter into covenants in all respects the same, or at least as stringent, as the covenants in the headlease ... Now this the under-lessees are not content to do; it would be useless to them; they wish to substitute for cl 4 of the headlease a new clause widening the purpose for which they may use the property. I am not prepared to oblige the plaintiff to put up with this, and therefore in this instance also I refuse relief.'

Thus, although the court has a discretion as to the terms of the new lease, it appears that the discretion will be exercised most sparingly.

The vesting does not have retrospective effect to the date of service of the court claim, but has effect from the order only and does not cause reinstatement of derivative interests (*Hammersmith and Fulham v Top Shop* [1990] Ch 237). During the interim period, whilst the subtenant's action for relief is being heard there is a 'twilight' period during which both the tenant and the subtenant are trespassers as against the landlord (see para 4.8), and for which period the landlord will be able to maintain an action against the occupiers for mesne profits.

If the relevant breach is one other than non-payment of rent the subtenant's application for relief may be made pursuant to the Law of Property Act 1925, s 146(2) as a subtenant has been held to be a 'lessee' within the terms of the subsection (*Escalus Properties Ltd v Dennis* [1996] QB 231, CA). In this case relief will be available upon the subtenant remedying the breaches of the headlease. The relief reinstates the lease and sublease with retrospective effect and the landlord cannot maintain an action for mesne profits.

It seems, however, that if there has been a disclaimer of the lease prior to forfeiture of the interest of the subtenant or mortgagee, the subtenant or mortgagee seeking relief cannot rely upon the Law of Property Act 1925, s 146(2); it is not deemed appropriate to grant relief in a manner expressed to reinstate the disclaimed lease since this might frustrate the effect of the disclaimer (*Barclays Bank plc v Prudential Assurance Co Ltd* [1998] BCC 928).

Relief of mortgagee

A mortgagee has an independent right to seek relief under the same statutory provision – the Law of Property Act 1925, s 146. The section refers to an application by an 'under-lessee', which includes a mortgagee who has taken a sublease by way of security. Nowadays most mortgages are by way of charge rather than by way of sublease, but, since a chargee by way of legal mortgage has the same rights as if there was a sublease (Law of Property Act 1925, s 87), the chargee may likewise apply for relief (*Belgravia Insurance Co Ltd v Meah* [1964] 1 QB 436, CA). If, however, the chargee has only an equitable (rather than legal) charge, the chargee has no independent right to relief in the High Court (*Bland v Ingram's Estates Ltd* [2002] 1 All ER 221, CA) but may obtain relief by joining the tenant as applicant and relying upon the tenant's right to relief.

Where relief is given to a mortgagee he holds the new lease as a substituted security for the tenant's debt. He may be entitled to possession and to sell under the terms of the charge. Meanwhile he must pay the rent and observe the other terms of the lease pending realisation of the security. The mortgagee does not take over the lease and the insolvent tenant's equity of redemption continues even though he has not applied for relief, and even though relief might have been refused to him, as a person not fit to be tenant. This appears to be a strange result, but when the court is considering giving relief to a mortgagee there is a dilemma as explained by Upjohn J in *Chelsea Estates Investment Trust Co Ltd v Marche* [1955] Ch 328:

> 'If this new lease is not treated as part of the mortgage security, then I can see no reason in law why the mortgagee should not keep his new lease and at the same time sue the plaintiffs for the whole mortgage money under the covenants in the mortgage; for the position in law can be no different from that where the leasehold security has expired not by forfeiture, but by effluxion of time; that would seem to be a hardship on the [mortgagor]. On the other hand, if the [mortgagors] are right the anomalies certainly arise the other way. It is clear that the mortgagee receiving a new lease will remain liable on the covenants throughout the residue of the term, although the mortgage might be redeemed by the mortgagor the next day. If there were an application for relief by a mortgagor, who was found to be quite unsuitable, because, for instance, he had used the demised premises as a brothel and relief was refused on that ground, but a new lease was granted to the mortgagee, as happened in the recent case before me of *Grand Junction Co Ltd v Bates*, then, if the [mortgagors] are right, if the mortgagor is in a position to redeem the mortgage, the landlord, who has been compelled to grant a new lease to the mortgagee, finds that the wholly unsuitable mortgagor is again in possession of the demised premises. That would seem strange.'

His Lordship did not see any easy way of resolving the dilemma, so, instead, he proceeded on the basis that the purpose of the legislature was to protect the mortgagee as mortgagee so that the new lease must be treated as substituted security, with the former tenant having an equity of redemption.

4.6.6 EFFECT OF RELIEF

If relief is given to a head tenant the original lease continues unaffected by the attempted forfeiture (*Dendy v Evans* [1910] 1 KB 263, CA). If before relief has been given the landlord has relet to a third party the effect of relief is that the mere equity which the tenant had to apply for relief is binding upon the third party if the third party had notice, and the tenant may repossess.

If, however, the third party had no notice of the tenant's equity to apply for relief the third party will have obtained a good right and relief will operate to make the tenant the immediate landlord of the third party (*Fuller v Judy Properties Ltd* (1991) 64 P & CR 176, CA). It is submitted that the dictum in

Bhojwani v Kingsley Investment Trust Ltd [1992] 2 EGLR 70, to the effect that the reinstated lease as a legal estate in land is binding upon the purchaser is misleading and inconsistent with *Fuller v Judy Properties Ltd.*

If relief is given subject to and with the benefit of the new lease granted, the terms of relief will probably include that the landlord should account to the tenant (or mortgagee) for any premium paid by the new occupational tenant – since such premium will likely represent value attributable to the tenant's interest in the property (*Bank of Ireland Home Mortgages v South Lodge Developments* [1996] 1 EGLR 91).

4.6.7 TRANSFER OF RIGHT TO RELIEF

The right to relief is an assignable chose in action so that it will vest in a tenant's trustee in bankruptcy, and a trustee or liquidator will be able to transfer it to a purchaser (*Howard v Fanshawe* [1895] 2 Ch 581).

4.7 Costs of forfeiture

If the landlord obtains an order for possession no doubt he will seek an award of costs in his favour in the order. On the face of it a landlord is entitled to recover the costs of forfeiture under the Law of Property Act 1925, s 146(3), which provides that a landlord shall be entitled to recover as a debt due to him 'all reasonable costs and expenses properly incurred ... in the employment of a solicitor and surveyor or valuer, or otherwise, in reference to any breach giving rise to a right of re-entry or forfeiture which, at the request of the lessee, is waived by the lessor, or from which the lessee is relieved, under the provisions of this Act'.

Thus the landlord will normally get the costs of the forfeiture. The basis of awarding costs is in the discretion of the court, which in the past has sometimes awarded them on a standard basis (*Scala House Ltd v Forbes* [1974] QB 575, CA) or on an indemnity basis (*Southern Depot Co Ltd v British Railways Board* [1990] 2 EGLR 39), and in doing so the court might be influenced by a term in the lease stating upon which basis costs are to be paid. Lord Templeman doubted whether costs of forfeiture should be awarded on an indemnity basis in *Billson v Residential Apartments Ltd* [1992] 1 AC 494.

Not only will the landlord be entitled to the costs of the forfeiture, but he will also be entitled to the costs of any application for relief, since even the relief proceedings are normally the consequence of the tenant's breach of covenant. In the case of an application for relief made by a subtenant, although the proceedings may not have ensued as a result of the subtenant's behaviour, the subtenant will normally have to pay the head landlord's costs (*London Bridge Building Co v Thomson* (1903) 89 LT 50). The landlord is entitled to costs even if the tenant responds to the landlord's section 146 notice by remedying the breach, since the Law of Property Act 1925, s 146(3) states that costs are due even if the 'lessee is relieved' from the forfeiture, and the tenant is 'relieved' where the landlord is prevented from forfeiting by the tenant's compliance with the notice (*Nind v Nineteenth Century Building Society* [1894]

1 QB 472). It should be noted, however, that where a landlord serves a section 146 notice in respect of dilapidations and the tenant serves a counter-notice under the Leasehold Property (Repairs) Act 1938, the landlord does not have the benefit of the Law of Property Act 1925, s 146(3) unless he proceeds to make an application to court for leave to forfeit. This does not, however, preclude the landlord from recovering costs if the terms of the lease oblige the tenant to pay (*Bader Properties Ltd v Linley Property Investments Ltd* (1967) 19 P & CR 620).

Although an order for costs will not normally be made against a landlord, nevertheless, the court does have a discretion, and in exceptional circumstances will make such an order. Such circumstances would include, for instance, where the landlord failed to send a letter before action, the tenant paid the arrears of rent, and the matter only proceeded because there was uncertainty as to the amount of the service charge to be paid by the tenant (*Woodtrek Ltd v Jezek* [1981] 1 EGLR 45). Another example is where the landlord has increased the costs of proceedings by unreasonably opposing relief, and a landlord might be ordered to pay the costs of an unsuccessful appeal (*Belgravia Insurance Co Ltd v Meah* [1964] 1 QB 436, CA).

4.8 Effect of forfeiture

The effect of forfeiture is to end the lease. The lease is ended from the date of re-entry or service of the claim for possession. In the latter case any court order has retrospective effect to the date of service. If, however, the tenant gets relief from forfeiture the lease will be reinstated. The position of the landlord and tenant in such circumstances was described by Parker LJ in *Liverpool Properties Ltd v Oldbridge Investments Ltd* [1985] 2 EGLR 111:

> 'There is a period of limbo during which it cannot be predicated for certainty whether the lease will ever truly come to an end, for if there is a counterclaim for relief in an action for forfeiture and that counterclaim for relief succeeds and any conditions are complied with the original lease continues. It is only when the forfeiture is operated by physical re-entry that there is a determination of the original lease. In such circumstances, if a separate claim for relief succeeds, there is then a new and separate lease upon the same terms and conditions as the old. But when the forfeiture is sought to be effected by action and the counterclaim succeeds, the original lease is reinstated as if nothing had happened.'

So, since there will be some time before any application for relief is heard, or before the tenant's right to apply for relief expires, there is a period of time during which it is not clear whether or not the lease is at an end, and this period of limbo causes some difficulty. What has been held is that during the period the landlord cannot enforce the tenant's covenants in the lease, as this would be inconsistent with the election to forfeit (*Wheeler v Keeble* [1920] 1 Ch 57), and if the forfeiture succeeds the tenant is only liable on its covenants up to the date of service of the claim (*Associated Deliveries Ltd v Harrison* (1984) 50 P & CR 91). The tenant, on the other hand, has not elected that the lease be at an end and is able to enforce the landlord's covenants (*Peninsular Maritime Ltd v Padseal Ltd* [1981] 2 EGLR 43, CA).

4.8.1 SUBTENANTS, MORTGAGEES AND THE 'TWILIGHT PERIOD'

If the forfeiture of the lease has effect but a subtenant or mortgagee obtains a vesting order there is a 'twilight' period from the date of service of the claim for possession and the vesting order when neither the tenant nor the subtenant or mortgagee has an interest in the property. The forfeiture terminates the existing lease and sublease on the date of service and the new lease in favour of the subtenant does not come into being until created by the vesting order, which does not have retrospective effect to the date of service of the claim (*Official Custodian for Charities v Mackey* [1985] Ch 168, CA; *Official Custodian for Charities v Mackey (No 2)* [1985] 2 All ER 1016). This is because the court has no jurisdiction to deprive the landlord retrospectively of his rights as the owner of the property (*Viscount Chelsea v Hutchinson* [1994] 2 EGLR 61, CA).

4.8.2 RIGHTS TO RENT AND MESNE PROFITS

During the 'twilight' period the tenant and any subtenants are trespassers against whom the landlord is entitled to proceed for mesne profits, normally calculated by reference to the letting value of the property (*Viscount Chelsea v Hutchison*, see above). Where the aggregate of rents under subleases exceeds the rent under the headlease the landlord might consider an action against the tenant or its receiver for an account of the subrents by waiving the tort of trespass (see Goff & Jones, *Law of Restitution* (4th edn) ch 38). As far as the relationship between tenant and subtenant is concerned it is not clear whether the tenant is entitled to the subrents. If the lease is forfeit the subtenants might try to recover from the tenant any rent paid during the twilight period. The subtenant could argue that money paid to the tenant or its receiver was money paid under a mistake of fact (*Official Custodian for Charities v Mackey (No 2)* [1985] 2 All ER 1016), at least where the subtenants were unaware of the forfeiture proceedings. If such an argument was to prove successful and the tenant was held not to be entitled to retain the subrents, a possible consequence for the landlord would be that any action for an account by the landlord should fail.

4.8.3 EFFECT VIS-À-VIS THIRD PARTIES

Forfeiture ends the lease vis-à-vis any party to it, even though a particular party may not have been named as defendant in proceedings which occurred prior to re-entry. In *Eaton Square Properties Ltd v Beveridge* [1993] EGCS 91, CA, the landlord brought proceedings against an assignee believed to be tenant – but an earlier tenant claimed that she was entitled to the tenancy. The landlords obtained judgment against the assignee and executed by changing locks. The earlier tenant claimed that her lease was not forfeit. The Court of Appeal rejected the former tenant's argument and ruled that peaceable re-entry was valid against her notwithstanding that she was not party to the proceedings. Forfeiture also marks an end to the lease vis-à-vis non parties – such as public bodies. This may cause, for example, the tenant to be relieved from liability from local rates and a transfer of such liability to the landlord (*Kingston Upon Thames Royal London Borough Council v Marlow* [1996] 1 EGLR 101, CA).

4.8.4 FINALITY OF FORFEITURE

A landlord should consider carefully the commercial benefit of forfeiture before embarking upon a peaceable re-entry or proceedings, since forfeiture is an unequivocal election to determine the lease and the landlord may not easily retract and keep the lease on foot once the election to forfeit is made. The point is well demonstrated by reference to *GS Fashions Ltd v B & Q plc* [1995] 1 EGLR 62. In that case a landlord elected to determine a lease for the tenant's breach of covenant in allowing a prospective assignee of the lease to occupy the premises without first obtaining the landlord's consent. The landlord served a writ to forfeit. The tenant accepted the forfeiture and required the prospective assignee to leave. The landlord, presumably then realising the commercial disadvantage of losing the tenant, wanted to withdraw the forfeiture. Lightman J decided that the lease had ended by the landlord's election to forfeit and could not be reinstated at the landlord's request. His Lordship did, however, point out that the landlord could have avoided this problem and kept his options open '... by claiming in the alternative in his writ forfeiture and relief ... which presupposes the continued existence of the lease, leaving his election between remedies ... to the trial ...' (but see *Calabar Properties Ltd v Seagull Autos Ltd* [1969] 1 Ch 451).

Although a landlord cannot unilaterally reinstate a lease which he has elected to forfeit, the reinstatement of the lease can be achieved by mutual consent by the landlord and tenant agreeing to dismiss the forfeiture action (*Hynes v Twinsectra Ltd* [1995] 35 EG 136, CA).

4.8.5 RIGHTS TO FIXTURES

A tenant's right to remove tenant's fixtures endures only so long as the lease subsists. Forfeiture therefore ends the tenant's right to remove tenant's fixtures and once a landlord has peaceably re-entered the tenant does not have the right to access the property to remove such fixtures (*Re Palmiero, Debtor (No 3666 of 1999)* [1999] 38 EGLR 27).

4.9 Rescission of lease

A lease possesses the dual nature of being both an interest in land and a contract. In certain circumstances a contract may be rescinded, usually if the parties entered into it upon the basis of some mistake. In the case of insolvency there is a special jurisdiction permitting the High Court or any county court to rescind contacts entered into by a person who is subsequently adjudged bankrupt (IA 1986, s 345), or entered into by a company which has gone into liquidation (IA 1986, s 345). It is arguable that a lease is a 'contract' within the meaning of the section, and that a landlord can apply to have the lease rescinded, although there is no reported case applying to a lease. If a contract is rescinded the other party to it may prove for damages in the winding up or bankruptcy.

4.10 Appointment of receiver by court

In some cases a landlord who is proceeding to forfeit may be concerned that the tenant is not taking proper care of the property. If it is necessary for the preservation of the property the landlord will be able to obtain an interlocutory order for the appointment of a receiver by the court under the jurisdiction of the Supreme Court Act 1981, s 37. The sort of case in which this might be useful is where it is necessary to preserve the premises as an hotel, restaurant or public house, and it is necessary to preserve licences necessary for the carrying on of business at the property (*Charrington & Co Ltd v Camp* [1902] 1 Ch 386; *Leney & Sons Ltd v Callingham and Thompson* [1908] 1 KB 79, CA). Another possible example is where the premises are sublet in multiple occupation in which case it may be necessary as a temporary expedient to appoint a receiver to deal with the provision of services and management of the premises.

4.11 Law reform

As is shown above the law of forfeiture is very complex, and it may be argued that some of its rules operate illogically or unfairly. The Law Commission (see Law Com 221, 1994 and Law Com consultation paper, 1998) has identified a number of defects which it recommends should be reformed. It has recommended abolition of the strict doctrine of waiver in favour of a rule that the landlord would lose the right to forfeit by conduct which is such as to show that he does not intend to forfeit; and abolition of the different procedures for forfeiture and relief for non-payment of rent and other breaches.

In place of the present system there would be a new regime whereby a landlord would in most cases have to apply to the court for a 'termination order'. The court would normally grant a 'remedial order', a sort of termination order nisi, providing that the lease will end on a specified date unless the tenant remedies the breach. In exceptional cases the court might make a termination order absolute, that the lease will end unconditionally on a specified date. Also, in certain cases the right to re-enter physically without court order would remain available but subject first to having served notice requiring remedial action.

CHAPTER 5

Liability of original tenant, assignees and sureties

The problems encountered by a landlord in enforcing rights against an insolvent tenant (see chapters 2–4) can often be circumvented by pursuing claims for rent and other breaches against other persons who are responsible for the performance of the obligations in the lease. The law relating to such claims was the subject of overhaul by the Landlord and Tenant (Covenants) Act 1995, and a distinction must be made between 'new tenancies' and old tenancies (see para 5.1.6 below). The following third parties may be responsible to the landlord for the failure of the insolvent tenant:

(a)   an original tenant (where the lease has been assigned and it is the ultimate assignee who is insolvent);
(b)   an intermediate assignee (where the lease has been assigned several times);
(c)   a surety for the current tenant or a former tenant; and
(d)   a mortgagee of the lease who is in possession (in the case of a 'new tenancy' – Landlord and Tenant (Covenants) Act 1995, s 15).

If there is any such person or persons remaining liable a landlord will be able to seek recovery from both the insolvent tenant and the other person or persons. If the other person or persons are solvent, it makes economic sense for the landlord to require payment of them immediately rather than to bother with what is likely to be a partially or wholly unsuccessful claim against the current tenant. Whether such persons may be pursued depends partly upon contract (upon the terms of the lease and any associated written or oral agreement) and partly upon the statutory limitations which have been imposed by the Landlord and Tenant (Covenants) Act 1995 and which are explained below.

If there are a number of different persons to whom the landlord can look for payment the landlord can choose freely which to pursue, and is not obliged to look first to the person who might be regarded as having primary liability. Suppose, for instance, the lease has been assigned by the original tenant (T) to an assignee (A), and there is a surety (S) for the assignee. Upon the default and insolvency of A the landlord can choose to pursue a claim against T only (assuming that T remains liable). The landlord is not under any obligation to seek payment from S before looking to T (*Norwich Union Life Insurance Society v Low Profile Fashions Ltd* (1991) 64 P & CR 187, CA).

5.1 Liability of original tenant

An original tenant is prima facie liable upon the terms of the lease for the whole of the term even though he later assigns the lease to a third party. In some cases, however, the tenant may be released from liability upon assignment, either because an agreement between the landlord and tenant so provides or by dint of statute (see para 5.1.6).

5.1.1 BASIS OF LIABILITY

The basis for the tenant's continuing liability is simply that he is liable upon the contract which he entered into with the landlord. By entering into the lease contract the tenant covenants that for the period of the lease its terms will be complied with (*Walker's Case* (1587) 3 Co Rep 22a). The original tenant is liable for performance of all of the terms of the lease, whether by himself or any later assignee, since the tenant's covenant is normally in such form that neither the tenant nor any of his successors in title will breach the obligations.

Even if the tenant does not expressly covenant 'for himself and his successors in title' it will be implied (except where the lease is a 'new tenancy') that the tenant is agreeing to be liable for his successor's default by the terms of the Law of Property Act 1925, s 79 which states that any covenant which relates to land is deemed to be made by the covenantor on behalf of himself and his successors, unless the lease expresses a contrary intention. Occasionally, but rarely, a lease does express such a contrary intention. A landlord's adviser must therefore check the terms of the lease in order to ascertain whether the original tenant is liable for the breaches of an insolvent assignee. Section 79 does not apply in relation to a 'new tenancy' (the Landlord and Tenant (Covenants) Act 1995, s 30) and in the absence of an express covenant by the tenant on behalf of its successors in title it is not clear, in respect of such tenancies, whether there will be any continuing liability following assignment (see para 5.2.1). The decision in *Walker's Case* (see above) might be relied upon by the landlord, but it would be best if the lease were to contain an express covenant.

5.1.2 EXTENT OF LIABILITY

The tenant's liability includes a liability for any changes in circumstances for which the lease provides, since the tenant has contracted to be liable in such circumstances. Thus, the tenant is not only liable for the initial level of rent, but if there is a rent review clause in the lease and the rent has been increased since an assignment, the tenant is liable for the level of the increased rent upon a default in payment by the assignee (*Centrovincial Estates plc v Bulk Storage Ltd* (1983) 46 P & CR 393). Similarly, if a lease contains an option for extension or renewal, and the option is exercised by an assignee, the original tenant will be liable upon the lease for the period of the extension (*Baker v Merckel* [1960] 1 QB 657, CA).

The original tenant's liability will include liability for payment of interest on late payments where the lease so provides. In the absence of a clause requiring payment of interest the landlord may rely upon the Supreme Court Act 1981, s 35A, but in this case a court is likely to award interest only from the date that the landlord makes a demand of the original tenant (*Estates Gazette Ltd v Benjamin Restaurants Ltd* [1995] 1 All ER 129, CA).

It is no defence that the original tenant is not in a position to prevent a breach of the terms of the lease by an assignee. So the original tenant is responsible if the ultimate assignee fails to deliver up the premises, or fails to deliver them up in good repair (*Thames Manufacturing Co Ltd v Perrotts (Nichol & Peyton) Ltd* (1984) 50 P & CR 1). The original tenant may, however, have protection through rights of indemnity and subrogation (see para 5.4) or through release from liability (see paras 5.1.6 and 5.1.7).

Liability during statutory continuation

Where a business lease protected by the Landlord and Tenant Act 1954 has been assigned, the contractual term has expired, and the assignee remains in occupation by right of a statutory continuation, the issue may arise as to whether the original tenant remains liable during the statutory continuation. In one decision (*City of London Corpn v Fell* [1993] QB 589, CA) it was held that a tenant was not liable during the period of statutory continuation. In that case the contractual term of ten years was referred to in the lease as 'the term'. The Court of Appeal decided that the Landlord and Tenant Act 1954 continued the tenancy but not the term, and that the tenant's liability during the term did not include liability for the period of statutory continuation of the tenancy. The result was different in *Herbert Duncan Ltd v Cluttons* [1993] QB 589 where the wording of the lease was such that the term was defined to include any statutory extension (cf the position of a surety, para 5.3.1). Accordingly the Court of Appeal held that the original tenant was liable for the contractual rent during the statutory continuation.

Assuming that the original tenant does remain liable the liability will not, however, extend to liability to pay any interim rent fixed by the court under the Landlord and Tenant Act 1954 (*Herbert Duncan Ltd v Cluttons*, see above) unless the lease expressly so provides.

Death/bankruptcy/liquidation of original tenant

Generally, if a contracting party dies he is not discharged from contractual obligations, which continue to affect his estate (Law Reform (Miscellaneous Provisions) Act 1934 and see Williams, *Executors, Administrators and Probate*, 16th edn, p 433). Thus if the former tenant has died his estate is probably liable by privity of contract for the duration of the lease (*Youngmin v Heath* [1974] 1 All ER 461, CA). The general rule may be excluded by an express provision to the contrary (Roxburgh J in *Kennewell v Dye* [1949] Ch 517), and some leases do provide that the former tenant is to be released from liability upon death.

It is not absolutely clear whether bankruptcy of the former tenant discharges the tenant from liability. It has been held that the liability of a surety is not discharged on bankruptcy, and the position of a former tenant is analogous to that of a surety (see *Boyd v Robins* (1859) 5 CBNS 597). But it is more likely that the former tenant's liability should be the subject of proof, as a contingent liability and that if the landlord fails to prove in the bankruptcy the debt is discharged (see *Hardy v Fothergill* (1888) 13 App Cas 351, HL and *James Smith & Sons (Norwood) Ltd v Goodman* [1936] Ch 216, CA).

Where the former tenant is a company in liquidation the dissolution of the company will deprive the landlord of the benefit of the company's covenant. Accordingly it has been held that the landlord is able to prove in the liquidation for the loss of the right of indemnity (*James Smith & Sons (Norwood) Ltd v Goodman*, see above), being the difference between the value of the lease with or without the right of indemnity against the former tenant (*Re House Property & Investment Co* [1954] Ch 576). In calculating the quantum of the loss the financial position of the assignee will be taken into account (*Cohen v Popular Restaurants Ltd* [1917] 1 KB 480).

If the landlord does not receive notice of the liquidation of the former tenant and the dissolution of the former tenant is complete, the landlord can apply to court to have the dissolution avoided so as to make a claim against the company. There will usually be little point in avoiding the dissolution since more often than not all of the company's assets will have been distributed and distributions which have been properly made cannot be set aside. In exceptional cases, however, assets may become available out of which a claim may be met (*Stanhope Pension Trust Ltd v Registrar of Companies* [1994] 1 BCLC 628, CA).

The landlord cannot usually forfeit the lease for the insolvency of the former tenant (*Smith v Gronow* [1891] 2 QB 394).

5.1.3 EFFECT OF SUBSEQUENT VARIATION OF THE LEASE

Although the original tenant has sometimes been dubbed a 'quasi surety', his responsibility differs from that of a surety in that it is viewed as a 'primary' liability rather than the secondary liability which a surety has (see para 5.3 below). Rowlatt on the *Law of Principal and Surety*, 5th edn, p 6 explains that:

> 'The covenant of the lessee is not collateral to the liability of the assignee of the lease, to pay if he does not, but is a covenant that the lessee or his assignee shall pay ... The liability of the assignee to the lessor upon the privity of estate is, as regards the lessee, an accident.'

No discharge

Because of this 'primary' liability the tenant is not so easily discharged from his duties as 'quasi surety' as a normal surety would be. A guarantor, for instance will normally be discharged if a co-surety has been released by the creditor (but see para 5.3.2); but if a landlord releases a surety of a lease from an obligation to pay rent arrears the original tenant is not necessarily discharged from the obligation to pay the arrears (*Allied London Investments Ltd v Hambro Life Assurance Ltd* [1984] 1 EGLR 16).

Since the original tenant is a 'quasi surety' one might also have thought that he, like any ordinary surety, would be discharged following any variation of the terms of the lease agreed between the landlord and an assignee. In *Baynton v Morgan* (1888) 22 QBD 74, however, an assignee surrendered part of the premises to the landlord. A later assignee became bankrupt and the landlord sued the original tenant for an apportionment of rent for the retained premises. The Court of Appeal held that the variation by the assignee did not release the tenant from liability, and the tenant was liable for the rent.

Liability for increased obligations?

Sometimes a lease variation will increase the tenant obligations. It should be noted that the former tenant's continuing liability will normally be limited to the terms of the original contract and that variations agreed between the landlord and assignee will not bind the former tenant. Suggestions to the contrary in *Selous Street Properties Ltd v Oronel Fabrics Ltd* [1984] 1 EGLR 50, and in *GUS Property Management Ltd v Texas Homecare Ltd* [1993] 27 EG 130, have recently been disapproved of by the Court of Appeal. In *Friends Provident Life Office v British Railways Board* [1996] 1 All ER 336, a landlord and assignee varied a lease to permit the assignee to grant sub-tenancies and licences more freely; in return for the relaxation of the lease terms the assignee agreed to pay an increased rent. A subsequent assignee then defaulted in payment of the increased rent, whereupon the landlord sought to recover the increased rent from the original tenant. The Court of Appeal decided that the original tenant remained liable following the variation – but only to the extent of the original rent and not to the extent that it had been increased. It appears that the principle is that after assignment an original tenant who has not been released remains liable on all of the original terms by virtue of privity of contract, but after assignment he is no longer privy to the estate and any alterations made to it do not affect him. The rule in *Baynton v Morgan* is not that the 'tenant was bound by the estate as altered irrespective of the terms of the original contract ... [but] that the tenant was bound by the original contract notwithstanding alterations to the estate' ([1984] Conv 443).

The original tenant's continuing liability on the lease terms will, however, include liability for changes in circumstances which have been provided for in the contract, e g an increase in rent pursuant to a rent review clause (*Centrovincial Estates plc v Bulk Storage Ltd* (1983) 46 P & CR 393). If, however, the landlord and assignee depart from the lease rent review procedure and agree a stepped rent this might constitute a variation for which the former tenant is not liable (see *Beegas Nominees Ltd v BHP Petroleum Ltd* [1998] 2 EGLR 57, CA).

The rule in *Friends Provident* (see above) may, however, give rise to difficulties in some circumstances. Suppose, for instance, a landlord and an assignee of the lease agree to vary the lease by increasing the tenant's repairing obligations and decreasing the rent. On the basis of *Friends Provident* it might be argued that the landlord could, by virtue of the contract, sue the original tenant for the balance of the original rent while enjoying the benefit of the assignee's increased repairing responsibilities. However, in most cases the assignee will have covenanted with the original tenant (see para 5.4.1) to indemnify the original tenant against the landlord's claim. The assignee could then end up paying the full amount (indirectly) and have an increased repairing liability, and the basis of the variation will have been frustrated. In such circumstances, in order to give business efficacy to the variation, the law might imply a restraint upon the landlord pursuing the original tenant. In order to avoid the complications of these arguments, an assignee should ensure that any deed of variation contains appropriate provisions to deal with any such potential problem.

Statutory restriction upon increased liability

The position is now further affected by the Landlord and Tenant (Covenants) Act 1995, s 18 which provides (in relation to lease variations after 1 January 1996) that any former tenant of a lease is not liable to pay any amount to the extent that the amount is referable to any 'relevant variation' of the lease agreed between the landlord and an assignee. Further, if the lease is a 'new tenancy' and the former tenant's continuing liability is under an 'authorised guarantee agreement' only, the variation may completely discharge the former tenant since s 16(8) of the 1995 Act declares that the rules of law relating to the release of sureties are (subject to its terms) applicable to an authorised guarantee agreement just as they are in respect of any other guarantee agreement.

A variation is a relevant one if the landlord has at the time of variation an absolute right to refuse it. A variation is also relevant if the landlord originally had an absolute right to refuse such variation if requested by the former tenant but since the assignment of the lease there has been a variation which has deprived the landlord of such right as against the assignee. For example, the lease may have contained an absolute restriction upon change of use but may have relaxed this to a qualified restriction not to change use without the landlord's consent, such consent not to be unreasonably withheld. If the landlord later consents to a change of use it is suggested that the consent may amount to a relevant variation within the meaning of the Landlord and Tenant (Covenants) Act 1995, so that the former tenant will not be liable for any increase in rent to the extent that the increase is referable to the new permitted use.

In the common case where a tenant seeks consent to assignment and variation or change of use at the same time a landlord might consider ensuring that the relaxation in respect of use is given in favour of the tenant immediately prior to the assignment so as to ensure that the assigning tenant is bound by the lease as varied and any later rent review to the full extent.

Implied surrender and regrant

Sometimes an agreed variation of the lease is so fundamental that in law it can only have effect through an implied surrender of the existing lease and the implied grant of a new lease. This will occur if the extent of the property let is increased, or if the duration of the lease is lengthened. In such cases the implied surrender should be sufficient to discharge the original tenant. The principle does not, however, apply if a lease is lengthened by an assignee exercising an option to extend the lease, which had been given to the original tenant (*Baker v Merckel* [1960] 1 QB 657, CA). Neither does the principle apply simply because the covenants in the lease have been varied and the rent increased (*Friends Provident Life Office v BRB*, see above).

5.1.4 EFFECT OF DISCLAIMER

Upon a disclaimer of the lease by a liquidator or a trustee in bankruptcy for the assignee the original tenant's liability will remain, but the original tenant may be able to obtain an order vesting the lease in him or some other party, e g in a sub-tenant or mortgagee. The original tenant's rights are considered in depth in chapter 6 (para 6.6.1).

5.1.5 EFFECT OF VOLUNTARY ARRANGEMENT BY ASSIGNEE

A voluntary arrangement on the part of the assignee does not reduce the liability of the former tenant to the landlord (*RA Securities Ltd v Mercantile Credit Co Ltd* [1995] 3 All ER 581 and *March Estates plc v Gunmark Ltd* [1996] 2 EGLR 38). The former tenant has the right to claim in full for its indemnity against the assignee (*Mytre Investments Ltd v Reynolds* [1995] 3 All ER 588), and will be able to proceed against the assignee in the usual way notwithstanding the voluntary arrangement (*Re a Debtor (No 64 of 1992)* [1994] 2 All ER 177).

5.1.6 STATUTORY RELEASE OF LIABILITY

An original tenant under a 'new tenancy' will usually benefit from a statutory release of liability upon an assignment of the lease (Landlord and Tenant (Covenants) Act 1995, ss 5 and 11). A new tenancy is one granted after 1 January 1996 (being the date of commencement of the Landlord and Tenant (Covenants) Act 1995) except:

(a) where it is granted pursuant to an agreement or option (including a right of pre-emption) entered into before that date; or
(b) where it is granted pursuant to a court order made before that date; or
(c) where it is an overriding lease granted pursuant to the Landlord and Tenant (Covenants) Act 1995, s 19 in relation to a tenancy which is not a new tenancy.

In addition it should be noted that a new tenancy may arise upon a variation of an existing tenancy if such variation is fundamental enough to give rise to an implied surrender and regrant (Landlord and Tenant (Covenants) Act 1995, s 1(5)).

The tenant is released from the 'tenant covenants', including any 'term condition and obligation' and any term of any collateral agreement, including any agreement for lease – but only if the covenant falls 'to be complied with by the tenant of premises demised by the tenancy' (Landlord and Tenant (Covenants) Act 1995, s 28). The release is a release in respect of future liability only and does not affect liability for existing breaches of obligation (1995 Act, s 24(1)).

A release is not, however, available (1995 Act, s 11) if the assignment of the lease is in breach of a covenant of the lease, nor if the assignment is by operation of law (e g a vesting of a bankrupt's lease in a trustee in bankruptcy). Such assignments are termed 'excluded assignments' and in such cases the tenant remains liable upon the lease until the next assignment (if any) which is not an excluded assignment.

Sometimes a tenant may unlawfully assign a lease without consent but then obtain a retrospective licence from the landlord. It is not clear, under the new law, whether the giving of such licence will automatically result in a release. If not then the question may arise as to whether the landlord can reasonably refuse a release upon the giving of such retrospective licence.

Even though a tenant under a new lease will usually benefit from the statutory release, he may in some circumstances be required to enter into an 'authorised guarantee agreement' by which a degree of liability is retained for the period that the incoming assignee is liable under the lease (see chapter 7, para 7.3).

5.1.7 STATUTORY RESTRICTION UPON ENFORCEMENT OF LIABILITY

A former tenant's liability for arrears of rent, service charge and interest for late payment is subject to the usual time limits upon enforcement contained in the Limitation Act 1980. It has often been thought that these time limits were unfair to former tenants who often were unaware of the defaults of assignees, and sometimes landlords allowed arrears of rent to mount for months or years before notifying former tenants of the problem. Since 1 January 1996, landlords have had to comply with the Landlord and Tenant (Covenants) Act 1995, s 17 which provides that a former tenant is not liable for rent, service charges or liquidated sums such as default interest unless, within the period of six months from the date when the sums become due, the landlord serves a written notice upon the former tenant in prescribed form or a form substantially to the same effect.

Sometimes it will be difficult for a landlord to ascertain precisely how much is due (particularly in the case of service charges). If so, the landlord may serve the statutory notice while notifying the tenant that the liability may be later determined at a sum greater than that known at the date of notice. Provided that the landlord then serves a further notice within three months beginning with the date upon which the further sum is determined, the landlord may recover the further sum so specified.

There is a transitional provision so that sums which became due prior to 1 January 1996 are treated as having become due on that date. The statutory restrictions on recovery do not, however, apply where proceedings for recovery of the sums due were commenced before 1 January 1996.

As to method of service, it appears that a notice is validly served if sent by recorded delivery in time – even if the mail is not actually delivered because there is no one at the relevant address to accept service on behalf of the former tenant (*Commercial Union Life Assurance Co Ltd v Moustafa* [1999] 2 EGLR 44).

5.1.8 EFFECT OF PAYMENT BY SURETY

If a surety makes a payment of rent or other sums due under a lease, the tenant's liability will be reduced to the extent of such payment. The landlord cannot, in order to preserve the right to pursue the tenant for the full amount of the original sums due, maintain that the payment by the surety is a contractual payment of indemnity which does not diminish or avert default on the part of the tenant (*Milverton Group Ltd v Warner World Ltd* [1995] 2 EGLR 28, CA).

The surety payment is treated as payment of sums due under the lease. This is so even if the payment is made in consideration of the release by the landlord of the surety's obligation. In *Milverton Group Ltd v Warner World Ltd* (see above), the lease had been assigned and the ultimate tenant became insolvent. Some payments were in arrears and the lease still had time to run – so future payments were yet to become due. The landlord released three guarantors from their obligations in consideration of payments which were, in total, greater than the arrears but less than the aggregate of the arrears and all future payments due. The future dilapidations liability was not yet quantified. The landlord then pursued the original tenant for all sums which had become due under the lease. The original tenant argued that the landlord should give credit for the sums which had been received from the sureties. The Court of Appeal accepted this argument in respect both of payments which were already due and in respect of future liabilities. The court considered that the landlord would be 'unjustly enriched' if he obtained payments from the sureties for their release while remaining entitled to the full debt from the original tenant.

There must be some doubt as to whether the court's decision in *Milverton* is sound. Insofar as a release payment may be attributed to sums already due under the lease it is difficult to see what value is received by the landlord in return for the release of the surety. In the absence of any benefit to the landlord, the landlord might as well demand payment under the surety agreement and keep the surety on the hook; accordingly, the court's decision is likely to have the effect of discouraging landlords from agreeing to release sureties.

To the extent that a release payment may be attributable to future liabilities, it could be argued that a landlord receives consideration for the release by virtue of having received some payment early. Since, however, the court in *Milverton* held that the tenant was entitled to be credited with interest from the date of receipt of the release payment until the date upon which the lease payment fell due, the landlord will not even have the commercial benefit of interest on the money. It would appear that the only possible consideration received by the landlord is the security of having the money early and a cash flow advantage – assuming the payment does become the immediate property of the landlord.

Neither should it be thought that treating the release payment as a lease payment will assist a tenant. In the usual case of landlord, original tenant and surety, a payment by the surety which is treated as a lease payment will entitle the surety to an indemnity from the tenant (see para 5.4.3). Accordingly the ultimate effect of *Milverton* (where the tenant is solvent) is that the surety will be released for nothing.

By reference to the above it is suggested that the decision in *Milverton* is suspect. It is submitted that a creditor and surety should be able to negotiate a release at any price agreed between them and the court should not consider either the adequacy of the consideration nor reclassify its nature. The tenant's obligations to the landlord are not increased by such an arrangement and the mere fact that the landlord has made a good bargain with the surety as third party is not sufficient reason to decrease the tenant's liability.

5.1.9 EFFECT OF RELEASE OF OTHER PARTIES

The tenant or former tenant is not necessarily released from liability simply because the landlord releases some other party from liability under the lease.

This principle is exemplified in the court decision in *Sun Life Assurance Society plc v Tantofex (Engineers) Ltd* [1999] 2 EGLR 135. That case involved an 'old' tenancy. The tenant (T) had assigned to a first assignee (A1). There was a second assignment from A1 to a further assignee (A2). At the time of the second assignment the landlord released A1 from its liability to the landlord. A2 later defaulted in payment of rent whereupon the landlord claimed against T. T in turn claimed an indemnity from A1. In defence of the landlord's claim it was argued on behalf of T and A1 that the release by the landlord of A1 also operated to release T. If this were not the case, then the release of A1 given by the landlord was of little benefit to A1. The court rejected the defence, holding that each of T and A1 had a several and separate liability to the landlord and the release of one did not release the other. This is to be contrasted with the position where there is joint liability and the release of one co-debtor may well release the other (see para 7.4.3).

5.2 Liability of assignees

Where the lease has been assigned several times, a landlord looking for some person to sue other than the insolvent tenant might consider whether any intermediate assignee is liable to him. The extent of the liability of an intermediate assignee, or indeed of the ultimate insolvent assignee, depends upon the following: the nature of the obligation which the landlord seeks to enforce; the time when the relevant obligation was due to be performed; whether the intermediate assignee entered into a direct contract with the landlord; and whether the landlord has a right to forfeit for the relevant default.

5.2.1 PERIOD FOR WHICH ASSIGNEE IS LIABLE

The basic rule is that an assignee is only directly liable to a landlord during the period of the assignee's ownership of the lease (*Valliant v Dodemede* (1742) 2 Atk 546). The reason for this is that if the assignee has simply taken a transfer of the lease and has not contracted with the landlord, the assignee's liability to the landlord arises from his ownership of the leasehold estate, which gives rise to a relationship between landlord and assignee of 'privity of estate'. An assignee is therefore not directly liable for breaches committed by a prior tenant, although the landlord might have a right to forfeit for such breaches (see below); and once an (intermediate) assignee transfers the lease to a further assignee there is no longer any relationship between the intermediate assignee and the landlord, and the landlord will only be able to pursue an action against the intermediate assignee in relation to the period of the assignee's ownership of the estate, and not in relation to any breach by a subsequent assignee.

In the case of a new tenancy (see para 5.1.6) the Landlord and Tenant (Covenants) Act 1995, s 3 provides that the burden of tenant covenants are annexed to the premises demised and will pass on an assignment of the premises; it further provides that the assignee becomes bound by the tenant covenants. Ordinarily, the assignee's liability will endure only for so long as the assignee has the lease, since the assignee will usually benefit from a statutory release of liability upon a subsequent assignment (see para 5.1.6).

Liability for breaches of subsequent assignee

Although an intermediate assignee is not normally liable to the landlord for a subsequent assignee's failure to perform the terms of the lease there are some instances where an intermediate assignee may be liable in respect of obligations falling due after the assignment. If rent is payable in arrears and the subsequent assignee fails to pay rent which relates partly to the period of ownership of the intermediate assignee the liability for rent may be apportioned under the Apportionment Act 1870 so that the intermediate assignee is liable to the landlord for part of the rent later due, apportioned on a daily basis up to the date of the assignment (*Parry v Robinson-Wyllie Ltd* (1987) 54 P & CR 187; *Swansea Bank v Thomas* (1879) 4 Ex D 94). If, however, rent is payable in advance, so that a payment is due and payable before the date of the assignment, there is no apportionment and the earlier assignee is liable to the landlord for the payment in full.

Another instance where an intermediate assignee may be liable for breaches committed by a subsequent assignee is where the landlord has obtained from the intermediate assignee a direct covenant that the intermediate assignee and its successors in title to the lease will perform and observe the covenants in the lease. If the landlord has the benefit of such a covenant from an intermediate assignee the landlord will (at least in the case of a pre-1996 tenancy) be able to look to that intermediate assignee in the event of the insolvency of a later assignee in possession (*Estates Gazette Ltd v Benjamin Restaurants Ltd* [1995] 1 All ER 129, CA).

In the case of a new tenancy an intermediate assignee can remain liable following a subsequent assignment in several circumstances. First, the intermediate assignee may be required to enter into an authorised guarantee agreement in respect of its immediate successor assignee, if the landlord is entitled by law to impose such a requirement (see para 5.1.6 and chapter 7, para 7.3). Second, an intermediate assignee who unlawfully assigns the lease without the landlord's consent (where required) does not enjoy the benefit of a statutory release from liability (Landlord and Tenant (Covenants) Act 1995, s 11(2)). In such circumstances, it is (arguably) implicit that the intermediate assignee should be responsible for default by its subsequent assignee. The statute does not, however, expressly provide for such liability. Accordingly, it is arguable that the intermediate assignee is only responsible for its unlawful successor if the intermediate assignee has given to the landlord a direct covenant on behalf of itself and its successors in title.

An intermediate assignee as former tenant will not be liable under any direct covenant or authorised guarantee agreement to the extent that any amount due is referable to a relevant variation of the lease agreed between the subsequent assignee and the landlord on or after 1 January 1996 (see para 5.1.3).

Liability for breaches of prior tenant

It has been noted above that an assignee is not directly liable for breaches of the terms of the lease committed by a prior tenant (and see the Landlord and

Tenant (Covenants) Act 1995, s 23(1)). So, strictly, the assignee is only liable to make good his own breaches and not those of his assignor. If, however, the breach is a continuing breach such as wrongful user or disrepair, the assignee will be liable to the landlord even though the breach first occurred prior to the assignee's ownership, since the assignee may be liable for the continuing breach by, for example, failing to remedy the disrepair (*Middlegate Properties Ltd v Bilbao (Caroline Construction Co Ltd)* (1972) 24 P & CR 329).

Also if, as will often be the case, the landlord has a right of re-entry for the breach the landlord will be able to forfeit the lease for the breach of the assignor, and the right to forfeit, being a proprietary right will bind the assignee who may in practice have to remedy the breach to prevent a forfeiture. In some cases, however, the landlord may have waived the right to forfeit for the breach (perhaps by consenting to the assignment) or, exceptionally, the landlord's right to forfeit might be void (as it was in *Parry v Robinson-Wyllie Ltd* (1987) 54 P & CR 187, see below).

One might have thought that the landlord's right to distrain would be treated similarly, and that being a security right could be enforced upon the goods of an assignee following assignment. It has been decided, however, that this is not the case and that a landlord cannot distrain upon goods upon the premises and goods of the assignee in respect of arrears of rent owed by an assignor (*Wharfland Ltd v South London Co-operative Building Co Ltd* [1995] 2 EGLR 21).

The principle requiring apportionment of rent payable in arrears means that an assignee of a lease is only directly liable to the landlord for an apportionment of the rent from the date of the assignment (but subject to the landlord's right to forfeit, above). The principle extends to a case where there is an outstanding rent review at the date of the assignment. In *Parry v Robinson-Wyllie Ltd* (see above), a lease contained a rent review clause and a review commenced whilst the original tenant had the lease. The original tenant suffered financial difficulties and a receiver was appointed, following which the lease was assigned to an assignee. By the time the new rent was determined by a surveyor, there was no hope of recovering any part of the arrears from the receiver for the original tenant, and the landlord sought to recover from the assignee the arrears of increased rent backdated to the review date. Browne-Wilkinson V-C applied, by analogy, the rule that 'on an assignment of the term between two quarter days, the assignor alone is liable to the landlord for rent in respect of the period down to the date of the assignment and (notwithstanding the covenant to pay the whole quarter's rent in arrear on the quarter day) the assignee is only liable for the rent referable to the period after the date of the assignment'. Similarly, where there is a rent review clause, although there is a liability to pay the backlog following determination of the new rent, the assignor alone is liable for the apportionment of the backlog relating to the period of his ownership.

5.2.2 TERMS UPON WHICH THE ASSIGNEE IS LIABLE

Pre-1996 leases

In the absence of a contract augmenting his liability an assignee will not necessarily be liable upon all the terms of the lease. Because liability depends upon his ownership of the leasehold estate the assignee is only liable upon terms in the lease which relate to that estate, or which are said to 'touch and concern' the land

(*Spencer's Case* (1583) 5 Co Rep 16a). Terms of the lease which are personal in nature so as to be relevant to the original tenant but not to the land itself do not normally affect assignees. Most terms in a lease will 'touch and concern' the land so as to bind assignees. Such terms include a covenant to pay rent (*Parker v Webb* (1693) 3 Salk 5); a covenant to repair (*Williams v Earle* (1868) LR 3 QB 739); a covenant to use the premises for a specified use only (*Wilkinson v Rogers* (1864) 2 De GJ & Sm 62); a restriction upon alienation (*Goldstein v Sanders* [1915] 1 Ch 549); and insolvency conditions (*Horsey Estate v Steiger and Petrifite Co* [1899] 2 QB 79, CA).

It is exceptional for a term in a lease to be held not to affect an assignee. A covenant to pay money to someone other than a landlord has been held not to touch and concern the land and not to bind an assignee (*Mayho v Buckhurst* (1617) Cro Jac 438); and a covenant not to employ on the demised property workers from other parishes has been held not to affect an assignee (*Congleton Corpn v Pattison* (1808) 10 East 130).

The underlying rule may have been displaced by a direct covenant by the assignee to perform and observe 'all of the terms of the lease', so that, in the unlikely event that the lease contains a tenant's obligation which does not relate to the land, the landlord will be able to rely upon the direct covenant of the assignee. In practice if the assignee is well advised and has sufficient bargaining power the covenant will be limited so that the assignee only covenants to perform the terms of the lease 'insofar as they relate to the land and are capable of being enforced'.

Post-1995 leases

Where a 'new tenancy' (see para 5.1.6) is assigned the Landlord and Tenant (Covenants) Act 1995, s 3 provides that an assignee will normally be bound by all tenant covenants in a lease without making any general distinction between those which 'touch and concern' the leasehold estate and those which do not. The assignee will not, however, be bound by an obligation which is expressed to be personal to the assignor. Furthermore, the assignee is only bound to the same extent that the assignor was bound immediately prior to the assignment; if there has been any variation or waiver which is not expressed to be personal to the assignor then the assignee will benefit from it.

5.2.3 STATUTORY RESTRICTION UPON ENFORCEMENT OF LIABILITY

The right to pursue an intermediate tenant in respect of arrears is subject to the need to serve a statutory notice within six months of the sums becoming due (see para 5.1.7).

5.3 Liability of sureties

Just as an original tenant has sometimes been termed a quasi surety (see para 5.1.3), a surety has been dubbed a quasi tenant. In *P & A Swift Investments v Combined English Stores Group plc* [1989] AC 632, CA, Lord Templeman said that 'A surety for a tenant is a quasi tenant who volunteers to be a substitute or twelfth man for the tenant's team and is subject to the same rules and regulations as the player he replaces'. As may be seen from a comparison between the rules appearing immediately below and above (see para 5.1), however, the rules which apply are not quite the same for both tenant and surety, and the tenant bears a greater amount of responsibility.

There may be one or more sureties, which surety or sureties may have undertaken obligations upon the original grant of the lease or upon a later assignment. Upon the tenant in possession becoming insolvent the landlord or his legal advisers will need to check the documents relating to the lease to check what sureties were taken on the original grant of the lease and any assignment, and whether any surety has been released from liability. Care must also be taken to check whether any surety obligation has been varied since it was first entered into, particularly since it is arguable that a guarantee may be varied orally even if it initially had to be in writing (*Re a Debtor (No 517 of 1991)* (1991) Times, 25 November, CA).

5.3.1 EXTENT OF LIABILITY

Once a surety has been identified the extent of liability will need to be considered. The extent of a surety's liability depends primarily upon the terms in which the surety has covenanted. The surety covenant may be drafted with the intent that it be a contract of 'guarantee', or that it be a contract of 'indemnity'. In the context of a surety for a lease the distinction is maybe a slightly artificial one, but theoretically a guarantee is regarded as a 'secondary' liability, whereas an indemnity is often described as a 'primary' one.

The resulting practical consequences of the distinction include first, the fact that where the main contract is void or unenforceable a guarantee, being secondary to the main contract, is also unenforceable. On the other hand the validity or enforceability of an indemnity, being a primary liability, does not depend upon the validity of the main contract. Second, a guarantee being dependent upon the main liability, will be discharged when the principal debtor is discharged; whereas an indemnity will persist notwithstanding discharge of the principal debtor. Third, a guarantee must either be in writing, or must be evidenced in writing, and in each case signed by the person giving the guarantee, or by that person's agent (see the Statute of Frauds 1677, s 4 and *Elpis Maritime Co Ltd v Marti Chartering Co Inc* [1992] 1 AC 21 , HL). No formality is required for an indemnity.

Whether on the facts of a particular case the surety is to be regarded as having given a guarantee or an indemnity, turns upon the wording used and the substance of the transaction. The distinction may be appreciated by reference to the report in *Birkmyr v Darnell* (1704) 1 Salk 27, where it is stated:

> 'If two come to a shop, and one buys, and the other, to gain him credit, promises the seller, if he does not pay you, I will; this is a collateral undertaking [a guarantee] ... but if he says, Let him have the goods, I will be your paymaster, or I will see you paid, this is an undertaking as for himself, and he shall be intended to be the very buyer, and the other to act but as his servant.'

In practice surety covenants in leases tend to include wording appropriate to both guarantees and indemnities, the draftsmen presumably hoping that all angles will be covered one way or another. It is suggested that in the case of this type of hybrid surety the obligation is initially likely to be that of a guarantee, but that upon discharge of the tenant for some reason the contract takes on the character of an indemnity so as to leave the surety as principal debtor (*General Produce Co v United Bank Ltd* [1979] 2 Lloyd's Rep 255). The distinction is probably of no significance while the lease continues (*NRG Vision Ltd v Churchfield Leasing Ltd* [1988] BCLC 624). In any case, in the absence of express provisions to the contrary the following rules normally apply.

Liability for reviewed rent

Where rent is reviewed between landlord and tenant pursuant to the terms of the lease which the surety has guaranteed then the surety should be liable for any increase in rent, notwithstanding that the surety was not a party to the review procedure. If, however, the lease envisages that the surety should be a party to the review procedure then a rent determined between the landlord and tenant only will not be binding upon the surety (*Cressey v Jacobs* (14 October 1977, unreported), see *Rent Review and Lease Renewal*, Vol 15 No 1 1995, pp 7–9).

Liability during statutory continuation

If the lease is a business lease protected by the Landlord and Tenant Act 1954 in respect of which the contractual term has expired, and which is continuing by virtue of s 24 of the 1954 Act, the surety's liability does not, in the absence of a contract to the contrary, extend into the statutory extension of the lease (*Junction Estates v Cope* (1974) 27 P & CR 482, McKenna J). The wording of the surety obligations may, however, indicate that the liability is to be so extensive and according to French J in *Plesser & Co Ltd v Davis* [1983] 2 EGLR 70, the courts will give effect to such clear wording. His Lordship said:

> '... it is clear that a contractual term and a statutory continuation are distinguishable as concepts. A document may be couched in language which without doubt or equivocation points to a guarantee of liability in respect of contractual term obligations or in respect of statutory continuation obligations or it may be of both.'

Liability after forfeiture

If the lease ends through forfeiture the surety will of course be liable to the landlord for any antecedent breaches by the tenant. This includes the liability for all rent due in advance prior to the service of the writ (*Capital & City Holdings Ltd v Dean Warburg Ltd* (1988) 58 P & CR 346, CA). It has been further decided that the surety is liable for any breaches which occur upon the termination itself. In *Associated Dairies Ltd v Pierce* (1982) 43 P & CR 208; affd (1983) 265 Estates Gazette 127, CA, it was held that the surety's liability extended to breach of the tenant's covenant to yield up the premises upon the termination of the lease. After service of a writ to forfeit the proper claim by the landlord is a claim for damages for the breach of contract caused by the failure to yield up, and not a claim for mesne profits for trespass, the latter claim being a claim against the tenant in tort and not covered by the guarantee.

If rent is payable quarterly in advance and a writ is served during the quarter, the rent is not apportioned up to the date of service, with the tenant and guarantor being liable for mesne profits from the date of service. Instead, the whole of the quarter's rent is due, with mesne profits payable from the beginning of the quarter following the date of service (*Capital & City Holdings Ltd v Dean Warburg Ltd*, see above).

Liability after compromise of proceedings

Where the tenant has compromised proceedings between himself and the landlord in relation to the lease it might be thought that the surety drops out of the picture, since the usual effect of a settlement or compromise is to supersede the original cause of action. It has been held, however, that this is not the case, and if the tenant fails to comply with his obligations under a settlement out of court the surety will be liable to the landlord under the terms of the settlement, notwithstanding that the surety was not a party to such settlement (*Collin Estates Ltd v Buckley* [1992] 2 EGLR 78, CA). This conclusion may be regarded as strict compared with the usual rule that a surety is discharged by any variation in terms agreed between landlord and tenant (see para 5.3.2), and it may be that the better view is that it should be up to the landlord to join the surety in the proceedings and the settlement in order to make the surety liable upon its terms.

Liability to former tenant

The surety normally contracts with the landlord only, and it might be thought therefore that he would only be liable to the landlord. The normal rules of contract ought to preclude any stranger to the contract from claiming any benefit under it. Notwithstanding the rules of contract it has been held that a surety for the obligations under a lease may be bound to indemnify other persons who are liable for violation or non-performance of the lease terms. In *Becton Dickinson UK Ltd v Zwebner* [1989] QB 208, McNeil J held that a surety for an assignee could be held responsible to an original tenant. The problem is considered in more depth at para 5.4.1.

Liability to successors of landlord

Another issue of import is whether, where a surety has contracted with a landlord, a successor in title to the landlord's reversion will have the benefit of the surety obligation. The basic rule is that the benefit of the surety obligation passes with the reversion to an assignee of it on the basis that it is an obligation which relates to the land. In *P & A Swift Investments v Combined English Stores Group plc* [1989] AC 632, the House of Lords decided that at common law any benefit which relates to or which 'touches and concerns' land will pass with the land. Their Lordships thought that the benefit of a surety contract related to the reversion on the lease and they were accordingly of the opinion that the benefit would be automatically conveyed to any person who took the landlord's reversion.

Dissolution of tenant

If the tenant is a company then unless the terms of the guarantee provide otherwise the dissolution of the tenant will end the liability of the surety, since liability under a simple guarantee is secondary to the liability of the principal debtor. A landlord can, however, circumvent the loss of a surety covenant in this way by seeking the restoration of the tenant to the Register of Companies, and reinstatement of the principal debtor will effect also the reinstatement of the guarantee (*City of Westminster Assurance Co Ltd v Registrar of Companies* [1997] BCC 960.

5.3.2 DISCHARGE OF SURETY

Sometimes a surety will be able to avoid liability where there has been some change in the relationship between the landlord and the tenant occurring since the surety obligation was entered into. A surety will normally be discharged following any modification in the contract which he has guaranteed, unless he is a party to such modification. In *Holme v Brunskill* (1878) 3 QBD 495, CA, a landlord leased a farm together with a flock of 700 sheep to a tenant and a third party acted as surety and gave a bond that at the end of the tenancy the sheep should be returned to the landlord in good condition, and that if the sheep at the end of the lease should be reduced in number or quality the surety would compensate the landlord. Subsequently the tenant agreed the surrender of one field to the landlord and a consequential rent reduction, but the surety was not a party to the variation. At the end of the lease the flock had reduced in number and quality and the landlord sought to hold the surety liable on the bond. The Court of Appeal by a majority held that the variation in the terms of the lease discharged the surety. Brett LJ dissenting thought that for a variation to discharge a surety it must be a material variation and that a minor variation which does not prejudice the surety would not release him. The other members of the court thought that it should be left to the surety to decide whether a variation was or was not material.

The surety may, however, remain liable after a deviation from the terms of the original lease if the surety agreement expressly states so. In practice, most properly drawn surety covenants will state that the surety is to remain liable notwithstanding any giving of time or variation of the terms of the lease, and the courts have held such drafting to be effective (*Selous Street Properties Ltd v Oronel Fabrics Ltd* [1984] 1 EGLR 50). But the wording will be construed restrictively, and if at all ambiguous will not preserve a guarantor's liability following a variation (*West Horndon Industrial Park Ltd v Phoenix Timber Group plc* [1995] 1 EGLR 77; *Howard de Walden Estates Ltd v Pasta Place Ltd* [1995] 1 EGLR 79).

Sometimes a surety may be a surety for a former tenant in circumstances that the surety is not released upon the assignment of the lease. In this case, if there is a variation agreed between landlord and later assignee, the surety for the former tenant will not be released; the variation of the lease in the hands of the assignee does not constitute a variation of the covenant given by the former tenant, whose obligations have been guaranteed (*Metropolitan Properties Co (Regis) Ltd v Bartholomew* (1995) 72 P & CR 380, CA). Nevertheless, in such circumstances the surety for the former tenant is not liable to make any payment to the extent that the payment is referable to any 'relevant variation' (see para 5.1.3 above) of the lease (Landlord and Tenant (Covenants) Act 1995, s 18(3)).

A surety may be discharged even though there is no actual variation of the terms of the contract other than the giving of extra time for payment (*Overend, Gurney & Co Ltd (Liquidators) v Oriental Financial Corpn Ltd (Liquidators)* (1874) LR 7 HL 348, HL) even though there is no evidence that the surety has actually suffered through the arrangement, since the failure to enforce on time may lead to delay during which time the tenant's financial position deteriorates further and makes it more likely that the surety will be called upon. For the surety to be discharged there must be an actual agreement between landlord and tenant for the giving of time and not merely a failure by the landlord to strictly enforce the terms of the lease.

Whether the release of the tenant will discharge the surety is a question of fact and law. Depending upon its terms a surety may be released by a voluntary arrangement on terms releasing the tenant (*Johnson v Davies* [1998] 3 EGLR 72, CA).

If the lease in question is a 'new tenancy' (see para 5.1.6) the surety will obtain an automatic release from future liability upon a voluntary lawful assignment of the lease in the same circumstances that the tenant whose obligations have been guaranteed obtains a release (see para 5.1.6 and the Landlord and Tenant (Covenants) Act 1995, s 24(2)).

In a case where the guarantor is discharged it appears that such discharge will include a release of any obligation to take a substitute lease (Hutchison J in *Selous Street Properties v Oronel Fabrics Ltd* [1984] 1 EGLR 50) except where the discharge arises following a disclaimer by a liquidator or trustee for the tenant (*Re Yarmarine (IW) Ltd* [1992] BCLC 276).

5.3.3 DEATH/BANKRUPTCY OF SURETY

Although death of a surety can sometimes discharge the surety from liability, whether this is the case depends upon the nature of the obligation guaranteed and the wording of the guarantee itself. Where the guarantee is designed to support obligations of the principal debtor which constantly change, the guarantee is prima facie revocable, as is usually the case with a guarantee of a running account with a bank. However, if the obligation guaranteed is fixed in nature it is much less likely to be discharged by the death of the surety. It appears that a lease falls into the latter category so that the surety is not discharged on death. The issue was considered briefly by the Court of Appeal in *Lloyd's v Harper* (1880) 16 Ch D 290, where Lush LJ said:

> 'Now it will be found, I think, that guarantees may, for the purpose of this case, be divided into two classes, the one in which the consideration is entire, and the other in which the consideration is fragmentary, supplied from time to time, and therefore divisible. An instance of the first is where a person enters into a guarantee that in consideration of the lessor granting a lease to a third person he will be answerable

for the performance of the covenants. The moment the lease is granted there is nothing more for the lessor to do, and such a guarantee as that of necessity runs on throughout the duration of the lease. The lease was intended to be a guaranteed lease, and it is impossible to say that the guarantor could put an end to the guarantee at his pleasure, or that it could be put an end to by his death contrary to the manifest intention of the parties.'

This reasoning is reflected in the decision in *Basch v Stekel* (2000) 81 P & CR D1.

If a surety for the obligations under a lease becomes bankrupt the landlord will be able to prove in the bankruptcy in respect of any arrears of rent or other liability accrued due at the time of the bankruptcy (*Re Houlder* [1929] 1 Ch 205). It has been held that the surety's possible liability for future breaches is not a contingent liability which can be proved for, and that the guarantee therefore continues notwithstanding the bankruptcy (*Boyd v Robins* (1859) 5 CBNS 597). This rule may, however, be inconsistent with the decision of the House of Lords in *Hardy v Fothergill* (1888) 13 App Cas 351, where it was held that where an assignee of a lease became bankrupt the assignee's liability to an original tenant was a contingent liability which should be proved in the bankruptcy and which would be discharged by it. Where the surety is a company in liquidation the landlord will lose the benefit of the surety's obligations upon dissolution and it is suggested that the landlord will have a right to prove in the liquidation for the loss of the surety.

5.3.4 EFFECT OF DISCLAIMER

The effect of disclaimer upon the liability of a surety is dealt with in depth in chapter 6. Essentially, disclaimer discharges the tenant as principal debtor from future obligation under the lease. Whether or not the surety is discharged may depend upon the form of the guarantee. If the surety remains liable the surety is not entitled to indemnity from the tenant but the surety will be able to make a claim in the liquidation for the loss arising as a result of the disclaimer.

Obligation to take substitute lease

Some surety contracts provide that, in the event of disclaimer by a trustee or liquidator, the surety is to take a new lease, normally on the same terms as the disclaimed lease and for a term equal to the residue which remained immediately before disclaimer. It has been held that such an obligation is a personal obligation of the guarantor which survives a disclaimer (*Re Yarmarine (IW) Ltd* [1992] BCLC 276).

If, however, there has been any variation of the terms of the lease the surety may have been released from the obligation to take a new lease (*Selous Street Properties Ltd v Oronel Fabrics Ltd* [1984] 1 EGLR 50.

The surety's covenant to take a new lease creates a contract conditional upon the tenant entering liquidation or becoming bankrupt, the liquidator or trustee disclaiming the lease, and the landlord requiring the surety to take a new lease. If pursuant to the terms of the surety covenant the landlord requires the surety to take a new lease, the contract is specifically enforceable with the result that the surety is considered in equity to be the tenant and is liable for the rent and other sums which would have been payable if a new lease had been taken by the surety. Accordingly, the landlord can make a statutory demand for any amounts due (*Re A Company (No 00792 of 1992), ex p Tredegar* [1992] 2 EGLR 39).

5.3.5 ENFORCEMENT OF LIABILITY

In general the surety's liability under a guarantee arises as soon as the obligation guaranteed has arisen, but has not been performed. In the case of liability for rent the surety's obligation is complete as soon as the due date for payment arrives. It is not, however, necessary for notice of the tenant's default to be given to the surety unless the terms of the surety contract so provides (*Halsbury's Laws*, 4th edn, Vol 20, paras 158–9). Neither, in the absence of agreement or statute (see below), does prior demand for payment need to be made of either principal or surety unless, again, this has been stipulated for.

It has been suggested that before the surety can be made liable he has an equity against the creditor which might require the creditor to pursue the principal debtor first (*Rouse v Bradford Banking Co* [1894] 2 Ch 32, 75, CA; affd [1894] AC 586, HL), but the existence of this right has been questioned and it is submitted that a court would not be likely to require a landlord to be put to the trouble of suing a tenant before the landlord could rely upon the guarantee (*Ewart v Latta* (1865) 4 Macq 983, HL). If such a right does exist the surety cannot compel the landlord to proceed against the tenant unless he indemnifies the landlord for the risk, expense and delay (*Wright v Simpson* (1802) 6 Ves 714).

The surety on being sued by the landlord may rely upon any right to set off or counterclaim which the tenant has against the landlord (*Bechervaise v Lewis* (1872) LR 7 CP 372, CPR 16.6 and CPR 20; *Anglo-Italian Bank v Wells* (1878) 38 LT 197, CA); but the surety is not bound to argue set-off, even if the tenant could (*Davis v Hedges* (1871) LR 6 QB 687), and the surety should be entitled to be indemnified by the tenant in full for all amounts paid, leaving the tenant to make a separate counterclaim against the landlord (*Thornton v M'Kewan* (1862) 1 Hem & M 525).

The surety might not be certain whether the amount demanded is properly due. If in these circumstances the surety pays money to the landlord in ignorance of relevant facts he should be able to claim restitution of the money as a payment made under a mistake of fact (*Mills v Alderbury Union Guardians* (1849) 3 Exch 590). The right to restitution may apply even in case of mistake of law (*Westdeutsche Landesbank Girozentrale v Islington London Borough Council* [1994] 1 WLR 938, CA).

The limitation period for pursuing a rent claim against a surety is six years (*Romain v Scuba TV* [1996] 1 EGLR 103, CA).

The landlord must also bear in mind the statutory restriction upon enforcement of liability imposed by the Landlord and Tenant (Covenants) Act 1995. In the case of a surety for a former tenant, s 17 of the 1995 Act makes rent and other sums irrecoverable unless the landlord serves a prescribed form of notice upon the surety within six months of the relevant sums becoming due (see para 5.1.7 below). It is not necessary that the landlord should also have served notice upon the tenant (*Cherwell Estates Ltd v Harris* [1998] 1 EGLR 27). Perhaps surprisingly, the procedure does not apply in respect of a surety for the current tenant. Although such a surety is likely to be closely connected with the tenant it will not necessarily be aware of the tenant's rent arrears.

5.4 Indemnity and contribution

If the landlord, seeking payment, receives sums from a former tenant, or surety, the person making the payment may be entitled to an indemnity or contribution from other persons who are under similar obligations in respect of the lease. Unfortunately the legal position is much neglected, and consequently it is not possible to state with certainty all of the rights and obligations which tenants, assignees or sureties might share amongst themselves. Some principles, particularly those based upon express agreement, can be stated with a high degree of certitude; but some such rights, being based upon the undeveloped law of restitution are beset with doubt. In so far as the discussion is reliant upon the latter undeveloped law it must be viewed as tentative only and subject to review by the courts.

5.4.1 RIGHTS OF FORMER TENANT

If a former tenant satisfies his obligation to the landlord by paying arrears of rent or by compensating the landlord for any other breach of obligation on the part of the insolvent assignee, the tenant has a right to be indemnified by the assignee. The former tenant's right of indemnity may stem from a covenant which has been given to the tenant by the assignee, or it may be based upon an equitable restitutionary right. The right is, of course, in many cases of academic interest only since the insolvent assignee is likely to be unable to satisfy the demand for an indemnity in full, or even in part. If in a bankruptcy or liquidation of an assignee a dividend is being paid to ordinary creditors, an original tenant who has paid the rent will be able to prove in the bankruptcy or liquidation of the assignee for the indemnity. It should be noted, however, that if the lease has been assigned several times the immediate assignee of the lease from the original tenant may be solvent and able to indemnify the original tenant, even if an action against the current assignee would be fruitless.

Indemnity or reimbursement from immediate assignee

The former tenant may have a right against its immediate assignee, by virtue of an express contract of indemnity. If an express covenant has not been given a covenant will (except in relation to 'new tenancies' – the Landlord and Tenant (Covenants) Act 1995, s 14) be implied into the conveyance from the tenant to the assignee, the Law of Property Act 1925, s 77 (and see the Land Registration Act 1925, s 24). The implied covenant is in terms that the assignee, or those deriving title under him, will pay all rent and observe and perform all the tenant's obligations in the lease, and that the assignee will indemnify the tenant in respect of any breach.

The implied covenant under the Law of Property Act 1925, s 77 only applies where the assignment is for 'valuable consideration' – so it might be thought that it would not apply where there is an assignment of a lease at no premium. The Court of Appeal held, however, in *Johnsey Estates Ltd v Lewis and Manley (Engineering) Ltd* (1987) 54 P & CR 296, that the fact that the assignee takes the obligation to perform the terms of the lease is sufficient consideration to invoke the implied covenant. Bingham LJ said that:

'The assignor obtained an obvious benefit because, although remaining liable to the landlord under his original contract, he ceased to be primarily liable and gained the benefit of another party being also liable. The assignee for his part undertook a responsibility to pay rent to the original landlord. Looking at the matter as a commercial transaction and ignoring the £1, it is in my judgment quite impossible to regard this transaction as one otherwise than for valuable consideration.'

This decision tends to render the words 'valuable consideration' in the section superfluous, since on this basis any person who takes a lease will be giving valuable consideration.

The former tenant, if made liable upon his contract with the landlord, will be able to rely upon the assignee's covenant in order to obtain an indemnity. It should be noted, however, that the implied covenant is sometimes modified so that the assignee only covenants to perform obligations which relate to the land, so that any obligation of a personal nature might be binding upon the former tenant by virtue of the contract, but the tenant will not be able to obtain an indemnity in respect of such obligations from his assignee.

The right to an indemnity from an assignee persists even though the assignor is primarily responsible for the breach. In *Gooch v Clutterbuck* [1899] 2 QB 148, CA, the lease contained a covenant that the tenant would keep the demised premises in repair. The defendant (A1) was an assignee who assigned the lease to A2 at a time when the premises were in serious disrepair. A2 covenanted with A1 that he would thenceforth pay the rent and perform the tenant's covenants in the lease and keep A1 indemnified in respect of any breach. The premises, in the hands of A2, remained in disrepair and the landlord sued A1 on the covenant. A1, having been made liable, sought an indemnity from A2, who argued that since the breach had endured during the period of A1's ownership, A1 was not entitled to an indemnity against what was, at least to some extent, his own breach. The Court of Appeal rejected the argument and held that A2 was liable on the covenant for indemnity since A2 knew of the breach when the premises were assigned and must have known that he was giving A1 an indemnity in respect of any claim that the landlord might make (see also *Middlegate Properties Ltd v Bilbao (Caroline Construction Co Ltd)* (1972) 24 P & CR 329).

The covenant of indemnity may contain provisions making it clear that the assignee must not only reimburse the tenant for sums paid, but also for costs incurred. Even in the absence of an express provision for costs it is an incident of such a covenant that the costs of legal proceedings properly incurred are recoverable from the tenant (*Duffield v Scott* (1789) 3 Term Rep 374) but this does not usually include the costs of an appeal (*Maxwell v British Thomson Houston Co Ltd* [1904] 2 KB 342). The implied covenants under the Law of Property Act 1925, s 77 and the Land Registration Act 1925, s 24 provide respectively that the assignee must indemnify the tenant against 'all proceedings, costs, claims and expenses' and 'actions, expenses, and claims'. In the absence of special circumstances the indemnity for costs will probably be limited to reasonable costs rather than a full indemnity (*Maxwell v British Thomson Houston Co Ltd*, see above).

In some cases the covenant given may be stronger than an indemnity, and may be a covenant of direct obligation. In other words the covenant may allow the assignor to proceed whenever there is a breach by the assignee even though the landlord has not proceeded against the assignor. The assignor could then, at least theoretically, seek an injunction to limit the damage being caused by the assignee. It is thought that the implied covenant under the Law of Property Act 1925, s 77 is one of indemnity only (*Reckitt v Cody* [1920] 2 Ch 452), so that the assignee is not liable to the assignor until the landlord has made a claim, but the wording is appropriate to an obligation and it has been suggested that the section may create an obligation (*Emmet on Title*, para 26.143). The effect of an express covenant will depend very much upon its wording and the circumstances. It is at least clear that a covenant by an assignee to observe and perform the covenants in the lease and which does not refer to indemnity is a covenant of obligation (*Butler Estates Co Ltd v Bean* [1942] 1 KB 1, CA), so that the assignor can enforce the covenants even if the landlord has not taken any action against him.

Even if there is no express covenant for indemnity, and the implied covenant under the Law of Property Act 1925, s 77 is excluded by agreement – or because the lease is a 'new tenancy' (Landlord and Tenant (Covenants) Act 1995, s 14), there is nevertheless an implied right of restitution under the rule in *Moule v Garrett* (1872) LR 7 Exch 101, unless this implied right has been excluded by clear words (*Re Healing Research Trustee Co Ltd* [1992] 2 All ER 481).

Indemnity from subsequent assignee

If the lease has been assigned more than once, and if the immediate assignee of the original tenant is either insolvent or not liable to him, the original tenant may wish to claim compensation from a subsequent assignee. In these circumstances, and assuming that the subsequent assignee is an intermediate assignee and not the ultimate assignee, the original tenant has no right of indemnity from the subsequent assignee, except in the unlikely circumstance that the subsequent assignee gave to the tenant an express covenant of indemnity. Neither can the original tenant compel an immediate insolvent assignee to use its right of indemnity to recover on behalf of the original tenant an indemnity from the subsequent assignee. In *Re Mirror Group (Holdings) Ltd* [1993] BCLC 538, a tenant (T) had assigned a lease to an assignee (A1), who in turn assigned the lease to a second assignee (A2), who then assigned to the ultimate assignee (A3). A3 became insolvent and the landlord sued T for the rent. Although T had a right of reimbursement from A3 (see *Moule v Garrett*, above and below) the right was of little use because of the insolvency of A3. T had a right to be indemnified by A1, but A1 was insolvent also. A2, however, was solvent and T wanted to obtain payment by making A2 liable. T could not sue A2 directly as A2 had not entered into any direct covenant with T. T argued, however, that A1's liability by virtue of the implied covenant under the Land Registration Act 1925, s 24(1)(b) (see above) meant that A1 should ensure that its successor, A2, paid the rent, and T sought an order that A1 should sue A2 or, alternatively, that A1 should assign to T its right to sue A2. Sir Donald Nicholls V-C held that s 24 did not impose any such obligations upon A1.

Where, however, the original tenant wishes to claim compensation from the ultimate assignee in possession there exists, independent of covenant or contract, a restitutionary right whereby if one person is made to satisfy the obligations of another, the first person is entitled to reimbursement from the other. An original tenant can rely upon this right to obtain reimbursement from an assignee in possession irrespective of whether the assignee has contracted with the original tenant. One of the leading cases is the decision in *Moule v Garrett* (1872) LR 7 Exch 101, where the tenant had assigned the lease and the assignee in turn had assigned to a second assignee. When the second assignee defaulted on the repairing obligations the landlord sought to hold liable the original tenant, who sought reimbursement from the second assignee. It was held that the second assignee was liable to reimburse the original tenant. Cockburn J explained that 'Where the plaintiff has been compelled by law to pay, or being compellable by law, has paid money which the defendant was ultimately liable to pay, so that the latter obtains the benefit of the payment by the discharge of his liability; under such circumstances the defendant is held indebted to the plaintiff in the amount'.

It should be noted that it has been stated that the restitutionary right is a right to reimbursement of money paid only and not a right to a complete indemnity for all loss. Goff and Jones (*The Law of Restitution*, 5th edn, p 453) assert that it does not, for example, include the right to recover legal costs of resisting the landlord's claim. Putnam (*Suretyship*, 1st edn, p 73), however, rejects this view for the opinion that the restitutionary right is treated in exactly the same manner as the normal contractual right to indemnity.

On a more academic note the restitutionary right is often referred to as a 'quasi contractual' one (see Putnam, *Suretyship*, p 62); i e that the right is based upon an implied contract of indemnity between the person ultimately liable and the person who has actually paid. The more modern approach is to consider the right as based upon the idea that one person should not be unjustly enriched at the expense of another (*Lipkin Gorman v Karpnale* [1991] 2 AC 548, HL); or in the present context that the tenant or assignee in possession, and primarily responsible for the rent, should not be unjustly enriched by having its obligations discharged through the payment made at the expense of an earlier tenant or surety.

If the lease has been assigned several times the original tenant may, of course, rely upon the express or implied covenant for indemnity given to him by his immediate assignee (see above) rather than to rely upon the restitutionary right to reimbursement from the insolvent tenant, which, in any case, is likely only to result in a proof in bankruptcy or liquidation.

If there has been an assignment of part of the land leased only, the position depends upon whether the rent has been legally apportioned with the consent of the landlord or not. If the rent has been apportioned with the consent of the landlord the assignor has a right of indemnity in respect of the apportioned rent and in respect of any breach of covenant as if the lease related solely to the land conveyed (Law of Property Act 1925, s 77(1)(c)). If the apportionment was made without the landlord's consent there is implied a covenant by the assignee that he will pay the apportioned rent and observe the other covenants in the lease so far as they relate to the land conveyed; in addition, there is implied a covenant by the assignor to pay the balance of the rent and perform the covenants in the lease so far as they relate to the land retained. The landlord may proceed against either assignor or assignee in respect of the entire rent but if one of them pays the whole amount under threat of distress the apportionment may be recovered from the other (*Whitham v Bullock* [1939] 2 KB 81, CA). Moreover, the right to indemnity may be enforced through distress or by taking the receipt of any income from the part of the land conveyed, until the indemnity is satisfied (Law of Property Act 1925, s 190). If the lease is a 'new tenancy' (see para 5.1.6) an agreement between assignor and assignee as to apportionment will bind a landlord provided that the assignor and assignee serve notice upon the landlord within four weeks after the assignment and (1) the landlord does not serve notice of objection within four weeks of service; or (2) he serves a notice of objection but the court declares that it is reasonable for the apportionment to be binding; or (3) he serves notice consenting to the apportionment (Landlord and Tenant (Covenants) Act 1995, s 10).

Whether the assignment was of whole or of part of the land, the assignor may reserve a right of distress (Law of Property Act 1925, s 189) or may charge the land conveyed with the indemnity (Law of Property Act 1925, s 77(7)). The charge is not registrable as a general equitable charge (Land Charges Act 1972, s 2(4)), if it is given in respect of apportioned rent and is charged on land in exoneration of other land.

Reimbursement from a surety for an assignee

The restitutionary right to reimbursement has also been held to be available to enable an original tenant to recover the rent from a surety for the assignee, despite the absence of any relationship between the tenant and the surety. In *Becton Dickinson UK Ltd v Zwebner* [1989] QB 208, the original tenant assigned the lease and a licence for assignment was entered into between the landlord, the original tenant, the assignee and a director of the assignee company as surety. The director of the assignee covenanted with the landlord that the terms of the lease would be performed by the assignee. The assignee defaulted on payment of rent and went into liquidation and the landlord demanded payment from the original tenant. The original tenant demanded an indemnity from the director of the assignee company as surety. Notwithstanding that there was no contractual relationship between the original tenant and the surety, the surety covenant in the licence being for the benefit of the landlord only, McNeill J ruled that the tenant was entitled to an indemnity from the surety, for the reason that, as between the original tenant and the surety, the liability of the surety is the 'primary' liability and that of the original tenant is 'secondary'. This reasoning has been criticised (McLoughlin [1989] Conv 29) on the basis that the liability of the original tenant and the surety is similar in that each has covenanted that the terms of the lease will be performed, and that a fairer result might be to hold that all parties who have 'guaranteed' the obligations in the lease are entitled to contribution as amongst themselves. It might be argued that if an original tenant wishes to dilute his liability at the expense of later sureties he should negotiate for a term in the lease or a supplemental document which provides that his consent will be required to any second or subsequent assignment, and that as a condition of such assignment he may require a surety to enter into a direct covenant to indemnify him. In conclusion it is suggested that the liability of a surety for an assignee ought not to include an obligation to reimburse completely the original tenant, but *Becton Dickinson UK Ltd v Zwebner* (see above) is an authority to the contrary and it has recently been followed at first instance in *Re a Debtor (No 21 of 1995)* [1995] NPC 170.

The problem may become more acute in a case where there have been several assignments of the lease and the original tenant claims restitution not from a surety for the insolvent assignee, but from an intermediate assignee or a surety for an intermediate assignee. Can it be said that the liability of the later intermediate assignee and its surety is primary to that of the original tenant?

5.4.2 INTERMEDIATE ASSIGNEE'S RIGHTS

If an intermediate assignee has been made to pay he has (unless the lease is a 'new tenancy' – see above) a right to indemnity from his immediate subsequent assignee on the basis of the implied covenants of indemnity under the Law of Property Act 1925, s 77 and the Land Registration Act 1925, s 24, mentioned in para 5.4.1. Presumably he too, like the original tenant, would have a restitutionary right of reimbursement from an insolvent assignee in possession (on the principle in *Moule v Garrett*, see above) or the surety for the assignee in possession (on the basis of *Becton Dickinson UK Ltd v Zwebner*, see above) even if there was no direct relationship between them.

5.4.3 SURETY'S RIGHTS

The normal rule relating to the liability of several sureties is that if there are several sureties, S1 and S2, who are liable under the same document then, in the absence of agreement to the contrary, the general rule would be that they should be liable *aequali jure* – to contribute equally to the debt (*Deering v Earl of Winchelsea* (1787) 2 Bos & P 270; see *Rowlatt on Principal and Surety* (5th edn) at pp 164–165). So in a straightforward case, where S1 and S2 are directors of the tenant company and have guaranteed the company's compliance with the lease, covenanting to be jointly and severally liable, either or both may be held responsible, and if one of them pays arrears of rent the other will be liable to contribute 50%.

The basic rule of equal contribution holds good even though S1 and S2 became sureties at different times under different agreements and were unaware of each other's existence (*Scholefield Goodman & Sons Ltd v Zyngier* [1986] AC 562, PC). So, applying this principle, if S1 became surety when the lease was granted, and S2 became surety on a later assignment; if the assignee defaulted in payment of rent and either S1 or S2 paid the landlord, whichever of S1 or S2 had paid would be entitled to a contribution from the other. But it is not clear whether in this type of case the general rule would apply. The general rule of equal liability, though based upon equitable principles, may be modified by contract (*Craythorne v Swinburne* (1807) 14 Ves 160) and would give way to any express agreement that their liabilities would be on an unequal footing. So if a second surety agreed to pay only in the event that the first should not, then the second surety would be entitled to full indemnity from the first (see *Craythorne v Swinburne*). This is unlikely to have occurred in the usual case involving several sureties for the performance of the terms of a lease; but the normal rule would also be displaced if the circumstances were such as to indicate that one of the sureties was to be ultimately liable so as not to be entitled to a contribution from the other and so as to be liable to indemnify the other if the other paid (*Re Denton's Estate, Licences Insurance Corpn and Guarantee Fund Ltd v Denton* [1904] 2 Ch 178, CA).

The general rule of equal contribution applies only to the debt or liability which co-sureties have mutually agreed to undertake. In the event that one co-surety undertakes some other different or greater obligation such co-surety cannot, in respect of such other obligation, claim contribution from the co-sureties. In *BSE Trading Ltd v Hands* [1996] 2 EGLR 214, CA, a surety who negotiated the surrender of a lease on terms which included the making of a large capital payment to the landlord was not entitled to claim from the other co-sureties a contribution to the capital payment.

A surety's right to claim contribution from a co-surety is a matter of substance which is not affected by procedural or evidenciary matters. Accordingly, if a surety satisfies a landlord's demand, the surety can claim contribution from a co-surety notwithstanding that the demand may not strictly have been in accordance with the procedure required by the surety agreement (*Stimpson v Smith* [1999] 2WLR 1292, CA).

Indemnity from later surety

One court decision indicates that in the context of a lease, where there are several sureties who have become obligated at different times, and for the benefit of different parties, it is to be implied that a surety for a later assignee is to have a 'primary' liability vis-à-vis a surety for an original tenant or earlier assignee. In *Selous Street Properties Ltd v Oronel Fabrics Ltd* [1984] 1 EGLR 50, the parties were the plaintiff landlord, and the defendants, being the original tenant, a surety for the original tenant, an intermediate assignee, the assignee in possession and a person who acted as surety for both the intermediate assignee and the assignee in possession. Hutchison J had to consider the respective liabilities and rights of indemnity or contribution of the defendants. One of the questions considered by his Lordship was whether there was a primary and secondary liability as between the surety for the original tenant on the one hand and the surety for the assignees on the other. He decided that there was and that the liability of the original surety was secondary to that of the later one. Unfortunately the extent to which the basic rule of equal contribution would have been appropriate or otherwise was not discussed. From a technical point of view the position of the two sureties was little different. Both had covenanted that the terms of the lease would be performed by the assignee in possession. In addition, it might be unfair to displace the normal rule so as to saddle the later surety with sole responsibility, particularly since the later may have entered into the surety commitment relying upon the fact that there was another surety who would be liable. After all, if there was no later surety for the assignee the surety for the original tenant would bear the full brunt of the liability; and the coming into existence of a later surety will be of fortuitous benefit to him even if there are rights of contribution. Why should he have the additional windfall of a complete indemnity when the later surety has not agreed to give him one?

Sureties' rights against the tenant

A surety who owes an obligation to a landlord has rights, both before and after payment, against the tenant whose liability he has guaranteed. Before payment the surety has an 'equity of exoneration', which entitles the surety to require the tenant to pay the rent or perform other obligations under the lease as soon as the liability falls due or arises, even if the landlord has not yet demanded payment (*Earl of Ranelaugh v Hayes* (1683) 1 Vern 189; *Lee v Rook* (1730) Mos 318; *Bechervaise v Lewis* (1872) LR 7 CP 372, 377). This might be useful in a case where the surety is aware that the tenant is beginning to suffer severe financial difficulties. The surety may require the tenant to perform the terms of the lease, leaving the tenant to default on other debts or contracts rather than the lease. Even before there is default it might be possible to obtain quia timet relief, obtaining an injunction to require the tenant to pay rents as they fall due, although the law is not clear on this point (Putnam *Suretyship*, p 74).

An alternative which a surety of a tenant company might consider if his contingent liabilities are increasing due to the tenant's failure to comply with the terms of the lease is to present a petition to bankrupt or wind up the tenant in an effort to force the tenant to pay (Putnam *Suretyship*, p 77). A petition may be presented on the basis of the company's inability to pay its debts taking into account its contingent liabilities (Insolvency Act 1986 ('IA 1986'), s 123(3), s 122(1)(g)).

If the surety pays money to the landlord he has a right to be indemnified by the tenant for the amount which he has paid together with interest (*Re Fox Walker & Co, ex p Bishop* (1880) 15 Ch D 400, CA). If under the terms of the lease the rent or other payments carried interest, then the surety is entitled to interest upon the entire sum, including interest, from the date of payment (*Rigby v Macnamara* (1795) 2 Cox Eq Cas 415; County Courts Act 1984, s 69; Supreme Court Act 1981, s 35A). If the tenant is an insolvent company which is being wound up the surety is entitled to interest up to the date of commencement of the winding up but not to any interest accruing subsequently (see para 2.10.4 above).

If the surety reasonably defended proceedings by the landlord the surety is probably also entitled to an indemnity for the costs from the tenant (*Baxendale v London, Chatham and Dover Rly Co* (1874) LR 10 Exch 35, 44).

The surety's cause of action may be upon an express agreement for indemnity or upon an implied indemnity and an action for money paid to the use of the tenant (*Toussaint v Martinnant* (1787) 2 Term Rep 100). The tenant may, of course, be joined in an action brought by the landlord against the surety, by a third party notice (CPR 20).

Claim on insurance policy

The surety may have the benefit of an insurance policy against tenant default, in which case the surety if made liable may rely upon this. This type of policy is considered briefly below (para 5.9). If the insurer pays he will be subrogated to the surety's rights against other parties, including the right to prove in the tenant's bankruptcy or liquidation.

5.4.4 ASSIGNMENT OF RIGHT OF INDEMNITY

The right of indemnity possessed by a former tenant or surety is apparently property which itself may be assigned. This may be of value in some negotiations so that a trustee or liquidator of an insolvent individual or company may sell the right, possibly to some other person liable under the terms of the lease. In *Re Perkins, Poyser v Beyfus* [1898] 2 Ch 182, CA, property was let to a tenant (T), and the lease was then assigned successively to A1, A2 and A3. A1 was bankrupt. A2 had died, and it was A2's executors who had assigned to A3. A3 was impecunious and failed to pay the rent. The landlord sought and obtained payment from T. T's right of indemnity from A3 under the rule in *Moule v Garrett* (see above) was of little value because of the impecuniosity of A3. T had a right of indemnity as against A1, but this had been reduced to a right of proof. So T negotiated with A1's trustee in bankruptcy to take from him A1's right of indemnity against the estate of A2. The Court of Appeal held that an assignment of the right of indemnity was valid and gave T the right to proceed against A2.

5.5 Subrogation to landlord's rights?

It is possible that a surety, or former tenant who has paid rent or other sums due in respect of a lease might be able to take over some or all of the landlord's rights against the tenant in respect of that rent or those other sums. Normally, if a surety pays a creditor the surety is entitled by way of 'subrogation' to stand in the shoes of the creditor and pursue that creditor's rights against the debtor. The principle applies not only to contracts of guarantee but also to any contract of indemnity, such as an insurance contract. In principle it ought also to apply to where an original tenant or an assignee is made to indemnify the landlord for non-performance by the tenant in possession.

5.5.1 GENERAL RULE

The rights available through subrogation are greater than the contractual right to indemnity or restitutionary right to reimbursement described above. As Sir Samuel Romilly said arguendo in *Craythorne v Swinburne* (1807) 14 Ves 160:

> '... a surety will be entitled to every remedy which the creditor has against the principal debtor; to enforce every security and all means of payment; to stand in the place of the creditor; not only through the medium of contract, but even by means of securities, entered into without the knowledge of the surety; having a right to have those securities transferred to him; though there was no stipulation for that; and to avail himself of all those securities against the debtor. The right of a surety stands, not upon contract but upon a principle of natural justice ...'

So the surety, or former tenant who has made payment to the landlord may be able to take over the landlord's rights against the current tenant (*Duncan Fox & Co v North and South Wales Bank* (1880) 6 App Cas 1, HL). To what extent this may be done is yet to be fully explored by the courts. The person making payment of rent or paying for disrepair (*Andrews v Patriotic Assurance Co of*

Ireland (No 2) (1886) 18 QB 355) should at least be subrogated to the landlord's right to sue the tenant for the rent paid, in the name of the landlord (*Swire v Redman* (1876) 1 QBD 536, 541), giving the landlord a proper indemnity for costs. Since, however, the person paying will also have a right to sue in his own name upon an express indemnity or restitutionary right of reimbursement, this particular right of subrogation is likely to be of little advantage.

5.5.2 RENT AS A LIQUIDATION/BANKRUPTCY EXPENSE

The right to be subrogated to the landlord's rights, rather than simply having the right to an indemnity, can be of significant value in some circumstances. One such circumstance is where the tenant is a company in liquidation and the liquidator is using the premises for the purposes of the liquidation. It has been established that a person paying rent to the landlord is entitled to be subrogated to the landlord's right to claim the rent as a liquidation expense with priority over other creditors. In *Re Downer Enterprises Ltd* [1974] 2 All ER 1074, a lease was assigned from the original tenant (T) to an assignee (A1), and then to a further assignee (A2) which was a company which then went into a creditors' voluntary winding up. The landlord recovered rent, including rent due both before and after the commencement of the winding up, from T, who recovered by way of indemnity from A1, who, in turn, sought to prove in A2's liquidation for the pre-liquidation arrears; and in respect of rent for the period of the liquidation, to be subrogated to the landlord's right to claim the amount as an expense of the liquidation. Pennycuick V-C decided that A1 could be subrogated to the landlord's claim to recover the rent for the period of the liquidation, as a liquidation expense in priority to other creditors.

5.5.3 RIGHTS AGAINST OTHER SURETIES

In conformity with the rule that the payer of a debt is entitled to the benefit of any securities that the creditor has, it has been held that where the assignee in possession cannot pay and a former tenant pays the landlord, the former tenant can, through subrogation, rely upon the landlord's right to sue a surety (*Selous Street Properties Ltd v Oronel Fabrics Ltd* (1984) 270 Estates Gazette 643 at 749). It is submitted, however, that this application of the basic rule relating to securities is not well founded. If it were it would follow that if one surety paid a debt he would be entitled to an indemnity from another. This is plainly not the rule, since in the absence of a contrary indication all sureties are liable to contribute equally. If a former tenant is to have an indemnity from a later surety it is suggested that the right must rest upon the idea that one party has primary liability and the other's is secondary (see para 5.4.3).

5.5.4 DISTRESS

A landlord's right to distrain upon the goods of the tenant for unpaid rent is another right which could be useful to a surety or previous tenant who has paid the landlord. The point was raised briefly in the litigation in *Selous Street Properties Ltd v Oronel Fabrics Ltd* [1984] 1 EGLR 50, but it was not necessary to decide the matter and Hutchison J expressed no opinion upon it. Until the matter is considered a person paying the rent would not be well advised to distrain, because of the risks attendant upon wrongful distress. If the question did come before the courts it is likely that they would take into account the fact that distress might give the payer a priority in bankruptcy or liquidation which he might not otherwise have.

In a case where there has been assignment of part of land comprised in a lease, and the landlord, in circumstance where the landlord is not bound by an apportionment of the rent, compels the assignor to pay the entire rent (or the amount due for the part assigned), or makes the assignor liable for breaches of the assignee, the assignor is, by the Law of Property Act 1925, s 190, entitled to distrain upon the premises assigned in order to obtain an indemnity. In practice this will be quite rare since most modern commercial leases specifically prohibit an assignment of part.

5.5.5 RIGHT TO SUBRENTS

It may also be considered whether other rights of the landlord are available to the payer by way of subrogation. Could a surety be subrogated to a landlord's rights to require a subtenant to pay the subrent direct to him under the Law of Distress Amendment Act 1908, s 6? It is arguable that the answer is 'yes' since it has been held in other circumstances that a person may be subrogated to the statutory rights of another (Goff and Jones, *The Law of Restitution*, 5th edn, p 140).

Where there has been a partial assignment of the land leased, and the assignee is in breach of covenant, the Law of Property Act 1925, s 190 gives the assignor the right to take subrents in order to obtain an indemnity from the assignee.

5.6 Rights to possession

5.6.1 RIGHT TO AN OVERRIDING LEASE

Under the law prior to 1996 a former tenant or his guarantor could often be required to make a succession of payments under a lease even though the former tenant or guarantor had no right to a reassignment of the lease, or to the grant of any relevant interest from the landlord. The perceived injustice suffered by such persons in having to pay rentals in respect of properties from which they were excluded has to some extent been remedied by the Landlord and Tenant (Covenants) Act 1995, s 19. This gives such a person the right, in specified circumstances, to require the landlord to grant to such person a lease (an 'overriding lease') slightly longer that the defaulting tenant's lease. This will place the person making payment in the position of intermediate landlord, and the defaulting tenant's lease will become a sublease. The person making such payment will then be able either to intercept subrents or to forfeit the relevant tenancy and take possession or (subject to the terms of the overriding lease) to assign or sublet to a third party.

The Landlord and Tenant (Covenants) Act 1995, s 19 raises a number of questions which may have to be resolved by the courts in due course. Its provisions are complex and a detailed analysis is not attempted here. The following points may, however, be noted.

Persons who may claim

An overriding lease may be claimed by a person who 'has duly been required to pay in accordance with s 17'. Section 17 applies to former tenants and to guarantors for former tenants; so these are the persons who can make a claim. A guarantor for the current tenant does not appear to be included and peculiarly may be obliged to pay rents and other sums but with no right to claim an overriding lease. Instead, such a guarantor may be able to procure an assignment of the lease from the tenant, but this may require landlord's consent and may prove difficult if the tenant is under the control of a receiver, liquidator or administrator.

Making the claim

The right only applies where the person paying 'makes full payment' of the amount together with any interest payable. A part payment will not entitle the guarantor, or other person making payment, to the grant of a lease.

The payer must have been 'duly required to pay in accordance with s 17' (see para 5.1.7 above). Thus it seems that the payer will not qualify for an overriding lease if the payment has been made prior to the service of the necessary statutory notice.

The person making payment must make written request to the landlord within 12 months beginning with the date of payment, and specifying the relevant payment.

The request can be protected vis-à-vis third parties (e g a purchaser from the landlord) by registration as a land charge and may be the subject of a notice or caution under the Land Registration Acts as if it were an estate contract.

Termination of the relevant tenancy

The landlord will not be under an obligation to grant an overriding lease if the relevant tenancy has been determined. It is not clear whether this will have the effect that the landlord can escape the obligation if the lease has been disclaimed by a trustee in bankruptcy or liquidator. A disclaimer ends the liability of the insolvent tenant and ends the lease but rights and liabilities of third parties may continue 'as if' the lease had continued (see chapter 6, para 6.6). In such circumstances there are statutory provisions regulating rights to possession by means of the granting of vesting orders. It may be that in such cases the IA 1986 provisions operate to the exclusion of the overriding lease provisions – but this remains to be seen.

Multiple requests

The landlord is not under any obligation if he has already granted an overriding lease to another person. Although the Landlord and Tenant (Covenants) Act 1995, s 19 is not clear on the point, it must be assumed that the section is referring to an overriding lease granted to another claimant and not, for instance, the grant of a lease to an associate of the landlord.

The landlord is not under any obligation if another person has already requested an overriding lease and the request has not been withdrawn or abandoned. So it seems that one claimant may be left in limbo, making payments due but unable to utilise the property, while another dallies – perhaps without very serious intent of taking up a lease.

Where two or more requests are made on the same day then a request made by a former tenant is treated as made before a request made by a guarantor. A request made by a person whose liability in respect of the tenancy commenced before the liability of another person is treated as made before the request of the other person.

Consents required?

An overriding lease is deemed to be authorised as against any mortgagee of the landlord's interest (Landlord and Tenant (Covenants) Act 1995, s 20(4)). The 1995 Act does not, however, deal with the situation where the landlord's reversionary interest is leasehold and the terms of the landlord's superior lease contain prohibitions in respect of the granting of a sublease. In some such circumstances the grant of the overriding lease may be a breach of the superior lease which will render it (and the overriding lease and the relevant lease) liable to forfeiture.

Duration of the overriding lease

The lease is to be for a term equal to the remainder of the term of the lease in respect of which payment has been made plus three days or the longest period (less than three days) that will not wholly displace the landlord's reversionary interest. If the landlord has a reversion which is only one day longer than the relevant lease it appears that the person making payment will not be able to procure the grant of an overriding lease. It is possible that a property owner who has a freehold or long leasehold interest might take advantage of this limitation by structuring his property holdings in such a way that premises intended to be let are held by a company (owned by him) under a lease or leases which are one day longer than the period for which it is intended to grant occupational leases. It will then never be possible for the intermediate landlord company to grant overriding leases pursuant to the Landlord and Tenant (Covenants) Act 1995. It is not clear whether such an arrangement between owner and landlord prior to any agreement with any occupier would be 'an agreement relating to a tenancy' which would fall foul of the anti-avoidance provisions which declare void any such agreement which would frustrate the operation of the 1995 Act (s 25).

Other terms of the overriding lease

The lease will contain the same covenants as the relevant tenancy with the following qualifications:

(i) The covenants are to be the same as they have effect immediately before the grant of the lease (s 19(2)(b)).

(ii) The lease need not reproduce any covenant of the relevant tenancy which is expressed to be a personal covenant (s 19(3)).

(iii) If any term is determined or operates by reference to the commencement of the relevant tenancy, the corresponding lease covenant will fall to be determined or will operate by reference to the relevant tenancy, and the overriding lease need not reproduce any covenant to the extent that it has become spent by the time that the overriding lease is granted (s 19(4)(b)).

(iv) The parties may agree to modify the terms if they wish (s 19(2)(b)).

(v) The overriding lease will, of course, be subject to and with the benefit of the relevant tenancy and accordingly the existence of the relevant tenancy will not constitute a breach of any restriction in the overriding lease against subletting or parting with possession (s 20(5)).

Formalities

Section 20 of the Landlord and Tenant (Covenants) Act 1995 requires that every overriding lease shall state that it is a lease granted under s 19 and whether it is or is not a new tenancy for the purpose of the 1995 Act. It will only be a new tenancy if the relevant tenancy was a new tenancy.

The landlord must grant and deliver to the claimant an overriding lease within a reasonable time after receipt by the landlord of the request. The claimant is thereupon to deliver to the landlord a duly executed counterpart and if he fails to do so then he is not able to exercise any rights which are given by the overriding lease.

Costs

The claimant is liable for the landlord's reasonable costs of and incidental to the grant of the lease. If the claimant withdraws or abandons the request before the grant of the lease the claimant shall be liable for the landlord's reasonable costs incurred in pursuance of the request down to the time of withdrawal or abandonment. For these purposes any withdrawal of a request must be in writing and a claimant is regarded as having abandoned his request if the landlord has made a written request that the claimant take all remaining steps needed before the grant of the lease and the claimant has failed to comply with the landlord's request.

Breach of statutory duty

A claim that the landlord has failed to comply with the obligation to grant the overriding lease is a breach of statutory duty and may be the basis of a damages claim.

5.6.2 RIGHT TO POSSESSION AFTER DISCLAIMER?

It has been noted above that the right of a surety or previous tenant to take an overriding lease may not apply if the lease has been disclaimed. Notwithstanding a disclaimer, however, a surety or former tenant may remain liable to pay rent or satisfy other obligations as if no disclaimer has taken place.

The surety or earlier tenant liable under the terms of the lease can apply for an order to have the lease vested in him, but such an application normally needs to be made within three months of the last notice of disclaimer having been served by the liquidator or trustee, or within three months of the applicant becoming aware of the disclaimer, whichever is the earlier. If the time limit is missed there may be a right to apply for an extension of the time limit (IA 1986, s 376, Insolvency Rules 1986, ('IR 1986') r 4.3).

However, what if the time limit has passed and the court is unwilling to make a vesting order out of time? On the face of it the landlord is entitled to possession since the disclaimer accelerates his reversion (*Re Hyams* (1923) 93 LJ Ch 184, CA) and the tenant is excluded from the property (*Smalley v Quarrier* [1975] 2 All ER 688, CA). But this is the position vis-à-vis landlord and tenant and not necessarily as between the landlord and other parties. The reversion is not, for instance, considered to be accelerated as against a subtenant (see para 6.6.3) and it may be that the position is similar as between landlord and surety or earlier tenant. It is likely that the lease will be regarded as ended if the landlord chooses to retake possession, in which case he will not be entitled to the benefit of a guarantee, which is then discharged (Manisty J in *Harding v Preece* (1882) 9 QBD 281, and Keane J in *Maurice Tempany v Royal Liver Trustees Ltd* [1984] BCLC 568, High Court of Ireland). If the landlord does not take possession it may be that as between landlord and surety the lease is regarded as continuing so that the surety remains liable for the term. In this case it is arguable that the surety is entitled to possession (Manisty J in *Harding v Preece*, see above). It was assumed without argument in *Re Carruthers, ex p Tobit* (1895) 2 Mans 172, by Vaughan Williams J, that in these circumstances an earlier tenant made liable following disclaimer was entitled to relet the premises, and that for this reason he could not prove for rent for the remainder of the term, but only for any reduction in rent (see para 5.10.2).

Sometimes the terms of a conveyance from an earlier tenant to a later one provide that if a later tenant fails to observe the terms of the lease and the earlier tenant is called upon to do so by the landlord, the earlier tenant has a right of re-entry upon the property. This would appear to create an equitable right of re-entry which is enforceable and is not registrable as a land charge (*Shiloh Spinners Ltd v Harding* [1973] AC 691, HL). Since the right of re-entry will not enable the assignor to enforce the lease against the landlord the right of entry is often supplemented by terms which oblige the assignee to transfer the lease back to the assignor if the assignor so requests; although if the landlord's consent is needed to the transfer back the consent will not necessarily be forthcoming.

5.7 Duty on landlord to mitigate loss?

It is sometimes suggested that a landlord is under a duty to mitigate possible loss arising through tenant insolvency or default so as to reduce the burden which might fall upon a former tenant or surety. A landlord might, for example, repossess and seek to re-let premises sooner rather than later. The authorities indicate, however, that there is no such duty.

A case providing a useful analogy is *China and South Sea Bank Ltd v Tan Soon Gin* [1990] 1 AC 536. In that case a loan was secured by a mortgage of shares and by a guarantee. After default by the debtor the mortgagee did not immediately exercise its power of sale and the shares reduced in value until they became worthless. The mortgagee then sought payment from the guarantor. The guarantor claimed that the mortgagee owed a duty to sell the shares once they had begun to decline in value. The Privy Council decided that the mortgagee owed no duty to the guarantor to sell the shares at the best time or at all, and that the guarantor had no defence to the mortgagee's claim upon the guarantee. Thus, it is likely that a landlord owes no duty to a surety or ex-tenant to enforce the terms of the lease against the tenant in possession.

Specifically, if a lease is disclaimed by a liquidator for the current tenant, a landlord is not required to repossess and re-let, but can rely upon rights of indemnity against a former tenant or surety (*Bhogal v Cheema* [1998] 2 EGLR 50). If the former tenant or surety wants to limit financial loss it can itself seek to possess and re-let by applying to court for a vesting order (see chapter 6).

Similarly argument has been put that a former tenant who is entitled to indemnity from a later surety should make efforts to mitigate the loss by negotiation with the landlord prior to making payment to the landlord and claiming indemnity from the surety. This argument has been rejected by the court (*Re a Debtor (No 21 of 1995)* [1995] NPC 170).

It has also been decided that a landlord owes no duty of care to a former tenant to procure that later assignees of the lease are of sufficient financial standing to pay the rent and perform the other obligations in the lease. In *Norwich Union Life Insurance Society v Low Profile Fashions Ltd* (1991) 64 P & CR 187, CA, the original tenant (T) had assigned the lease to an assignee (A1). A1, in turn, with the consent of the landlord, assigned the lease to a second assignee (A2). A2 failed to pay rent, and was then wound up. The landlord sued T, who defended, arguing that a landlord giving licence to assign a lease owes a duty to the original tenant to take reasonable care in approving the assignee, and that in this case the landlord was in breach of duty by approving an unsatisfactory assignee. The Court of Appeal rejected the argument.

5.8 Rent deposits and bank guarantees

The landlord may also, or alternatively, be able to rely upon a bank guarantee or rent deposit in the event of tenant default. In many cases the landlord will through such devices have valuable priority over other creditors.

5.8.1 BANK GUARANTEES AND PERFORMANCE BONDS

A bank guarantee is perhaps the most certain form of security but is usually quite restricted in its terms, as it is not the business of a bank to take upon itself liabilities of its customers. Usually the guarantee will be up to a specified amount only, and in some cases will be limited to liability for non-payment of rent, and will not include liability in respect of other breaches by the tenant. The tenant will often have had to make a specific deposit with the bank, separate from any existing deposit, to meet the liability. Sometimes the bank's assurance will take the form of a performance bond whereby the bank or possibly an insurance company will undertake to pay 'on demand'. The bonds are similar to letters of credit or promissory notes payable on demand (*United City Merchants (Investments) Ltd v Royal Bank of Canada* [1983] 1 AC 168, HL).

5.8.2 RENT DEPOSITS

Rent deposits are more complex and take a variety of forms. In the case of insolvency of a tenant there may be a problem as to what rights a landlord may have over the moneys; and in the case of insolvency of a landlord there may be a question as to whether the moneys may be distributed as assets of the landlord.

Where a tenant who has given a rent deposit is insolvent there are a number of questions which might be posed in relation to the deposit. The first question is whether the landlord has any priority claim to the deposit. The answer to this query depends upon the wording of any rent deposit deed or correspondence regulating the deposit, and upon the mechanics of the deposit. If the moneys have been deposited with the landlord or the landlord's agent or solicitor, or in a specially designated bank account in the landlord's name, the landlord might claim that the money belongs to him, subject to the return of any balance to the tenant at the end of the lease (see *Re Chelsea Cloisters Ltd (in Liquidation)* (1980) 41 P & CR 98, CA). It is arguable, however, that in some such circumstances the landlord is not the owner of the deposit but holds it as security for payment of sums due. If the tenant is a company the rent deposit, being a charge over property of a company should be registered under the Companies Act 1985, s 396; otherwise it will be void and will give the landlord no priority.

A similar but slightly different analysis which might be applied is that the moneys are being held upon trust for the primary purpose of satisfying liabilities under the lease, and that to the extent that they are not required for such purpose there is a resulting trust in favour of the tenant on the basis of *Barclays Bank Ltd v Quistclose Investments Ltd* [1970] AC 567, HL. Since the rules of law and equity do not recognise a purpose trust it may be that the proper analysis of this type of arrangement is that the moneys still remain the property of the tenant but subject to the contractual arrangement in favour of the landlord (Millett (1985) 101 LQR 269). Similarly, if the deposit is held with the tenant's solicitor, or with someone else on behalf of the tenant it might be argued that there is a trust of the *Quistclose* variety, and that the tenant has the better claim to the property, leaving the landlord to enforce his contractual rights in the tenant's liquidation or bankruptcy.

If the rent deposit is being held by someone as stakeholder, the position might be slightly different again. A stakeholder normally acts as agent of both parties to the stakeholding. Pending the outcome of the contingency upon which the stake is held, the money is held upon trust to satisfy the contingencies (*Skinner v Trustee of Property of Reed (a bankrupt)* [1967] Ch 1194). The stakeholder is trustee, but who owns the beneficial interest? It is arguable that the beneficial interest is shared between landlord and tenant subject to the contingency that if there is no breach by the tenant during the period of the deposit agreement, the tenant shall become absolutely entitled, but if there is a breach, the landlord will become absolutely entitled. Meanwhile each of them has a contingent interest only. If the tenant becomes insolvent and defaults the landlord can call upon the stakeholder to release the deposit to him, thus gaining priority over other creditors, but if there is no default the liquidator or trustee has nothing more than a contingent interest which will be of little or no value to anyone unless the lease can be assigned together with the contingent rights.

The second question is whether the landlord can enforce the deposit without leave of the court. Assuming that the deposit constitutes a charge, in bankruptcy or liquidation a chargee is generally free to enforce the charge without the leave of the court. If, however, it is necessary to bring court proceedings, because, for example, the deposit is outside of the landlord's control and the liquidator or trustee refuses to surrender the deposit, leave may be necessary before the landlord can take proceedings to enforce the charge. In a voluntary liquidation no leave is required, but an application may be made by other parties to stay court proceedings (IA 1986, ss 112, 126). In a compulsory liquidation, proceedings may be stayed in the period between petition and winding-up order (IA 1986, s 126), and leave of the court is required to commence or continue proceedings once a winding-up order is actually made (IA 1986, s 130). The position is similar in bankruptcy (IA 1986, s 285). If leave to continue or commence proceedings is required the court will normally give such leave (*Lloyd v David Lloyd & Co* (1877) 6 Ch D 339, CA). If the tenant is a company in administration leave of the court will be required to enforce any security once a petition has been presented, and once an order is made the landlord may only enforce the deposit with the leave of the court or the consent of the administrator (IA 1986, ss 10, 11). If the deposit is in such a form that it gives the landlord contractual rights only rather than proprietary rights the landlord is unlikely to be able to persuade a court to allow enforcement in a liquidation, bankruptcy or administration and the landlord will have to take his place as an ordinary unsecured creditor.

Another problem with rent deposits is that there may be difficulties upon a change of landlord, or of tenant. In *Hua Chiao Commercial Bank Ltd v Chiaphua Industries Ltd* [1987] AC 99, the Privy Council determined that a landlord's obligation to repay a rent deposit was not an obligation which ran with the land so as to bind an assignee of the landlord's reversion. If the obligations under a rent deposit do not 'touch and concern' the leasehold estate it should also follow that the tenant's obligation to allow the landlord to use the deposit will not pass with the lease to an assignee, and in some circumstances it might be possible for the tenant to assign the lease and then claim that the landlord is no longer entitled to the benefit of the deposit. Most well-devised rent deposit deeds will provide for these eventualities, but it is all too easy for a point to be missed and for the deposit deed to give rise to a dispute.

5.9 Insurance against tenant default

A landlord sometimes, but rarely, will have the benefit of an insurance policy known as a tenant default indemnity which will compensate him in the event of the insolvency of the tenant (see (1983) 4 PLB 37; (1986) 277 Estates Gazette 944). Such a policy may be expensive and will normally be subject to a maximum agreed limit of indemnity. An institutional landlord will wish to include the cost in the service charge or insurance charge under the lease so that the premium is passed on to the tenant. A tenant of good financial standing is likely to oppose this as an unnecessary expense, just as he might oppose the giving of a surety or rent deposit. If the insurer is made to indemnify the landlord for a tenant's default it will of course be subrogated to the landlord's rights including the right to prove in a bankruptcy or liquidation.

5.10 Proof by former tenant or surety

A surety or former tenant who is liable under the terms of the lease has rights to prove in the bankruptcy or liquidation of the insolvent tenant. If any such person has actually paid the landlord rent or other sums due under the lease, then the person may prove for the amount paid. Although, at least in most cases, it will make little or no practical difference, the proof may presumably be for a contractual right of indemnity, or, by way of subrogation, a proof for the landlord's rights.

Even if the person liable has not yet been made to pay it might be thought that he has a right to prove for an indemnity in respect of his contingent liability to make payment upon the debtor's future failure to do so. The law in relation to proof by sureties and other persons liable is, unfortunately, not quite as clear as it might be.

5.10.1 PROOF WHERE NO DISCLAIMER

If there is no disclaimer the position in bankruptcy appears to be that a surety or earlier tenant can prove for sums already paid by him. Proof may also be lodged in respect of the contingent liability for future default and the trustee may, taking into account all circumstances, estimate the value of the liability. If such a person is, after the bankrupt's discharge, made liable, no indemnity can at that time be claimed against the discharged bankrupt (*Hardy v Fothergill* (1888) 13 App Cas 351, HL). There can be no objection to the proof on the basis that it is difficult to estimate the liability. In *Re Hinks* (1886) 3 Morr 218, the lease in question had been assigned three times and the ultimate assignee became bankrupt and defaulted in payment of rent. The landlord (L) sued the original tenant (T). T sued the first assignee (A1), who joined the second assignee (A2) by a third party notice. A2 sought to prove in the bankruptcy of the third assignee (A3) for the amount which he had been forced to pay (£240) and a further sum (£2,000) for the contingent liability for the remaining eight years of the term. The trustee rejected the proof on the ground that it was incapable of estimation, but Cave J held that the trustee was wrong to do so and that the proof should be admitted, subject to estimation by the trustee.

There appears to be no direct authority where the tenant is a company in liquidation, but the general principle (that the contingent claim is provable) ought to be the same. In valuing the claim the liquidator will probably have to take into account the fact that upon dissolution of the company the lease will vest in the Crown, which might then disclaim.

5.10.2 PROOF WHERE DISCLAIMER

If the trustee or liquidator disclaims, the surety or earlier tenant should be able to prove for the liability under the lease. Where, in addition to the insolvent tenant, there is only one other person liable under the lease, the effect of the disclaimer will be to transform that person's liability from a contingent one into an actual liability for performance of all covenants under the lease for the remainder of the term. The landlord might, however, take possession, in which case he should not be entitled to any remedy greater than the diminution in the letting value of the property.

However, the person liable may, of course, obtain a vesting order, or may be entitled to possession of the property (see para 5.6.2). If so, he will not be able to prove for the whole rent but only for any reduction in the letting value of the premises (cf para 6.9.2). In *Re Carruthers, ex p Tobit* (1895) 2 Mans 172, a landlord let premises in High Street, Kensington to Phillips for 21 years at a rent of £100 per annum. Phillips assigned the lease to Tobit, who, in turn, transferred it to Carruthers, who gave his covenant to indemnify Tobit. Carruthers subsequently became bankrupt and his trustee in bankruptcy disclaimed the lease, of which four years remained unexpired. The premises were also in serious disrepair so as to be virtually unlettable. The law report does not explain what had happened to Phillips, but presumably the primary liability fell to Tobit. Tobit, in reliance upon his right to indemnity sought to prove in Carruther's bankruptcy for £400, being the rent for the remainder of the term, and to prove also for disrepair. Vaughan Williams J assuming that Tobit would be entitled to possession and able to relet decided that Tobit's basic right of proof was the reduction in the rental value of the premises, which he assessed at £30 (i e the then letting value was reduced from £100 per annum to £70 per annum). He was also able to prove for dilapidations and for two quarters' rent to allow a period for Tobit to put the premises in repair prior to reletting.

5.10.3 DOUBLE PROOF

The position is further complicated by the rule against double proof. In simple terms the rule prohibits two separate persons from proving in bankruptcy or liquidation for the same debt, since to allow this would result in a double dividend being paid for a single amount. Applying this rule the Court of Appeal has held that a creditor and a surety cannot both prove in a debtor's bankruptcy for the same debt (*Re Fenton, ex p Fenton Textile Association Ltd* [1931] 1 Ch 85, CA). Thus if the landlord has put in a proof, a surety who is liable to the landlord, but who has not paid the debt, cannot also prove.

If the landlord lodges a proof and is then paid in full by the surety, the surety will be entitled to any dividends paid in respect of the landlord's proof (*Re Sass* [1896] 2 QB 12); and the landlord is entitled to prove in full notwithstanding any payments to him by the surety, and may afterwards pursue the surety for any balance (*Re Rees* (1881) 17 Ch D 98, CA). But if after receiving a sum from the surety and a dividend the landlord has more than the amount of the debt, he will have to repay the surplus to the surety.

5.10.4 SUBROGATION TO PROOF

The surety or earlier tenant, apart from having a proof for the indemnity is also entitled to be subrogated to rights of proof which the landlord might have. This may be valuable where the landlord has a pre-preferential right to have the rent treated as an expense of the liquidation or bankruptcy. It has been held that, if an earlier tenant pays to the landlord rent in respect of a period during which a liquidator is using the property for the purposes of the liquidation, the earlier tenant or other person making payment may be subrogated to the landlord's right to claim the payment with priority as an expense of the liquidation (*Re Downer Enterprises Ltd* [1974] 2 All ER 1074, see para 5.5.2).

5.11 Law reform

The first edition of this book stated that the balance of legal relationships in respect of commercial leases was weighted in the landlord's favour. The popular understanding of the Landlord and Tenant (Covenants) Act 1995 is that its principal purpose is to redress that balance. The extent to which such redress has come about should become clear with time and with judicial decision upon those aspects of the 1995 Act which are susceptible of argument.

The Landlord and Tenant (Covenants) Act 1995 contains an anti-avoidance provision so that any agreement relating to a tenancy is void to the extent that it would have effect to exclude, modify or frustrate the operation of the 1995 Act. Such an agreement is also void to the extent that it provides for the termination or surrender of the tenancy or the imposition on the tenant of any penalty, disability or liability as a consequence of, in connection with or in the event of the operation of any provision of the 1995 Act (s 25). Commercial practice and judicial decision should in due course test the efficacy of these anti-avoidance provisions, and investigate whether further reform will be needed in the future.

CHAPTER 6

Disclaimer of lease by trustee in bankruptcy or liquidator

Where assets are being collected in, realised and distributed in bankruptcy or liquidation, the trustee in bankruptcy or liquidator is entitled to walk away from continuing obligations arising in relation to onerous property, by the process of 'disclaimer'. In the context of landlord and tenant the obvious property which will fall within the category of 'onerous' property is the lease.

If the lease has a capital value the trustee or liquidator will normally sell or surrender it at a premium so as to realise as much as possible for creditors; but if the lease is at a full rack rent and has no realisation value, and if it is not needed for the purpose of the bankruptcy or liquidation, the trustee or liquidator will often wish to disclaim it so that the rents cannot be claimed from the trustee personally or claimed as an expense in the bankruptcy or liquidation (see chapter 2). A liquidator (whether in voluntary or compulsory liquidation) or trustee in bankruptcy may disclaim the lease under the powers given by the Insolvency Act 1986 ('IA, 1986'), ss 178–182 (for liquidation) and ss 315–320, which consolidate and modify the law formerly set out in the Bankruptcy Acts and the Companies Acts. In so far as it may be relevant to take into account the old law it should be remembered that the power of a trustee in bankruptcy to disclaim was first introduced in 1869, and a similar power was first given to a liquidator by the Companies Act 1929. It may seem unjust that landlords' contractual rights may be defeated by a disclaimer but landlords do at least have rights to prove in bankruptcy or liquidation for loss suffered (see para 6.9.1). Landlords may also be able to pursue rights against sureties and previous tenants (see para 6.6 and chapter 5).

The power to disclaim is available to liquidators and trustees to enable the assets of the company or the bankrupt's estate to be effectively wound up. Where the tenant is in receivership or administration the objective is generally not to wind up affairs and there is therefore no power for a receiver or administrator to disclaim.

6.1 Interests which may be disclaimed

The liquidator or trustee can disclaim 'onerous property', which means any unprofitable contract and any other property which is unsaleable or not readily saleable or is such that it may give rise to a liability to pay money or perform any other onerous act (IA 1986, ss 178 and 315). A lease will normally be onerous property since most leases give rise to a liability to pay money and contain other onerous covenants (*Eyre v Hall* (1986) 18 HLR 509).

6.1.1 CONTRACTUAL INTERESTS

Most interests by way of lease may be disclaimed. A fixed term lease may be disclaimed, however short. It would appear to make no difference whether the lease was made by deed or is merely one created orally or in writing not being a deed (i e a lease at the best rent reasonably obtainable without taking a fine and taking effect immediately in possession for a term not exceeding three years within the Law of Property Act 1925, s 54(2)). There appears to be no reason why a periodic tenancy should not be disclaimed and it was assumed in *Alloway v Steere* (1882) 10 QBD 22, that a yearly periodic tenancy could be disclaimed (although with a shorter period e g a weekly tenancy, a notice to quit might be simpler for the trustee or liquidator).

Any unprofitable contract falls within the definition of 'onerous property', and accordingly it has also been held that an agreement by a bankrupt to take a lease can be disclaimed (*Re Maughan, ex p Monkhouse* (1885) 14 QBD 956).

If there is an existing agreement by a bankrupt to *sell* a lease, and the trustee wishes to disclaim, the position is different. It has been held that the contract for sale passes an equitable interest in the lease to the purchaser. The equity of the purchaser is binding upon the trustee in bankruptcy and it would be unfair to allow the trustee to disclaim the contract so as to allow the trustee to have the full legal and equitable interest in the lease, leaving the purchaser as an unsecured creditor for any deposit paid (*Capital Prime Properties plc v Worthgate Limited* [2000] 1 BCLC 647).

If, however, the continuing obligations under the lease are onerous the trustee might be able to disclaim the contract for sale, but only if at the same time he disclaims the lease itself (*Re Bastable, ex p Trustee* [1901] 2 KB 518, CA; *Pearce v Bastable's Trustee* [1901] 2 Ch 122). As to the enforceability of contracts to take or sell a lease, see para 7.2.4.

Sometimes liabilities under a lease survive its termination, e g liability for terminal disrepair; it has been decided that a trustee in bankruptcy can disclaim, even though the lease has terminated (whether by expiry of time or forfeiture), so as to be freed from such liability (*Re Throckmorton, ex p Paterson* (1879) 11 Ch D 908, CA; *Re Morrish, ex p Sir W Hart Dyke* (1882) 22 Ch D 410, CA), from the date of his appointment.

The disclaimer, if made, must be in respect of the entire property and not part only. A trustee or liquidator cannot sever the contract, disclaiming part only. In *Re Fussell, ex p Allen* (1882) 20 Ch D 341, land and chattels had been leased under a single contract and the trustee wished to disclaim in respect of the land but not the chattels. The Court of Appeal held that the trustee could not opt for such a partial disclaimer.

6.1.2 STATUTORY RIGHTS OF OCCUPATION

Sometimes a tenant's right to occupy property is by virtue of a statutory right. In the case of a commercial lease a tenant will often have rights under the Landlord and Tenant Act 1954. If the contractual term of such a lease expires (whether by effluxion of time or by landlord's notice), but the lease has not been terminated in accordance with the 1954 Act, the lease continues by virtue of s 23 of the Act. The continuation lease is not simply a personal right of occupation, but is a proprietary interest which is assignable, and it is likely that it will vest in the trustee in bankruptcy of a bankrupt tenant and is an interest which can be disclaimed by a trustee in bankruptcy or liquidator.

Rights which do not vest in a trustee in bankruptcy

In the case of residential leases most rights of occupation given by statute to individual tenants are merely personal. They do not vest in the individual tenant's trustee in bankruptcy and they cannot be disclaimed by the trustee. For example, a statutory tenancy under the Rent Acts, being purely personal in nature, does not vest in a trustee in bankruptcy and cannot be disclaimed (*Sutton v Dorf* [1932] 2 KB 304). Similarly a secure tenancy under the Housing Acts cannot be disclaimed. In *City of London Corpn v Bown* (1990) 60 P & CR 42, CA, it was held that the fact that such a tenancy is not assignable (Housing Act 1985, s 91) means that it is not a proprietary interest which a trustee can realise or disclaim.

The rules in relation to some such tenancies have now been codified so that it is now expressly provided by statute that secure tenancies, and certain assured tenancies and protected tenancies, which contain restrictions on assignment do not automatically vest in the trustee (IA 1986, s 283(3A)) and cannot be disclaimed. A secure tenancy which is periodic or which is a fixed term granted on or after 5 November 1982 does not vest in the trustee. In the case of an assured tenancy, an assured agricultural occupancy, or a tenancy where the bankrupt is a protected occupier under the Rent (Agriculture) Act 1976, the tenancy does not vest in the trustee if by the terms of the lease the tenant is prohibited from assigning or underletting, or if the terms allow assignment or underletting but on condition that the landlord may require a premium or that the tenant offers to surrender.

There are, in addition to the above, several other circumstances in which leases will not vest in a trustee in bankruptcy. A lease which a bankrupt tenant holds upon trust is not part of the bankrupt's estate and does not vest in the trustee; and a lease acquired by the bankrupt after the commencement of the bankruptcy does not automatically vest in the trustee in bankruptcy (see para 1.5.7).

Notice requiring vesting in the trustee

Although the leases mentioned above do not automatically vest in the trustee in bankruptcy, the trustee can (except in the case of a lease held upon trust) serve a notice upon the bankrupt whereupon the tenancy will vest in the trustee and the vesting relates back to the commencement of the bankruptcy, or, in the case of after acquired property, the date upon which the property vested in the bankrupt (IA 1986, ss 308A and 333). The notice must be served within 42 days beginning with the day on which the tenancy first came to the knowledge of the trustee, although it may be served later with the leave of the court. In the case of an after acquired lease the tenant must notify the trustee of the lease within the 21 days following its acquisition, and the 42 days runs from the date of notification. If such a notice is served so as to vest the tenancy in the trustee, he cannot later disclaim the tenancy without the leave of the court (IA 1986, s 315(4)). There is protection for a purchaser in good faith of any such interest from the bankrupt who does not have notice of the bankruptcy.

6.1.3 STATUTORY LICENCES

There are rights other than occupational rights which can be disclaimed. For instance, a waste management licence under the Environmental Protection Act 1990 can be disclaimed notwithstanding that the Act provides that the licence is to continue until determined by that Act (*Official Receiver v Environment Agency* [1999] 3 EGLR 21, CA). On the other hand sometimes statute may specifically provide that a certain licence is not to be regarded as property for the purpose of the IA 1986 or cannot be disclaimed as is the case of a licence under the Coal Industry Act 1994.

6.2 Leave of court

Under previous legislation leave of the court was required before a trustee or liquidator could disclaim. The fact that leave was necessary gave landlords and other interested parties the opportunity to object to the disclaimer on the ground that they would be prejudiced by disclaimer. Now, under the IA 1986 leave is not normally necessary, and a landlord or other interested party's right is limited to the making of an application for an order to have the lease vested in himself or some third party (see para 6.7), and it has been decided that there is no general discretion to interfere with a decision by a trustee or liquidator to disclaim in the absence of bad faith or perversity which would justify a challenge under the IA 1986, s 168(5) (*Re Hans Place Ltd* [1993] BCLC 768). The fact that a landlord or other party may be prejudiced will not be sufficient to persuade the court to interfere with the decision of a trustee or liquidator acting in the interests of the insolvent tenant and its general creditors (*Re Hans Place Ltd*, see above).

In bankruptcy there are exceptions where leave is necessary before a trustee in bankruptcy can disclaim (see para 6.1.2). Where leave is required a disclaimer without leave will be void (*Metropolis Estates Ltd v Wilde* [1940] 2 KB 536, CA).

If leave is necessary the court will consider whether the disclaimer will benefit the creditors of the bankrupt (*Re Clarke, ex p East and West India Dock Co* (1881) 17 Ch D 759, CA). It is not clear to what extent prejudice to third parties such as the landlord, former tenant or surety will be taken into account. In *Re Katherine et Cie Ltd* [1932] 1 Ch 70, possible prejudice to a landlord was considered but the case was concerned with whether, under previous legislation, leave should be given to a liquidator to disclaim. It was emphasised that considerations differed between liquidation and bankruptcy because in the latter the trustee will be personally liable on the lease if he is unable to disclaim (see also *Re Müller, ex p Buxton* (1880) 15 Ch D 289).

6.3 Timing of disclaimer

Under previous law there was a one-year limitation upon the power to disclaim. Now, under the IA 1986 the trustee or liquidator can disclaim at any time that is desired, unless he has previously been put to an election to disclaim (see below). A decision whether or not to disclaim does not have to be made immediately the trustee or liquidator is appointed, and the property might be used for the purposes of the bankruptcy or liquidation for some time before disclaimer. This may be inconvenient for a landlord or surety who for commercial reasons may wish to know with certainty whether there is or is not to be a disclaimer. If, for example, a landlord has a prospective new tenant for the property the landlord may not want to lose the prospective tenant, only to find that a disclaimer occurs shortly after and the premises are then vacant.

Putting liquidator or trustee to election to disclaim

In order to assist landlords and other interested persons the IA 1986 allows any person interested in the property to impose a 28-day time limit upon the trustee in bankruptcy or liquidator by written notice requiring him to disclaim within that time or not at all (IA 1986, ss 316 and 178(5)). The notice must be delivered to the liquidator or trustee personally or by registered post and must be in the form of a 'notice to elect' (see Insolvency Rules 1986, 'IR 1986', rr 4.191, 6.183 and IA 1986 Sch 4, Forms 4.54, 6.62).

This option may be useful to a landlord who wants to relet the property and who cannot procure a surrender; he can put the trustee or liquidator to his election in an attempt to force his hand. If the trustee or liquidator fails to disclaim he runs the risk that rents will be an expense for the whole period of the bankruptcy or liquidation, and, in the case of a trustee in bankruptcy, the risk of personal liability.

The liquidator or trustee does not necessarily lose the opportunity to disclaim for all time, since the court has jurisdiction to extend time if the liquidator or trustee wishes to disclaim later (IA 1986, ss 178(5), 376), but, in order to provide sufficient certainty for the landlord, the application to extend time should normally be made within the 28-day period, unless there is some special circumstance, such as illness or fraud on the part of the landlord, to justify a late application (*Re Jones, ex p Lovering* (1874) 9 Ch App 586). The mere fact that the landlord has required a trustee or liquidator to pay rent in advance is not a sufficient reason to justify a late application by the trustee or liquidator for leave to disclaim (*Re Richardson, ex p Harris* (1880) 16 Ch D 613). Even if leave is given the court might decide to impose a condition upon the trustee or liquidator; such as a requirement that the trustee or liquidator personally pay rent and costs (*Re Page, ex p Mackay* (1884) 14 QBD 401).

6.4 Procedure for disclaimer

In order to disclaim, the liquidator or trustee must file a prescribed notice of disclaimer in court (IR 1986 4.187, 6.178) and must within seven days of its return to him serve a copy upon (so far as he is aware of their existence): any subtenant or mortgagee; any person claiming an interest in respect of the disclaimed property – such as the landlord (*Re Morgan, ex p Morgan* (1889) 22 QBD 592); and any person who is under a liability in respect of the disclaimed property which is not discharged by the disclaimer, such as a former tenant or a surety (IR 1986, rr 4.188 and 6.179). If it appears to the trustee or liquidator that there may be some other person interested in the property the liquidator or trustee may serve notice on that person requiring him within 14 days to declare whether he claims any interest and, if so, what interest. If no response is received within 14 days the trustee or liquidator is entitled to assume that the person concerned has no interest in the property which would prevent or impede a disclaimer.

In addition, in bankruptcy a disclaimer of an interest in a dwelling-house does not take effect unless a copy of the disclaimer has also been served (so far as the trustee is aware) on every person in occupation of or claiming a right to occupy the dwelling-house.

Although the formalities above may appear to be strict, they have not always been strictly applied. In *MEPC plc v Scottish Amicable Life Assurance Society* (1993) 67 P & CR 314, the Court of Appeal took a relaxed view of a notice of disclaimer which purported to disclaim a documentary licence to assign a lease and held that the notice was effective as a disclaimer of the lease itself.

If the disclaimed lease was registered at the Land Registry, an application will usually need to be made to the Registry for closure of the title and if the landlord's interest is registered for the cancellation of the notice of the lease in the register of the landlord's title. The original lease and land certificate should be lodged together with the necessary evidence to prove the bankruptcy or liquidation and the disclaimer. A certificate of the trustee or liquidator should be obtained to the effect that the prescribed notices have been served and no application has been made for a vesting order.

6.5 Effect of disclaimer in relation to landlord, tenant and trustee

The effect of a disclaimer is quite complex. In general it ends the relationship of landlord and tenant. It also absolves a trustee in bankruptcy from personal liability. Notwithstanding the determination of the lease vis-à-vis landlord and tenant, however, rights and liabilities of third parties subsist *as though the lease had continued* as explained in para 6.6.

6.5.1 POSITION OF LANDLORD AND TENANT

In liquidation and bankruptcy a disclaimer 'operates so as to determine, as from the date of the disclaimer, the rights, interests and liabilities of [the company] [the bankrupt and his estate] in or in respect of the property disclaimed' (IA 1986, ss 178, 315). The disclaimer, as between landlord and tenant, puts an end to any future liabilities under the lease and the landlord and tenant lose the benefit of any covenants which take effect on the expiry of the term, as if there was a surrender which did not preserve those liabilities (*Re Morrish, ex p Sir W Hart Dyke* (1882) 22 Ch D 410, CA). Where rent is payable in arrears it is likely that it can be apportioned up to the date of the disclaimer under the Apportionment Act 1870, s 3, but the amount due prior to the bankruptcy order or petition for winding up can be the subject of proof only. It is likely that sums due from the date of the bankruptcy order or winding-up petition, up to the date of disclaimer, may be claimed as an expense of the bankruptcy or liquidation (see paras 2.3.2, 2.4). The loss of the future rents is a loss which the landlord can prove for in the bankruptcy or liquidation (para 6.9.1).

Landlord's right to possession

On disclaimer the landlord's reversion is accelerated and he may require that possession of the property be delivered up to him (*Re Hyams, ex p Lindsay v Hyams* (1923) 93 LJ Ch 184, CA). The tenant has no right to remain in the property after the disclaimer takes effect (*Smalley v Quarrier* [1975] 2 All ER 688, CA). It appears, however, that the landlord does not have to repossess, and if the landlord cannot relet and has the benefit of the covenant of a former tenant or surety he can rely upon such covenant to require continuing payments instead of repossessing. If the landlord does repossess he is not still entitled to the benefit of any such covenants (*Harding v Preece* (1882) 9 QBD 281), so that he cannot have the full benefit of both the land and the right to sue the former tenant or surety (see further para 5.6.2). It is a question of fact as to whether the landlord has repossessed, which question may be difficult to determine in some cases – e g where the landlord is not aware of the disclaimer and an entity associated with the tenant continues to occupy the property (*Cromwell Developments Ltd v Godfrey* [1998] 2 EGLR 62, CA).

Right to remove fixtures

If no application for a vesting order has been made (see para 6.7), the position in bankruptcy used to be that by disclaimer the trustee lost any right to remove fixtures, and the landlord was entitled to all fixtures removed whether before or after the disclaimer (*Re Roberts, ex p Brook* (1878) 10 Ch D 100; *Re Latham, ex p Glegg* (1881) 19 Ch D 7, CA; *Re Lavies, ex p Stephens* (1877) 7 Ch D 127, CA). This was on the basis of the previous statutes providing that the lease was deemed to be surrendered from the date of the appointment of the trustee. Under the modern law the effect of the disclaimer is that the rights and liabilities in respect of the property are ended from the date of the disclaimer, and this ought to be the relevant date before which the liquidator or trustee should remove any tenant's fixtures.

6.5.2 PERSONAL LIABILITY OF TRUSTEE IN BANKRUPTCY

In the case of bankruptcy, disclaimer of property 'discharges the trustee from all personal liability in respect of that property as from the commencement of his trusteeship' (IA 1986, s 315). Thus if there are arrears of rent for the period from the trustee's appointment to disclaimer the trustee cannot be sued (*Titterton v Cooper* (1882) 9 QBD 473, CA), and the court cannot order him to pay a sum for use and occupation for the time that the premises were vested in him (*Re Sandwell, ex p Zerfass* (1885) 14 QBD 960; *Metropolis Estates Co Ltd v Wilde* [1940] 2 KB 536, CA).

If, however, the trustee needs leave to disclaim (see para 6.2) the court might order him to pay rent up to the date of the disclaimer as a condition of giving leave. In cases decided under previous legislation the court would order the trustee to take personal responsibility for rent up to the date of disclaimer if he unreasonably delayed disclaiming (*Re Page, ex p Mackay* (1884) 14 QBD 401). If the trustee kept the property for the purpose of the bankruptcy the court would order the trustee to pay the rent but with a right to an indemnity from the bankrupt's estate (*Re Witton, ex p Arnal* (1883) 24 Ch D 26, CA). Under the current legislation, and bearing in mind that in many cases no leave is required, it is submitted that in similar circumstances it is more likely that the rent from the date of the bankruptcy order will be treated as an expense of the bankruptcy (see para 2.4).

Disclaimer of the lease will not, of course, absolve the trustee from torts committed by him in respect of the premises. The trustee may, for instance, be liable for the tort of waste in removing landlord's fixtures from the premises (*Re Roberts, ex p Brook* (1878) 10 Ch D 100, CA). In addition, the trustee may be personally responsible for an active breach of a term of the lease. If, for instance, the trustee in breach of the lease terms, has wrongfully taken produce which is grown upon the property, he cannot escape liability through the device of disclaiming (*Schofield v Hincks* (1888) 58 LJQB 147).

6.5.3 VALIDITY OF DISCLAIMER

A disclaimer is presumed to be valid and effective unless it is proved that the trustee or liquidator has been in breach of his duty with respect to the giving of notice of disclaimer or otherwise, under the IA 1986, ss 178 to 180 (in the case of a liquidator), under ss 315 to 319 (in the case of a trustee) or under the IR 1986 (*Re Hans Place Ltd* [1993] BCLC 768).

6.6 Effect of disclaimer in relation to third parties

The effect of disclaimer on the rights and obligations of third parties is quite complex, and discussion of the result of a disclaimer is best prefaced by the wording of the 1986 Act, ss 178 and 315 which provide that a disclaimer 'operates so as to determine from the date of the disclaimer, the rights, interests and liabilities of [the company][the bankrupt] in or in respect of the property disclaimed; but does not, except so far as is necessary for the purpose of releasing [the company] [the bankrupt] from liability, affect the rights or liabilities of any other person'. Thus a disclaimer relieves the insolvent tenant from liability in respect of the lease – including any liability to indemnify any third party, such as a former tenant or guarantor, in respect of payments made by them instead of the insolvent tenant (*Hindcastle Ltd v Barbara Attenborough Associates Ltd* [1996] 1 EGLR 94, HL). The position of such third parties is, however, as if the lease had continued (see para 6.6.3).

6.6.1 POSITION WHERE LEASE HAS NOT BEEN ASSIGNED

Where the lease has not been assigned and it is an original tenant in possession who is insolvent it was previously the rule that disclaimer ended the liability of a surety despite the normal rule that obligations of third parties are unaffected. The House of Lords in *Hindcastle* (see above), however, has now ruled that there is no automatic discharge of a surety upon disclaimer. The terms of the relevant guarantee should, however, be considered so as to ascertain whether its extent is such as to cover the period following disclaimer (see *Murphy v Sawyer-Hoare* [1994] 2 BCLC 59).

6.6.2 POSITION WHERE LEASE HAS BEEN ASSIGNED

Where the insolvent tenant is an assignee of the lease there may be a number of other persons who are liable under the terms of the lease; e g the original tenant, intermediate assignees, and sureties for original tenant, intermediate assignees and the insolvent assignee.

Liability of former tenants

Following the general rule that disclaimer does not, except so far as is necessary for releasing the bankrupt or company from liability, affect the liabilities of any other person it has been held that if the insolvent tenant is an assignee disclaimer does not end any liability which a former tenant may have. In *Warnford Investments Ltd v Duckworth* [1979] Ch 127, an assignee of the lease, being a company, went into voluntary liquidation and the liquidator disclaimed. The original tenant had a continuing lease liability under the privity of contract doctrine applicable to 'old tenancies' (see para 5.1) and the landlord sought to recover from the original tenant the rent accruing due under the lease after the date of disclaimer. Megarry V-C held that the original tenant remained liable on the terms of the lease.

The position is no different in respect of an intermediate assignee who has taken on a lease liability which has not been released. In *Hindcastle Ltd v Barbara Attenborough Associates Ltd* [1995] QB 95 (affd [1996] 1 EGLR 94, HL), the Court of Appeal regarded the position of an intermediate assignee as indistinguishable from the position of an original tenant who remains liable notwithstanding a disclaimer on behalf of the ultimate assignee.

Liability of surety for assignee

Similarly it has been held that a surety for the insolvent assignee remains liable, notwithstanding the discharge of the assignee. In *Harding v Preece* (1882) 9 QBD 281, the original tenant (T) assigned the lease to A and took the covenant of a third party (S) as surety for the payment of the rent and compliance with the lease by A and for the duration of the term. On the bankruptcy of A the lease was disclaimed and the landlord recovered the next half-year's rent from T who in turn sought indemnity from S. The court held that S remained liable, since the disclaimer did not affect the liability of S as third party.

In the more usual case, where it is the landlord who has the benefit of the surety covenant, the same rule applies – i e that the disclaimer of the lease on behalf of the assignee will not affect the liability of the surety (*Hindcastle Ltd v Barbara Attenborough Associates Ltd*, see above). In some cases, however, it may be possible as a matter of construction to avoid this conclusion. In *Murphy v Sawyer-Hoare* [1994] 2 BCLC 59, a landlord granted consent to an assignment of a lease by a formal consent document in which a surety for the assignee covenanted with the landlord that '... the assignee will pay the rent reserved by the lease and will perform and observe all the covenants on the part of the tenant therein contained ...'. Following a disclaimer by a liquidator for the assignee the question arose as to whether the surety remained liable for the rent and other tenant's obligations. Grabiner QC held that the surety was discharged by the disclaimer. Although he recognised that the surety could be kept on the hook, as a matter of construction he was of the view that the surety obligation in the case before him was not clear enough to achieve this objective. Further, it was drafted in terms which made the surety liable only following default by the tenant. After disclaimer there could be no such default, and no liability on the part of the surety.

6.6.3 EFFECT ON SUBTENANT

The effect of disclaimer of a headlease upon subtenants is most peculiar. Although the headlease is determined it might be unfair to the landlord if the subtenant were allowed to remain upon the terms of the sublease, particularly if the rent under the sublease was lower than that under the headlease. The solution adopted by the judiciary is to allow the subtenant to occupy (for the remainder of the sublease) as long as the terms of the headlease are complied with. The effect is perhaps best summarised by Vinelott J in *Re AE Realisations* [1987] 3 All ER 83 (and see *Re Levy, ex p Walton* (1881) 17 Ch D 746, CA), where he described the effect of disclaimer upon the headlease, thus:

> 'The position under [the earlier statute] as interpreted in *Re Levy, ex p Walton*, (1881) 17 Ch D 746, was simply this: as between the lessor and the bankrupt lessee, the disclaimer operated as a surrender. As between the lessor and the underlessee, the lease was to be treated as still in existence, the underlessee was entitled to remain in possession during the term of the underlease. However, the lessor retained his rights in rem – that is his rights to distrain for rent due under the lease and to forfeit for non-payment of rent or for breach of covenant. If the right to forfeit for non-payment of rent became exercisable then, subject to the statutory power of the court to relieve against forfeiture, the underlease and the underlessee's right to continue in possession fell with it.'

Vinelott J continued to explain that the effect of the disclaimer upon the sublease is that the sublease no longer binds the head tenant and does not become binding upon the head landlord; it remains in existence only in so far as is necessary to support the subtenant's right to remain in possession during the term granted by the sublease and so long as the headlease does not become liable to forfeiture.

So the subtenant can remain in possession for the duration of the original sublease as long as the landlord does not re-enter for breach of the disclaimed headlease terms. The terms of the headlease, however, are not directly enforceable between the parties (*Re Finley, ex p Clothworkers' Co* (1888) 21 QBD 475, CA). The subtenant's right to remain in possession is not to be regarded as the continuation of the sublease (*Re AE Realisations*, see above) but is a bundle of rights in the property which is assignable and is regarded as a good title for the purposes of satisfying a contract for sale of the subtenant's interest (*Re Thompson and Cottrell's Contract* [1943] Ch 97). If the sublease is protected by the Landlord and Tenant Act 1954 it is probable that the subtenant remains protected and has the usual renewal rights.

The landlord may re-enter for any breach of terms of the disclaimed lease – and notwithstanding that the subtenant may have applied for a vesting order under IA 1986, s 181 (*Pellicano v MEPC plc* [1994] 1 EGLR 104). The landlord's right, however, is subject to the subtenant's right to apply for relief from forfeiture under the Law of Property Act 1925, s 146(4) (*Hill v Griffin* [1987] 1 EGLR 81, CA; *Barclays Bank Plc v Prudential Assurance Co Ltd* [1998] BCC 928.

6.6.4 EFFECT ON MORTGAGEE

The effect upon a mortgagee is similar to the effect in relation to a subtenant. So long as the head rents are paid and the other covenants in the headlease performed the mortgagee may have the benefit of the property (*Re Wilson* (1871) LR 13 Eq 186) and may sell the rights to a third party (see *Re Thompson and Cottrell's Contract*, above).

6.6.5 ELECTION FOR VESTING ORDER

Since neither the terms of the headlease nor the sublease are directly enforceable between head landlord and subtenant or mortgagee the position following disclaimer is not entirely satisfactory. For instance, if the headlease contained a rent review clause which was designed to operate on the basis of obligations between landlord and tenant it will not be enforceable between landlord and subtenant. In order to give the parties a chance to remedy the situation legislation has given interested parties such as the landlord the right to put the subtenant to an election to have the lease vested in him or to be excluded from all interest in the property. The subtenant or mortgagee too can make an application for a vesting order to regularise the position (see para 6.7).

6.6.6 OBLIGATION TO TAKE NEW LEASE

Some lease guarantees provide that upon disclaimer the guarantor will take a new lease of the property – usually for the residue of the term of the original lease and otherwise upon the same terms as the original lease. Such an obligation is a personal obligation of the guarantor which is apparently not discharged by the disclaimer, and which does not carry with it any right of indemnity from the tenant (*Re Yarmarine (IW) Ltd* [1992] BCLC 276).

6.7 Vesting of lease in surety or other party

It has been explained above (paras 6.5, 6.6) that disclaimer can have unfortunate effects for some of the persons who are interested in the lease or any sublease. The difficulty was recognised as early as the nineteenth century so that a solution was incorporated into the Bankruptcy Act 1883 which permitted interested persons to apply to the court to order that the lease be vested in an appropriate person. The current statutory provisions for liquidation and bankruptcy provide (IA 1986, ss 179 and 317) that the disclaimer does not take effect unless either:

'(a) no application [to court under s 181 or s 320] is made ... before ... 14 days [of service of the last copy of the disclaimer]; or
(b) where such an application has been made, the court directs that the disclaimer [shall] [is to] take effect.'

So if no application to court is made within 14 days of service of the disclaimer and any copy notices then the disclaimer takes effect, with the results described in paras 6.5 and 6.6 above. If an application is made the effect of the disclaimer is postponed and will not have effect until the application has been heard.

6.7.1 PERSONS ENTITLED TO APPLY TO COURT

The application to court is made under IA 1986, s 181 or s 320. The sections provide that any person who 'claims an interest in the disclaimed property' or any person 'who is under any liability in respect of the disclaimed property, not being a liability discharged by the disclaimer' may apply to the court for an order. Persons who can apply under these provisions will include the landlord (*Re Cock, ex p Shilson* (1887) 20 QBD 343), subtenants, mortgagees, original tenants, intermediate assignees, and sureties whose liability is not discharged by the disclaimer.

The 'disclaimed property' for the purpose of the section is the lease – but for a person to be entitled to apply for a vesting order he need not have a direct proprietary interest in the lease; it is sufficient that the applicant has a financial interest which is adversely affected by the disclaimer. For this reason a subtenant with a statutory tenancy is included in the class of persons who can apply (*Re Vedmay Ltd* (1993) 69 P & CR 247). So too is a local authority which has registered a local land charge for amounts to be secured on the property (*Hackney London Borough Council v Crown Estate Commissioners* [1996] 1 EGLR 151). But an intended assignee of the lease who occupies the property under the terms of an agreement for lease does not have a sufficient interest in the disclaimed lease to enable him to apply for a vesting order – at least where the agreement is conditional upon obtaining landlord's consent and such consent has not been given (*Lloyds Bank SF Nominees v Aladdin Ltd* [1996] 1 BCLC 721, CA).

If a surety's obligations have been discharged by the disclaimer the surety is not entitled to apply for a new lease (*Re Yarmarine (IW) Ltd* [1992] BCLC 276 and *Re No 1 London Ltd* [1991] BCC 118). The mere fact of disclaimer, however, does not by itself cause the discharge of the surety (*Hindcastle Ltd v Barbara Attenborough Associates Ltd* [1996] 1 EGLR 94, HL)

Procedure

The application must be made within three months of the applicant becoming aware of the disclaimer (IR 1986, rr 4.194, 6.186), whether he becomes aware by receipt of notice from the trustee or liquidator, or otherwise. The application must be accompanied by an affidavit stating whether the applicant applies as a person claiming an interest in the lease, or as a person under a liability in respect of it, or in bankruptcy as an occupier of a dwelling. The affidavit must also specify the date upon which the applicant became aware of the disclaimer and must specify the grounds of the application and the order which he desires the court to make (IR 1986, rr 4.194, 6.186). The court may give directions as to who should be given notice of the application. If at the time that the application is heard any interested person has not been notified, the court may order that they be notified and they may issue separate applications in their own right (*Re Baker, ex p Lupton* [1901] 2 KB 628, CA). If there are several applications pending concurrently the disclaimer is not to have effect until all applicants have been heard (IR 1986, rr 4.194, 6.186).

The time limits applying to the effect of disclaimer and the application for a vesting order appear confusing. Sections 179 and 317 of the IA 1986 provide that disclaimer will not have effect unless no application for an order is made within 14 days of service of the last copy of the notice of disclaimer, or, if such an application is made, the court directs that the disclaimer should have effect. This appears to indicate that the application for a vesting order needs to be made within 14 days; but the rules state that the application for an order must be made within three months of service of the last notice, or of the applicant becoming aware of the disclaimer through some other means. It appears that if no application to court has been made within 14 days the disclaimer has effect and the rights and obligations of landlord and tenant cease, but, notwithstanding this 'determination' of the lease, it can be reinstated if an application for a vesting order is made within the three months prescribed by the rules.

Even if the time limits are missed it appears that in both bankruptcy and liquidation time can be extended. In relation to bankruptcy the 1986 Act, s 376 states: 'Where by any provision in this Group of Parts or by the rules the time for doing anything is limited, the court may extend the time, either before or after it has expired, on such terms, if any, as it thinks fit.' In liquidation the IR 1986, r 4.3 provides: 'Where by any provision of this Act or the Rules about winding up, the time for doing anything is limited, the court may extend the time, either before or after it has expired, on such terms, if any, as it thinks fit'. An appropriate case for extending time would appear to be where a party did not receive a notice of and was not aware of the disclaimer. It is possible, however, that the provisions allowing extension of time may be limited to procedural matters only and may not apply to the extension of time for the making of vesting orders (*Re a Debtor (No 416 of 1940), ex p Official Receiver v Hubbard* [1950] Ch 423, CA).

6.7.2 PERSONS IN FAVOUR OR AGAINST WHOM ORDERS MAY BE MADE

A person making an application may be seeking an order for the vesting in the lease in himself. A subtenant, for instance might seek an order in favour of himself. On the other hand the applicant might request that the lease be vested in some other person. For example, a landlord may seek to have the lease vested in a subtenant; or in a mortgagee (*Re Baker, ex p Lupton* [1901] 2 KB 628, CA); or in a surety. A former tenant, as a person under a liability in respect of the disclaimed property might seek an order vesting the lease in a subtenant or mortgagee (*Re Finley, ex p Clothworkers' Co* (1888) 21 QBD 475). In the case of bankruptcy and a disclaimer relating to a dwelling house an order may be made in favour of any person who at the time when the bankruptcy petition was presented was in occupation of or entitled to occupy it.

It appears that there is a 'pecking order' whereby some applicants for a vesting order are to be preferred over others. Vinelott J in *Re AE Realisations* (para 6.6.3 above) said:

'. . . it is, I think, clear that what is contemplated by [ss 181 and 320] is that an application for a vesting order may be made, first, by a person claiming under the bankrupt as underlessee or mortgagee (and, if more than one, in the order of priority of their respective interests inter se); secondly, if none is willing to take a vesting order by any person "liable either personally or in a representative character, and either alone or jointly with the bankrupt to perform the lessee's covenants"; and thirdly, by "any person claiming [an] interest in [the lease] or under any liability not discharged by it."'

So a subtenant or mortgagee must be offered the lease first. Second in line for a vesting order is a surety or a former tenant who has not been released from liability. Last, in the event of the persons first and second entitled declining to take a vesting, the landlord may have the property vested in himself (per Cave J, *Re Cock, ex p Shilson*, above). The pecking order cannot be altered simply by virtue of one party making application in priority to another – as occurred in *Sterling Estates v Pickard UK Ltd* [1997] 2 EGLR 33, where a landlord sought a vesting order with the intent of taking the property with the benefit of subleases. The subtenants successfully argued that they should first be offered a vesting order and at their option they could be excluded from the property – leaving the landlord without the benefit of the subleases.

If asked to make a vesting order the court will normally do so (*Re Britton* (1889) 37 WR 621), although if the person applying for a vesting is a surety who is bound to take a new lease under the terms of a covenant with the landlord the court may decline an order (see para 6.7.4, *Re AE Realisations*, para 6.6.3 above). It should also be noted that an order cannot be made vesting the lease in a person who is under any liability not discharged by the disclaimer unless it appears that it would be just to do so for the purpose of compensating that person (IA 1986, ss 181(4), 320(4)).

6.7.3 TERMS OF THE ORDER

In liquidation

In liquidation the court will not normally order a vesting in a subtenant or mortgagee except on terms either that the subtenant or mortgagee is subject to the same liabilities as the company was subject to at the commencement of the winding up (IA 1986, s 182(1)). This will have the result that the subtenant or mortgagee is liable for breach of any covenants, even though they occurred prior to the vesting (*Re Walker, ex p Mills* (1895) 64 LJQB 783). This puts the mortgagee or subtenant in a similar position to that they would have been if there had not been a vesting order: i e that in order to avoid a forfeiture by the landlord all the terms of the lease, including payment of arrears of rent would need to be complied with. The mortgagee or subtenant cannot avoid the liability by transferring its interest to a person of straw as trustee for itself; the court may still order that the vesting is directly to such mortgagee or subtenant (*Re Smith, ex p Hepburn* (1890) 25 QBD 536, CA, cf *Re Holmes, ex p Ashworth* [1908] 2 KB 812).

The court does have a discretion to vest the lease in the subtenant or mortgagee on the basis that it takes subject to the same liabilities as there would have been if the subtenant or mortgagee had taken an assignment at commencement of the winding up. If an order is made in these terms the subtenant or mortgagee will be in the position of an assignee and will therefore only (unless the tenancy is a 'new tenancy', see para 5.1.6) take subject to covenants which touch and concern the land. In addition, since an assignee of a lease is liable to the landlord for the period of its own ownership only the effect of such an order is that the subtenant or mortgagee would not be liable for past breaches (*Re Walker, ex p Mills*, see above). Although an assignee is not directly liable to a landlord for past breaches, the landlord can still usually rely upon his proprietary right to forfeit the lease in respect of such a breach, but it is probable that the effect of a vesting order on terms that the subtenant or mortgagee is in the position of an assignee is to deprive the landlord of the right to forfeit; otherwise there would be little difference between the two forms of vesting order since the assignee would probably have to make good the past breaches in order to obtain relief from forfeiture.

It was held in *Re Walker, ex p Mills* (see above) that the court is very unlikely to exercise its discretion to order that the subtenant or assignee should only be subject to such liabilities as there would be if there had been an assignment, unless there are very exceptional circumstances (see also *Re Müller, ex p Buxton* (1880) 15 Ch D 289, CA). In *Re Carter and Ellis, ex p Savill Bros* [1905] 1 KB 735, the Court of Appeal allowed the exercise of the discretion since in the circumstances there would be no unfair prejudice to the landlord, as it was not considered just for the landlord to have the benefit of the mortgagee as a solvent tenant in place of the insolvent tenant whose lease was disclaimed.

The vesting will generally be of a lease on the same terms as existed at the date of the vesting – including any formal lease variation which has taken place (*Beegas Nominees Ltd v BHP Petroleum Ltd* [1998] 2 EGLR 57, CA). Apart from this general principle, however, it seems that the court in exercising its discretion assumes a jurisdiction to impose such terms as it thinks fit upon the parties. In *Re Walker, ex p Mills* (see above) the vesting order in favour of a mortgagee was made on terms that the landlord should at any time accept a surrender upon the mortgagee giving six months' notice in writing and performing all the covenants and obligations of the lease down to the date of the disclaimer. In *Lee v Lee* [1998] 2 BCLC 219 the court ordered that a vesting in a mortgagee could be subject to conditions as to the allocation of any surplus money after payment of the mortgage debt.

Where the vesting order is in favour of some person other than a subtenant or mortgagee the court is not limited to the forms of order explained above. Further, the court can vest the lease in the person freed and discharged from all estates, encumbrances and interests created by the company.

In bankruptcy

In bankruptcy the court will not order a vesting in any person except on terms either that the person is subject to the same liabilities as the bankrupt was subject to on the day the petition was presented or the same liabilities as there would have been if the person had taken an assignment on that day (IA 1986, s 321(1)). The exercise of the court's discretion is likely to be influenced by the decisions in *Re Walker, ex p Mills* and *Re Carter and Ellis*, mentioned above.

If no person is willing to accept an order on these terms the court may vest the lease in any person who is liable to perform the tenant's covenants in the lease, and freed from all estates, incumbrances and interests created by the bankrupt (IA 1986, s 321(3)).

Removal of fixtures

If an application has been made for a vesting order and the court orders that the disclaimer should have effect it also has a discretion to make such order as it thinks fit in respect of any fixtures or tenant's improvements (IA 1986, ss 179(2) and 317(2)). It is likely that the court will apply the normal rule which would be applicable on the determination of a lease, that the tenant should be allowed to remove tenant's fixtures (*Re Moser* (1884) 13 QBD 738).

6.7.4 EFFECT OF VESTING ORDER

The vesting order is in itself enough to give title to the person in whose favour the order is made; it is not necessary to complete the vesting by a conveyance, assignment or transfer (IA 1986, ss 181, 320). In the case of a registered lease the vesting order must direct the alteration of the register in favour of the person in whom the lease is vested, and the registrar must, upon being served with the order, alter the register (Land Registration Act 1925, s 42(2), as amended).

Although a vesting order is normally on the same or similar terms to those of the original lease, the order does not have the effect of reinstating the position in respect of the property as if there was no disclaimer. The court order must contain a direction giving effect to the disclaimer (IR 1986, rr 6.186(7), 4.194(7)), and the rights of parties will be affected accordingly by the disclaimer.

Subleases, for example, do not remain unaffected. In *Re AE Realisations* (1985) Ltd [1987] 3 All ER 83, the lease contained a surety covenant which provided that on disclaimer the surety would, if required, take a lease on identical terms. The liquidator of the original tenant disclaimed and the landlord required the surety to take a new lease. The surety applied to the court for an order that the existing lease subject to and with the benefit of an existing sublease should be vested in it. The subtenant did not wish to continue its subtenancy. Vinelott J held that the determination of the bankrupt's rights interests and liabilities necessarily involved the extinction of the liabilities of the bankrupt under the sublease and the extinction of those liabilities necessarily involved the extinction of the liabilities of the subtenant. The subtenant had the option to be excluded from an interest in the property and the surety could not require the subtenancy to continue. Further, since a vesting of the existing lease would not achieve any more than the creation of a new lease under the terms of the covenant no order should be made.

6.7.5 VESTING ORDER IN RESPECT OF PART OF THE PREMISES

An order can be made in respect of part only of the premises under IA 1986, ss 182(2) and 321(2) but on terms that the tenant of part will be subject to the same obligations as the tenant of the whole was. Unfortunately the sections do not make any clear provision for apportionment of rent, or in relation to other provisions appropriate to a tenancy of the whole but not of parts. There may also be other difficulties arising from a vesting order. For example, suppose the headlease was protected by the Landlord and Tenant Act 1954, but in order to avoid a protected tenancy of part the alienation clause provided that any subtenancy should be contracted out. Would a vesting order in relation to part be contracted out of the Act? Presumably also a former tenant of the whole or a surety in respect of the whole may remain liable for the whole of the original head rents, notwithstanding the vesting of part in a subtenant. If the landlord relets the other part his claim against the original tenant or surety should reduce accordingly.

Another matter which is unclear is whether an applicant who is a subtenant of part is only entitled to apply for a vesting in relation to that part only, or whether, as under earlier legislation, the court retains a discretion to vest the whole in the applicant (*Re Holmes, ex p Ashworth* [1908] 2 KB 812).

6.7.6 REFUSAL OF VESTING ORDER BY SUBTENANT OR MORTGAGEE

If in a liquidation a person, say a landlord, applies to have the lease vested in a subtenant or mortgagee, the subtenant or mortgagee can elect whether to take the lease or to be excluded from all interest in the property (IA 1986, s 182(4)). The right of a subtenant to elect whether to take the lease or alternatively to vacate the property cannot be circumvented by the landlord seeking a vesting order in itself subject to and with the benefit of the sublease (*Sterling Estates v*

Pickard UK Ltd [1997] 2 EGLR 33). The court may specify a time limit within which the mortgagee or subtenant is to decide whether to take on the obligations under the lease, and if the opportunity is not taken up within the specified time the right to take the lease will be lost (*Re Baker, ex p Lupton* [1901] 2 KB 628, CA).

A statutory tenant is not a subtenant for the purpose of these provisions and accordingly cannot be required to take the disclaimed lease or otherwise be excluded from the property. The statutory tenant can continue to rely upon the statutory right to occupy afforded by statute (*Re Vedmay Ltd* (1993) 69 P & CR 247).

If no person claiming under the company as subtenant or mortgagee is willing to accept a vesting order the court can order that the lease be vested in any person who is liable to perform the tenant's covenants in the lease, e g a former tenant. The court is only to do so, however, where it is just to do so for the purpose of compensating such former tenant or other person.

The drafting of the statutory provisions relating to bankruptcy is slightly different with the wording of s 321 of the IA 1986 differing from that of s 182. In s 321 there is no special reference to subtenants or mortgagees. It is suggested, however, that the section is intended to have similar effect to s 182 and that if the order is made by virtue of s 321(3) the person liable cannot elect to decline the order. Admittedly the drafting is unclear and if the problem arises it may well prompt further consideration.

6.8 Effect if no disclaimer

In bankruptcy if there is no disclaimer the effect is that the trustee in bankruptcy will be liable upon the terms of the lease by virtue of the statutory vesting of the lease in the trustee and the liability which attaches to the trustee as current tenant. If the bankrupt tenant was the original tenant in respect of the lease he will remain liable by privity of contract. Liability for all rent accruing after the date of the bankruptcy order will persist notwithstanding the discharge of the tenant from bankruptcy (*Metropolis Estates Co Ltd v Wilde* [1940] 2 KB 536, CA). If the trustee wishes to be released from liability he will need to disclaim the lease, procuring an extension of any time limit, if applicable; or the trustee can assign the lease to some third party.

If the liquidator of a company does not disclaim the lease the landlord may be able to claim rent for the duration of the liquidation as an expense of the liquidation (see chapter 2), but failure to disclaim does not make a liquidator personally liable upon the terms of the lease (*Stead, Hazel & Co v Cooper* [1933] 1 KB 840). Upon the completion of the winding up the company is dissolved (IA 1986, ss 201–205) and title to the lease will vest in the Crown as *bona vacantia* (Companies Act 1985, s 654, *Re Wells* [1933] Ch 29, CA).

The Crown has the option to disclaim the lease (Companies Act 1985, s 656) but it must do so within 12 months of the date upon which the vesting in the Crown came to the Treasury Solicitor's notice, or, within three months of receipt of a notice from a person interested in the property requiring him to decide whether or not to disclaim. The effect of Crown disclaimer is that the lease is deemed not to have vested in the Crown and s 178(4) and ss 179 to 182 of the

IA 1986 apply as if the liquidator had disclaimed the lease immediately before the dissolution of the company.

One effect of such disclaimer may be to discharge a guarantor from liability under the lease (*Allied Dunbar Assurance plc v Fowle* [1994] 2 BCLC 197). But any such discharge is precarious, as the guarantor's liability may be resurrected if the company is restored to the register, since such restoration has the effect that the lease is deemed never to have vested in nor been disclaimed by the Crown (*Allied Dunbar Assurance plc v Fowle*, see above).

If, however, the company is not restored to the register and the Crown disclaimer is left to have its effect the usual provisions relating to vesting orders apply and interested persons, or any person under a liability not discharged by the disclaimer, can apply to the court for a vesting order, and persons who suffer loss through the disclaimer may prove for their injuries.

Although Crown disclaimer is treated as if it is a disclaimer by a liquidator, there is not deemed to have been a liquidation of the company, and provisions in a lease which would follow if there had been a liquidation (e g an obligation upon a guarantor to take a new lease) do not necessarily have effect (*Re Yarmarine (IW) Ltd* [1992] BCLC 276) where the dissolution of the company was for some reason other than liquidation.

6.9 Proof for injury for disclaimer

The landlord, and any other person sustaining loss or damage in consequence of the disclaimer is entitled to prove for the loss or damage (IA 1986, ss 315(5), 178(6)). Proof may lie whether the sum is liquidated or not (see para 2.10).

6.9.1 PROOF BY LANDLORD

Where the lease is disclaimed and the landlord is unable to recover the rent from an original tenant or other party he can prove in the liquidation under the IA 1986, ss 178 or 315 on the basis that there is a loss which is consequential upon the disclaimer. It should not be thought that a landlord will be able to prove for all future rents since the landlord through the disclaimer will get the property back and will, in most cases be able to mitigate its loss through reletting. If the landlord is only able to relet at a reduced rent it will be able to prove for the difference between the contractual rent under the disclaimed lease and the rent which the landlord is able to get for the property following the disclaimer (*Re Hide, ex p Llynvi Coal and Iron Co* (1871) 7 Ch App 28) for what would have been the remainder of the term, or the earliest date upon which the lease might have been determined by a tenant's option (*Re McEwan, ex p Blake* (1879) 11 Ch D 572, CA). Presumably a similar rule would apply if there was a landlord's option.

It appears that if the landlord has not relet at the time of proof he is entitled to prove for 'the difference between the rent which he reserved and the rent which the premises are fairly worth' (James LJ in *Ex p Llynvi Coal and Iron Co*, see above). If he has actually relet, and 'if he can get as much rent for the property afterwards as before, then the damages would be nil; if he gets less, it will be the difference' (Mellish LJ in *Ex p Llynvi Coal and Iron Co*, see above). Allowance can also be made to cover a void period for reletting and an amount to compensate the landlord for breach of repairing covenant by the insolvent tenant (*Re Carruthers, ex p Tobit* (see para 5.10.2)).

Although the starting point for quantifying the landlord's loss is to calculate the difference between the rent reserved by the disclaimed lease and the rent which the landlord will or is likely to receive following disclaimer, the quantification must take into account the fact that the landlord will receive a present capital sum rather than a future income stream. Accordingly, the computation has to make allowance for any advancement that has occurred. The basis of such allowance was considered in detail through the High Court, the Court of Appeal and ultimately the House of Lords in *Christopher Moran Holdings Ltd v Bairstow* [1999] 1EGLR1. The most difficult issue for the House of Lords was the formula for determining discount and the level of such discount. One possible basis for determining discount would be by application of IR 1986, r 4.94 together with r 11.13 which apply a statutory discount rate (currently 5% per annum with monthly rests) in a case where a creditor claims in respect of a debt where payment is not due when the company goes into liquidation. The House of Lords rejected this basis for determining discount – reasoning that following a disclaimer there is no debt just a statutory right to compensation and therefore IR 1986, r 11.13 is inapplicable. Instead, their Lordships were of the opinion that the best evidence of the appropriate discount rate was the yield on gilt-edged securities for a term equivalent to the lease term (or the remainder of the lease term). On the evidence before the Court the relevant discount rate was 8.5%.

Further, if a vesting order is made this must also be taken into account in assessing the landlord's loss (IA 1986, ss 181(5), 320(5)). It is questionable how far the landlord has a loss in respect of which he can prove. If the order vests the lease in a subtenant the landlord might claim that the determination of the sublease has deprived him of the right to recover subrents under the Law of Distress Amendment Act 1908; or if the lease is vested in a surety the landlord might argue that his position has been weakened by not having a new surety. If the terms of the order relieve the recipient of the lease from liability for past breaches (see para 6.7.3) then there will obviously be a loss to prove for.

6.9.2 PROOF BY ORIGINAL TENANT OR SURETY

The disclaimer will result in the loss to a former tenant or surety of the right to claim indemnity from the insolvent tenant (*Hindcastle Ltd v Barbara Attenborough Associates Ltd* [1995] QB 95, CA; affd [1996] 1 EGLR 94, HL) and the former tenant made liable to the landlord after disclaimer is able to prove for his loss as an 'injury' arising from the disclaimer. Accordingly, the former tenant or surety who has made payments will be able to prove to the extent of such payments and should also be able to prove for the loss representing the liability to make future payments. The level of proof is likely to be affected by any right of the former tenant or surety to take possession of the property (see paras 5.6 and 5.7). As to the amount of such proof, see paras 5.10.2 and 6.9.1.

6.9.3 PROOF BY SUBTENANT

A subtenant may be prejudiced by disclaimer in that he will only be able to remain in possession if the head rents are paid. The subtenant may pay the head rents either after taking a vesting order or if he does not take a vesting, by voluntarily paying the head rents in order to avoid a forfeiture. If the subtenant does so and the head rents exceed the subrents, then the subtenant can prove in the liquidation for the difference (*Re Levy, ex p Walton* (1881) 17 Ch D 746, CA) subject to discount for early settlement.

CHAPTER 7

Surrender or assignment

The previous chapters of this work have explored the rights and liabilities of insolvent tenants and of landlords and other creditors. Examination of a landlord's rights and remedies discloses that there may be considerable difficulty in enforcing them against the tenant, particularly where the tenant is bankrupt, in liquidation or in administration. Study of the right to disclaim, which is possessed by a trustee in bankruptcy or liquidator, shows that its outcome can be accompanied by awkward complexities and conceptual difficulties. Because of these problems it is very often more attractive to the parties interested in the lease if the insolvency of the tenant can be dealt with by agreement, usually by an assignment of the lease to a solvent assignee or by a surrender of the lease to the landlord. Through assignment or surrender a liquidator, administrator or trustee in bankruptcy can realise the capital value, if any, of the lease, for the benefit of creditors; or rationalise the tenant's affairs, even if the lease has no capital value. The landlord will be benefited if, through assignment a solvent tenant replaces an insolvent one, or if through surrender the landlord is able to re-let the property to a solvent tenant, possibly on more advantageous terms, or repossess the property himself.

7.1 Dealings by the insolvent tenant

A tenant who is insolvent, or who is in severe financial difficulties, may negotiate a surrender or assignment before any formal insolvency procedure results in the tenant's control of its own affairs being affected by the appointment of some other person, such as a receiver, a trustee, an administrator or liquidator. A landlord or prospective assignee of an insolvent tenant should be aware that a dealing with the lease is liable to be set aside notwithstanding that there is no apparent existing restriction upon the tenant's powers. If a petition for bankruptcy or liquidation has been presented before the transaction is effected, the transaction will be void. Even if the transaction occurs before presentation of any petition, it might later be challenged as a fraudulent preference or transaction at an undervalue.

7.1.1 VOID TRANSACTIONS

Where a transaction is entered into after the presentation of a petition for bankruptcy or liquidation of the tenant, any disposition of the tenant's property made pursuant to the transaction may be void. Consequently, if a person dealing with a tenant makes payments to the tenant in return for an interest in property the person dealing will find himself without the property, and an unsecured creditor for payments which he has made. In addition any payment made by the tenant may be recovered by the trustee in bankruptcy or liquidator.

Bankruptcy

Where a person is adjudged bankrupt, any disposition of property made by that person in the period beginning with the day of the presentation of the petition and ending with the vesting of the bankrupt's estate in a trustee is void except to the extent that it is or was made with the consent of the court, or is ratified by the court (Insolvency Act 1986 ('IA 1986'), s 284). 'Disposition' is not defined, but includes an assignment of a lease (see 'liquidation' below), and is likely to include a surrender. It probably does not, however, embrace a sale by a mortgagee (see 'liquidation' below). So a surrender or assignment made by a bankrupt tenant during the relevant period is prima facie void. Not only will any disposition of property be void, but so also will any payment made by the bankrupt. A person receiving such payment, for example, a landlord or assignee receiving a reverse premium, must hold it as part of the bankrupt's estate (IA 1986, s 284(2)).

There is, however, an important protection for a disposition made to a person who receives property or payment in good faith, for value and without notice that a petition has been presented (IA 1986, s 284(4)). Under the different wording of earlier legislation it has been held that a person is not acting in good faith where he takes a transfer of substantially the whole of the debtor's property in satisfaction of a past debt, while knowing that there are other creditors (*Re Jukes, ex p Official Receiver* [1902] 2 KB 58). Once property disposed of has passed into the hands of a person protected by the IA 1986, s 284(4) any person taking an interest derived from it will likewise be protected without having to prove that he purchased in good faith for value without notice of the petition.

Where the relevant disposition is a dealing with the lease the rules governing the protection of a purchaser are altered by the requirements of registration and the protection provided by the Land Charges Act 1972 and the Land Registration Act 1925. Where the title to the lease is not registered at HM Land Registry the position is governed mainly by the requirements of the Land Charges Act 1972. When a petition in bankruptcy has been presented the registrar of the court in which it is filed must have it registered in the register of pending land actions under the Land Charges Act 1972, s 5 (Insolvency Rules 1986 ('IR 1986'), r 6.13). If the petition is registered then a purchaser of a lease of unregistered land will be deemed to have notice of the petition (Law of Property Act 1925, s 198). If the petition is not so registered it shall not bind a purchaser of a legal estate in good faith, for money or money's worth (Land Charges Act 1972, s 5). Once a bankruptcy order is made the Official Receiver must arrange for its registration in the register of writs and orders affecting land (IR 1986, 6.34). If the order is registered the purchaser will be deemed to have notice of it. If the order is not registered, and the petition is not registered either, the title of a trustee in bankruptcy is void against a purchaser of a legal estate in good faith for money or money's worth. If the order is not registered, but a petition is, the title of the trustee is, nevertheless, good against the purchaser (Land Charges Act 1972, s 6).

Where the title to the lease is registered at HM Land Registry, and a petition has been registered as a pending action, or an order has been registered as an order affecting land, the land registrar must as soon as practicable after the registration of the petition register a 'creditor's notice', and as soon as practicable after registration of the order register a bankruptcy inhibition against the title to any lease or leases registered in the name of the bankrupt. The registration in both cases is to be made in the proprietorship register (Land Registration Act 1925, s 61 and Land Registration Rules 1925, r 179). If the petition or order has been properly protected the purchaser will be affected accordingly, but if there is no entry on the registered title a disposition to a purchaser in good faith for money or money's worth is protected and the title of the trustee in bankruptcy is void against the purchaser. A purchaser who has actual notice of the petition or adjudication is not protected, but there is no obligation upon the purchaser to make a search of the registers of pending actions or of writs and orders affecting land, and the fact that the petition or order may have been registered in either register will not prejudice a purchaser without actual notice (Land Registration Act 1925, s 61).

So, in general, a purchaser of the lease will find that the disposition is void unless the petition or order, or (in the case of a registered lease) the creditor's notice or inhibition, as appropriate, was not registered at the time of purchase, and the purchaser had no actual notice of the petition or order. To be protected a purchaser must have given money or money's worth. It has been held that this does not have to be full value (*Midland Bank Trust Co Ltd v Green* [1981] AC 513, HL), but it is not clear whether an assignee of the lease at no premium is to be regarded as having given money's worth by taking from the bankrupt tenant the burden of the obligations in the lease. For other purposes it has been held that the taking on of such obligations is 'valuable consideration' so as to make the assignee a purchaser for value (*Johnsey Estates Ltd v Lewis and Manley (Engineering) Ltd* (1987) 54 P & CR 296, CA. See para 5.4.1).

In practice there ought to be few cases where the petition and order have not been registered, since as mentioned above the court and the Official Receiver respectively are under a duty to give notice of the petition and order respectively, to the Chief Land Registrar, who, in turn, in the case of registered land, is obliged to enter a creditor's notice or bankruptcy inhibition upon the register.

Compulsory winding up

Where the tenant is an insolvent company or limited liability partnership which is ultimately wound up by the court any disposition of the company's property made after the presentation of a petition is, unless the court otherwise orders, void

(IA 1986, s 127). 'Disposition' is not defined, but it includes any assignment of a lease (*Re AI Levy (Holdings) Ltd* [1964] Ch 19), any charge (*Re Park Ward & Co Ltd* [1926] Ch 828), and is likely to include a surrender. It also includes a payment made from a company's bank account, and a payment into an overdrawn bank account (*Re Gray's Inn Construction Co Ltd* [1980] 1 All ER 814, CA), but it does not include a payment into an account which is in credit (*Re Barn Crown Ltd* [1994] 4 All ER 42).

Where a lease is subject to a mortgage or other charge, any sale of the lease by the mortgagee, chargee or any receiver is not a disposition for the purpose of the IA 1986. The disposition of property is considered to have taken place when the charge was created. Neither, if the company rather than the chargee has sold the property, is any payment to the chargee out of the proceeds of sale of charged property a void disposition (*Re Margart Pty Ltd, Hamilton v Westpac Banking* [1985] BCLC 314). Similarly, the completion of an existing unconditional contract for sale of a lease is probably not a disposition made after the commencement, since the disposition takes place when the contract is made (*Re French's (Wine Bar) Ltd* [1987] BCLC 499). It is possible, however, that a waiver or variation of the terms of an existing contract may be a disposition (*Re French's (Wine Bar) Ltd*). In practice, if there is any doubt as to whether the pre-existing contract is specifically enforceable an order of the court might be sought before completing any transfer pursuant to the contract.

The disposition is void 'unless the court orders otherwise'. So the disposition may be validated by a court order. An application for a court order may be made by the company or by any interested person (*Re Argentum Reductions (UK) Ltd* [1975] 1 All ER 608), and the application may be made before or after the order for winding up, and in respect of an existing or proposed disposition (*Re AI Levy (Holdings) Ltd* [1964] Ch 19).

The aim of the provision is to ensure that all creditors share the company's property rateably, so in general a transaction will be validated by the court so long as its effect is not to reduce the assets available to creditors (*Re Tramway Building and Construction Co Ltd* [1988] Ch 293), and in particular a transaction should not operate to prefer one creditor over others (*Re Gray's Inn Construction Co Ltd* [1980] 1 All ER 814, CA). In the case of payments made, the test is not whether the payment causes damage to the company but is rather whether the payment is a benefit to the company, e g if it is made to obtain supplies on a contract which is profitable (*Re Webb Electrical Ltd* [1988] BCLC 382). Benefit to the creditors is also taken into account, but the court can reasonably assume that what is for the benefit of the company is also for the benefit of the general body of creditors (*Denney v John Hudson & Co Ltd* [1992] BCLC 901, CA).

There is no special protection afforded to a purchaser in good faith, and no special provisions of the Land Charges Act 1972 or Land Registration Act 1925 which apply. If a contract for the sale of a lease is entered into prior to the petition the later completion should be protected by the rule in *Re French's (Wine Bar) Ltd* (see above), but where there is no prior contract, or where the contract is entered into after the presentation of the petition the disposition would appear to fall foul of the IA 1986, s 127.

Where the title to the land is not registered it has been argued that the winding up petition is registrable as a pending land action under the Land Charges Act 1972, s 5. It is unlikely, however, that this is the case, since to be so registrable there must be an action claiming a proprietary interest in land (*Calgary and Edmonton Land Co Ltd v Dobinson* [1974] Ch 102) and a winding-up petition is not an action claiming such an interest. It may be of note that the Land Charges Act 1972, s 5 expressly provides for registration of a petition in bankruptcy, but provision for registration of a winding-up petition is conspicuous by its absence.

Where the title to the land is registered interests which in the case of unregistered land would be registrable under the Land Charges Act 1972 may be protected by lodging a creditor's notice, a bankruptcy inhibition or a caution against dealings, but as it is unlikely that a winding-up petition is capable of registration under the Land Charges Act 1972, it is doubtful that it can be protected on the register in the case of registered land. It must remain a moot point whether a purchaser would be protected by the general protection provisions of the Land Registration Acts, or whether, if the register was rectified to show the company as the proprietor, the purchaser would be entitled to indemnity (see Ruoff & Roper, *Registered Conveyancing* at para 34.26).

So, notwithstanding that a purchaser may be a purchaser in good faith without notice of the petition, there is no special protection for the purchaser of a commercial lease, and it may be that the purchaser can only look to the discretion of the court under the IA 1986, s 127 to validate the transaction. It may be of interest that the provisions of the Land Registration Act 1925 were not referred to in *Re French's (Wine Bar) Ltd* (see above), nor in *Re Tramway Building and Construction Co Ltd* (see above). In order to avoid the complications discussed above an intending purchaser would be wise to carry out a search at the Central Compulsory Winding Up Registry of the Companies Court, immediately before entering into the contract for sale, in order to discover whether a petition has been presented.

Once an order for the compulsory winding up of the company is made and a liquidator has been appointed (whether in voluntary or compulsory winding up) the order and appointment must be advertised and notified to the registrar of companies (IA 1986, ss 109, 130, IR 1986, rr 4.21, 4.106). There is, however, no compulsion for notification to the Chief Land Registrar, although if land of the company is registered land the liquidator may apply to have his appointment noted on the register (Land Registration Rules 1925, r 185). A purchaser of land from a company should therefore search the companies register before purchase in order to discover whether the company is in liquidation.

Effect of void transaction

If a disposition of a lease is caught by the provisions discussed above it is void ab initio. It has been said that it nevertheless passes the legal title to the transferee who then holds the property upon trust for the bankrupt or the company (per Vinelott J in *Re French's (Wine Bar) Ltd*, see above). In relation to earlier legislation, however, it has been held that if a lease contains a restriction upon the tenant assigning, and the tenant, in breach of the restriction, purports to assign the lease under a void transaction, there will be no breach of the covenant not to assign, and the landlord will not be able to rely upon the purported disposition as a ground for forfeiting the lease (*Doe d Lloyd v Powell* (1826) 5 B & C 308). It is possible, however, that the transaction may have some validity for the purpose of imposing obligations upon a third party. In *Stein v Pope* [1902] 1 KB 595, a tenant assigned a lease and the assignee defaulted in payment of the rent. The landlord began legal proceedings for the rent against the assignee, and shortly afterwards the tenant was made bankrupt. In the circumstances the assignment was void ab initio. In the hearing of the legal proceedings, started by the landlord before the bankruptcy, against the assignee, the assignee objected that, as the assignment was void, he was not liable for the rent which had accrued due for the interval between the date of the assignment and the date that the tenant was adjudicated bankrupt. The Court of Appeal decided that the assignee was liable for the rent which had accrued due during the period that he had the property. Romer LJ's reasoning is wide enough to establish a general principle that an assignee is liable up until the date of a bankruptcy order, or, in the case of a company, an order for winding up. But Collins MR was more reserved and might have limited *Stein v Pope* to its particular facts, i e that the assignee is liable where the landlord has started legal action against the assignee before the bankruptcy or liquidation.

Where a disposition of a lease is caught by section 127 the lease remains the property of the company. Consequently, the lease will be subject to any crystallisation of a floating charge which occurs following the presentation of the petition (*Merton v Hammond Suddards* [1996] 2 BCLC 470) and a lender with a floating charge will acquire a fixed charge over the lease.

7.1.2 PREFERENCES

Transactions entered into before a petition in bankruptcy, liquidation or administration are not automatically void, but if a transaction operates to prefer one creditor over another it may be set aside, or the court may make such order as it thinks fit for restoring the position which existed before the transaction was entered into (IA 1986, ss 239, 340). The discretionary jurisdiction of the court is available upon an application by an administrator, a liquidator or a trustee in bankruptcy and the conditions set out below must be satisfied.

There must be a 'preference'

A 'preference' is given to a person who is a creditor or surety for any liability of the individual or corporate tenant and the tenant 'does anything or suffers anything to be done which (in either case) has the effect of putting that person into a position which, in the event of [bankruptcy][insolvent liquidation], will be better than the position he would have been in if that thing had not been done'.

There must be a 'desire' to prefer

It must be shown that '[the company which][the individual who] gave the preference was influenced in deciding to give it by a desire to produce' the preference. Unlike under the old law, the desire to prefer does not have to be the only or dominant intention of the transaction. 'It is no longer necessary to establish a dominant intention to prefer. It is sufficient that the decision was influenced by the requisite desire' (per Millett J in *Re MC Bacon Ltd* [1990] BCLC 324).

The mere fact that the transaction will operate to prefer a particular creditor is not a sufficient ground for setting it aside. In *Re MC Bacon Ltd* in order to avoid the calling in of an unsecured bank loan, owed by a company which was virtually insolvent, the company gave a debenture to the bank. Although the natural consequence of the giving of the debenture was to prefer the bank, Millett J decided that the directors of the company had no desire to produce the preference, their desire simply being to enable the company to continue to trade. In a similar vein, a floating charge granted by a company in favour of one of its directors was held to be valid to secure sums advanced in *Re Fairway Magazines Ltd* [1993] BCLC 643, where the reason for granting the floating charge was to raise finance from the director.

So, it seems likely that if an insolvent tenant makes payments of rent to a landlord in order to avoid a forfeiture, there will be no fraudulent preference, unless there are other circumstances to show that the tenant had a 'desire' to prefer the landlord. Similarly where a surrender is made, and part of the consideration for the surrender is that the landlord foregoes arrears of rent, the surrender will not necessarily be a fraudulent preference of the landlord over other creditors. Even though the landlord will get the property at least partly in place of rent arrears, the tenant's desire may simply be to rid itself of the onerous obligations in the lease, rather than to prefer the landlord, and the preference of the landlord may simply be a by-product of the transaction.

Where the transaction in question is entered into between the tenant and an 'associate' (in the case of an individual tenant) or a 'connected' person (in the case of a corporate tenant) it will be presumed, unless the contrary is shown that there is a desire to prefer (IA 1986, ss 239(6), 340(5)). The meanings of 'connected' person and 'associate' are defined at length in the IA 1986, ss 249 and 435, and include, in the case of an individual tenant, relatives, and in the case of a corporate tenant, directors and companies within the same group. Employees are generally taken not to be connected persons or associates.

The presumption of a desire to prefer is certainly capable of rebuttal in appropriate cases. In *Re Beacon Leisure* [1992] BCLC 565, a company running a billiard saloon was run by A, B and C each of whom was a director and shareholder. The saloon was owned by A and leased to B and C, who in turn permitted use of the saloon by the company in return for payment of the rent by the company. In December 1987 a quarter's rent due on 1 January 1988 was paid early. The company went into insolvent liquidation at the end of January 1988. By virtue of the IA 1986, s 239(6) it was to be presumed that the payment by the company was made with a desire to prefer B and C. B and C gave evidence that they had no such desire and that the rent had never been paid regularly on the due date. In the absence of strong documentary evidence to prove the liquidator's contention that other creditors were pressing for payment, the court decided that the presumption of a desire to prefer had been rebutted.

In contrast to *Re Beacon Leisure* is the decision in *Re Exchange Travel (Holdings) Ltd* [1996] BCC 933. In that case a family-owned company owed money to various family members. At a time when the company was technically insolvent, the company made payments to family members in discharge of the debts owed to such family members. Accordingly, the presumption of a desire to prefer arose. In an attempt to rebut the presumption it was argued that the relevant payees did not know of the technical insolvency, that the particular director did not intend a preference and that the family members believed that sums paid represented money held by the company on trust rather than moneys owed by way of debt. None of these arguments succeeded to rebut the presumption of a desire to prefer.

The time for testing whether the requisite desire to prefer exists is the time when the preference occurs (*Wills v Corfe Joinery Ltd* [1998] 2 BCLC 75).

The preference must be within the 'relevant time'

The preference must be made within the 'relevant time'. The relevant time will usually (but see 'inability to pay debts' below) be the six months or the two years immediately preceding the presentation of a bankruptcy petition or, in the case of a company, the two years before the 'onset of insolvency', depending upon the circumstances (IA 1986, ss 240, 341). The 'onset of insolvency' in the case of a company means the date of the petition for administration, if either the company is presently in administration, or where it is in liquidation, having gone into liquidation immediately following the discharge of an administration order. Where the liquidation occurs at any other time the onset of insolvency is the date of the commencement of the winding up. A transaction is also made at a relevant time if it occurs between the date of presentation of a petition for administration and the date of an order for administration.

Where the preference is in favour of a 'connected' person (in the case of a corporate tenant), or is in favour of an 'associate' (in the case of an individual tenant), the relevant time is the period of two years prior to the bankruptcy, administration or winding up. If the person dealing with the insolvent tenant is not a 'connected' person or 'associate' the relevant time is six months before the bankruptcy, administration or winding up.

There must be inability to pay debts

A preference will only be set aside if the tenant is insolvent at the time or immediately after the relevant preference is created. If the tenant is solvent, and remains so despite the preference, the preference is considered not to have occurred at a 'relevant time' (see above).

In the case of an individual tenant the transaction is not made at a relevant time unless at the time of the transaction, or immediately after and in consequence of it, he is unable to pay his debts as they fall due, or the value of his assets is less than the amount of his liabilities, taking into account his contingent and prospective liabilities (IA 1986, s 341(2), (3)). If the transaction is with an associate of the tenant these requirements are deemed to be satisfied unless the contrary is shown.

In the case of a corporate tenant the transaction is not made at a relevant time unless at the time of the transaction, or immediately after and in consequence of it, the company is unable to pay its debts. A company is unable to pay its debts if it has failed to satisfy a statutory demand from a creditor, if execution has been returned unsatisfied in whole or part, if it is proved to the court that the company is unable to pay its debts as they fall due, or the value of the company's assets is less than the amount of its liabilities, taking into account its contingent and prospective liabilities (IA 1986, ss 123, 240). If the transaction is with a connected person these requirements are deemed to be satisfied unless the contrary is shown.

Orders which may be made

The court may make such order as it thinks fit for restoring the position to what it would have been if the preference had not been given (IA 1986, ss 239(3),

340(2)). The orders which may be made include, inter alia, orders to vest property in the tenant, to discharge any security given by the tenant, and to pay money to the tenant (IA 1986, ss 241, 342).

Protection for third parties

Although the court has a wide discretion as to the making of an order to restore the position to what it would have been had there not been a preference, an order cannot be made so as to prejudice any interest in property which was acquired from a person other than the tenant and was acquired in good faith, for value and without notice of the relevant circumstances, or prejudice any interest deriving from such an interest. Neither can the court require a person who received a benefit from the preference in good faith, for value and without notice of the relevant circumstances to pay any sum unless he was a party to the transaction causing the preference (IA 1986, ss 241, 342). A person is presumed not to have acted in good faith if he had notice of the relevant circumstances (i e the preference) and of the relevant insolvency proceedings, or if he was an associate of or connected with the person to whom the tenant gave the preference. The presumption of bad faith can be rebutted by evidence to the contrary (IA 1986, s 241(2A)). It is unlikely that a third party's position will be impugned simply because he has knowledge of a transfer by way of gift, but if such knowledge is accompanied by knowledge of the donor's insolvency then action against the third party may be appropriate.

7.1.3 TRANSACTIONS AT UNDERVALUE

A transaction at an undervalue may be set aside on an application to court by a liquidator, administrator or trustee in bankruptcy, for the benefit of creditors of a company or bankrupt. The following conditions must be met (IA 1986, ss 238, 339).

There must be a transaction

A transaction includes a gift, agreement, arrangement or other transaction (IA 1986, s 436). In some cases there may be difficulty in identifying the relevant transaction. This may occur if the relevant transaction forms part of a series of transactions or several concurrent transactions with several connected parties (eg connected companies). If in reality there is one transaction the combined consideration may be taken into account when considering undervalue (*Phillips v Brewin Dolphin Bell Lawrie Ltd* [2001] 1 BCLC 145, HL.

The transaction must be at an undervalue

There must be a transaction at an undervalue. A transaction is at an undervalue if it is a gift or if the consideration received by the company or individual has a value in money or money's worth which is significantly less than the value of the consideration provided by the company or individual. In the case of a bankrupt a transaction is also at an undervalue if marriage is the only consideration for it.

Use of the term 'significantly less' indicates that a transaction may be set aside if the value received by the insolvent tenant is well below the level of equality; it is not necessary to show that the value received is nominal or insignificant. In *Re MC Bacon Ltd* (see above) Millett J said that, in order to decide whether a transaction with a company is at an undervalue, it is necessary to make a comparison between the value obtained by the company, and the value provided by the company, both values being measured in money or money's worth, the valuation being made from the point of view of the company. A similar exercise may be undertaken where the insolvent is an individual (*Re Kumar (a bankrupt), ex p Lewis* [1993] 2 All ER 700).

It might be thought that almost anything done for or by the insolvent tenant could be regarded as having value. In *Re MC Bacon Ltd* (see above) Millett J thought that a forbearance from calling in a loan was value given by a bank to an insolvent company. On the other hand, his Lordship thought that the giving by the company of a debenture was not value because it did not deplete the company's assets. It is submitted that his Lordship was mistaken in this latter view, since on one basis of valuing a company's assets the existence of a debenture would reduce the valuation, since the existence of a debenture will make it difficult for the company to raise money upon the security of its assets.

The transaction must be made at the 'relevant time'

The transaction must be made at the 'relevant time'. In the case of a company this normally (but see the paragraph immediately below) means two years before the 'onset of insolvency' (see above) or, where the company is in administration, the time between petition and the making of an administration order (IA 1986, s 240). In the case of an individual the 'relevant time' is the period of five years ending with the presentation of the bankruptcy petition upon which the individual was made bankrupt (IA 1986, 341).

The tenant must be insolvent at the time of the transaction

As is the case with fraudulent preferences (see para 7.1.2) a transaction at an undervalue is not made at a relevant time unless the tenant was insolvent at the time. In the case of an individual tenant a transaction entered into in the period two to five years before petition is not made at a relevant time unless at the time of the transaction, or immediately after and in consequence of it, he is unable to pay his debts as they fall due, or the value of his assets is less than the amount of his liabilities, taking into account his contingent and prospective liabilities (IA 1986, s 341(2), (3)). So a transaction at an undervalue made in the two years immediately preceding bankruptcy may be set aside irrespective of whether the tenant was insolvent at the time, but a transaction in the period two to five years before bankruptcy can only be set aside if the tenant was, at the time, insolvent.

In the case of a corporate tenant a transaction is not made at a relevant time unless at the time of the transaction, or immediately after and in consequence of it, the company is unable to pay its debts, within the meaning of the IA 1986, s 123 (IA 1986, s 240(2)). That is, the company has failed to satisfy a statutory demand from a creditor, execution has been returned unsatisfied in whole or part, it is proved to the court that the company is unable to pay its debts as they fall due, or the value of the company's assets is less than the amount of its liabilities, taking into account its contingent and prospective liabilities.

Where the transaction in question is made with an 'associate' (in the case of a tenant who is an individual) or with a 'connected' person (in the case of a corporate tenant) it will be presumed, unless the contrary is shown that the tenant is insolvent (IA 1986, ss 240(2), 341(2)). The meanings of 'connected' person and 'associate' are defined at length in the IA 1986, ss 249 and 435, and include, in the case of an individual tenant, relatives, and in the case of a corporate tenant, directors and companies within the same group. Employees are generally taken not to be connected persons or associates.

The transaction may be with 'any person'

The jurisdiction is available where a transaction is entered into with 'any person'. It has been held that this enables proceedings to be served upon a person or company outside of the jurisdiction (*Re Paramount Airways Ltd* [1993] Ch 223, CA). The court does, however, have a discretion whether or not to make an order and the person against whom the order is made should normally be sufficiently connected with England to justify the making of an order. The court also has a discretion as to whether to grant leave for service of an application outside of the jurisdiction, and before leave will be given a strong case must be shown, including a strong case that the person served has sufficient connection with the jurisdiction (*Re Paramount Airways Ltd*, see above).

Good faith

A court shall not make an order in respect of a transaction entered into by an insolvent company if it is satisfied that the transaction was entered into in good faith, for the purpose of carrying on its business, and there were reasonable grounds for believing that it would be beneficial to the company (IA 1986, s 238(5)). There is no similar provision in relation to transactions entered into by individuals.

Orders which may be made

The court may make such order as it thinks fit for restoring the position to what it would have been if the transaction had not been made (IA 1986, ss 238(3), 339(2)). The orders which may be made include, inter alia, orders to vest property in the tenant, to discharge any security given by the tenant, and to pay money to the tenant (IA 1986, ss 241, 342).

Protection for third parties

Although the court has a wide discretion as to the making of an order to restore the position to what it would have been had there not been a transaction at an undervalue, an order cannot be made so as to prejudice any interest in property which was acquired from a person other than the tenant and was acquired in good faith, for value and without notice of the relevant circumstances, or prejudice any interest deriving from such an interest. Neither can the court require a person who received a benefit from the transaction in good faith, for value, and without notice of the relevant circumstances, to pay any sum unless he was a party to the transaction at an undervalue (IA 1986, ss 241, 342). A person is presumed not to have acted in good faith if he had notice of the relevant circumstances (i e the undervalue) and of the relevant insolvency proceedings, or if he was an associate of or connected with the insolvent tenant or the person with whom the tenant entered into the transaction. The presumption of bad faith can be rebutted by evidence to the contrary.

7.1.4 TRANSACTIONS DEFRAUDING CREDITORS

There is a further provision which is likely to be of relevance to a transaction entered into with a tenant which is in financial difficulties, but which operates irrespective of whether the tenant is insolvent and without any necessary connection with bankruptcy, administration or liquidation, and without any time limit. The IA 1986, s 423 provides that certain transactions entered into at an undervalue, with an intention to defraud creditors, may be set aside.

There must be a transaction at an undervalue

A transaction can only be set aside if it is a transaction at an undervalue. The meaning of 'undervalue' is much the same as for the IA 1986, ss 238 and 339 (see paras 7.1.2 and 7.1.3). That is, it must be a gift or a transaction where the consideration received by the tenant has a value of which in money or money's worth is significantly less than the value of the consideration provided by the company or individual. In the case of an individual a transaction is also at an undervalue if marriage is the only consideration for it.

A transfer, for a nominal price, of valuable land subject to a mortgage is not at an undervalue if the amount secured on the property far exceeds the value of the property so that the value of the equity of redemption is negative or nil (*Pinewood Joinery (a firm) v Starelm Properties Ltd* [1994] 2 BCLC 412).

If one party to a transaction receives benefits significantly greater in value, in money or money's worth than the consideration given then the transaction is at an undervalue. The benefit in money's worth may include indirectly safeguarding a family home and business. In *Agricultural Mortgage Corpn plc v Woodward* [1995] 1 BCLC 1, a borrower was in arrears under his mortgage and following him being given a deadline to clear the arrears he granted a tenancy at a commercial rent of the mortgaged property to his wife. The value of the mortgaged property with vacant possession was £1m but subject to the tenancy was £500,000. By the arrangement the wife was able to safeguard the home, continue the family farming business and she procured a potential surrender value of £500,000 in respect of the tenancy. The Court of Appeal held that the benefits received by her exceeded the consideration which she paid by way of rent and that the transaction could be set aside under the IA 1986, s 423. A similar decision was reached by the Court of Appeal on somewhat similar facts in *Barclays Bank plc v Eustice* [1995] 4 All ER 511 (see below).

Intention to defraud

The jurisdiction is designed to prevent 'fraudulent' transfers; so there must be a requisite intention. Proof of dishonesty, however, need not be adduced, and the fact that lawyers have advised that the transactions are proper does not mean that the requisite intention does not exist (*Arbuthnot Leasing International Ltd v Havelet Leasing Ltd (No 2)* [1990] BCC 636). In this context the intention is expressed in terms that the court must be satisfied that the transaction was entered into by the tenant 'for the purpose (a) of putting assets beyond the reach of a person who is making, or may at some time make, a claim against [the tenant], or (b) of otherwise prejudicing the interests of such a person in relation to the claim which he is making or may make'. The purpose of putting assets beyond the reach of a person who is or might make a claim against the tenant does not need to be the only purpose of the transaction. It is enough that it is the dominant purpose (*Chohan v Saggar* [1992] BCC 306; now see [1994] 1 BCLC 706, CA) or possibly simply a substantial purpose (*Royscot Spa Leasing Ltd v Lovett* [1995] BCC 502).

The intent need not be a specific intent to defraud particular creditors. A general intent to avoid creditors is sufficient. So, for example, in *Jyske Bank (Gibraltar) Ltd v Spjeldnaes* [1999] 2 BCLC 101 a transfer by a company of the benefit of a contract at an undervalue at a time when the company's financial position was 'shaky' was sufficient to show an intention to put the contract beyond the reach of creditors generally and this was sufficient to justify an order for setting aside. Even an intent to avoid possible future creditors may be sufficient to justify an order for setting aside. In *Midland Bank plc v Wyatt* [1995] 1 FLR 697, a declaration of trust in favour of a wife and children and intended to put property beyond the reach of future creditors was capable of being set aside under the IA 1986, s 423. The jurisdiction to set aside was held to be not limited to cases in which the transferor is about to begin a risky business; it is sufficient that the transaction is intended and designed to keep assets from the reach of potential creditors.

Evidence of intent

Direct evidence of intent may be hard to come by and often a claimant may need to begin proceedings and seek an order for discovery of relevant documents in those proceedings in an effort to prove the necessary intent. Discovery may even be sought of communications between the debtor and his legal advisers. Usually such communications will be privileged and a court will not easily order discovery of them (*Royscot Spa Leasing Ltd v Lovett* [1995] BCC 502). If, however, there is a strong prima facie case against the debtor such discovery may be ordered. A strong prima facie case may exist where there is a transfer of assets at an undervalue to members of the debtor's family at a time when the debtor clearly anticipates action by a creditor and where the assets remaining in the debtor's hands barely cover the debt, if at all (Schiemann LJ in *Barclays Bank plc v Eustice*, see above).

Further, in order to show that the tenant had the relevant purpose in mind it is not necessary to have direct evidence of his state of mind; it is enough that the surrounding circumstances indicate that the tenant had such a purpose. In *Moon v Franklin* (1990) Independent, 22 June, Franklin was an accountant facing a negligence action for £99,000. He decided to sell his business and at the same time to transfer money and the matrimonial home to his wife. Following the transfer of the house to her, Mrs Franklin proposed to sell the house. The plaintiffs in the negligence action sought an order under the IA 1986, s 423 to prevent the sale. Mr Franklin claimed that the transfer of the house to his wife was not made for the purpose of avoiding the negligence claim, but was simply an impetuous display of affection and gratitude to her. The court rejected Mr Franklin's evidence and decided that the purpose of the transfer of the house was to avoid the negligence claim, and an order was made restraining any dealing with the house.

All of the circumstances can be taken into account in order to ascertain whether or not there was the necessary intention, including the timing of the transaction and consideration of advice received by the transferor with regard to liability for debts and evidence of asset-stripping (*Re Schuppan (a bankrupt) (No 2)* [1997] 1 BCLC 256).

Persons who may apply

The great advantage of the IA 1986, s 423 is that it can be used by any person who is a 'victim' of the transaction in question, and it is not necessary that there be any formal insolvency procedure. A 'victim' is any person who is, or is capable, of being, prejudiced by the transaction. In *Moon v Franklin* (see above), for example, it was relied upon by plaintiffs who had begun a negligence action against the debtor, and who were concerned that transfers of property would put the property out of their reach.

Where there is bankruptcy, liquidation or administration the provision can be relied upon by a trustee in bankruptcy, Official Receiver, liquidator, administrator, or, with the leave of the court, a victim. In a case where a victim of the transaction is bound by a voluntary arrangement, the supervisor can apply or any person who (whether or not so bound) is a victim.

Where the application is made by a victim the application is treated as if it is made by the victim on behalf of all victims of the transaction (IA 1986, s 424). The effect of this stipulation is not clear, although it may mean that an unsecured creditor will not be able to take advantage of the IA 1986, s 423 so as to make a claim against property involved ahead of other creditors, at least where the tenant is insolvent at the time of the transaction.

Orders which may be made

The court has a general discretion to make such order as it thinks fit for restoring the position to what it would have been if the transaction had not been entered into, and protecting the interests of persons who are victims of the transaction. The orders which may be made include (inter alia) orders in relation to the vesting of property, orders for the application of proceeds of sale, and orders for the discharge of security (IA 1986, s 425). If the transaction in question is a transfer of business and assets from a transferor company to a transferee, the court may order that the transferee should hold all of its business and assets upon trust for the transferor, but without prejudice to the claims of any creditors of the transferee company (*Arbuthnot Leasing International Ltd v Havelet Leasing Ltd (No 2)* [1990] BCC 636).

Protection for third parties

Although the court has a wide discretion as to the making of an order in respect of a transaction at an undervalue, an order cannot be made so as to prejudice any interest in property which was acquired from a person other than the tenant debtor and was acquired in good faith, for value and without notice of the relevant circumstances, or prejudice any interest deriving from such an interest. Neither can the court require a person who received a benefit from the transaction in good faith, for value and without notice of the relevant circumstances to pay any sum unless he was a party to the transaction (IA 1986, s 425(2)).

Extent of jurisdiction

Jurisdiction under the IA 1986, s 423 is unlimited and extra-territorial and in an appropriate case an order may be made against a foreign beneficiary of the transaction whether or not such beneficiary has a connection with the jurisdiction (*Jyske Bank (Gibraltar) Ltd v Spjeldnaes* [1999] 2 BCLC 101).

7.1.5 EXTORTIONATE CREDIT TRANSACTIONS

Where the tenant is a company in liquidation or administration, or a bankrupt individual, a transaction entered into within the three years before liquidation or bankruptcy which involves the giving of credit to the tenant may be varied or set aside if the terms require payments which are grossly exorbitant, or if they otherwise grossly contravene ordinary principles of fair dealing (IA 1986, ss 244, 343). The provisions of the IA 1986 to this effect are modelled upon those contained in the Consumer Credit Act 1974. If the legal decisions upon the Consumer Credit Act provisions are anything to go by, it will not be easy for a trustee in bankruptcy, liquidator or administrator to invoke this jurisdiction successfully (see *Davies v Directloans Ltd* [1986] 2 All ER 783).

7.1.6 AVOIDANCE OF FLOATING CHARGES

Where the tenant is a company which is experiencing financial difficulties, a person to whom the tenant owes obligations may consider taking a floating charge over the company's assets. Such a floating charge would, of course, affect the lease. Most commonly a bank which is asked to provide further finance to an ailing company will seek a floating charge to secure past and future indebtedness. In such circumstances the bank should note that if the company is later affected by liquidation or administration a floating charge made at a 'relevant time' will only be effective to the extent of any fresh consideration, including reduction of debt (IA 1986, s 245).

The charge must be given at the 'relevant time'

A floating charge is only affected if it is made at a 'relevant time'. The time is usually (but see 'inability to pay debts' below) a relevant time if:

(a) it was made within the two years before the onset of insolvency in favour of a person connected with the company; or
(b) it was made within the 12 months before the onset of insolvency, in favour of any other person, and at the time the company is unable to pay its debts or becomes unable to pay its debts as a consequence of the transaction; or
(c) it is made between the date of presentation of a petition for an administration order and the date of making of the order.

The 'onset of insolvency' is, where the company has gone into liquidation, the date of commencement of the winding up of the company and, where the company is in administration, the date of presentation of the petition for administration.

There must be inability to pay debts

Where the charge is not in favour of a connected person it is not considered to be given at a 'relevant time' unless the tenant is insolvent at the time of or after the relevant charge is created. If the tenant is solvent, and remains so despite the charge, the charge is considered not to have occurred at a 'relevant time' (see above), unless it is granted to a connected person.

More precisely, the charge is not affected unless at the time of its creation, or immediately after and in consequence of the charge, the company is unable to pay its debts (IA 1986, s 240(2)). A company is deemed unable to pay its debts if it has failed to satisfy a statutory demand from a creditor, if execution has been returned unsatisfied in whole or part, if it is proved to the court that the company is unable to pay its debts as they fall due, or if the value of the company's assets is less than the amount of its liabilities, taking into account its contingent and prospective liabilities (IA 1986, s 123).

How the charge is affected by the IA 1986, s 245

The effect of the IA 1986, s 245 is that the floating charge will only secure fresh lending. The charge is not effective to secure any existing debt, although the debt, of course, remains as an unsecured one (*Re Parkes Garage (Swadlincote) Ltd* [1929] 1 Ch 139, CA).

Although the charge may be void it is not clear whether it is void ab initio or only upon the onset of insolvency. On the previous legislation it was held that the wording that the charge 'shall' be void meant that it was valid until winding up intervened and that an appointment of a receiver and sale of assets to repay the chargee prior to the winding up was valid (*Mace Builders (Glasgow) Ltd v Lunn* [1987] Ch 191, CA). The wording has been changed so that a charge made at the relevant time 'is' invalid, although this is unlikely to make any difference.

The charge is effective to secure debt for goods or services supplied or money paid to the company 'at the same time as, or after, the creation of the charge'. In the context of similar wording in the Companies Acts it has been held that a payment is made at the same time even though it was made shortly before the relevant charge, so long as it is a payment made in reliance upon the agreement for the charge (*Re Columbian Fireproofing Co Ltd* [1910] 2 Ch 120, CA; *Re F & E Stanton Ltd* [1929] 1 Ch 180). Whether a payment made in contemplation of the charge is made at the same time is, however, one of fact and degree. The question is whether a businessman having knowledge of the kind of time limits imposed by the legislation and using ordinary language would say that the payments had been made at the same time as the execution of the debenture. A debenture executed several months later might (*Re Fairway Magazines Ltd* [1993] BCLC 643) or might not (*Power v Sharp Investments Ltd* [1994] 1 BCLC 111, CA be considered to be made at the same time.

The payment must, however, swell the assets of the company B otherwise it will not be secured by the charge. So in *Re Fairway Magazines Ltd* a payment to a company's bank which reduced the company's overdraft, but which also reduced the liability of the payer under a guarantee of the company's liability, was held not to be secured by the floating charge.

7.1.7 ASSET STRIPPING IN GENERAL

The statutory regulation upon disposals at undervalue, preferences and other rules summarised above are designed to provide protection for creditors and investors against 'asset stripping', i e the removal from the tenant of assets to the detriment of general creditors and investors. There is, however, some doubt as to whether current legislation provides full and sufficient protection against asset stripping. It may be possible for a tenant with a business which is reasonably successful, but which is hampered by high lease rentals, to sell assets and liabilities (other than the lease) to a purchasing entity which would be able to use assets to continue the business and to pay off ordinary trade creditors while the landlord would be left with rights enforceable against a shell stripped of assets.

The issue has arisen in several decided cases which demonstrate the difficulties (and possibly inadequacies) of the present regulation. *Creasey v Breachwood Motors Ltd* [1993] BCLC 480 shows how a case of asset stripping can be successfully challenged. In that case a company ('the transferor company') transferred its assets and certain liabilities to another company ('the transferee company') controlled by the same persons who controlled the transferor company. At the time of the transfer an ex-employee was bringing a claim for wrongful dismissal against the transferor company. The effect of the transfer could therefore have been to leave the ex-employee with a claim against a shell company. R Southwell QC as judge took the view that '... the assets of one company cannot simply be stripped and removed to another company at the whim of common directors and shareholders, with the result that a creditor of the first company is left without recourse to any of the assets of the first company'. In the circumstances of the case, R Southwell QC thought that the directors and shareholders of the transferor and transferee had ignored the separate legal personalities of the two companies and the transfer of assets and business to the transferee had been made in disregard of their duties as directors and shareholders in respect of the transferor. In these circumstances, the court decided that the employee could pursue the outstanding claim against the transferee company.

It should be noted that the favourable outcome for the creditor in the *Creasey* case was not achieved easily nor without a fair degree of agonisation on the part of the court. The outcome might (just as easily) have been unfavourable – as it was in the recent Scottish decision of *Baillie Marshall Ltd v Avian Communications Ltd* 2000 GWD 27–1057. In that case an insolvent tenant company entered into an agreement with a second company. Both companies were under common control. The agreement provided for the purchase by the second company of various assets and liabilities and also provided for the first company to pay off the various trade creditors. The overall effect of the transaction was (as described in the judgement) '... selling the business to another company controlled by directors, paying off trade creditors (as was important for goodwill) but leaving the major disadvantageous creditor with rights only enforceable against a shell, or as in this case, a company with much reduced assets'. Following the transaction, the first company was put into liquidation and the liquidator challenged the transaction as a preference under the IA 1986, s 243. The challenge failed. The court considered that the IA 1986 provided no claim against the second company which had paid full value for the package of assets and liabilities which it had received. It is not clear whether the claim would have been successful if a remedy had been sought to undo the payments in favour of other creditors but, in the case, the liquidator had not requested such remedy. Similarly in *Dora v Simper* [2000] 2 BCLC 561 a receiver of a transferor company hived off assets and liabilities to a shelf company managed by the same persons who managed the transferor company. There was left in the transferor company a debt owed to a judgment creditor. A claim by the judgment creditor that the transfer should be set aside under the IA 1986, s 423 failed because the sale to the shelf company had not been shown to be intended to put assets beyond the reach of the creditor.

The packaging of assets and liabilities and the transfer of such package to a new entity is by no means an uncommon device. There is clearly scope for further development of the case law on the current IA 1986 regulation and possibly, in due course, for amendment to the IA 1986 itself should it be considered that creditors such as landlords are unfairly losing out through the use of such devices.

7.2 Dealings by persons other than the tenant

Where a tenant is seriously insolvent the landlord or prospective assignee of the lease is likely to find himself dealing with someone other than the tenant;

perhaps with a mortgagee, receiver, administrator, liquidator or trustee in bankruptcy.

7.2.1 DEALING WITH A MORTGAGEE

If the lease has been mortgaged the assignment or surrender may be by the mortgagee or by a receiver appointed by the mortgagee. The mortgagee's power to deal with the lease is dependent upon default by the tenant upon the terms of the mortgage and upon statute. In some cases leave of the court is required before a mortgagee can sell, for instance, if the tenant is a company in adminis-tration (IA 1986, ss 10, 11); or if the only relevant breach of the mortgage is that the debtor has become bankrupt or is in liquidation (Law of Property Act 1925, s 110). In general the landlord or prospective assignee need not be concerned with these matters and can rely upon the protection afforded by the Law of Property Act 1925, s 104(2) which provides that:

'Where a conveyance is made in exercise of the power of sale conferred by this Act ... the title of the purchaser shall not be impeachable on the ground B

(a) that no case had arisen to authorise the sale; or

(b) that due notice was not given; or

(c) ... that leave of the court, when so required, was not obtained; or

(d) ... that the power was otherwise improperly or irregularly exercised; and a purchaser is not, either before or on conveyance, concerned to see or inquire whether a case has arisen to authorise the sale, or due notice has been given, or the power is otherwise properly and regularly exercised ...'

So normally all a purchaser needs to satisfy himself of is that there has been a mortgage, that he is purchasing from the mortgagee, and that the statutory power of sale is available under the Law of Property Act 1925, s 101. The statu-tory power is available if the mortgage was made by deed and if the mortgage money is due. The purchaser does not need to check that the power has become exercisable through some event of default. However, if a purchaser has actual notice of an irregularity he will not get good title. It is not clear in law, however, whether a purchaser who only has constructive notice of an irregularity is deprived of the protection of the statute (*Bailey v Barnes* [1894] 1 Ch 25, CA). The purchaser does not need to be concerned with the insolvency of the tenant or whether leave of the court ought to be obtained by the mortgagee.

A sale by a mortgagee will be subject to any interests in the property which existed at the date of the mortgage (Law of Property Act 1925, s 104), including any prior mortgages, but the sale overreaches the interest of the mortgagor and subsequent mortgages (Law of Property Act 1925, ss 88, 2(1)(iii)), and will be free from any interests which arose subsequent to the mortgage, except to the extent that the mortgagee consented to or acquiesced in their creation.

Contract and completion

The mortgagee can contract with the purchaser in the normal manner and is entitled to recover from any person, who does not have priority to him, all deeds and documents necessary for the purpose of the sale (Law of Property Act 1925, s 106). The contract for sale extinguishes the tenant's right to redeem (*Property and Bloodstock Ltd v Emerton* [1968] Ch 94, CA). Completion of the sale will be by deed as usual, but the mortgagee should be expressed to sell 'as mortgagee', should give neither full nor limited title guarantee and give only a covenant that the mortgagee has not executed or done, or knowingly suffered, or been party or privy to, any deed or thing, whereby the title to the property may be impeached, or which might hinder the mortgagee from giving good title. The mortgagee can give a good receipt for the purchase money and the purchaser is not concerned to enquire whether any money remains due under the mortgage, or whether any balance is due to the mortgagor (Law of Property Act 1925, s 107).

7.2.2 RECEIVER APPOINTED BY MORTGAGEE

A mortgagee of the lease may decide to appoint a receiver to manage the property, and perhaps also to sell it. A receiver may be appointed even though the mortgagee has taken possession (*Refuge Assurance Co Ltd v Pearlberg* [1938] Ch 687, CA). Normally a receiver appointed by a mortgagee of the lease under the Law of Property Act 1925 (ss 109, 103) does not have power to dispose of the lease, but most charges expressly give receivers such powers. The receiver acts as agent of the tenant, and in the case of a tenant who is an individual, the receiver has no personal contractual liability. If the tenant is a company the receiver is personally liable upon any contract entered into unless the contract provides otherwise (see para 1.3.3). Since the receiver acts as agent of the tenant, the contract for sale will be expressed to be made by the tenant, as will any deed of assignment. Although the receiver is acting as agent of the tenant the receiver will not normally have available much information about the property, and, as a result, the receiver will not normally reply to detailed enquiries about the property which a purchaser would normally make of a vendor. The receiver will also endeavour to negotiate for the insertion of a disclaimer of personal liability in any contract or deed of assignment, and the receiver will not give any title guarantee, except perhaps a covenant that he has not knowingly done or suffered anything whereby the tenant is disabled from transferring the property.

From a purchaser's point of view a sale by the mortgagee is preferable to a sale by receiver for several reasons. First, a purchaser from a receiver does not have the protection afforded by the Law of Property Act 1925, s 104, which protects the title of a purchaser from a mortgagee, notwithstanding that the power to sell has not become exercisable, or has been irregularly exercised. Second, since the receiver acts as agent of the tenant, the receiver can probably only give such title as the tenant has, which title may be affected by subtenancies or other interests, created after the date of the mortgage. A sale by a mortgagee, on the other hand, will give the purchaser a title free from all interests to which the mortgage has priority (Law of Property Act 1925, 104). In practice the problem is sometimes circumvented by the contract for sale being entered into by the receiver, but with the actual transfer being by the mortgagee.

If the transfer is executed by the receiver rather than the mortgagee, the purchaser should also obtain upon completion a deed of release from the mortgagee, since it is arguable that the receiver, being merely the agent of the company, cannot sell free of the mortgage without such a release (see *Phoenix Properties Ltd v Wimpole Street Nominees Ltd* [1992] BCLC 737).

7.2.3 ADMINISTRATIVE RECEIVER

If the tenant is a body in respect of which an administrative receiver has been appointed the receiver will have the powers of disposal which are contained in the debenture under which he was appointed. In addition the debenture is deemed to include the powers listed in the IA 1986 Sch 1, except insofar as the terms of the debenture limits the powers (IA 1986, s 42). The powers in Sch 1 include a power to 'sell or otherwise dispose of the property of the company'; and a power to 'grant or accept a surrender of a lease or tenancy of any property of the company, and to take a lease or tenancy of any property required or convenient for the business of the company'. The power to sell or 'otherwise dispose' of property ought to be wide enough to cover both assignment and surrender of a lease.

Lease subject to prior fixed charge

Even if the lease is subject to a prior fixed charge in favour of a third party the administrative receiver may, with the leave of the court, dispose of the lease free from the charge (IA 1986, s 43). The holder of the charge must be given notice of the court hearing, at which the court must be satisfied that the disposal would be likely to promote a more advantageous realisation of assets than would otherwise be effected. If an order authorising sale is made, the net proceeds of sale must be utilised to pay the amount owing to the prior chargee. From the receiver's point of view there is a possible disadvantage with the procedure: it is a condition of the order that if the receiver sells at below market value the deficiency must be made good – but then a receiver would normally owe a duty to obtain the true market value on the sale of assets subject to a charge.

Contract by the receiver

As explained earlier (para 1.3.2) the administrative receiver is deemed to be an agent of the company, so that any contract for sale or surrender entered into prior to the receivership remains binding upon the company and an order for specific performance may be obtained by the purchaser notwithstanding the receivership (*Freevale Ltd v Metrostore (Holdings) Ltd* [1984] Ch 199, see para 1.3.3).

The receiver will normally enter into any fresh contract expressly 'without personal liability' so as to counteract the IA 1986, s 44 which gives rise to a presumption that the receiver is personally liable on any contract entered into by him, but subject to the right to be indemnified from the assets of the company.

If the tenant is in liquidation as well as receivership the receiver is not deemed to be the agent of the tenant (see para 1.3.2). The effect of this on the administrative receiver is not at all clear. In the absence of any evidence to the contrary the fact that he is not agent for the company does not necessarily make him an agent of the debenture holder. The company will not to be liable on any contract entered into by him and it is possible that the debenture holder will not be liable either. The receiver might be personally liable, although the contract will often stipulate otherwise. If the receiver does contract with personal liability he will only normally do so on the basis of his right to be indemnified from the assets of the company. If the receiver has contracted without personal liability it is not clear whether there is then a contract under the terms of which only the purchaser is liable, but which is wholly ineffective in creating any reciprocal obligation upon the tenant company, the debenture holder or the receiver.

Completion by the receiver

In order to allow the administrative receiver to complete the sale as agent of the company the debenture may state that the receiver can execute any deed and use the company's seal for this purpose. Even if the debenture is silent on the point, unless the wording of the debenture shows otherwise, the powers in the IA 1986, Sch 1 to 'use the company's seal' and 'to execute in the name and on behalf of the company any deed, receipt or other document' will be available.

Assuming that the agency of the receiver has not terminated the fact that the receiver is an agent of the company is of little comfort at the completion stage of a disposal since in practice, the receiver, whilst executing the deed in the name of the company, will usually negotiate terms whereby no covenant for title is given by the company or the receivers. The prevalence of the practice has little merit to it, since the deed is a deed of the company, and a company disposing of property would normally give a covenant that it disposes of the property as beneficial owner. The fact that a receiver executes a transfer or other disposition as agent ought to make little difference. Apart from the question of any covenant on the part of the company, it is common for receivers to covenant that they have not knowingly done or suffered any thing which would prevent the company from making the relevant disposal, and this would appear to be a reasonable covenant to procure from the receivers personally.

If the company is in liquidation the receiver is not agent of the company, and cannot bind the company to any new obligation. This does not, however, take away the powers of disposition given by the debenture for the purpose of enforcing the security. Thus the receiver may still exercise any power given by the debenture to execute any deed in the name of the company or to use a power to execute as attorney of the company, and the disposition will be binding upon the company (*Sowman v David Samuel Trust Ltd (in liquidation)* [1978] 1 All ER 616; *Barrows v Chief Land Registrar* [1977] CLY 315). Goulding J described the effect which a liquidation has upon a receiver as follows:

> 'Winding up deprives the receiver ... of power to bind the company personally by acting as its agent. It does not in the least affect his powers to hold and dispose of the company's property comprised in the debenture, including his power to use the company's name for that purpose, for such powers are given by the disposition of the company's property which it made (in equity) by the debenture itself.'

7.2.4 OFFICIAL RECEIVER OR TRUSTEE IN BANKRUPTCY

Where the tenant is an individual, a landlord or prospective assignee might find that he is faced with dealing with the Official Receiver, or with a trustee in bankruptcy. The presentation of a petition in bankruptcy is not necessarily followed by the interference of the Official Receiver, but in some cases the Official Receiver will be made interim receiver during the period between petition and order. Once an order is made, and until a trustee is appointed, the Official Receiver becomes the receiver and manager of the bankrupt's property. The Official Receiver's role is a caretaker role only and he should not normally dispose of the lease (see para 1.5.2). The lease does not vest in the Official Receiver, and although there is a rule allowing him to apply to become the registered proprietor of any lease which is registered at HM Land Registry (Land Registration Rules 1925, r 174), it is possible that the rule is applicable only in the rare cases where the Official Receiver has also to act as trustee in bankruptcy.

Once a trustee in bankruptcy has been appointed any lease vests in him automatically without the need for any assignment (IA 1986, s 306). If the lease is registered at HM Land Registry he can apply to become the registered proprietor, by applying to the registrar with a copy of the bankruptcy order, a certificate of his appointment, and a certificate that the lease is an asset divisible amongst the creditors (Land Registration Act 1925, s 42). The trustee has a power 'to sell any part of the property for the time being comprised in the bankrupt's estate'. The trustee has the ancillary powers to make contracts and to execute any power of attorney, deed or other instrument, in order to complete the sale. If, however, the deal negotiated by the trustee involves credit terms, the consent of the court, or of the creditor's committee, if there is one, must be obtained. The purchaser ought not to be concerned to discover whether the necessary consent has been obtained, since a person dealing with the trustee in good faith and for value 'is not to be concerned to enquire whether any permission required ... has been given' (IA 1986, s 314, and see *Weddell v Pearce & Major* [1988] Ch 26). The trustee will normally contract only to give such title as the bankrupt had (*Freme v Wright* (1819) 4 Madd 364). Since the trustee is an intermediate assignee of the lease and will not be liable on the terms of the lease for the period following sale it is not appropriate for the trustee to require the purchaser to covenant to indemnify the trustee in respect of future breaches (*Wilkins v Fry* (1816) 1 Mer 244 at 265, 268).

If there is an existing contract by the bankrupt to sell a lease, the trustee may wish to disclaim the contract. It has been held that the trustee cannot do so unless he also disclaims the lease (see para 6.1.1). Once bankruptcy intervenes the purchaser ought to pay the balance of the purchase price to the trustee rather than to the bankrupt. If the purchaser, being unaware of the bankruptcy, pays the balance to the bankrupt, he cannot compel the trustee to complete without again paying the balance to the trustee (*Re Pooley, ex p Rabbidge* (1878) 8 Ch D 367, CA). The purchaser is entitled to an order of specific performance requiring the trustee to complete the sale (*Re Taylor, ex p Norvell* [1910] 1 KB 562, CA), but the trustee cannot be required to perform a contract which requires him to carry out works to the premises (*Re Gough, Hanning v Lowe* (1927) 96 LJ Ch 239).

An existing agreement by a bankrupt to take a lease, or a transfer of a lease, can be disclaimed (*Re Maughan, ex p Monkhouse* (1885) 14 QBD 956). The landlord or seller can put the trustee to an election whether or not to disclaim (see para 6.3). If the trustee disclaims or fails to pay the full amount of the purchase money it seems that the seller can retain any deposit paid (*Re Parnell, ex p Barrell* (1875) 10 Ch App 512), and can prove in the bankruptcy for any loss over and above the amount of the deposit. The bankrupt purchaser is not entitled to an order for specific performance requiring the seller to complete the sale, but the trustee in bankruptcy of the purchaser may obtain such an order (*Jennings' Trustee v King* [1952] Ch 899). An order for specific performance requiring the trustee to complete the purchase will not be available (*Holloway v York* (1877) 25 WR 627).

7.2.5 ADMINISTRATOR

If the tenant is a company in respect of which a petition in administration has been presented a person can deal with the directors of the company until an administration order is made. Once an order is made and an administrator appointed, the administrator must take into his custody and control all of the company's property, including the lease. Any powers of the directors which might interfere with the actions of the administrator are not exercisable without his consent, and if he wishes he can remove any director of the company (IA 1986, s 14). The administrator has power to dispose of the company's assets including the lease (IA 1986, s 14), and has power to 'grant or accept a surrender of a lease or tenancy of any property of the company, and to take a lease or tenancy of any property required or convenient for the business of the company'.

If a lease is part of the company's property which is subject to a floating charge, the administrator can dispose of the lease free from the charge. After sale the charge holder will have the same priority to the proceeds of sale, or other property representing the product of the disposal of the lease, that he would have had in respect of the property subject to the charge (IA 1986, s 15).

If the lease is subject to a mortgage the administrator can apply to the court for leave to dispose of the lease free from the mortgage. It will be a condition of an order that the net proceeds of the disposal must be applied towards discharging the sums secured by the mortgage. The court can make an order if it is satisfied that the disposal of the lease, either by itself, or together with other property, would be likely to promote the purpose or one of the purposes for which the administration order was made. It is the scheme of the IA 1986 to allow creditors to have their say before any proposals of the administrators are implemented – so the court will not give the administrator leave to dispose of the lease free from a charge before the creditors have been given an opportunity to comment at the creditors meeting (*Re Consumer & Industrial Press Ltd (No 2)* (1987) 4 BCC 72).

If the mortgaged lease is being disposed of together with other property, such as the tenant's business, the court can take into account the fact that the proceeds of the disposal as a whole will be enough to pay the mortgagee, even if the value of the lease itself is less than the amount owed (*Re ARV Aviation Ltd* (1989) 4 BCC 708). The 'net proceeds of the disposal' are to be applied towards discharging the sums secured, even though those net proceeds arise partly from other property in the disposal to which the security does not extend (IA 1986, s 15).

Agency of administrator and protection of purchaser

In exercising the powers available to him the administrator is agent of the company, and his acts will, by the usual rules of agency bind the company. The IA 1986 also provides that a person dealing with the administrator in good faith and for value is not concerned to inquire whether the administrator is acting within his powers (IA 1986, s 14(6)). Bearing in mind normal agency principles, and the fact that the powers are drafted widely, it is not likely that this provision will often need to be invoked. The protection might perhaps be relevant to a purchaser of property free from a fixed charge, in which case the effect of the IA 1986, s 14 ought to be that it is not necessary for the purchaser to check that the leave of the court has been obtained.

7.2.6 LIQUIDATOR

Where the tenant is a registered company (or limited liability partnership) it may be necessary to deal with the Official Receiver, a provisional liquidator (usually the Official Receiver), or the liquidator.

In a voluntary winding up the company has to cease carrying on its business as soon as the resolution for winding up is made. The directors remain in the driving seat until a liquidator is appointed or nominated (see para 1.6.1), but they should only normally do what is necessary to preserve the company's assets (IA 1986, s 114), and should not normally dispose of any lease. Once a liquidator has been appointed, and any necessary creditors' meeting held, the liquidator will be able to exercise freely, without the sanction of the court, the power 'to sell any of the company's property by public auction or private contract, with power to transfer the whole of it to any person or to sell the same in parcels' (IA 1986, ss 165–166 and Sch 4, para 6). The liquidator also has power to do all such other things as may be necessary for the winding up of the company's affairs and distribution of its assets. Whether this would include taking a grant of a new lease or an assignment of a lease must be doubtful except in the most unusual cases.

In a compulsory winding up there may be a provisional liquidator or Official Receiver acting. The role of each is essentially a temporary one of caretaking, until a permanent liquidator is appointed after meetings of the creditors and contributories respectively. Apart from the fact that the role is a caretaking one, the appointment of a provisional liquidator may expressly limit his powers, so that in some cases a lease should not be sold before the appointment of a permanent liquidator (see para 1.6.3). Once a liquidator has been appointed he has the same power to sell any of the company's property described above that a liquidator has in a voluntary winding up (IA 1986, 167).

In order to complete any deed of surrender or assignment the liquidator can rely upon the power contained in the IA 1986, Sch 4, para 7, 'to do all acts and execute, in the name and on behalf of the company, all deeds, receipts and other documents and for that purpose to use, when necessary, the company's seal'. Since the liquidator acts in place of the directors as agent of the company, the transfer is by the company with the seal of the company attached in the presence of the liquidator. It is not necessary for the liquidator to execute the transfer as such unless he is entering into any personal obligations.

If the transfer is of registered land evidence of the liquidation should accompany the application to the Land Registry, unless the liquidation has already been noted on the register. In a member's voluntary winding up there should be a certificate by the company, or by the liquidator or his solicitor that a statutory declaration of solvency under the IA 1986, s 89 has been filed with the Registrar of Companies and a certified copy of the resolution appointing the liquidator. In a creditor's voluntary winding up there must be produced a certified copy of the resolution for winding up and either a certified copy of the resolution for appointment of the liquidator or a certificate by the liquidator that the meeting of creditors was held which confirmed his appointment or made no nomination of a liquidator. In a compulsory winding up there must accompany the application either a copy of the court order or appointment by the Secretary of State of the liquidator; or a certified copy of the winding-up order together with either a copy of the resolution appointing a liquidator, or his certificate that the meeting of creditors was held which confirmed his appointment or made no nomination of a liquidator.

There is some controversy amongst lawyers as to the correct method of execution of deeds in liquidation. Since the lease remains vested in the company, and the company's powers remain until it is dissolved; and since the liquidator's position as agent of the company is analogous to that of a director, it might be thought that the liquidator can deal with execution in the same way that the directors might, by signing as witness to the fixing of the company's seal. Some commentators, however, consider that the liquidator should join in the deed as a party, reciting the exercise of his statutory powers. It is submitted that the former view is the better one in theory. In practice, however, the latter view ought to be adhered to until the dispute is resolved by the courts, since the main criticism of it is simply that the liquidator's participation may be superfluous, but if it is not superfluous the deed might be ineffective (see *Emmet on Title*, para 11.192).

Another moot point is whether in any deed the company should convey with title guarantee so as to give the title covenants described in the Law of Property (Miscellaneous Provisions) Act 1994. It is suggested that the fact that the company is being wound up should not deprive a purchaser of the benefit of the covenants, which provide the purchaser with certain warranties that the company has a good title to the lease, and that the obligations in the lease have been complied with so that it is not voidable. It might be objected that the liquidator has no personal knowledge of the position in respect of the lease, but, assuming that the liquidator is not personally liable on the implied covenants, this should not be a strong enough reason for excluding them.

7.3 Assignment

The questions in relation to assignment which will be of most concern to the insolvent tenant and the landlord will be threefold. First, is landlord's consent required to the assignment? Second, can the landlord unreasonably withhold consent? Third, in the particular circumstances is it reasonable for the landlord to object to the proposed assignment? In exceptional circumstances an insolvent tenant, represented by a receiver, trustee in bankruptcy, administrator or liquidator, may wish to carry out some disposition other than an assignment, e g a subletting or mortgage. The questions considered here will also apply in such circumstances, with appropriate modification.

7.3.1 IS LANDLORD'S CONSENT REQUIRED?

Whether landlord's consent is required depends upon whether the lease so provides. If there is no restriction in the lease the tenant is free to assign without the landlord's consent, and a trustee in bankruptcy, receiver, administrator or liquidator can do likewise. In such a case the lease may be assigned to a pauper or a shelf company in order that the tenant gets rid of the lease. Such a transfer is not considered to be fraudulent (*Hopkinson v Lovering* (1883) 11 QBD 92). The tenant's freedom to so assign is simply a consequence of the landlord's failure to insist upon having a term in the lease restricting such assignment.

A modern commercial lease is likely, however, to contain a restriction in the form of a tenant's covenant not to assign (an absolute covenant), or not to assign without landlord's consent (a qualified covenant). In the case of an insolvent tenant there may be special considerations applicable in deciding whether a restriction affects the person acting for the insolvent tenant as appears immediately below.

Bankruptcy

Upon appointment of a trustee in bankruptcy there is an automatic vesting of the lease by operation of law in the trustee. The transfer of the lease to the trustee, being an involuntary event, is not a breach of a restriction upon assignment (*Re Riggs, ex p Lovell* [1901] 2 KB 16); although the terms of the lease may be such that the bankruptcy amounts to a breach of condition and gives rise to a right to forfeit the lease.

Whether an assignment by the trustee requires consent depends upon the terms of the lease. In some old legal decisions it has been held that a restriction upon the tenant's right to assign a lease does not necessarily restrict assignment by the tenant's trustee in bankruptcy. If the lease states that the original tenant, his executors, administrators and assigns shall not assign without the landlord's consent, an assignment by a trustee in bankruptcy is not fettered, since a trustee in bankruptcy is not an executor, administrator or assign (*Doe d Goodbehere v Bevan* (1815) 3 M & S 353). If the lease is drafted even more loosely to restrict only acts of the original tenant, his executors and administrators, the restraint will not affect the trustee in bankruptcy of the tenant, and further a purchaser from the trustee will not be affected and will be free to assign the lease without the landlord's consent (*Doe d Cheere v Smith* (1814) 5 Taunt 795).

If, however, the lease prohibits assignment by the tenant and any 'successors in title', the restraint will affect a trustee in the bankruptcy of the tenant, because the trustee is a successor in title to the lease (*Re Wright, ex p Landau v Trustee* [1949] Ch 729). A modern commercial lease will normally define the term 'tenant' to include all successors in title, so that all of the tenant's covenants are to be construed as binding upon any person in whom the lease vests, including a trustee in bankruptcy.

In any case, it is suggested that a trustee in bankruptcy should be bound by a restriction upon assignment in all cases, since as successor in title to the lease he ought to be bound by all covenants which bind an assignee (see para 5.2.2).

Company winding up, receivership and administration

In the case of a winding up of a registered company the lease does not vest in the liquidator, unless an order for vesting is made. Accordingly any assignment is an assignment by the company, which is bound by any covenant against assignment, and if landlord's consent is required the liquidator, as agent of the company, will have to obtain it, irrespective of whether the winding up is voluntary (*Cohen v Popular Restaurants Ltd* [1917] 1 KB 480), or compulsory (*Re Farrow's Bank Ltd* [1921] 2 Ch 164, CA). Where a company is in receivership or administration similar principles ought to apply, since a receiver or an administrator, like a liquidator, is simply an agent of the company.

Building leases

Where there is a building lease exceeding 40 years granted by a private landlord and there is a qualified covenant against assigning, underletting, charging or parting with the possession of premises or any part thereof then no consent is needed for dealings by the tenant or any subtenants effected more than seven years before the end of the term, provided written notice of the transaction is given to the landlord within the six months following the relevant transaction (Landlord and Tenant Act 1927, s 19(1)(b)). This rule does not apply to a 'new tenancy' (Landlord and Tenant Act 1927, s 19(1D) – inserted by the Landlord and Tenant (Covenants) Act 1995, s 22).

7.3.2 WHAT TRANSACTIONS ARE RESTRICTED?

Even if there is a restriction which appears to fetter dealings by the tenant and any trustee, receiver, administrator or liquidator, the wording of the restriction must be examined closely to determine whether the proposed transaction is within a category of dealing which is specifically restricted. A restriction upon assignment, for instance, will not restrict subletting. Each lease and proposed transaction must be considered upon its particular facts, but the guide below should assist in the most common cases.

Form of restriction	*Effect of restriction*
Covenant 'not to assign'	Prohibits an assignment, but not a mortgage (*Doe d Pitt v Hogg* (1824) 4 Dow & Ry KB 226), subletting (*Sweet & Maxwell Ltd v Universal News Services Ltd* [1964] 2 QB 699, CA), declaration of trust (*Gentle v Faulkner* [1900] 2 QB 267, CA), or giving of a licence (*Edwardes v Barrington* (1901) 50 WR 358).
Covenant 'not to assign part'	Prohibits an assignment of part or whole (*Field v Barkworth* [1986] 1 All ER 362), but not a subletting of part (*Russell v Beecham* [1924] 1 KB 525, CA).
Covenant 'not to underlet'	Prohibits subletting, including a mortgage by means of sublease (*Serjeant v Nash, Field & Co* [1903] 2 KB 304, CA), and probably an equitable sublease (*Folioshield Ltd v Pleamere Ltd* [1990] 28 EG 124), or tenancy at will but probably not an assignment

(*Marks v Warren* [1979] 1 All ER 29), nor subletting of part (*Cook v Shoesmith* [1951] 1 KB 752, CA), unless the whole is sublet part by part (*Chatterton v Terrell* [1923] AC 578, HL) and probably not a charge by way of mortgage.

Covenant 'not to part with possession'	Prohibits assignment or subletting (*Marks v Warren* [1979] 1 All ER 29), and a licence involving a parting with control (*Lam Kee Ying Sdn Bhd v Lam Shes Tong* [1975] AC 247, PC), but not if the tenant retains control, and not a sharing (*Holland v South London Supplementary Benefits Appeals Tribunal* [1978] CLY 1788).
Covenant 'not to share possession or occupation'	Prohibits any joint use of the premises.

7.3.3 CAN LANDLORD'S CONSENT BE UNREASONABLY WITHHELD?

Assuming that the lease does contain a restriction on assignment, the landlord's consent will, as explained above, be required for the assignment. To what extent the landlord is able to refuse consent or impose conditions in respect of a proposed transaction will depend upon whether the restriction is absolute or qualified.

Absolute restrictions

If the restriction is absolute, i e the tenant has simply covenanted 'not to assign', it is up to the landlord to decide whether or not to waive the restriction. The landlord does not have to act reasonably in making such decision, and can if he wishes require a premium as a condition of giving consent. The landlord is, however, affected by the Sex Discrimination Act 1975 and the Race Relations Act 1976, and is not able to refuse consent on grounds of race or sex but the restriction does not apply where there will be a sharing in 'small' residential premises in which the landlord or a near relative resides (Sex Discrimination Act 1975, s 31, Race Relations Act 1976, s 24).

Qualified restrictions

In the case of a commercial lease it is more likely that the restriction is qualified so that the tenant has covenanted 'not to assign without the landlord's consent'. This type of covenant may be further qualified by an express proviso that the landlord cannot unreasonably withhold consent. If a qualified covenant is not accompanied by such a proviso one will be implied by the Landlord and Tenant Act 1927, s 19.

Where there is a qualified restriction there is also deemed to be a proviso in the lease to the effect that no 'fine or sum of money in the nature of a fine shall be payable for or in respect of' the landlord's consent, except that the landlord can charge reasonable legal or other expenses incurred in relation to such licence or consent (Law of Property Act 1925, s 144). A demand for a break clause or other variation of lease terms in consideration of a consent is probably a fine for these purposes and if demanded may justify the tenant in assigning without consent (*Barclays Bank plc v Daejan Investments (Grove Hall) Ltd* [1995] 1 EGLR 68).

If the landlord's consent is required the tenant will be in breach of the lease terms if he effects a prohibited transaction without first asking for the landlord's consent, even if the landlord could not reasonably refuse consent (*Barrow v Isaacs & Son* [1891] 1 QB 417, CA). So, the proper procedure is for the tenant to request consent and if the landlord refuses consent, and the tenant believes such refusal to be unreasonable, the tenant can apply to the court for a declaration that the consent has been withheld unreasonably. Alternatively the tenant can take the risk of assigning, and if the refusal was unreasonable the tenant will not be considered to be in breach of the terms of the lease (*Treloar v Bigge* (1874) LR 9 Exch 151).

Making the application for consent

The tenant should make an application for consent in writing. If the landlord does not either give consent, or refuse on reasonable grounds, within a reasonable time the landlord will be in breach of a statutory duty under the Landlord and Tenant Act 1988 (s 1). If a landlord has been furnished with the heads of terms for the transaction he will probably have sufficient information to enable a decision on the merits to be made, subject to the status of the proposed assignee and any other material circumstances (*Dong Bang Minerva (UK) Ltd v Davina Ltd* [1995] 1 EGLR 41). What is a reasonable time depends upon the facts of the particular case. It would probably be unreasonable if the landlord did not respond at all for three months (*Midland Bank plc v Chart Enterprises Inc* [1990] 2 EGLR 59).

The landlord is required by the Landlord and Tenant Act 1988 to consent except where it is reasonable not to do so, and to serve upon the tenant written notice of his decision, with reasons for any refusal, and stating any conditions which the consent is subject to. The landlord should give a full response as usually the landlord will not later be able to adduce new reasons for refusal not relied upon at the time of notification of the decision (*Footwear Corpn Ltd v Amplight Properties Ltd* [1998] 2 EGLR 38). It may be reasonable for the landlord to impose interim conditions – e g that the consent is subject to the provision of further details – or to the tenant providing security for the landlord's costs (*Dong Bang Minerva (UK) Ltd v Davina Ltd* [1996] 2 EGLR 31, CA). As to other conditions it may be reasonable that the landlord approve the terms of a sublease but perhaps not the terms of an assignment and level of reverse premium, but this is a question of fact and circumstance (*Dong Bang Minerva (UK) Ltd v Davina Ltd and Kened Ltd and Den Norske Bank plc v Connie Investments Ltd* (1995) 70 P & CR 370, CA).

If the landlord fails to comply with the Landlord and Tenant Act 1988 the tenant can pursue a claim for the tort of breach of statutory duty, or for breach of the landlord's obligations in the lease.

Reasonableness

In determining whether the landlord is acting reasonably the principal consideration is that the basic purpose of a restriction upon assignment is so that the landlord may ensure that any assignee of the lease is able to pay the rent and perform the other obligations in the lease. The leading legal authority on the question is that of the Court of Appeal in *International Drilling Fluids Ltd v Louisville Investments (Uxbridge) Ltd* [1986] Ch 513, where Balcombe LJ laid down seven propositions which might be used as guidelines in deciding whether a landlord is acting reasonably:

(1) The purpose of a covenant against assignment without the consent of the landlord, is to protect the lessor from having his premises used or occupied in an undesirable way, or by an undesirable tenant or assignee.

(2) A landlord is not entitled to refuse his consent to an assignment on grounds which have nothing whatever to do with the relationship of landlord and tenant in regard to the subject matter of the lease.

(3) The onus of proving that consent has been unreasonably withheld is on the tenant.

(4) It is not necessary for the landlord to prove that the conclusions which led him to refuse consent were justified, if they were conclusions which might be reached by a reasonable man in the circumstances.

(5) It may be reasonable for the landlord to refuse his consent to an assignment on the ground of the purpose for which the proposed assignee intends to use the premises, even though that purpose is not forbidden by the lease.

(6) While a landlord need usually only consider his own relevant interests, there may be cases where there is such a disproportion between the benefit to the landlord and the detriment to the tenant if the landlord withholds his consent to an assignment that it is unreasonable for the landlord to refuse consent.

(7) Subject to the above, it is in each case a question of fact, depending upon all the circumstances, whether the landlord's consent to an assignment is being unreasonably withheld.

It should be noted that proposition numbered 3 is no longer valid in cases where the Landlord and Tenant Act 1988 applies, but the other propositions may be considered as a good general guide to the law. Apart from the general guidelines derived from the *International Drilling Fluids* case (see above), there is a plethora of case law which may be of assistance in deciding what is or is not reasonable. There is not enough space in this book to explain and debate the cases in depth, but there is listed below in brief outline some instances where landlords have been found to be acting reasonably or unreasonably:

Examples of reasonable refusal	*Examples of unreasonable refusal*
If references are not supplied (*Rossi v Hestdrive Ltd* [1985] 1 EGLR 50).	Requiring a guarantee in a case where the assignee is of sufficient financial standing (*Re Greater London Properties Ltd's Lease* [1959] 1 All ER 728), unless the lease reserves a right to guarantee irrespective of reasonableness (*Vaux*
If accounts of assignee are such that the assignee's financial standing is unsatisfactory (*British Bakeries (Midlands)*	

Ltd v Michael Testler & Co Ltd [1986] 1 EGLR 64).

If the transaction will diminish the value of the landlord's reversion (*Ponderosa International Development Inc v Pengap Securities (Bristol) Ltd* [1986] 1 EGLR 66), but not if the landlord has no intention of dealing with the reversion (*International Drilling Fluids Limited v Louisville Investments (Uxbridge) Ltd* [1986] Ch 513, CA).

If the assignee will acquire statutory security of tenure which the assignor did not have (*Leeward Securities Ltd v Lilyheath Properties Ltd* (1983) 17 HLR 35, CA), but it depends upon all of the circumstances.

Requiring the remedy of a serious breach of covenant (*Orlando Investments Ltd v Grosvenor Estate Belgravia* (1989) 59 P & CR 21, CA), but not if the breach is trivial.

If the assignee is likely to break a clause of the lease (*Ashworth Frazer Ltd v Gloucester City Council* (1999) 80 P & CR11, CA).

If the terms of a proposed subletting are unsatisfactory. In particular it may be reasonable to require a user restriction similar to that in the headlease (*Re Spark's Lease* [1905] 1 Ch 456), or that the sublease is at a full market rent (*Re Town Investments Ltd Underlease* [1954] Ch 301).

If the proposed assignment is to be a former tenant in respect of whom the lease gives any special personal right (e g the right to exercise a break clause) (*Olympia & York Canary Wharf Ltd v Oil Property*

Group plc v Lilley (1990) 61 P & CR 446 and the Landlord and Tenant Act 1927, s 19(1A)).

Insisting that a guarantee must be given by a United Kingdom company rather than by a foreign corporation (*Kened Ltd v Connie Investments Ltd* (1995) 70 P & CR 370).

Requiring a guarantor on assignment to guarantee the performance of the lease for the entire term, rather than just the period of the assignee's ownership (*Evans v Levy* [1910] 1 Ch 452).

The landlord probably cannot require the assignee to enter into a direct covenant with the landlord that the terms of the lease will be complied with for its duration (*Waite v Jennings* [1906] 2 KB 11, CA) unless there is an express requirement in the lease.

The landlord probably cannot require a subtenant to covenant to pay a rent equivalent to the head rent (*Balfour v Kensington Garden Mansions* (1932) 49 TLR 29).

It is not reasonable for the landlord to refuse on the ground that he wants the premises for himself (*Re Smith's Lease* [1951] 1 All ER 346).

A landlord cannot require a variation of the lease (*Roux Restaurants Ltd v Jaison Property Development Ltd*) (1996) 74 P & CR 357, CA.

The fact that a superior landlord or mortgagee's consent is not available does not justify refusal by the intermediate landlord (*Vienit Ltd v W Williams & Sons (Bread Street) Ltd* [1958] 3 All ER 621).

Investments Ltd [1994] 2 EGLR 48, CA).

Requiring security for payment of the landlord's costs. (*Dong Bang Minerva (UK) Ltd v Davina Ltd* [1996] 2 EGLR 31, CA).

Where an insolvent tenant or a receiver, trustee in bankruptcy, administrator or liquidator wishes to assign the lease the financial standing of the proposed assignee is likely to be the most important factor. If the proposal is to assign the lease to an insubstantial solvent subsidiary of the insolvent tenant the landlord may refuse consent on the ground that the replacement of the tenant by an insubstantial assignee is not to be foisted upon the landlord (*Geland Manufacturing Co v Levy Estates Co* (1962) 181 Estates Gazette 209, [1962] CLY 1700). This is so even though there is a substantial guarantor for the assignee (*Geland Manufacturing Co v Levy Estates Co* (1962) 181 Estates Gazette 209, [1962] CLY 1700). On the other hand if the proposed assignee is substantial and is backed by a substantial corporate guarantee a landlord is likely to be acting unreasonably by insisting that personal guarantees are given before he will consent (*Pakwood Transport Ltd v 15 Beauchamp Place Ltd* (1977) 36 P & CR 112, CA).

It is not reasonable for the landlord to refuse consent to a proposed assignment on the ground that a right to forfeit for the tenant's insolvency has arisen. If the landlord attempts to forfeit without giving due consideration to the proposal to assign the court may grant the tenant relief from forfeiture, together with a declaration that the landlord's refusal of consent is unreasonable (*Pakwood Transport Ltd v 15 Beauchamp Place Ltd* (1977) 36 P & CR 112, 121 Sol Jo 712, 245 Estates Gazette 309).

Conditions contractually agreed

In some circumstances consent may be withheld or conditions may be imposed upon grounds which have previously been agreed between landlord and tenant. The courts have traditionally been reluctant to uphold any agreement between landlord and tenant which would predetermine whether a landlord is acting reasonably or not in particular circumstances (*Re Smith's Lease* [1951] 1 All ER 346) and despite some movement to treating such agreements as valid (*Vaux Group plc v Lilley* (1990) 61 P & CR 446) it could be argued that any such arrangement contravened the statutory requirement of reasonableness in the Landlord and Tenant Act 1927, s 19. Since 1 January 1996, however, and except in the case of a residential lease, a landlord will not be regarded as refusing consent unreasonably if the ground for refusal is one specified in the lease or in some other agreement between the landlord and the tenant. Similarly, if the lease or some other agreement specifies conditions which the landlord may impose in connection with an assignment, the landlord will not be regarded as acting unreasonably by reason of imposing such conditions (Landlord and Tenant Act 1927, s 19(1A) – inserted by the Landlord and Tenant (Covenants) Act 1995, s 22).

If such a ground for refusal or such condition is framed by reference to any matter falling to be determined by the landlord or some other person (e g something is to be done to the satisfaction of the landlord or the landlord's surveyor), the agreement between landlord and tenant is not to have effect unless the agreement states that the landlord or other person is to act reasonably or the tenant is given an unrestricted right to have the determination of the landlord or other person reviewed conclusively by an independent person whose identity is ascertainable by reference to the agreement.

Authorised guarantee agreements

Where a tenant under a 'new tenancy' (see para 5.1.6) will be released from liability upon the assignment of the lease the landlord may require the tenant to stand as surety for the assignee, provided that such requirement is lawful (Landlord and Tenant (Covenants) Act 1995, s 16). The 1995 Act does not specify when such a requirement is lawful but it can be assumed that it will be lawful if it is a condition agreed between the parties within the Landlord and Tenant (Covenants) Act 1995, s 19(1A) (see above), or if otherwise it is reasonable in the circumstances to require such a guarantee (*Wallis Fashion Group Ltd v CGU Life Assurance Ltd* [2000] 2 EGLR 49).

A guarantee so given is governed by the Landlord and Tenant (Covenants) Act 1995, s 16 and its terms are only valid to the extent that they satisfy the criteria of an 'authorised guarantee agreement' within the 1995 Act. Accordingly for all of its terms to be binding any such agreement must meet the following conditions:

(a) the tenant cannot usually be required to guarantee performance of the lease terms by any person other than the immediate assignee;

(b) the tenant cannot be bound by any liability, restriction or requirement which relates to any time after the assignee will be released from the lease obligations by virtue of the 1995 Act;

(c) the agreement may take the form of an indemnity (imposing a primary liability) or a guarantee (imposing a secondary liability);

(d) the terms binding the tenant must be no more onerous than those binding the assignee;

(e) if the agreement requires the tenant to take a new lease of the property following a disclaimer by a trustee in bankruptcy or liquidator the terms of the new lease must be no more onerous than those of the disclaimed lease and the term must expire no later than the term of the disclaimed lease;

(f) the agreement may contain terms 'incidental or supplementary' to c, d, and e.

There is an exception to (a) above. Suppose by the terms of a lease a landlord's consent is required to any assignment. The tenant (T) unlawfully assigns a lease to an assignee (A1) without consent. A1 then wishes, with consent, to lawfully assign to a second assignee (A2). The Landlord and Tenant (Covenants) Act 1995, s 16(6) provides that if A1 enters into an authorised guarantee agreement with regard to A2, the landlord may require T to enter into a guarantee of A2's liability on terms corresponding to those of the authorised guarantee agreement entered into by A1.

7.3.4 FORMALITY

Any assignment of a lease must be made by deed (Law of Property Act 1925, s 52). This is so irrespective of the fact that the lease is one which was properly created without a deed (*Crago v Julian* [1992] 1 All ER 744, CA) due to the fact that it was for a period not exceeding three years, and was at the best rent reasonably obtainable without taking a fine (Law of Property Act 1925, s 54).

7.3.5 EFFECT OF ASSIGNMENT

Assignment will vest the lease in the assignee. This is so even if the assignment is in breach of a restriction upon assignment in the lease (*Old Grovebury Manor Farm Ltd v W Seymour Plant Sales and Hire Ltd* [1979] 1 All ER 573). The benefits and burdens of obligations in the lease will in general pass to the assignee (see chapter 5, para 5.2.2) . The assignor as former tenant may remain liable to the landlord or may be liable to indemnify some earlier tenant (see chapter 5).

Where a lease has vested in a trustee in bankruptcy, the trustee becomes liable under the terms of the lease (see para 5.2). Once, however, the trustee has assigned, the trustee is absolved from any continuing liability with effect from the date of the assignment, but without prejudice to the trustee's liability for the period that the lease was vested in him (*Re Johnson, ex p Blackett* (1894) 70 LT 381, and see chapter 5).

Where the lease is assigned by the liquidator of an insolvent company, the company's liability (if any) as original tenant, will be extinguished upon its dissolution. So a landlord who loses the benefit of the company's covenant can prove in the winding up for the loss. The measure of damages has been described as the difference in the value of the lease to the landlord with and without the benefit of the former tenant's covenant (*Re House Property and Investment Co* [1954] Ch 576). The measure of loss might be more clearly stated as the reduction in value of the landlord's reversion. The landlord cannot normally insist upon the liquidator setting aside a sum equal to the future liability for rent (*Re House Property and Investment Co Ltd* [1954] Ch 576).

7.4 Surrender

Surrender of the lease can produce benefits for both landlord and insolvent tenant. If the lease has a capital value a surrender for a premium paid by the landlord will realise value for the tenant's creditors, allowing the landlord to relet or repossess. Even if the lease is of no value a surrender might be the best way for the tenant to rid itself of its obligations, and may be simpler and neater for a liquidator or trustee than a disclaimer. A trustee in bankruptcy should bear in mind that if he surrenders rather than disclaims he will be personally liable under the terms of the lease up to the date of the surrender (*Re Solomon, ex p Dressler* (1878) 9 Ch D 252).

7.4.1 EFFECT OF SURRENDER

A surrender ends the lease, and the future obligations on the part of both land-lord and tenant end with it. Even obligations which would normally arise imme-diately upon the end of the lease do not arise. In *Re ABC Coupler Engineering Co Ltd (No 3)* [1970] 1 All ER 650, the tenant company was in liquidation and an informal surrender was agreed between the provisional liquidator and the landlord. The lease contained an obligation for the tenant to yield up possession of the premises 'at the expiration or sooner determination of the ... term'. After the surrender the liquidator left a substantial number of items upon the prop-erty. The landlord sought to prove in the liquidation for damages for the tenant's failure to comply with the yielding up obligation in the lease. Plowman J decided that the obligation to yield up died with the surrender and consequently the landlord could not prove in the liquidation for the breach of obligation. In order to avoid this problem the landlord ought, before completing any surrender, to check that the premises have been vacated and cleared.

Past breaches and obligation

Although no future obligations arise after the surrender has effect, the surrender does not impliedly release the landlord or tenant from any breach of a term of the lease which was perpetrated prior to the surrender. Unless an express release is obtained from the landlord, the tenant will remain liable for all arrears of rent, since the tenant's pre-existing obligation to pay is not dependent upon the con-tinuance of the estate in the land given by the lease (*A-G v Cox* (1850) 3 HL Cas 240). Similarly in *Dalton v Pickard* [1926] All ER Rep 371, the tenant was held liable for dilapidations following a surrender. Vaughan Williams LJ said: 'with respect to the future I think that the obligations have come to an end, but in so far as there have been breaches of covenant anterior to the surrender I think the right of action accrued'. Farwell LJ added that 'In order to get rid of a liability under the covenants the tenant would have to show either release or accord and satisfaction'.

Not only will the tenant who has not procured a release be liable for any prior breaches of obligation, but the tenant will also be bound to perform any obligation ascertained after the surrender, but in respect of a period prior to it. So where rent is payable in arrears an apportionment may be made up to the date of the surrender, even though the due date for payment under the terms of the lease is a date subsequent to the surrender (Apportionment Act 1870, s 3). Where rent is payable in advance the tenant may suffer from a converse problem. In this case the Apportionment Act 1870 does not apply and if the tenant has paid rent in advance for a period extending beyond the date of the surrender he is not entitled to have reimbursed to him an apportioned part of the rent unless there is an express agreement to such effect (*William Hill (Football) Ltd v Willen Key and Hardware Ltd* (1964) 108 Sol Jo 482).

The tenant who has not obtained a release is also at risk if a rent review date has passed before the surrender date, and after the surrender the new rent is determined so as to be backdated to the review date. The tenant is obliged to pay the backlog of reviewed rent for the period prior to the surrender, since this is an antecedent obligation which accrues due before the date when the surrender has effect (*Torminster Properties Ltd v Green* [1983] 2 All ER 457, CA).

7.4.2 NEED FOR FORMAL DOCUMENTATION

A lease may be surrendered formally by deed, or the surrender may be done informally by some dealing between landlord and tenant which shows that the lease has ended. Often, in the case of an insolvent tenant, a receiver, liquidator, trustee in bankruptcy or other party is tempted to have an informal surrender, by delivery of the premises to the landlord without formal documentation. The above cases show that such a policy is not a wise one, since in the absence of clear documentation the tenant may have an unexpected rental obligation (see *Torminster Properties Ltd v Green*, above), and may be liable for dilapidations (see *Dalton v Pickard*, above), and a landlord who had dealt informally may suffer the loss of the benefit of tenant's obligations which would arise on determination (see *Re ABC Coupler*, above).

Even if the parties have tried to deal with the situation by letter, rather than employing lawyers, there may be problems. In *Richmond v Savill* [1926] 2 KB 530, an informal surrender took place following a letter from the landlord's agent to the tenant stating that if the tenant 'gives up possession not later than the end of February next, [the landlord] is willing to release him'. The Court of Appeal decided that the surrender released the tenant from future obligations only, and that the tenant remained liable for existing breaches of the repair obligations in the lease.

If the lease is registered at HM Land Registry, it will be easier to procure the removal of the entry relating to it if there is a formal deed of surrender.

Formal surrender

If it is agreed that there will be a formal surrender the document used should be a deed (Law of Property Act 1925, s 52), unless the lease was a lease not exceeding three years at the best rent that could be reasonably obtained without taking a premium. In the latter case the surrender may be in writing (Law of Property Act 1925, s 53(1)). No particular form of words is required to effect a surrender, but it must be made clear that the lease is ended, and, since the surrender is a mutual dealing there must be both a surrender by the tenant and an acceptance by the landlord; a unilateral surrender by the tenant is not sufficient. The surrender document should also contain any release from prior liabilities which it is intended to give to either or both of landlord and tenant, and perhaps any third parties.

The surrender deed or document may be preceded by a binding contract for surrender, setting a date for the completion of the surrender, making provision for any apportionment of rent which should take place upon completion, and obliging the tenant to yield up vacant possession. This last provision is necessary because the surrender will release the tenant from any obligation to yield up which is contained in the lease (see *Re ABC Coupler Engineering Co Ltd*, above). A deed of surrender in draft form will normally be annexed to the contract, so that the terms of the surrender, including any release of liability, are clear.

Informal surrender

Although, as explained above, it is desirable that a surrender should be done formally, it is possible to have an informal surrender, even if the lease is one which had to be created by deed (Law of Property Act 1925, s 52(1)(c)). A lease may be surrendered informally by any mutual course of dealing between landlord and tenant which unequivocally demonstrates that the lease is at an end. Probably the most usual such course of dealing is the surrender of possession by the tenant to the landlord, and the acceptance of the key by the landlord (*Dodd v Acklom* (1843) 6 Man & G 672). But the test is one of the intention of the parties. If there is correspondence between the parties showing a clear desire on the part of both that a surrender should take place, then there will be one. But if the facts show that the tenant wished to surrender, but the landlord did not accept the surrender, then the lease will continue, and with it the liability for future rent.

If a tenant simply delivers the keys of the premises to the landlord's address, and the landlord does not return them, the lease continues if the landlord has not taken any action showing acceptance of a surrender (*Cannan v Hartley* (1850) 9 CB 634). Even if the landlord does not return the keys, but uses them, it is possible that he has not accepted a surrender. If, for instance, the tenant has vacated the premises and is in arrears with rent, the landlord may have had little choice than to seek a replacement tenant, but the existing tenancy should be regarded as continuing until a new one is granted (*Oastler v Henderson* (1877) 2 QBD 575, CA). Neither will there be a surrender where the landlord takes the key for the purpose of doing repairs (*Boynton-Wood v Trueman* (1961) 177 Estates Gazette 191, CA), or where the tenant has vacated and the landlord changes the locks in order to secure the premises (*Relvok Properties v Dixon* (1972) 25 P & CR 1, CA). It might be thought, however, that where a tenant abandons control of premises and the landlord seeks possession against a trespasser such action will be tantamount to the landlord accepting the premises by way of surrender. This was held not to be case in *McDougals Catering Foods Ltd v BSE Trading Ltd* (1997) 76 P & CR 312, CA.

If, on the other hand, the landlord has received the keys and has begun to market the premises for his own benefit a surrender will be presumed (*Phene v Popplewell* (1862) 12 CBNS 334), or if the tenant has surrendered possession and the landlord has actually relet to a new tenant (*Wallis v Hands* [1893] 2 Ch 75). Where, however, the tenant has allowed a related company to occupy as licensee and the landlord has accepted rent from the licensee, this circumstance will not cause a surrender if the landlord accepts rent from the occupier on account of rent owed by the tenant (*Bhogal v Cheema* [1998] 2 EGLR 50). Nor will acceptance of rent from a third party be taken as acceptance of a surrender if the landlord is unaware that there has been a dissolution of the tenant company and a disclaimer of the lease on behalf of the Crown (*Cromwell Developments Ltd v Godfrey Ltd* [1998] 2 EGLR 62, CA) or if the landlord is unaware that rent has been proferred by a third party on its own behalf (*Mattey Securities Ltd v Ervin* [1998] 2 EGLR 66, CA).

Other courses of dealing between landlord and tenant may demonstrate that a surrender has taken place, including the grant of a new lease to the existing tenant (*Gibbs Mew plc v Gemmell* [1999] 1 EGLR 43, CA) or the giving of a rent free licence to the tenant (*Foster v Robinson* [1951] 1 KB 149, CA). A variation of the existing lease, such as a change in the rent, does not normally amount to a surrender of it and a grant of a new lease (*Jenkin R Lewis & Son v Kerman* [1971] Ch 477, CA), but there will be implied surrender and regrant if the 'variation' is an increase in the length of the old lease, or an increase in the extent of the property leased (*Re Savile Settled Estates* [1931] 2 Ch 210; *Baker v Merckel* [1960] 1 QB 657, CA).

If the course of dealing between landlord and tenant envisages the satisfaction of a condition, there can be no surrender until the condition is satisfied. Accordingly, there is no present surrender where landlord and tenant intend a future surrender conditional upon the grant of a new lease to a surety (*Proudreed v Microgen* (1995) 72 P & CR 388, CA).

7.4.3 EFFECT ON SURETY AND ORIGINAL TENANT

If the tenant's liabilities have been guaranteed, a surety's liability is normally co-extensive with that of the tenant, so that a surrender by the tenant will stop any future obligations of the surety from arising. Similarly, it is a necessary incident of a surrender that the original tenant is discharged as to the future (*Clements v Richardson* (1888) 22 LR Ir 535). But the original tenant or surety will be liable for any prior obligations or breaches of obligation which continue to affect the tenant (*Torminster Properties Ltd v Green*, para 7.4.1). If, however, the tenant obtains an express release from liability for past breaches of obligation, it appears that the original tenant or surety will also be released. In *Deanplan Ltd v Mahmoud* [1993] Ch 151, A2 was the ultimate assignee of a lease which had been assigned several times. A2 was insolvent and the landlord (L) accepted a surrender of the lease from A2 and released him from obligations, past and future, in return for A2 handing over some of his stock of goods to L. Subsequently L made a claim against an intermediate assignee (A1) who had given to L an express covenant that the terms of the lease would be performed for the remainder of the term. The principal question which arose was whether the release of A2 also operated to release A1. Judge Paul Baker QC held that the release by accord and satisfaction of A2 also resulted in the release of A1. He reasoned that there was only one, rather than several, obligations, so that if the obligation was extinguished, all the parties subject to the obligation were released. He also noted that if A1 was not released A1 would have a right to indemnity from A2, in which case A2 would not have the release which L had agreed. He did state, however, that it would be possible for a landlord to agree not to sue the insolvent tenant, while reserving his rights against a surety or earlier tenant. In such a case, however, the insolvent tenant will remain exposed to indemnify the surety or earlier tenant if the landlord makes a claim against such person.

These comments must now been considered in the light of the decision in *Milverton Group Ltd v Warner* [1995] 2 EGLR 28 (see chapter 5, para 5.1.8) where the Court of Appeal held that any sum received by a landlord from a surety in consideration of a release from liability must be taken to be a payment of sums due or to become due under the lease, and the landlord's rights against the tenant are reduced accordingly.

7.4.4 EFFECT ON SUBTENANTS AND MORTGAGEES

A surrender of the insolvent tenant's lease does not operate to prejudice the interests of third parties, such as subtenants and mortgagees, whose interests are derived from the surrendered lease. After surrender any subtenant of the property becomes tenant of the head landlord upon the terms of the sublease (Law of Property Act 1925, s 139).

If the lease has been mortgaged the terms of the mortgage will in most cases restrict any dealing with the lease, including surrender, without consent of the mortgagee. In any case a surrender of the lease does not defeat the rights of a mortgagee of the lease (*ES Schwab & Co Ltd v McCarthy* (1975) 31 P & CR 196, CA), and the mortgagee is entitled to possession (*Ushers Brewery Ltd v PS King & Co (Finance) Ltd* (1969) 113 Sol Jo 815). It is not clear, however, what the mortgagee's rights will be in these circumstances. It is arguable that the tenant's equity of redemption is destroyed and that subsequent payment of money due to a mortgagee will not entitle the tenant to retake the lease, and the landlord will be entitled to possession. However, although the relationship between the landlord and tenant is considered to have gone, it is likely that in the event of a default on the mortgage, the mortgagee should have a power to sell to a purchaser a lease equivalent to that surrendered. If the mortgagee does so, and receives a sum greater than that outstanding under the mortgage, it is not clear who ought to receive the balance. It is arguable that the surplus proceeds represent value in the property which was surrendered to the landlord and that the landlord should be entitled to them.

Index